Quitting the Nation

ERIC R. SCHLERETH

Quitting the Nation
Emigrant Rights in North America

The University of North Carolina Press *Chapel Hill*

© 2024 The University of North Carolina Press
All rights reserved
Set in Arno Pro by Westchester Publishing Services
Manufactured in the United States of America

Complete Library of Congress Cataloging-in-Publication Data is available at
https://lccn.loc.gov/2024005601.
ISBN 978-1-4696-7852-8 (cloth: alk. paper)
ISBN 978-1-4696-7853-5 (pbk.: alk. paper)
ISBN 978-1-4696-7854-2 (ebook)

Cover art: Detail from Henry S. Tanner, "A Map of North America" (1833).
Courtesy of David Rumsey Map Collection, David Rumsey Map Center, Stanford Libraries.

For Hazel and Ruben

Contents

Illustrations and Maps

Quitting the Nation

A Nation of Emigrants

Perceptions of the United States as a nation of immigrants are so common-place that its history as a nation of emigrants is largely forgotten. However, from the moment the United States came into existence, its citizens asserted their rights to emigrate for new political allegiances elsewhere. As a writer with emigration sympathies proclaimed in a New York newspaper in 1798, "To contend that every man must invariably feel an exclusive attachment, or owe exclusive duties, to the soil which has brought him into existence, is as absurd as to say, that because a man is born in a stable, he shall always delight in the smell of horse dung." This evocative rejection of patriotic sentiments and natal obligations reveals the existence of citizenship rights that are absent in histories of the early United States. These unfamiliar rights are best described as emigrant rights, a bundle of privileges that includes the freedom of movement and of expatriation. Debates over the assertion and exercise of emigrant rights roiled public life in the United States from the 1770s through the 1860s. The advent of emigrant rights revealed doubts about republican governance during crucial decades of state formation. It seemed that the United States might never secure the popular consent necessary for lasting sovereignty if its citizens felt that their obligation to remain in their country was no more powerful than their reasons for quitting it. Although debates over emigrant rights raised fundamental questions about the nature of citizenship and were decided by the consequential movement of people throughout North America, the history of emigrant rights remains untold.[1]

This history began with individual decisions to leave the United States. In 1790, Ezekiel Forman quit Pennsylvania for Natchez, a Spanish colony on the lower Mississippi River, where he lived the rest of his life as a Spanish subject in possession of land and enslaved people. John Bell was a New York chair maker who traveled northward along the rivers and lakes that led him to Montreal, where he established residence in 1792. Once settled and practicing his trade in the city, Bell notified local officials of plans to bring his family "into this Province where I intend to remain and to Become a subject of the British Government." Several decades later, Leah Alsberry was among the many emigrants from the United States who settled in Texas during the 1820s.

Alsberry's husband adopted Mexican citizenship, which, combined with a subsequent choice of her own, forever changed her national status. By the 1850s, Texas was the westernmost state in the United States' cotton empire. Planter demand for labor forced an influx of enslaved people, including seven of Isaac Griffin's children. Griffin spent nearly his entire life enslaved in Kentucky. During that time, Griffin accompanied his enslaver on several voyages down the Mississippi River, occasionally stopping at Natchez, by then a thriving port in the state of Mississippi made rich by cotton and the enslaved people who cultivated it. Griffin witnessed the brutality of racial slavery on his forced river voyages that he experienced personally with the sale of his children. Unable to reconstitute his family, Griffin committed himself to escaping his enslavement in 1855 by claiming his freedom to leave the United States. Griffin settled in Chatham, Canada West, where, he proclaimed, "The law is the same for one as another."[2]

Each of these individuals, in one way or another, claimed emigrant rights for themselves or led lives determined by the emigrant rights of others. When considered together, their choices suggest the evolution of emigrant rights claims over time and the North American places where people exercised these rights. Tracing the development of citizenship rights within the United States through the choices people made at and beyond the republic's borders is the central subject of this book.

Histories of emigration usually begin in places other than the United States. An "exit revolution" occurred in the late eighteenth century, according to migration historians. Precipitated by population growth and economic demands, migrants left western Europe, often in violation of laws prohibiting their departure without government consent. In response, several European states adopted liberal emigration policies beginning in the 1840s. With more freedom of movement, internal emigration increased in Europe and internationally throughout the Atlantic world. The early United States appears in histories of this exit revolution primarily as a destination that attracted European emigrants by the millions, especially after 1840. Europe's exit revolution created the United States as a nation of immigrants, or so it seems.[3]

During the era of mass immigration to the United States, many newcomers became citizens on relatively easy terms provided they met specific conditions. Federal naturalization law limited citizenship to free white people of "good moral character" who swore allegiance to the United States after residing there for a minimum number of years. They then obtained civic and political rights within the United States and claims to the government's protection when abroad. Immigrants to the United States thus became naturalized citizens by exercising the same emigrant rights, often subject to similar character and race restrictions, that native-born citizens already claimed for themselves as they moved about North America seeking new allegiances. Ultimately, mass immigration to the United States belongs to a broader history of emigrant rights that began much earlier.[4]

With the advent of emigrant rights, the United States experienced an exit revolution of its own, one that put it on the vanguard of global emigration more generally. Pennsylvania representative Thomas Scott described the makings of this exit revolution. "There are seven thousand souls waiting for lands" in the western United States, Scott estimated before his House colleagues in 1789. Should this population fail to acquire land within the United States, they "would go to the Spanish or English colonies" that bordered the republic. During the 1790s, nearly 20,000 American citizens quit the United States for Spanish territory, including Scott's fellow Pennsylvanian Ezekiel Forman. Over 50,000 more eventually joined John Bell in British North America. Although nearly 100,000 people also arrived in the United States between 1790 and 1800, the history of human movement in the early United States is clearly not one of immigration alone. Moreover, enough people extolled their right to quit the United States over subsequent decades that emigration remained a perennial topic of politics, law, and popular understanding. It was also a choice many people continued to make for themselves into the nineteenth century. However, the United States' exit revolution remains hidden in plain sight because it unfolded in ways illegible to prevailing histories of citizenship and the North American borderlands.[5]

Emigrant rights originated in various challenges to the English common law doctrine of perpetual allegiance. First articulated in the early seventeenth century, this doctrine held that a subject's allegiance to a sovereign was fixed at birth in exchange for protection. Subjects were free to leave the territory of their sovereign, but they could not change their allegiance at will without violating a divine duty. During the seventeenth and eighteenth centuries, early law of nations writers disputed the doctrine of perpetual allegiance with social contract arguments for allegiance based on individual consent. Similar understandings of consensual allegiance proved appealing to settlers in Great Britain's Atlantic empire. Both developments provided the legal and intellectual basis for a notion of citizenship that rested on what James H. Kettner identified as "volitional allegiance." This concept of citizenship prevailed in the American Revolution to become the basis of citizenship in the new United States. Among other rights and expectations, citizenship based on volitional allegiance allowed its holders the freedom to move but also the freedom of expatriation; that is, an individual right to change allegiance at will. Combined, these two freedoms created a citizen's emigrant rights.[6]

Foundational histories of early US citizenship consider free movement or a right to expatriation but from perspectives that obscure their relationship in law and everyday life. Histories of free movement reveal how courts and governments limited this right to reinforce the racial, gender, and class boundaries of citizenship within the United States. From this perspective, legal and political contests over free movement stopped at the country's territorial boundaries. Most histories that address expatriation in the early United States begin from a decidedly national perspective, using expatriation debates to illuminate questions about the nature of political allegiance and civic membership for people already in the United States or as its basis for naturalization law. Studies of early expatriation debates thus concentrate on contests over obtaining citizenship in the United States rather than American citizens choosing civic membership elsewhere. By enclosing free movement and expatriation within the borders of the nation-state, prevailing histories cast them as separate citizenship rights.[7]

An emigrant rights perspective reveals why this distinction is untenable by showing that freedom of movement and expatriation constituted a single rights claim that individuals exercised both within and outside the United States. Before the ratification of the Fourteenth Amendment, citizenship claims within the United States arose from state and local laws rather than federal law. The absence of national citizenship under federal law empowered state and local governments to decide civic membership in a given community. This allowed for emigrant rights claims within the United States for those individuals entitled to the privileges and obligations of local allegiance based on their freedom to move across layered jurisdictional boundaries—be it from county to county, from one town to another within a single state, or from state to state. However, emigrant rights claims within the United States readily became emigrant rights claims beyond the United States. This seemed self-evident to contemporaries. There was not "a man in the world," Thomas Jefferson asserted, who did not hold an "innate feeling of right to live on the outside of an artificial line as he has to live within it," to use his faculties "in whatever place he can do it to the greatest promotion of his own happiness." Isaac Griffin claimed such a right for himself when he quit enslavement for a free life beyond the United States. The world imagined by the enslaver but created by a person once enslaved thus reveals the larger North American context for an emigrant rights history of the early United States, a context in which meaningful distinctions between internal and external emigration collapsed and crossing sovereign borders generated individual rights claims, not fore-closed them.[8]

American emigration occurred in the North American borderlands. Here individuals by the thousands moved about in pursuit of allegiances that best protected their interests amid larger contests over territorial sovereignty that embroiled Indigenous nations, the United States, and rival national powers. American citizens who settled under British, Spanish, or Mexican allegiance have not eluded borderlands historians. Such scholars often emphasize, above all else, economic motivations, both of those who left and the govern-ments that welcomed them. However, more elusive to borderlands historians is recognition that when Americans abandoned their citizenship for alle-giance elsewhere, they became participants in ongoing legal and political contests about a person's relative freedom to quit the nation. Viewing such people as emigrants not only aligns with common usage in the eighteenth and nineteenth centuries for people who moved about, the term also suggests an alternative relationship between individuals and the state. Immigrants gain rights at the forbearance of the state whereas migrant refers to people of uncertain legal standing not entirely of their own choosing. Both terms exist in a world in which states create borders to decide national belonging.[9]

On the contrary, an emigrant rights history of the borderlands begins without privileging state power. The announcement of emigrant rights within American law challenged dominant theories of sovereignty in which states possess nearly absolute power to regulate borders and to define the terms of civic belonging. Emigrant rights empowered individuals to cross in-ternational borders at will in expectation of full civic membership in the country of their choice. The history of emigrant rights to free movement and expatriation thus provides an opportunity to look outward from the United States, past its coasts and across its borders. Indeed, American citizens exer-cised their emigrant rights in places distant from the confines of legislatures and courtrooms. By the early 1800s, many people sailed the seas aboard the republic's mercantile fleet, but even larger numbers migrated throughout North America, a continent shaped by competing national interests and powerful Indigenous peoples. In North America's borderlands, thousands of American citizens exercised their emigrant rights for new political allegiances outside the republic. It was in the borderlands where claims to emigrant rights became the basis for forms of emigration right citizenship.[10]

Emigration right citizenship included several particular elements. The privileges of emigration right citizenship were not contained by state borders but reached across them. Moreover, emigration right citizenship did not presuppose or prescribe exclusive allegiance to one nation over another. Emigrant rights thereby created the category of emigration right citizenship by which free movement across borders and residence determined a person's legal status rather than birthplace. Emigration right citizenship existed in sharp contrast to notions of birthright citizenship. Birthright citizenship was, and still remains, a form of belonging most meaningful in a world of relatively fixed territorial boundaries and uniform state sovereignty. The conditions of birthright citizenship presume that most individuals born in a nation will likely remain there for life. Because birthright citizenship prevailed in the United States after the Civil War, it becomes easy to forget that before the 1860s the conditions for birthright citizenship—fixed borders and a strong central government—did not exist or were in formation. The early United States existed in a world of shifting borders and uneven sovereignty in which emigrant rights to free movement and expatriation often proved more useful than birthright claims to place. Emigration right citizenship proved most meaningful to people living in or near North America's major borderlands regions just as fluid political loyalty has benefited people living at the periphery of state power throughout history and across the globe. Individuals entitled to emigration right citizenship could thus mediate, limit, or accept—therefore choose—their relationship to state power.[11]

As with all forms of citizenship, the exercise of emigration right citizenship reinforced contemporary racial and gendered boundaries of civic belonging. Able-bodied, adult white men such as Ezekiel Forman and John Bell possessed emigrant rights. Proof of their genuine allegiance and potential standing within political communities outside the United States often depended on their command of the reproductive labor of wives, the physical labor of children, and sometimes the reproductive and physical labor of enslaved people. In return, laws and political decisions that limited or denied emigrant rights to free movement and expatriation inscribed the dependent status of children and of white women such as Leah Alsberry along with the unfreedom of enslaved people, at least until challenged by individuals such as Isaac Griffin. Finally, white men might exercise emigration right citizenship in the wake of Indigenous dispossession in some places, but Indigenous power might dictate its exercise in other places.

Individual emigrant rights provided a basis for legal personhood and self-ownership also denied to entire groups of people. This included Loyalists exiled for their political sentiments during the Revolutionary War. As the nineteenth century unfolded, the federal government dispossessed Indigenous nations of their land in the southeastern United States, the Ohio Valley, and the upper Midwest before forcibly removing them. Moreover, the various North American slave trades forced the migration of enslaved people, whose absence of legal rights inscribed their status as portable property. State governments, particularly in New York and Massachusetts, adopted laws that empowered authorities to stop Irish immigrants from disembarking in their ports and to deport those already settled even if they were naturalized citizens. Finally, the migration and settlement of religious communities such as the Mormons often met with local resistance and suspicion. When viewed against these various instances of forced, involuntary expatriation, full citizenship in the early United States seemed meaningless if the power to deny it or cast it aside belonged to someone else. Contests to define the boundaries of who possessed freedom of movement and expatriation characterized the emigrant rights history of North America through the 1860s.[12]

During the same period, movements for territorial secession, as expressions of collective expatriation, lost legal recognition against rising tolerance for an individual right to expatriation. Citizens were free to leave and adopt new allegiances beyond the United States, but they could not adopt new allegiances if doing so separated territory from the union. As a result, secession haunted American federalism from the 1780s onward. Such concerns began with the possibility of new republics forming west of the Appalachian Mountains. During the War of 1812, New England Federalists threatened to create a separate regional confederacy at the Hartford Convention. Finally, conflicts over slavery posed a constant threat to the union. Of course, debates in the United States over the legality of secession became most urgent in the 1860s. Critics of secession looked to the history of emigrant rights to discredit secessionist claims. One newspaper cited James Madison's distinction from the 1830s between expatriation and the "heresy of secession." "The expatriation party moves only in his person and his moveable property, and does not incommode those whom he leaves," Madison argued. However, he continued, "a seceding State mutilates the domain, and disturbs the whole system from which it separates itself." This distinction emerged in American law and politics in the late eighteenth century and persisted through the 1860s. Nevertheless, a collective act of expatriation by way of secession did not occur in the United States until 1861 with the slaveholders' insurrection that became the Civil War.[13]

Although a collective claim to expatriation rights proved central to the outbreak of the Civil War, by the 1860s American citizens had expatriated themselves for new allegiances beyond the United States for decades. *Quitting the Nation* focuses on this much longer history of individual emigrant rights. To tell the story of evolving individual rights to free movement and expatriation within and beyond the United States, *Quitting the Nation* braids the histories of US citizenship and the North American borderlands. This approach emphasizes that the allegiances of citizens in the United States were contingent rather than inevitable because the same was true for the nation's territorial boundaries. This approach also reveals that any history of personal mobility within and beyond the borders of the early United States is incomplete without accounting for the legal presumption of emigrant rights. Ultimately, *Quitting the Nation* situates the early United States in an Atlantic context ordered by the norms of international law and within a continental frame shaped by the choices of those living near North America's shifting national boundaries.

As a history of early US citizenship, *Quitting the Nation* explains the creation of emigrant rights within American law and the domestic controversies such rights engendered. This history centers on questions about the implications of a notion of citizenship in which the choice to belong is as equally powerful as the choice to leave. This is the history of legal and political documents regarding free movement and expatriation—including federal and state judicial opinions, local statutes, law treatises, congressional debates, and diplomatic correspondences—from which American citizens claimed their rights to leave the United States. It is also a history of ideas about the freedom of movement and expatriation within the larger culture that included debates over the right to quit the nation in American newspapers, pamphlets, and popular literature. The citizenship history of emigrant rights begins in the late eighteenth century. Although the American Revolution was a rebellion in favor of emigrant rights, an individual right to expatriation remained a disputed legal issue in the United States from the 1770s through the 1860s. In what amounted to contests over emigration control, these disputes concerned conflicting opinions about the necessary limits that governments and courts could place on a person's freedom to choose allegiance. At the state level, Virginia and Kentucky enacted laws allowing their citizens to expatriate while several other states adopted constitutional provisions regarding emigration that implied a right to expatriation. Congress frequently debated expatriation's standing as a right under federal law, and congressmen introduced several national expatriation acts. Moreover, between 1781 and 1868, state and federal courts, including the US Supreme Court, heard over thirty cases concerning a citizen's right to expatriation. Ultimately, Congress adopted the Expatriation Act of 1868, which declared expatriation a natural right of citizenship. This federal legislation combined with the 1867 Supreme

Court decision in *Crandall v. State of Nevada* that established a constitutional right to free movement codified emigrant rights within American citizenship law. Under the federal citizenship regime created by the Fourteenth Amendment, emigrant rights became birthright privileges by 1870. Citizens of the United States thus gained an unequivocal right to leave their country at a moment when the federal state seemed strongest and its national existence secured.

As a borderlands history, *Quitting the Nation* follows the exercise of emigration right citizenship through various regions and how this effected state formation beyond the United States. During the 1790s and early 1800s, this included the British colony of Lower Canada and the Spanish colonies of Lower and Upper Louisiana. During the 1820s and 1830s, such places included the British colony of Upper Canada and Texas, which at this moment was part of the Republic of Mexico and was governed as the larger state of Coahuila and Texas. Government officials in these places adopted policies to attract American emigrants that in each instance created decidedly different configurations of territory and sovereignty. Nevertheless, American emigrants in each of these places were white settlers. Many of the American emigrants in Spanish and later Mexican settlements owned enslaved people. Moreover, each region had a particular history of Indigenous people defending their own territorial claims that often decided where and how American settlers exercised their emigrant rights. During the 1830s, insurgencies erupted in both borderlands regions fueled by emigrant rights claims. The formation of the Republic of Texas and the failed republican revolutions in Lower and Upper Canada dictated the geography of emigration right citizenship in the decades to follow. This outcome was most evident in the British colony of Canada West, which provides the final regional center and counterpoint to the other emigrant settlements. In the 1850s, Canada West became the leading destination for nominally free Black Americans subjected to diminished legal status in the United States and for people who escaped enslavement in the American South. Canada West thus became the place where emigrant rights and emigration right citizenship found their most radical expression a decade before American law recognized the existence of both in the late 1860s. As the combined history of these places demonstrates, claims to the emigrant rights of free movement and expatriation not only shaped life in North America's borderlands, but in fundamental ways the exercise of emigration right citizenship created the continent's borderlands.

A comparative borderlands approach reveals why emigration is absent from histories of the United States and North America more broadly. This absence is most understandable for interpretations of the Spanish and Mexican borderlands. At first glance, emigration from the United States to Spanish and later Mexican allegiance reinforces narratives of inevitable American expansion. Indeed, the United States eventually conquered by treaty or warfare every place that large numbers of American emigrants settled under Spanish or Mexican sovereignty before 1848. This outcome invites interpretations of emigrant rights to free movement and expatriation as at most peripheral legal considerations for settlers who understood themselves as once and eventually American citizens. Histories of expansion thereby displace histories of emigration.

Emigration from the United States for British allegiance in Canada makes such dismissal difficult. American citizens who settled in British North America rarely returned, and the places they settled never became US territories. American citizens who adopted imperial allegiances in Canada largely expatriated themselves for good. Emigrant rights were a powerful source for permanently changing legal status in the Canadian borderlands. Yet without the privileges of hindsight, Americans in the eighteenth and nineteenth centuries had no reason to doubt that emigrant rights would operate differently in the Spanish and Mexican borderlands. Exploring American emigrant rights from a comparative borderlands perspective thus reveals how their exercise constituted North America's boundaries of territory and sovereignty in contingent ways that contemporaries found difficult to predict. In other words, the lasting power of emigrant rights in the Canadian borderlands forces a reckoning with their potential power in the Spanish and Mexican borderlands before the United States' territorial claims in the region seemed manifest or particularly destined.[14]

Quitting the Nation includes eight chapters, which are organized chronologically around the relationships between emigrant rights and emigration right citizenship. This structure reinforces one of the book's central claims about citizenship formation in the early United States. Although Americans defined and debated emigrant rights in their courts, legislatures, and the public sphere, emigrant rights did not become a meaningful citizenship privilege in the United States until American citizens crossed borders and adopted new political allegiances. Thus in the early United States, citizenship was not only a legal mechanism that state officials used to construct and enforce borders, but rather conditions in the borderlands dictated the forms of citizenship that state officials were forced to accommodate. Moreover, *Quitting the Nation* is organized in a way that clearly situates changing perceptions and expressions of emigrant rights in the United States within the evolving geography of North America's borderlands. Throughout the eighteenth and nineteenth centuries, North America's international borders changed over time. Within the United States during the same period, the legal standing of emigrant rights also changed. In fundamental ways, Americans thus defined and exercised their emigrant rights not in response to domestic considerations familiar to most histories of citizenship formation but rather in response to changes in territorial sovereignty that remade the era's borderlands.

Recounting the history of American emigration also provides an interpretation of political allegiance in the early United States with significance for the present. In important ways, American citizenship and patriotism before the Civil War were probationary. Although nationalist boosters extolled the virtues of steady loyalty to the United States, the history of emigrant rights accounts for the thousands of American citizens who traded their citizenship for civic membership in another country and for the opinions of those who insisted citizenship was meaningless without the freedom to cast it aside. The history of emigrant rights also accounts for those conditions of inequality that denied free movement and choice of citizenship to a vast array of people. Nevertheless, the advent of emigrant rights introduced a perspective with powerful implications, for it suggested that people should be free to move throughout the world at will and to decide for themselves the nation they belong to. This perspective is all the more relevant in the twenty-first century when limitations on personal mobility persist inside the United States and at its borders. The American Revolution in favor of emigrant rights remains incomplete until the freedom of every individual to cross borders and choose allegiances is no less lawful than state claims to border control.

CHAPTER ONE

Choice Not Chance

David Ramsay counted the Constitution's ratification in 1788 among the seminal events in the brief but auspicious history of the United States. A physician, politician, and the first historian of the American Revolution, Ramsay thought the inauguration of a new political order demanded a precise reckoning of how one became a citizen of the United States. To Ramsay, a citizen was "a member of the new nation" who shared sovereignty with every other citizen. Citizens could vote for their political representatives and hold elected office, among other privileges that distinguished them from mere inhabitants who resided in the United States but could not participate in its governance. In a pamphlet on the subject, Ramsay identified what he believed were "the only modes of acquiring this distinguishing privilege." Each mode rested on consent, although the form of which changed over time. As a historian, Ramsay recognized that citizens lived in unique historical moments that required them to express their consent accordingly. Adult men who accepted the Declaration of Independence in 1776 or swore their allegiance to one of the new state governments created thereafter, acquired their citizenship during a time of political change and warfare. With peace and the ratification of the Constitution, Ramsay observed a transition toward stable governance that he believed would persist into the future. Under these later circumstances, Ramsay identified citizenship as a privilege obtained by birth or naturalization.[1]

In a nation rapidly growing through natural increase, Ramsay predicted that birth would likely outpace naturalization as the common mode of acquiring citizenship in the United States. Nevertheless, "At twenty-one years of age, every freeman is at liberty to chuse his country, his religion, and his allegiance," Ramsay asserted. Those who stayed in the United States at maturity expressed their tacit consent to remain allegiant to the United States. "In this manner," Ramsay concluded, "young men are now daily acquiring citizenship." By recognizing individual choice as the basis of political belonging, Ramsay embraced the notion of volitional allegiance central to the prevailing view of citizenship that formed during the American Revolution. Moreover, he was confident that the maturation of each generation would yield a steady bounty of new citizens. With independence secured under a new constitutional order, Ramsay held a sanguine view of the republic's future. Ramsay's failure to consider that

Americans might choose alternatives to US citizenship satisfied nationalist aspirations in the 1780s and abetted nationalist myths thereafter. Of course, citizens might also refuse their birthright allegiance or later decide to withdraw it.[2]

During the 1770s and 1780s there were no legal or political controls to stop citizens from choosing another country or allegiance. Rather, state and federal governments took steps during the Revolution and its aftermath to establish a citizen's natural right to leave the place and allegiance of their birth for others of their own choosing. Recognizing citizens' liberty to decide their own allegiances rejected the English legal doctrine of perpetual allegiance, which permitted subjects to leave but not adopt new allegiances. By discarding English legal precedent, American legislators during the 1770s and the 1780s argued for individual emigrant rights to free movement and expatriation under the law of nations.[3]

Nationalist assumptions, such as Ramsay's, about the nature of citizenship as belonging to or becoming a member of a country, thus a matter of domestic law, masks the degree to which citizenship in a union of equal states was a matter of international law. Indeed, developing international law doctrines provided some of the clearest guidance in the eighteenth century about the privileges and obligations of citizenship in a particular nation or the world at large. Emigrant rights under international law thus ultimately helped bring the United States into being in 1776 while also defining fundamental aspects of citizenship in the new union.[4]

LEGAL SYSTEMS OFTEN rely on fictions about the past to assert rights and obligations in the present. The early modern law of nations was no different, according to which individuals possessed a natural right to emigration. The fiction behind this right was that of the world before sovereignty. Immanuel Kant referred to such a world as that in which "no-one originally has any greater right than anyone else to occupy any particular portion of the earth." Kant rejected the exclusive possession of a given territory based on claims that were somehow timeless or prior to general human needs to move freely about the world. To accept such claims, Kant argued, would violate "that right to the earth's surface which the human race shares in common." The Swiss legal philosopher Emer de Vattel looked to a past before humans created bounded political space in the form of kingdoms, empires, or states to establish the "right of passage." According to Vattel, the right of passage was "a remnant of the primitive state of communion, in which the entire earth was common to all mankind" and "passage was everywhere free to each individual according to his necessities." By imagining a world without the markers of territorial sovereignty, Kant and Vattel identified a past in which the concept of emigration did not exist. People moved about without ever exiting one sovereign territory for another. The advent of sovereign powers that claimed exclusive dominion over bounded territories and commanded the allegiance of inhabitants within those territories thus created emigrants out of people who once moved freely across a globe they possessed in common. This account of a fictional past of free movement without the burden of sovereign states provided the conceptual foundation upon which law of nations theorists established a right to emigration. Ultimately, Kant, Vattel, and other writers concerned with establishing the rules for international order found a right to free movement compelling. As an inheritance from a vanished world without claims to territorial sovereignty, a right to free movement proved essential to their larger theoretical ambitions.[5]

The growth of Atlantic empires beginning in the sixteenth century pushed European legal theorists to consider norms suitable for governing a colonial world increasingly bound together by commerce, settlement, and notions of stronger state sovereignty. From its advent, the burgeoning law of nations considered the relationship between freedom of movement and state sovereignty. For early international law writers, state sovereignty did not require strict limitations on freedom of movement. On the contrary, prominent international law theorists assumed that states would preserve territorial sovereignty over their colonial possessions at the same time that outsiders would move into and out of their empires at will. From the perspective of early international law, constant human movement was a fact of life that states should accommodate whenever possible, regulate if necessary, but rarely deny. A right to emigration became central to a functioning law of nations for its conceptual power to reconcile a world of nearly constant migration with the creation of norms necessary to govern orderly interactions among states. Moreover, establishing a right to emigration could guide judgments about how best to balance an absolute freedom of movement with the needs of sovereign governments to protect their territorial interests and command the allegiance of resident populations, including the degree to which parts of its population were free to emigrate. Thus a central question under the law of nations was how to determine the proper relationship between state power and emigrant rights.[6]

Preserving the unencumbered mobility that supposedly existed before the creation of territorial sovereignty provided the basis for emigrant rights under the law of nations. In *The Principles of Natural and Politic Law*, Jean-Jacques Burlamaqui asserted "a right inherent in all free people, that every man should have the liberty of removing out of the commonwealth, if he thinks proper." Samuel von Pufendorf claimed that the freedom to leave permitted emigrants to abandon allegiance altogether, thereby effectively removing themselves from the law of nations. For "it must be presumed," Pufendorf argued, "that every Man reserved to himself the Liberty to remove at Discretion, and that he chose rather to be a Citizen of the World (as Socrates said) than a Subject in any particular Commonwealth." Vattel accused governments of condemning their "subjects to an insupportable slavery" if leaving their borders became onerous or impossible. Indeed, joining oneself to a government was meaningless if this choice then foreclosed all opportunities to leave, for as Burlamaqui noted, "when a person becomes a member of a state, he does not thereby renounce the care of himself and his own private affairs." Taken together, the prominent law of nations theorists of the seventeenth and eighteenth centuries outlined the privileges of emigrant rights. People could choose to stay or leave. The absence of choice equaled enslavement. However, between an absolute right to leave and forced settlement akin to slavery, the same writers recognized that emigrant rights imposed obligations as well.[7]

Emigration demanded some regard for the society and government the emigrant left behind. Asserting that emigrant rights included obligations proved far less difficult than defining what these obligations entailed. For one, the law of nations required some way for governments to distinguish emigrants from mere sojourners, or populations that left but might return. In a world marked by maritime trade, colonization, and frequent migration, even people who intended to return might be absent from their home countries for months and years, often living in foreign jurisdictions. If movement throughout the world created new political obligations, then diplomatic confusion might abound as governments would find it difficult to determine individual allegiance. Vattel suggested a way to avoid this confusion by defining the qualities of an emigrant. "Those who quit their country for any lawful reason, with a design to settle elsewhere, are called emigrants," Vattel concluded. Moreover, Vattel continued, emigrants were those who chose to leave for good as evident in his notion of "settlement," which he defined as a "fixed residence in any place with an intention of always staying there."[8]

However, by demanding that potential emigrants have lawful reasons to leave, Vattel invited governments to regulate the right of emigration. Indeed, governments were obligated to regulate emigration as only an "imperfect society" would allow every citizen liberty to quit his country "whenever he thinks proper, without alleging any reason for it." The government that let its citizens quit their country at will invited its own destruction, for such an un-bridled liberty proved "contrary in its own nature to the welfare and safety of society." Just as governments were obligated to impose some limits on the right to emigration, lawful citizens were obligated to exercise civic-minded prudence before choosing to leave. As Vattel insisted, "Every man has a right to quit his country, in order to settle in any other, when by that step he does not endanger the welfare of his country." Whereas Vattel prioritized the state's power to regulate emigration, thereby bolstering the obligations of emigrant rights, other law of nations writers such as Burlamaqui were inclined to re-strain state power in favor of the privileges of emigrant rights. "In general, a man ought not to quit his native country without the permission of his sover-eign," Burlamaqui instructed, "but his sovereign ought not to refuse it to him, without very important reasons." By weighting obligation differently, Burlamaqui and Vattel revealed that a right to emigration under the law of na-tions was ultimately incoherent.[9]

Influential law of nations theorists failed to align the privileges and obliga-tions of emigrant rights. The liberty to leave existed with certainty whereas the conditions that permitted lawful departure seemed open to debate. This ten-sion between the privileges and obligations of emigrant rights appeared in the major treatises on the law of nations published into the eighteenth century, including Vattel's *The Law of Nations*, first published in French in 1758 and translated into English in 1760. *The Law of Nations* quickly became the authoritative treatise for anyone concerned with matters of international law in Europe and its colonies. Publishers introduced English translations of Vattel's work at a moment in North America when conceptual inconsis-tencies and unsettled legal questions proved politically useful. At such mo-ments, protean legal principles were ready-made for those willing to force revolutionary change.

The American Revolution began with a dispute over emigrant rights. Starting in 1763, Parliament attempted to expand its authority over Great Britain's North American empire by improving revenue collection, reforming colonial governance, and asserting sovereignty over a vastly enlarged terri-tory. Within a decade many colonists concluded that Parliament's efforts threatened the sovereignty of provincial governments. This dispute over su-preme legislative authority in the colonies rested on competing understand-ings about emigration's place in the origins of English colonies. To imperial reformers in Parliament, settlers left England with royal permission to create colonies abroad, which thereby extended the sovereignty of Crown and Par-liament to North America. Opponents of this view in the colonies argued that early English settlers did not extend England's sovereignty abroad but rather established provincial governments that were sovereign unto themselves. Out of this conflict between imperial reformers and their colonial critics emerged conflicting notions of emigrant rights. The reformers believed that early settlers were obligated to carry, establish, and then preserve royal authority in North America. After all, a functioning empire demanded the projection of English sovereignty abroad. Parliament's critics in the colonies emphasized that settlement endowed the colonists with privileges of self-governance. According to this view, a portable sovereignty gave emigrants the authority to create governments of their own wherever they set foot. The view that emigrant rights created local sovereignty gained broad appeal in many British colonies by the 1770s.[10]

Colonial elites such as John Adams and Thomas Jefferson appealed to this view of emigrant rights in their influential opposition writings. Writing as "Novanglus" in 1774, Adams argued that the original New England settlers could have created societies that within a generation owed no allegiance to the king. By emigrating, the first settlers "were not bound or obliged to submit to" the common law "unless they chose it," and only then they were bound "to just so much of it as they pleased to adopt, and no more." Jefferson asserted a similar view about the origins of English colonization in *A Summary View of the Rights of British America*, also published in 1774. Jefferson declared that English settlers established colonies in North America by exercising the natural right "given to all men, of departing from the country in which chance, not choice, has placed them." Adams and Jefferson thus both concluded that accidents of birth only bound people to a government if they decided not to leave.[11]

Those who decided otherwise had effectively decided to govern themselves. Adams took this view to explain the history of English settlement in Massachusetts. Although the original settlers derived their laws from colonial compacts with the king, once in North America, Adams insisted, the first settlers "had a clear right to have erected in this wilderness a British constitution, or a perfect democracy, or another form of government they saw fit." The charter generation owed loyalty to the king, but the governments they created imposed no such burdens on subsequent generations. The settlers' children born in the colonies "would not have been born within the king's allegiance, would not have been natural subjects, and consequently not entitled to protection, or bound to the king." Adams thus concluded that the Massachusetts colonists were loyal subjects in 1774 only because previous generations of colonists chose to sustain their allegiance to the Crown. What held true for settlers in New England also held true for settlers in all of England's colonies according to Jefferson. Once in North America, emigrants assumed a self-governing authority to create settlements, societies, and laws that "to them shall seem most likely to promote public happiness." By conquering Native peoples, creating colonial governments and provincial legal systems, and establishing commerce, English settlers overcame hardships following their migration to North America. This occurred at expense to emigrants, not the British public, so no relationship of dominion or obligation existed between English settlers in North America and Parliament in Great Britain. Instead, settlers in North America chose a "union" with Great Britain by "submitting themselves to the same common sovereign," the only shared connection throughout the empire. Of course, nothing ensured that Adams and Jefferson's generation of settlers would keep their inherited loyalties. Within two years many colonists cast aside their birthright royalism.[12]

Those who joined the emigrant's rebellion exercised a legal option to collectively dissolve their allegiance to the Crown, latent since the creation of English colonies. This view that emigrant rights put colonists in possession of their own sovereignty gained succinct expression in the Declaration of Independence with reference to "the circumstances of our emigration and settlement here." Moreover, other familiar passages from the Declaration of Independence such as the "pursuit of happiness," which Americans would eventually extol as the essence of national belonging, in 1776 more accurately captured the collective freedom to quit nations. Thus as an expression of emigrant rights, the Declaration of Independence was an instrument of the law of nations.

Delegates to the Continental Congress realized that without recognition by European powers, the independent union of states they announced into existence in 1776 would amount to nothing more than a paper confederation. In order to support the American cause, established European powers had to recognize the Continental Congress as an independent sovereign waging legitimate war against Great Britain rather than an illegal collection of insurgent provinces provoking civil war. Delegates to Congress wrote and approved the Declaration of Independence with just such an intention, to announce the advent of a sovereign state within an international order of states. Although the Continental Congress turned to the law of nations in its aspiration for sovereignty, it also relied on the law of nations to exercise actual sovereignty after it declared independence. However, assuming self-governance according to the law of nations meant that the Continental Congress also assumed certain burdens. In particular, by launching an emigrant's rebellion, the Continental

Congress forced itself to decide how to balance the privileges and obligations of emigrant rights during a war with Great Britain.[13]

Wartime security pushed revolutionaries to police freedom of movement in order to deny the emigrant rights of suspect populations. The outbreak of colonial rebellion precipitated an unprecedented level of slave mobility throughout North America. International law provided no support for freedom of movement to enslaved people. Nevertheless, Britain's wartime policy of liberating and arming runaway slaves created an entire population of potentially free people unwilling to see the empire collapse. Seizing opportunities to flee their enslavers, enslaved people sought freedom as British subjects. Furthermore, British officials such as Lord Dunmore, Virginia's last colonial governor, encouraged people enslaved by insurgent slave owners to run away for freedom under British protection. Loyalist strongholds, such as New York City, provided haven and nominal freedom for slaves fleeing insurgent domains. Black Loyalists formed regiments to defend the empire. Revolutionary governments, many of which enslavers controlled, had existing laws of slavery at their disposal to prevent or punish runaway slaves. Revolutionary leaders thus took substantial measures to prevent slave mobility. Insurgent forces also restrained freedom of movement for the significant white Loyalist population. Patriots violently coerced Loyalists to abandon their allegiance to the Crown or forced them into exile beyond the boundaries of the newly created, Patriot-controlled states. Nevertheless, the presence of Loyalist regiments prepared to fight Patriot forces, coupled with persistent fears of secret Loyalist subversion, made all free white people potentially suspect as they traveled outside their communities. Support for the insurgents thus determined freedom of movement once hostilities erupted in North America.[14]

Local Whig authorities and insurgent communities at large viewed strangers with suspicion, as possible Tories or royal agents, if they arrived without proof of their Whig sympathy. Committees of correspondence and private individuals of correct political principles issued passports that opened doors to people who traveled outside their communities. In an attitude of revolutionary consistency, Comfort Sands, a member of the New York Provincial Congress, solicited a passport from the local Committee of Safety before departing Albany. Much like the passports that the Albany Committee of Safety expected all outsiders to possess when they passed through the region, the Albany committee's passport for Sands conceivably protected him from harassment anywhere he encountered people sympathetic to the American cause by certifying that Sands "has steadily exerted himself as a sincere and active friend to the liberties of this country, and as such he is hereby most cordially recommended to all friends to *American* liberty." The revolutionary turmoil of the mid-1770s put even travel for private matters to the test of American loyalty. New Yorker Gerard G. Beekman's physician prescribed a visit to Bristol, Pennsylvania, in the hope that drinking local mineral water would cure a chronic illness. However, in order to take this recuperative journey in safety, Beekman obtained a passport from the New York Committee of Safety confirming that he was "a friend to the cause of *American* liberty." According to the committee, "It is therefore recommended to all the friends of liberty, to suffer him to pass unmolested" to Bristol. Widespread slavery and a divided population with fluctuating allegiances thus exposed the revolutionary governments' limited commitment to the principle of free emigration. However, the same governments that curtailed freedom of movement for suspect populations recognized that the remaining population needed individual emigrant rights for the revolution to succeed.[15]

After the Continental Congress declared independence, it had to prove itself worthy of recognition under the law of nations. The Continental Congress had to become treaty-worthy; that is, Americans had to prove to European powers that they could defend themselves against adversaries and maintain domestic order to gain equal standing with the sovereign states of Europe that set the terms of international law. And in order for the separate states to avoid internecine conflicts while preserving their independence, a confederation of republics bound by an agreement akin to a peace treaty was necessary. The Articles of Confederation and eventually the Constitution created a union of states governed by principles of diplomatic cooperation and mutual alliances rooted in the burgeoning law of nations. In order to satisfy the demands of independence under the law of nations, those who drafted the fundamental agreements of union included provisions for emigrant rights.[16]

The law of nations provided guidance to American lawmakers in their need to transform emigrant rights from a justification for colonial rebellion into an instrument of orderly republican governance. This transformation concerned the role of consent in balancing the privileges and obligations of emigrant rights. According to all of the leading law of nations theorists, people should not emigrate without the consent of the government they left behind while governments should rarely withhold consent. Pufendorf maintained that free people could choose to abandon their "General Duties" to government provided they had "the express or tacit Consent of the Nation" to settle beyond its borders. Any government that did not adopt laws to prohibit emigration granted its population tacit consent to leave at will, Pufendorf argued. Vattel identified the ways that governments could grant express consent to emigration. Emigrant rights could "be secured to the citizens by a fundamental law of the state." Moreover, multiple governments might recognize a right to emigration in treaties. According to Vattel, a right to emigration "may be derived from some treaty made with a foreign power, by which a sovereign has promised to leave full liberty to those of his subjects, who, for a certain reason . . . desire to transplant themselves into that power." Beginning in 1776, Americans created governments that consented to individual emigrant rights for their citizens according to standards established under the law of nations.[17]

The Articles of Confederation provided the first governing charter for the United States once adopted by its constituent states in 1781. As drafted and approved by the Continental Congress in 1777, the articles were widely understood as a treaty between sovereign republics to create a union, or "firm league of friendship," intended to achieve shared but circumscribed ends of mutual defense and cooperation. Also understood as a confederation, the member states remained independent, sovereign entities with wide power over affairs within their boundaries. Citizenship remained the domain of state law under the Articles of Confederation as each state preserved the authority to determine whom to include or exclude from its political community. Moreover, states, not the union, bestowed citizenship. A person's civic standing stemmed from residence in a state that constituted the union, not from the union as such. Thus according to the Articles of Confederation, citizens in one state were effectively foreigners to citizens in another. Migration from state to state was akin to crossing an international border so that changing residence in one state for that in another also required trading allegiance from one sovereign entity to another. Thus in nearly every way, a citizen's freedom of movement throughout the confederated states exemplified a right to emigration under international law, the very system of custom and treaties that the Articles of Confederation relied on for its authority.[18]

The Articles of Confederation established emigrant rights in Article IV. According to this provision, free people in one state could not be denied citizenship in any other except for "paupers, vagabonds, and fugitives from justice." In addition, "the people of each state shall have free ingress and regress to and from any other State." When considering the Articles of Confederation as a treaty among several sovereign republics, Article IV met one of Vattel's standards of express consent to emigration. It recognized emigrant rights according to a multilateral international agreement. According to the terms of union, all states party to the Articles of Confederation recognized a right to emigration.[19]

The Constitution replaced the Articles of Confederation in 1789. The new charter gave the central government stronger powers in certain domains in order to create a more effective federal union, and, like the charter it superseded, the Constitution also functioned much like a treaty among sovereign states. For the Constitution to maintain peace and cooperation among the member states, the migration of people from state to state became one of the many diplomatic considerations before the delegates who drafted and ratified it. The drafters of the Constitution preserved the principle from the Articles of Confederation that citizens possessed freedom of movement with the expectation that citizenship in one state guaranteed citizenship in another, but in a more succinct fashion than their predecessors in 1777. According to Article IV, Section 2 of the Constitution, "The Citizens of each State shall be entitled to all Privileges and Immunities of Citizens in the several States." At its most basic, the privileges and immunities clause ensured that citizens of one state would not become aliens upon entering the jurisdiction of any other state. Free people thus had the right to emigrate from one state to another where they would then obtain all of the citizenship rights available to them under municipal law. Although residence in a federal republic granted emigrant rights to many Americans, so did residence in particular states.[20]

Lawmakers in Pennsylvania established emigrant rights for its citizens soon after declaring independence from Great Britain. In 1776, Pennsylvania adopted a constitution with a Declaration of Rights that announced that "all men have a natural inherent right to emigrate from one state to another that will receive them, or to form a new state in vacant countries, or in such countries as they can purchase, whenever they think that thereby they may promote their own happiness." In 1790, Pennsylvania lawmakers revised the state's constitution to include a less prolix statement of emigrant rights, merely declaring that "emigration from the state shall not be prohibited." Nevertheless, convention delegates did not intend for the amended language to limit a citizen's freedom to leave, for they defeated a motion to add the words "unless in time of war" to the article. Instead, convention delegates in Pennsylvania actually expanded the privileges of emigrant rights in ways that become apparent only when compared to contemporary developments in other states.[21]

Legislators in Virginia adopted the most definitive statement of emigrant rights during the revolutionary era. In 1779, Thomas Jefferson, as a member of the Virginia House of Delegates, successfully introduced a bill that defined citizenship in Virginia to include "that natural right, which all men have of relinquishing the country, in which birth, or other accident may have thrown them, and, seeking subsistence and happiness wheresoever they may be able, or may hope to find them." Although the Virginia citizenship statute echoed Pennsylvania's Declaration of Rights, Jefferson wrote the statute to codify a right to expatriation, which meant citizens' freedom to both leave a state and to cast aside their former allegiances. Although emigrant rights under the law of nations implied the freedom and necessity of changing allegiance, the Virginia legislature made this relationship explicit in its definition of citizenship. Jefferson believed that expatriation was a natural right, so he wrote the bill to avoid uncertainty in its exercise. Citizens of Virginia who chose to relinquish their citizenship could do so in person before the county court where they resided or the general court, or in writing before three witnesses. Once they publicly stated their intention to expatriate and left the commonwealth, they severed all ties of allegiance to Virginia, and Virginia's government could claim no further authority over them. Most importantly, the bill did not empower state officials to prevent citizens from expatriating. The bill guaranteed all state citizens the opportunity to avail themselves of Virginia's expatriation procedures. Virginians could eventually expatriate themselves without declaring their intent so long as the person left and "entered into the service" of a state at peace with Virginia and the United States or by "any act whereby he shall become a subject or citizen of such state," according to the revised citizenship statute of 1784.[22]

Ultimately, Virginia's citizenship statute announced a natural right to expatriation implied but left unstated in Pennsylvania's Declaration of Rights. Citizens were free to leave both states without the law first requiring a stark choice between keeping or abandoning their citizenship. In this regard, Virginia and Pennsylvania established a portable, individual right to expatriation, a right reserved for its citizens to exercise wherever and whenever they pleased. Together, the state laws allowed citizens to absolve their allegiance without demanding that they transfer their allegiance to a sovereign elsewhere, and to preserve the benefits of state citizenship until they saw fit to shed this status. Virginia and Pennsylvania thus allowed their citizens to effectively become citizens of the world, just as Pufendorf understood the right to emigration.

By the late 1780s, the federal structure of American government allowed conflicting forms of emigrant rights to take hold in the United States. The Constitution protected emigrant rights to facilitate the movement of people, property, and commerce throughout the United States. To encourage comity and cooperation among states that preserved much of their independence, the right to emigration functioned as a treaty provision intended to make the union more cohesive. Citizens who exercised their federal emigrant rights did so in furtherance of the nationalist aspirations behind calls for a stronger constitutional union. State emigrant rights could further nationalist ends, but they could just as easily undermine them. The freedom to expatriation recognized under Virginia and Pennsylvania law provided citizens the right to leave not just their states but the United States. Moreover, according to one perspective from the law of nations, the right to expatriation might belong not only to citizens of Virginia and Pennsylvania but to every citizen of the United States. By Pufendorf's measure of tacit consent, all citizens were free to leave their respective states because none of the original thirteen states adopted laws to prohibit their exit. Thus state-level recognition of an individual right to expatriation during the 1780s created a citizenship privilege that existed without nationalist duties or sentiments.

As a citizenship right, freedom of expatriation was fundamentally a right to free movement before all else. Although it was a right that often came to include more familiar citizenship privileges such as voting, property ownership, or holding political office, expatriates gained these privileges only with settlement outside the United States. Moreover, freedom of expatriation was a citizenship right that did not presuppose or prescribe exclusive allegiance to one nation over another. Indeed, its privileges were not contained within state borders but reached across them. Freedom of expatriation thus created a citizenship right that was cosmopolitan in its operation because it existed apart from any particular nation.

The cosmopolitan underpinnings of a right to expatriation were evident to all who explained how freedom to leave defined adopted citizenship elsewhere. The elevation of choice over chance denigrated accidents of birth as sources of political allegiance and civic status. To those who included expatriation as an emigrant right, such as Thomas Jefferson, a person's place of birth was no more special than any other patch of earth. Traditional ties of belonging through family, community, or tradition could be set aside for pursuits elsewhere in the world. Positions such as Jefferson's were backed by law of nations writers such as Vattel. People should always kindle a sentimental attachment to their country of birth because this was the place that provided their parents with the necessary means to bring them into adulthood. However, this was a debt of gratitude to one's past, insisted Vattel, not a patriotic duty that must be upheld in the future. Should a person remain in their native country into adulthood, then their gratitude became the basis of patriotic duty, but "various lawful reasons may oblige him to chuse another country." For Vattel, duty to country is reserved to "the state of which a man is an actual member" for it is this state above all others "that he is bound to serve with his utmost efforts." Changing countries thus changed people's object of patriotic duty because they transferred their consent from one government to another. Indeed, a commentator in a Georgia newspaper from the late 1780s suggested that choosing to leave one country for life in another made an expatriate's adopted citizenship more meaningful than citizenship acquired by birthright. After all, this writer asked, "is not the foreigner who, from the expectation of living free, quits his native country, settles here, pays his taxes, bears his proportion of the public burthen, and performs every other duty of a citizen as good and useful a man as him whose only merit perhaps consists in his being accidentally born here?" Ultimately, the freedom of expatriation allowed for the performance of emigration right citizenship, a form of belonging obtained by free movement across relatively open borders followed by intentional participation in the civic life of another nation, kingdom, or empire.[23]

Once the notion of emigrant rights came to include the freedom of expatriation, a fundamental privilege of republican citizenship became inseparable from the era's larger discourses surrounding cosmopolitanism. When eighteenth-century writers referred to a "citizen of the world," they typically did so as part of a broader exploration of cosmopolitanism as an ideal or an outlook. Throughout the 1700s, the citizen of the world was a familiar type in an array of writings from political treatises to cultural commentary in newspapers and pamphlets published in Europe and North America. By the 1780s, writers in the United States found the notion of cosmopolitanism useful in their attempts to discern the meaning of citizenship. In nearly every instance, references to world citizenship were set against alternative forms of local allegiance and particular attachments to a place, society, or belief system. According to a succinct definition of world citizenship published in 1784 in the *Massachusetts Centinel*, a "cosmopolitan" was a person "unattached to nation, party or profession." It is unclear from this conception of cosmopolitanism if it was an ideal worthy of aspiration. Other writers, however, were less ambiguous, upholding cosmopolitanism for its virtues or excoriating its vices.[24]

Eighteenth-century writers who celebrated cosmopolitanism, or world citizenship, did so because it taught suspicion of local, parochial allegiances and disregard for international borders. Cosmopolitanism reminded those who embraced it to be humble in their patriotism. As a writer in New York's *Daily Advertiser* cautioned in 1787, "a laudable regard to one nation is frequently the parent and nurse of an illiberal contempt for all others." Those without a cosmopolitan outlook, the same writer continued, might too easily believe that virtue was unique only to the places or customs they called their own. This notion of virtue as "the peculiar growth of any certain countries, sects, or religions, is a sentiment that can," this writer concluded, "spring only from hypocrisy, bigotry, ignorance, illiberality—or the union of all." Rather than substituting parochialism for genuine virtue, citizens of the world could distinguish between the particular and the universal, perhaps relishing the former but obligated to uphold the latter no matter their place in the world. According to a writer in a New Jersey newspaper in 1786, government was one such universal institution without which society would falter. Foreigners who defended governments besides their own acted according to their duties as "a citizen of the world." At its most ambitious, champions of world citizenship would claim no single nation as their own because people had duties that transcended national borders, duties that remained with them as they exercised their natural right to freedom of movement. In this regard, American writers understood cosmopolitanism in ways familiar to European writers. "All the countries are the same to me" and "[I am] changing my places of residence according to my whims," proclaimed Fourget de Montbron in his 1753 treatise, *Le Cosmopolite*.[25]

Cosmopolitanism's tendency to attenuate national allegiance disturbed its eighteenth-century critics. One account of world citizenship from a Pennsylvania newspaper in 1791 described it as encouraging an encompassing but absurdly thin notion of allegiance. In the words of a fictional citizen of the world, "I'd forget the family where I was born, yes, and the town—yes, and the country, and the world. I'd belong to the universe, and if any body had the impudence to ask my native place—I'd tell 'em the *solar system*." Although a satire of cosmopolitanism, it cautioned readers that allegiance spread too far provided no meaningful forms of civic inclusion or community. Any appeal to world citizenship was thus hobbled by a contradiction of terms at the very center of the concept. Other American skeptics of world citizenship focused on its pernicious consequences. The editor of the *Royal Gazette*, a Loyalist newspaper published in New York during the Revolutionary War, disdained the Whigs for dissolving their allegiance to the Crown and rejecting the empire that had protected them and their ancestors in North America. Rather than remaining loyal subjects bound to the Crown by perpetual allegiance and affection, they were selfish; they had "become entire citizens of the world, governed by interest alone." Even after the fraught political conflicts of wartime ended, the ideal of world citizenship did not lose its association with selfishness and duplicity. As Gouverneur Morris argued at the Constitutional Convention, all nations had a right to set limits on membership. Although other delegates at the convention might naively entrust their government to "citizens of the world," he could not do the same, for "he did not wish to see any of them in our public councils." According to Morris, "The men who can shake off their attachments to their own country can never love any other." On the contrary, Morris concluded, "these attachments are the wholesome prejudices which uphold all governments."[26]

Just as American exponents of world citizenship held views that aligned with like-minded writers in Europe, cosmopolitanism's opponents in the United States argued against it for reasons similar to writers across the Atlantic. Johann Georg Schlosser celebrated nationalist patriotism, the antithesis of world citizenship. "It is better to be proud of one's nation than to have none," he announced in his poem, "Der Kosmopolit." Jean-Jacques Rousseau argued that cosmopolitans "boast that they love everyone, to have the right to love no one." Ultimately, for those disdainful of world citizenship, cosmopolitanism was equal parts immoral and dangerous. It glorified reckless self-interest over the common good.[27]

Despite conflicts over cosmopolitanism's virtues, its ideals proved essential to those eager to incorporate emigrant rights into the meaning of republican citizenship. Without cosmopolitanism, the revolutionary generation could not have put consent to remain a citizen on an equal conceptual footing with a person's right to revoke consent and abandon citizenship. The terms of consensual citizenship were clearly defined and broadly understood in the eighteenth century. From John Locke's social contract philosophy to the new state laws and constitutions after 1776, Americans accepted that citizens were those who freely consented to obey and support the government in exchange for protection. The other side of consent, which was a citizen's right to withdraw it from one government and transfer it to another, was a broadly recognized but less clearly articulated right during the late eighteenth century. In part this is not only because it reflected the undoing of citizenship but also because its exercise, at least in the minds of many, depended on a person's choice to leave the jurisdiction of one government for life and allegiance within another. In this way, a coequal element of consent in republican citizenship was best defined according to cosmopolitan principles backed by the law of nations.

Although emigrant rights, including the freedom to expatriate, constituted full citizenship during the 1770s and 1780s, they were strictly proscribed in law and practice. In the most basic sense, only the able-bodied could exercise emigrant rights. Only the physically capable could move from place to place for choice, not chance, to determine their lives. However, the law of nations, as well as federal and state laws, granted full citizenship to some people by denying the privileges of emigrant rights by gender and race. Emer de Vattel underscored that emigrants were men—patriarchs, in particular—when he explained that they depart with "their families and property" to form new settlements. Federal emigrant rights under the Articles of Confederation and the Constitution assumed economic independence as a precondition for free movement throughout the union, but in practice the status of nominally free people who changed residence from state to state varied widely by locale. Adult white men possessed full citizenship in the federal union in part because they were entitled to full rights wherever they settled. For adult Black men and all women and children, changing residence from one state to another might result in a diminution of rights or the exchange of civic disabilities in one place for those in another. A state's right to emigration also defined full citizenship in exclusionary ways. Under Virginia's 1779 citizenship statute, Jefferson awarded citizenship to "all white persons" born in Virginia and resident there since independence, and to the children of the commonwealth's natural-born citizens. The law also empowered Virginia to naturalize white immigrants who swore an oath of allegiance to the state and established residency. By limiting birthright citizenship and naturalization to Virginia's white inhabitants, Jefferson proscribed the concomitant right to expatriation along similar racial lines. From the law of nations to state statutes, theorists and lawmakers limited full citizenship in the United States to able-bodied, propertied white men in part by denying emigrant rights to everyone else.[28]

Should laws fail to deny emigrant rights to those whom governments wanted to exclude from full citizenship, cosmopolitan ideals could achieve the same ends. Cosmopolitanism suggested that freedom of movement existed along a spectrum with citizens of the world on one end and the stateless at the other extreme. World citizenship was a status reserved for free white men because they possessed nearly absolute emigrant rights to free movement and expatriation. For them, cosmopolitanism provided moral ballast to move throughout the world seeking happiness where they saw fit. In effect, cosmopolitanism provided its beneficiaries the freedoms to move about the globe and possess land that supposedly existed in the world before sovereignty—that fictional past created by law of nations theorists—but under the protection of emigrant rights recognized by sovereign powers. Cosmopolitan values combined with emigrant rights to assure free white men that governments could not reduce them to slavery by preventing them from leaving. In fact, to deprive free men their emigrant rights reduced them to slavery, they insisted. Of course, enslaved people occupied the other end of the spectrum. As property according to the law, they possessed no individual freedom of movement or civic standing to transfer. Without personal liberty, meaningful government protections, and freedom of movement, enslaved people were stateless. Moreover, a free white man's rights to free movement and expatriation allowed him to take his enslaved property when he traveled from one sovereign nation to another. Provided the laws of the receiving state allowed slavery, slave owners exercised their emigrant rights by depriving them to the people they enslaved.

Married women and dependents in the United States inhabited a status without the privileges of world citizenship but protected from the dangers of statelessness. The English common law of coverture and patriarchal authority subsumed the legal identity of wives and children within that of their husbands and fathers. Although considered citizens in the early United States, any privileges and obligations wives and children possessed came through those enjoyed by their husbands or fathers. Wives and children did not possess individual emigrant rights. Instead, their mobility and status reflected the choices that male authorities in their lives made about where to move and to what government to grant their allegiance. Occasions when married women and children moved about often registered their absence of emigrant rights but not those of their husbands and fathers. A husband or father's cosmopolitan liberty of free movement and transferable allegiance rested, for its full and unencumbered exercise, on the denial of such liberty to his household dependents.[29]

AMERICAN NOTIONS OF CITIZENSHIP included the freedom to revoke consent—articulated within international law and justified by appeals to cosmopolitanism—and established a spectrum of citizenship rights already evident by the late 1780s. Constitutional and legal developments at the state and federal levels from 1776 onward made this clear. These developments together created a robust legal framework to support the view that freedom of movement often entailed freedom to change allegiance, that emigrant rights underwrote a free person's natural right to expatriation. From this perspective, the freedom to adopt and shed citizenship at will was fundamental to personal liberty in a republic. James Wilson succinctly expressed this view in 1790. According to Wilson, a leading legal theorist and an original justice on the US Supreme Court, "It is both inhuman and unjust to convert the state into a prison for its citizens, by preventing them from leaving it on a prospect of advantage to themselves." Although citizens might choose to leave the United States for allegiance elsewhere, Wilson, like David Ramsey, was confident that citizens would decide otherwise. The United States did not have to become a prison because its citizens would never have reason to escape. Instead, the United States was the destination for outsiders seeking advantages, not a place that people fled to improve their fortunes.[30]

Nevertheless, Wilson and Ramsay wrote at a moment when citizens had already quit the United States for allegiance to neighboring sovereigns. By moving to territory in the lower Mississippi Valley controlled by the Spanish Crown or forming settlements in British North America, citizens expatriated themselves using emigrant rights protected by the law of nations but won in the American Revolution. If the early United States was an island nation instead of a single sovereignty among several striving for power in North America, the unsettling potential of individual emigrant rights would have remained unrevealed. However, the prospect of US citizens actually pursing their happiness in other nations shook the foundation of republican citizenship. Could the United States last as a union if its citizens chose to cast their allegiance abroad? Might the United States ultimately be undone by principles from the very body of international law that it relied on for its existence? Expatriated Americans who settled in regions beyond the nation's inchoate borders held the power to decide such questions.

CHAPTER TWO

A Spirit of Emigration

During the 1780s, Americans by the thousands settled west of the Appalachian Mountains. This territory comprised the republic's claim to a North American empire, although Indigenous people possessed much of this land. Many Americans feared that without firm control of its western territory, the Confederation's independence was hollow and possibly fleeting. "A spirit of emigration," as contemporaries described it, offered hope to federal officials that industrious, allegiant white settlers would occupy the republic's western domains, thereby upholding the republic's territorial sovereignty. For a nation that secured its independence from Great Britain in a revolution for emigrant rights, populating territory was an act of citizenship.

However, as Americans exercised emigration right citizenship in the republic's western territory, it became apparent that a personal freedom to move and choose allegiance also threatened national sovereignty. In a region defined by Indigenous power and European imperial interests, nothing guaranteed that loyalty to the United States would determine personal allegiances or the limits to individual mobility for white inhabitants. Indeed, the choices of white settlers west of the Appalachians first revealed the unsettling implications of a notion of citizenship in which the freedom to quit the nation equaled the obligations to remain. The spirit of emigration was effectively unbound. Once citizens exercised their rights to move from state to state, they claimed their freedom to emigrate beyond the United States. Government efforts after 1783 to harness emigrant rights for building an empire rather than resisting one ultimately put the Confederation on a precarious foundation.

THE REGION WEST of the Appalachian Mountains was a landscape of vast waterways and woodlands. The Ohio River divided this landscape as it flowed southwest to its confluence with the Mississippi River, thereby connecting the Great Lakes region to the Gulf Coast. Indigenous people moved along this region's lakes and rivers and overland through forest trails for purposes of trade, communication, and warfare. Human movement made this world, including Native emigrants who moved in pursuit of national sovereignty and land. Throughout the eighteenth century, several Algonquin- and Iroquois-speaking peoples settled the Ohio Valley from other parts of North

America, including Miami, Shawnee, Delaware, and Seneca among the more powerful nations. These waves of Native emigration imposed an Indigenous political geography on this region.[1]

Beginning in the 1760s, white emigrants claimed Native land in this region for themselves. British subjects established isolated settlements in Native territory at places in the upper Ohio and the eastern Tennessee River Valleys. British officials enacted policies to regulate emigration and settlement in its territory west of the Appalachians. The Proclamation of 1763 was the most categorical in its effort to prevent warfare with the Native nations that controlled much of the Ohio and Mississippi Valleys by stanching all English migration west of the Appalachian Mountains. At the same time that the Crown imposed the proclamation line, it also created colonial governments for the new provinces of East and West Florida. British colonial officials thus hoped to restrict white settlement to existing colonies or to its new Gulf Coast possessions. Montfort Browne, the lieutenant governor of West Florida, summarized Great Britain's colonial policy after 1763 as an effort to keep white colonists from becoming "commercially annihilated to the State." The dislocation wrought by the Revolutionary War and Great Britain's eventual surrender only increased white emigration west of the Appalachians.[2]

The Peace of Paris in 1783 recognized the United States as an independent republic with a territorial empire. American and European diplomats created a republican empire under the law of nations by shuffling sovereignty in North America. The United States assumed authority over all of the territory south of the Great Lakes and between the Appalachian Mountains and the Mississippi River formerly claimed by Great Britain. Moreover, Great Britain ceded its colonies of East and West Florida to Spain. Madrid thereby gained dominion over territory stretching from the Florida peninsula northwestward along the Gulf Coast to the Mississippi River where its new possessions met the Louisiana District, a vast region of New Spain stretching northward along the Mississippi's western bank deep into the continental interior. The United States and, to a greater extent, Spain thus expanded their territorial claims in North America at the expense of Great Britain, which was left with a diminished North American empire centered on the St. Lawrence River and the northern Great Lakes.

European and American diplomats imposed dramatic changes on the political geography of North America that invited border disputes. Great Britain continued to exercise influence throughout the Great Lakes by maintaining a military and commercial presence in territory that nominally belonged to the United States. Even greater uncertainty prevailed along the

Gulf Coast and the lower Mississippi River. Great Britain and the United States maintained that Spanish West Florida existed along a narrow coastal strip. This claim put the confederation's southern border about sixty miles inland from the Gulf of Mexico. Spain insisted that the United States possessed a far more limited dominion. West Florida extended one hundred miles north of the boundary recognized by the United States and Great Britain. Moreover, Spanish officials argued that the law of conquest and a debt of gratitude from the United States gave Spain control over significant territory east of the Mississippi and north between the Ohio and Tennessee Rivers. Spain's claims thus put its border with the United States adjacent to territory claimed by Virginia, North Carolina, and Georgia.[3]

The Europeans and Americans vying for dominance west of the Appalachians during the 1780s often found it difficult to enforce their ambitious territorial claims. State officials were few, sites of official power were thinly populated and widely dispersed, and the respective military forces were relatively small. The Confederation Congress could rarely muster an army in the Ohio Valley with more than 350 soldiers. In the absence of evident and enforceable state power throughout most of the region, populations that acted largely beyond the control of imperial governments in Quebec City, Philadelphia, or New Orleans often determined actual sovereignty over a given territory.[4]

Despite European and American claims to regions on maps, land west of the Appalachians largely remained Native country during the 1780s. In the Ohio Valley, a confederation coalesced in the villages of the Shawnees, Delawares, Miamis, and several other Algonquin peoples to protect their land and autonomy from diplomatic accords decided in Paris at negotiations to which Indigenous delegates were not invited. Should Great Britain decide to reclaim parts of its lost empire in North America, peaceful relations and commerce with the emerging Algonquin confederacy and the Cherokee farther south would prove essential. Indigenous power forced similar considerations on Spanish officials in North America. Apart from isolated Spanish colonial settlements and occasional trading posts, Seminoles controlled much of East Florida while the Creek, Choctaw, and Chickasaw were powerful in West Florida and the disputed territory to its north. Spanish colonial officials found themselves in a similar position to British colonial authorities in Canada. Spain could not assert control over its expanded empire on the Gulf Coast and the lower Mississippi without Indigenous support, or at least compliance. Whereas Great Britain and Spain might hope to use alliances with various Native peoples to preserve their North American empires, Indigenous

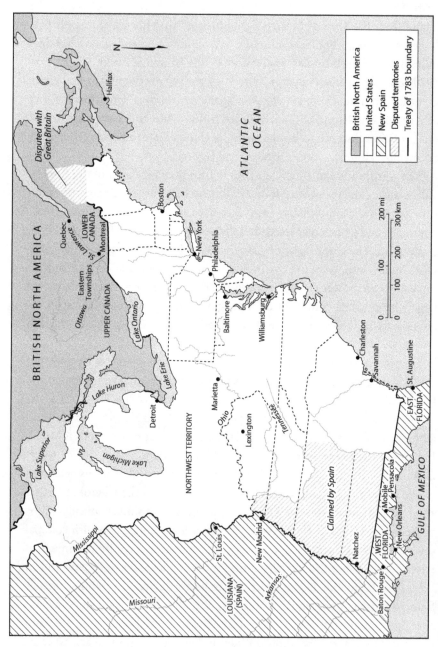

Eastern North America, ca. 1794

power also determined the kind of empire that the American confederation might become.[5]

The United States inherited an old imperial conundrum over how best to govern a mobile settler population seeking land already possessed by Indigenous nations. Although it needed to secure the economic benefits of its territorial empire without inviting needless warfare with a burgeoning Algonquin confederacy, the Confederation Congress could not achieve these ends by preventing its citizens from emigrating westward. First and foremost, individual states, not the Congress, initially claimed jurisdiction of the confederation's western territory. Atlantic Seaboard states including Massachusetts, Connecticut, New York, and Virginia claimed much of the land north of the Ohio River. By the mid-1780s, the Confederation Congress gained jurisdiction over the territory north of the Ohio River after the seaboard states ceded their western land claims. Nevertheless, Congress's authority over western land ended at the Ohio River. Territory to the south comprised the westernmost reaches of Virginia and North Carolina along with Georgia's vast claims to the Yazoo lands that stretched to the Mississippi River. With western land under a welter of jurisdictions, the Confederation Congress was powerless to restrain emigration with a single colonial policy.

Moreover, the confederation's fiscal needs required American settlement west of the Appalachians. Only through the dispossession of Indigenous land by force and treaty could the American Confederation begin to exercise colonial dominion over its western territory. Although dispossession risked warfare with Indigenous nations and meddling from Spain and Great Britain, federal officials pursued it in response to American citizens who demanded western land and the revenue this demand might bring to the Confederation Congress. Transforming dispossessed Native land into private property promised a lucrative source of government revenue, but without white settlers, western land remained valueless to Congress.[6]

Any effort by Congress to prevent westward emigration would have also been inconsistent with revolutionary principles. American colonists claimed their emigrant rights as they transformed themselves from subjects to citizens in rebellion against Great Britain. As citizens, they protected their emigrant rights in the Articles of Confederation, in various state constitutions, and under the law of nations that created the union. Finally, emigrant rights included citizenship privileges uncontained by jurisdictional limits or state borders. Those citizens free to move and choose their allegiance within the union as it existed in 1776 possessed the same liberty in the union's western territorial domain after 1783.

White settlement surged after 1783. Through mountain gaps and over waterways, white men entered the republic's western territory to exercise their privileges of emigration right citizenship. Emigrants rooted this privilege in property, which they obtained by dispossessing Native land to create a landscape of family farms devoted to cultivating various grain crops. White settlers created the Kentucky region of western Virginia by exercising emigration right citizenship. Settlers effectively dispossessed Shawnee of their Kentucky land, which forced them into the Ohio country and precipitated growth in the white emigrant population from 12,000 people in 1783 to 73,000 people by 1790. White emigrants also settled on dispossessed Cherokee land in the Tennessee River Valley of western North Carolina. The white men who brought their families to Kentucky or the Tennessee Valley exercised their emigrant rights in order to obtain full citizenship that only land ownership could provide. The settlers expected responsive governments that would secure their land claims through laws of private property and a military that would protect them and their property in instances of Native warfare, so authorities in Virginia and North Carolina created western counties in an effort to secure emigrant allegiance.[7]

Responsibility for governing American territory north of the Ohio River belonged to the Confederation Congress. Throughout the 1780s a series of federal land ordinances created a public domain out of territory that Congress dispossessed from Indigenous nations by force and treaty. Congress expected to raise essential government revenue by selling land from the public domain, so in 1785 it adopted a land ordinance that provided for the surveying and division of the territory into equal-sized townships that buyers could purchase at public land auctions. Congress intended for the Land Ordinance of 1785 to begin the rapid but orderly settlement of the public domain. Federal officials expected the Land Ordinance of 1785 to attract settlers with the promise of secure land titles so that every time citizens claimed their emigrant rights to settle western territory, it redounded to the fiscal and imperial interests of the Confederation Congress.[8]

Officials in Congress and in states with western land claims ultimately found it difficult to govern emigrants. They held uncertain allegiance to the federal union and were quick to declare themselves independent of all distant governments. Hugh Williamson, a North Carolina representative to the Confederation Congress, described the republic's western reaches as territory where an insurrectionary "Spirit of Migration" combined with "the Spirit of making new States." Efforts by emigrant settlers in 1784 to create the state of Franklin out of North Carolina's westernmost counties confirmed fears such as

Williamson's. Although Franklin existed only as a paper state because the Confederation Congress never recognized its existence, emigrant demands for local control over land allocation and Native dispossession also threatened Virginia's control over its Kentucky counties. State officials in Virginia managed to prevent emigrant rebellions in the Ohio Valley with eventual guarantees of statehood for Kentucky. Congress attempted to preclude movements for emigrant state-making in the Ohio country by including provisions in its later land ordinances for the creation of new states in the region with equal standing in the union.[9]

Although creating effective local governments in the union's western territory presented one possibility for securing emigrant allegiance, promoting western commercial development seemed equally important. Transforming dispossessed Native territory into private property met two immediate needs: settler demands for citizenship through secure land ownership and government revenue. However, future commercial potential determined western land values. If western settlers found it difficult to transport their produce to eastern markets, then dominion over a territorial empire was meaningless to the union. Promoters of western commercial development during the 1780s thus supported efforts to secure emigrant allegiance in order for the union to realize the profits of colonialism. George Washington was a leading proponent of this view. In 1784, he lobbied the Virginia government to create a company for improving navigation on the Potomac River and linking it to the Ohio River. Washington and other prominent investors in Virginia expected to profit from the project's success. Indeed, "upon a commercial scale alone," Washington boasted, the project is "sufficient to excite our endeavors." Yet Washington easily braided personal enrichment with the public good, for he argued that the project's "political object is, in my estimation, immense." As Washington concluded in regard to the Ohio Valley, "the closer we bind that rising world (for indeed it may be so called) to our interests . . . the greater strength shall we acquire."[10]

Those who supported the formation of local governments in the West and the region's commercial development hoped that both measures would encourage western settlers to exercise their emigrant rights in favor of the union. Instead, such hopes faded against the realization that western settlers often claimed their emigrant rights to move and possess land without regard for the governing institutions or economic incentives that eastern leaders depended on to secure their allegiance. Moreover, emigrants frequently attacked Native villages, either in small bands or organized under the Kentucky militia. These armed emigrants seized Indigenous land north of the Ohio

River in disregard of actual Native possession and notional federal authority over the region. The Algonquians of the Ohio region formed their confederacy during the 1780s in large part to defend their villages and hunting lands from invading American emigrants. Despite his optimism about the possibilities of commercial development, on various occasions George Washington described American emigrants as "wavering Inhabitants" and as a "people who are not very subordinate to Law & Good Government." Squatters embodied why emigrant rights remained largely ungovernable in the republic's western empire.[11]

Squatting was inevitable west of the Appalachians. The region's welter of confusing land claims, combined with its inadequate legal and governing institutions necessary to secure settler property ownership, guaranteed as much. Movement onto land constituted possession, and agricultural improvements entailed ownership, regardless of claims from distant governments, land speculators, or Native people. In this regard, emigrant rights endowed American citizens with squatters' rights. This relationship between emigration and squatting became most evident in the waves of Pennsylvania, Virginia, and Kentucky citizens who populated territory north of the Ohio River in contravention of Congress's land ordinances. Squatters provoked retaliation from Native people in Ohio and undermined Congress's policy for the orderly sale and settlement of land in the region, so federal troops frequently destroyed squatter settlements in order to force their inhabitants to return to the states from whence they emigrated.

However, squatters asserted that their emigrant rights allowed them to remain in the Ohio country. In 1785, squatter John Amberson called for a constitutional convention to create a new state north of the Ohio. Amberson's assertion of squatter popular sovereignty was that possessed "by all mankind agreeable to every constitution formed in America" of "an undoubted right to pass into vacant country, and there to form their constitution." Many of the white men squatting on Ohio lands left states such as Pennsylvania and Virginia with laws that recognized emigrant rights. Pennsylvania's 1776 constitution included a declaration of rights that protected freedom of emigration in terms similar to those used by Amberson. Virginia's 1779 citizenship statute, which applied to Kentucky settlers as well, recognized free men's natural right to seek "subsistence and happiness wheresoever they may be able, or may hope to find them." State laws recognizing emigrant rights, derived as they were from the law of nations, allowed Amberson to claim citizenship privileges for squatters that no state boundaries or jurisdictional limits could contain. Instead, squatters possessed freedom of movement and portable allegiance that characterized the world before sovereignty posited by law of nations theorists. By wrapping squatter claims to land in the legal authority of emigrant rights, Amberson allowed that Americans settled on Ohio lands were the ultimate citizens of the world, people free to move about and to choose their allegiance.[12]

Other squatters on Ohio land understood their rights in similar ways. A group of Kentucky emigrants who settled on Ohio land petitioned the Confederation Congress for secure title despite claims to the land by Virginia speculators. The petitioners asserted that their emigrant rights not only allowed them to possess the land but also gave them recourse should Congress deny their request. The petitioners announced their good standing as patriarchs who quit Kentucky with their families and portable property to improve Ohio lands. They exposed themselves to Native retaliation, which they responded to with like violence. As settlers, therefore, the petitioners argued that they exercised their emigrant rights for personal gain and the good of the union. By dispossessing Indigenous land for reduction to settled agriculture, the petitioners believed they helped "advance the Common cause of Liberty" but were "subject to the United States at Large, and no other State or power whatsoever." By exercising their emigrant rights, the Kentucky petitioners articulated a notion of national citizenship well before this concept existed under law, which allowed them to claim that the Confederation Congress alone could recognize their liberty to adopt "regulations amongst themselves as they shall find necessary to Govern themselves." If Congress failed to recognize this novel notion of national citizenship, then they were left with few options. They must return to Kentucky to live as "slaves to those Engrossers of Lands and to the Court of Virginia," a choice that diminished their liberty, or they might exercise their emigrant rights beyond the borders of American territory where they could "remove down the River Ohio, and land on some part of Mexico and become Subjects to the King of Spain."[13]

In outlining their options, the Kentucky petitioners muddled their geography but not their rights. The Kentucky petitioners possessed an express right to expatriation under Virginia citizenship law. However, freedom of expatriation was a privilege common to all citizens of the confederation. As the federal government sought to prohibit squatting on Ohio lands, the fundamental threat of its citizens' emigrant rights to the confederation's sovereignty and its independence became apparent. The federal government had no power to prevent its citizens from choosing allegiance to another sovereign once they left its jurisdiction or that of its constituent states. Freedom of emigration allowed American citizens to move at will throughout the confederation as well as beyond its borders. The Confederation Congress could never secure its territorial domain if a spirit of emigration carried away American citizens in significant numbers.

Spanish officials at New Orleans viewed rising emigration to the western United States from existing imperial concerns of their own. Increased American strength in the Mississippi Valley by way of emigration and settlement threatened Louisiana's standing as a strong buffer to protect Spain's lucrative possessions in Mexico. Spanish authorities reasoned that the western United States would remain undesirable if the region lost access to New Orleans and Atlantic commerce more broadly. In reaching this conclusion, Spain ended its nominal alliance with the United States in favor of imperial rivalry over territory and control over the movement of settler populations. With the intention of directing American settlement away from Louisiana, Spain closed the Mississippi River to American navigation in 1784.

Initial signs from the Confederation Congress suggested that the American government might accept Spain's closure of the Mississippi. During negotiations over a commercial treaty between the United States and Spain the following year, John Jay, the secretary for foreign affairs under the Confederation Congress, proposed surrendering American usage of the Mississippi River for at least twenty-five years when Don Diego de Gardoqui, Spain's minister to the United States, insisted on Spain's control over the lower Mississippi Valley. Jay concluded that commercial ties with Spain were more important to the United States' immediate interests than access to a distant river. Northern delegates to Congress agreed by offering their unanimous support for Jay's proposal while southern delegates unanimously rejected it. Although northern votes in Congress outnumbered southern votes, treaty negotiations continued for several years without resolving the Mississippi question.[14]

By closing the Mississippi, Spain also provoked a crisis of governance and allegiance outside of Congress. A confederation that was too weak to secure the potential of its western territory was also too weak to secure the citizens within its borders. Western inhabitants expressed this position in stark terms. "America is ruined!" exclaimed Thomas Green in a letter that he sent from Louisville, Kentucky, to a correspondent in New England. So long as the United States acquiesced to Spain's control over the Mississippi, Green believed that "Spain has placed the rock upon which they are like to split." Green was unburdened by the potential wreckage of the United States because he blamed Congress's neglect of western needs for the Confederation's perilous state. If Congress and state authorities ultimately failed to address western concerns, Green argued that its citizens would exercise their emigrant rights to assume any form of self-government deemed necessary. "In case we are not countenanced and succored by the United States," Green proposed, "our allegiance will be thrown off, and some other power applied to." Green suggested that Kentuckians might also cast their allegiance to Great Britain through trade and military ties with colonists in Canada. Even Kentuckians with stronger affections for the United States were certain that western citizens might seek other allegiances if necessity dictated this choice. A letter writer who also purported to be from Kentucky disputed Green's observations about western sentiment, asserting that he did not capture "the voice of the people of Kentucky." The majority, this author continued, "have too high a veneration for federal government to betray such disrespect." Nevertheless, the author concluded that "it must be a repetition of injuries that will drive them to seek connexion with a people lately so hostile to their liberties." Despite this author's paean to western loyalty, he warned readers and politicians in the East against taking it for granted. The competing dispatches from Kentucky circulated throughout the West and eventually found widespread publication in newspapers on the Eastern Seaboard. Delegates to Congress entered copies of Green's letters into the official record during debates over how the government should respond to Spain's policies regarding the Mississippi. Eastern audiences in the 1780s found that reports from the western United States exposed the confederation's weakness, its inability to exercise power at its borders.[15]

Conflicting positions on the Mississippi question revealed clashing configurations of sovereignty and mobility. Those who supported concessions to Spain believed that US sovereignty relied on maritime commerce, which it should protect even at the expense of limiting American emigration in the West. Those who demanded American rights to navigation on the Mississippi River insisted that the republic's sovereignty was hollow if the confederation's citizens were unable to freely move about and use its territory. If the United States was too weak to protect the people's emigrant rights, then the people, western inhabitants most immediately, were free to create or seek allegiance to alternative sovereign powers. George Washington recognized this possibility in light of the West's growing population from the "emigration of foreigners who will have no particular predilection towards us, as well as from the removal of our own Citizens." When it came to western settlement, birth in the United States versus birth elsewhere was a distinction with little meaning for Washington. He believed that both populations would, under the right circumstances, quit the United States. From necessity, western citizens could "be *driven* into the arms of, or be made dependent upon foreigners." As

Washington warned, "The Western settlers stand as it were upon a pivot—the touch of a feather, would turn them any way." Ultimately, western citizens had several options for turning away from the United States.[16]

Westerners might secede from the union to form independent republics or separate confederacies. For some observers, northern support for surrendering the Mississippi to Spain, against southern opposition, portended a confederation fractured into at least three separate, smaller confederacies. The new borders of the various confederacies would likely follow existing regional divisions among New England, the mid-Atlantic states, and the South. A contributor to a New York newspaper speculated that a fourth confederacy west of the Appalachians would include Kentucky and other Ohio River settlements. Although many American observers anticipated this outcome, they also recognized that new republics or regional confederacies could not provide for their own defense or commerce. Indigenous power alone would force American settlers in the region to seek stronger sources of government protection in exchange for their allegiance.[17]

This led to the second possibility that western citizens might enter alliances with North American powers besides the United States. Many Americans believed that Spain was the most likely partner for such alliances. George Washington predicted that if Spain pulled western settlers into its orbit, then the United States would be powerless "to apply the cement of interest, to bind all parts of the Union together by indissoluble bonds." Indeed, throughout the 1780s and 1790s, Spanish colonial officials entertained clandestine American schemes to bring parts of the western United States under Spanish sovereignty. Spanish officials were reluctant to provide open support because doing so violated norms of international law against fomenting domestic insurrections inside friendly nations.[18]

This left a third option for western American citizens eager for access to the Mississippi River. They could expatriate themselves to Spanish allegiance by migrating to Spanish territory. Ultimately, a future United States splintered by regional interests or seditious plots existed only in nationalist fears. However, a sizeable American population did pursue its emigrant rights to free movement and expatriation. They concluded that if the United States could not guarantee their access to the Mississippi, then they would become Spanish subjects. Beginning in the 1780s, a steady flow of American citizens settled in Spanish territory, with the largest concentration of emigrants in Natchez, a colonial settlement on the lower Mississippi River.

Each European power that claimed the Mississippi Valley regarded Natchez as an important military and trading post. Early in the eighteenth

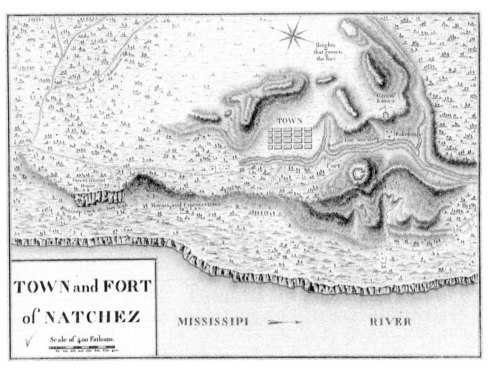

"Town and Fort of Natchez," from Georges-Henri-Victor Collot, *Voyage dans l'Amérique Septentrionale* (Paris: A. Bertrand, 1826). Library of Congress, Geography and Map Division, Louisiana: European Explorations and the Louisiana Purchase.

century, warfare between the Indigenous Natchez nation and French colonists resulted in the destruction of Natchez villages. Natchez survivors fled the region for refuge in Chickasaw, Creek, and Cherokee villages, but the French kept their name on the conquered territory. Great Britain then created the Natchez District as part of West Florida after victory in the French and Indian War. Spain took control of the region after Great Britain's defeat in the Revolutionary War, but it preserved the colonial boundaries established by the British. Authority over Natchez during the 1780s belonged to Esteban Miró, the governor of Louisiana and West Florida from 1782 to 1791. Soon after Miró became governor, Natchez had a population of approximately 1,000 people concentrated in three areas known as St. Catherine Creek, Second Creek, and Coles Creek. Francisco Bouligny, the Spanish military officer who commanded Fort Panmure at Natchez, described the sentiments of the settler population in 1785. He believed "that many of those who by birth and inclination are Americans are filled with gratitude for the benefits which they have received from our government." Moreover, Bouligny observed, the Americans "loudly proclaim that it would be impossible to have a control that could be milder or more advantageous." Despite the overall satisfaction with Spanish colonial government in Natchez, Bouligny recommended steps that Miró should take to guarantee that local opinion did not turn against Spanish rule.[19]

Natchez needed a regular military presence along with local government to protect settlers and adjudicate legal disputes. Bouligny provided a list of trustworthy Natchez settlers of good character, among them many emigrants from the United States, whom Miró could appoint as officers in the district's three militia units. As militia service was a hallmark of freedom and civic inclusion in the eighteenth century, Bouligny's proposal burnished the Americans' status as Spanish subjects in good standing by further enmeshing them in matters of colonial defense. Bouligny argued that his various reforms would fill the American settlers "with the most complete satisfaction, and this would represent a new tie that would cement their loyalty and promote peace." Bouligny endorsed his recommendations for Natchez with an architectural metaphor familiar to empire builders in the United States such as George Washington. The shared language revealed a common understanding that governments in possession of vast territorial domains could not command allegiance from settlers, but instead settlers must find reasons to attach their allegiance to a given government. If Spain wanted to secure its sovereignty over Natchez, then the settlement needed effective local institutions to convince American citizens to expatriate themselves from the United States. Allowing for meaningful subjecthood at Natchez might create an opportunity for Spanish officials to turn the emigrant rights fundamental to republican citizenship into a force for bolstering their monarch's North American empire. In response to Bouligny's recommendation, Miró separated Natchez into two parishes in 1787, one for Santa Catalina Creek and Second Creek, and the other for Cole's Creek, the latter of which provided facilities for an officer and soldiers to maintain law and security. By 1788, Natchez's population approached 3,000, many of whom were American emigrants.[20]

The prospect of a thriving Natchez soon captivated Americans because the settlement appeared to be a refuge from problems besetting the United States. From accounts published in American newspapers, people familiar with Natchez explained how life in the settlement compared positively to life in the United States. In 1787, a Massachusetts newspaper reprinted a portion of a letter from a resident of New Orleans to a correspondent in Philadelphia. The letter described Spanish colonial officials respected by the local population.

Absent factionalism and chicanery, the governor of Louisiana competed with other officials only to see who could best promote the prosperity of the colony. Favorable prices for tobacco harvested on generous property allotments demonstrated that "his majesty is very indulgent to his new subjects at the Natchez." This radiant account of Louisiana, and Natchez in particular, appeared in American newspapers amid tumult throughout the United States. Several insurgencies erupted in 1786 and 1787, most notably Shays' Rebellion in western Massachusetts, to protest distant state governments deemed unresponsive to local needs and beholden to wealthy land speculators. Moreover, state taxes were high and the federal government under the Articles of Confederation was underfunded and relatively weak, thus unable to adequately suppress the insurrections that challenged governments throughout the confederation. This tale of two governments drew a stark comparison from "A Citizen of Philadelphia," a pseudonymous correspondent writing in the shadows of the Confederation Congress. The dispatch from New Orleans revealed "the wisdom, and at the same time the policy of Spain, by promoting and encouraging the settlement of the back country." Spain would "secure the hearts of a great people now settling on the western waters, while the United States are divided, and about abandoning them for ever."[21]

Encouraging emigration from the United States became part of Spain's official colonial policy for West Florida and Louisiana in 1788. Aware of the growing and discontent western population, along with the likelihood that Americans were and would continue seeking land in Spanish territory by legal or illegal means, Miró concluded that Spain could best protect its interests in the Mississippi Valley by entertaining requests from American citizens who expressed genuine interest in becoming Spanish subjects. Miró created a colonization policy for the region that provided incentives and a legal pathway for Americans to expatriate themselves by settling in Louisiana, thereby exchanging citizenship in the republic for allegiance to the Spanish Crown. With the Crown's consent to continue the colonization policy already in effect for the territory he governed, Miró issued a general invitation for American citizens to settle in Louisiana, which he published in English in 1789. The invitation initially targeted inhabitants of Franklin and Cumberland, the western reaches of North Carolina and Virginia. The details of Miró's invitation soon spread throughout the United States.[22]

To attract American citizens, Miró offered free land in proportion to the number of enslaved laborers and dependents in each emigrant family. Miró surmised that American men who removed their families and portable property to Louisiana intended to settle permanently in the province. Out

of self-interest, such emigrants would commit themselves to their new settlements in order to protect their families and property. Miró thus tied generous
land allocations to family size in order to attract the type of people most inclined to become dependable and diligent subjects. The prosperity of Louisiana and West Florida required emigrant populations outwardly loyal to the
Spanish Crown and willing to defend its interests in exchange for protection
and secure land title. However, for the colonies to flourish over time, Miró
expected that American settlers or at least their children would develop affective, patriotic attachments to the Spanish Crown and the Spanish colonial
communities in which they lived.

Spain's colonization policy for Louisiana gained wide public awareness in
the United States amid debates over the creation, ratification, and implementation of the Constitution. The coincidence of fundamental changes to the
national government with emigration from the United States seemed ominous
to the republic's viability over time. Advocates of the Constitution insisted that
only a strong federal government could project sovereignty throughout its territory and command the allegiance of its citizens, but they found their nationalist aspirations deflated every time an American quit the republic to settle in
Spanish territory. With the very legitimacy of the new United States government at stake, prominent American officials followed the movement of sojourning western citizens to calculate the national costs of emigration.[23]

Proximity to Spanish territory produced the most pessimistic predictions.
Arthur St. Clair surveyed developments at the United States' western border
from his position as governor of the Northwest Territory. A major-general
and Revolutionary War veteran, St. Clair was an astute observer of how America's imperial rivals might secure the allegiance of the republic's western citizens. In St. Clair's estimation, Spain was most likely to answer this demand. "It
seems likewise to be the Expectation of that Court, that the Country they possess upon the Mississippi may be peopled from the united States," St. Clair
observed. With the enticements of free land and access to New Orleans for all
who settled in Louisiana, St. Clair believed that Spain's new colonization policy would succeed. "Many will make the Experiment and they and their Progeny be lost." St. Clair harbored no nationalist illusions that emigrants in
Louisiana would preserve their patriotic affection for the United States or in-
still their children with love for the nation they left behind. To the contrary,
"they will become Spaniards to all intents and purposes." Moreover, Americans who transformed themselves from citizens in the United States to Spanish subjects would likely defend the interests of their adopted sovereign with
zeal. "Should many People be induced to remove into that Country they will

soon imbibe the Spanish prejudices, and be more active" in preserving Spanish control of the Mississippi River "than the Spaniards themselves." St. Clair was a military officer and colonial governor like Esteban Miró. St. Clair shared Miró's certainty that American citizens would choose to become loyal Spanish subjects willing to defend the interests of their adopted sovereign against the pretensions of the country where they abandoned their birthright. The prospect of American citizens expatriating themselves to Spanish Louisiana thus engendered St. Clair's pessimistic concerns about the loss of population that mirrored Miró's optimistic hopes that receiving American settlers would strengthen Spanish Louisiana.[24]

Kentucky's burgeoning settler population seemed most likely to challenge the United States' pretense of territorial sovereignty. St. Clair singled out Kentuckians for whom "land being the first Object of their pursuit, they are ready to go to any Country where it can be easily obtained." George Nicholas—a resident of Louisville, Kentucky, and a prominent legal figure in the region—confirmed St. Clair's description of Kentuckians, and the deleterious effects of unrestrained emigrant rights more broadly, in a letter to James Madison. Nicholas reminded Madison that Kentucky remained subject to Indigenous power and separated from Atlantic markets by Spanish control of the Mississippi River. Unless Congress granted Kentucky statehood and achieved an agreement with Spain for American access to New Orleans, Nicholas argued that the federal government effectively treated Kentucky settlers like "enemies or aliens." A population that expected the benefits of citizenship by virtue of their birth and residence thus found themselves abandoned by the federal government within its own territory. "No people will remain long under a Government which does not afford protection," Nicholas asserted, so the United States Congress "has no right to expect our support." Indeed, Nicholas counted himself among the Kentuckians who "shall be ready to join in any other Mode for obtaining our rights." Nicholas thus intimated that his attachment to the United States was strong at the moment but not indissoluble, and the attachments of others were even weaker. Nicholas reported that disaffected Kentuckians were already expatriating themselves in such numbers to "depopulate this country and carry most of the people to the Spanish settlements." If Spain's colonization policy persisted and former American citizens flourished as new Spanish subjects, Nicholas warned that within a few years "no man can say how far the emigration to that country may be carried" while "no obstacles will be sufficient to prevent the people who continue here from putting themselves into a situation that will enable them to avail themselves of those advantages" of adopting Spanish allegiance.[25]

Although Americans feared that Spain's colonization policy would depopulate the republic's western territory, one of its leading citizens welcomed this possibility. George Morgan, a colonel from New Jersey who served in the Revolutionary War as an Indian agent for Congress, speculated in Illinois Country lands in the late 1780s. When Congress failed to sell Morgan and his associates Illinois land at a satisfactory price, he turned his attention to Spanish territory west of the Mississippi. Just as Spanish officials in North America began implementing the empire's new colonization plans for Louisiana, Morgan proposed to create a colony settled by American families below the mouth of the Ohio River, which marked the boundary between Lower and Upper Louisiana, with St. Louis serving as the administrative capital of the upper district. All of Upper Louisiana sat just across the Mississippi from US territory. Moreover, because the United States controlled the Ohio River, Spain had a strategic interest in establishing a post on the west bank of the Mississippi near the mouth of the Ohio. This would be the first Spanish post Americans encountered after they entered the Mississippi on their downstream journeys. A local commander at this post could inspect boats and issue passports in an effort to control entry into Spanish territory. In 1788, Morgan sought permission from Don Diego de Gardoqui, Spain's foreign minister in the United States, to help secure this region vital to Spain's imperial claims by settling American emigrants in a colony called New Madrid.[26]

Morgan found a receptive audience for his proposed colony. Gardoqui answered Morgan's request by granting him permission to reconnoiter and establish his colony. Gardoqui supported Morgan's proposal because he believed its success would bolster Spain's control over the lower Mississippi River. "I consider him a very important acquisition for us," Gardoqui insisted, for "he will be a zealous servant for the conservation of the exclusion of the navigation of that river from all who are not His Majesty's vassals." Morgan's high esteem in the United States further bolstered Gardoqui's confidence in his proposal, as a person of the colonel's standing would have little difficulty "leading away many thousands under his protection." Thomas Hutchins, an American geographer and surveyor familiar with western opinion and conditions, suggested that Gardoqui's confidence was not unfounded. Without a doubt, Hutchins insisted, Morgan's settlement would "depopulate" western Pennsylvania, New Jersey, and Kentucky "of all its best Inhabitants, Farmers, Tradesman and Mechanics, who will take the Oath of Allegiance to the King of Spain and become most excellent Subjects." He was also eager to join the mass emigration. In words certain to please Morgan and Gardoqui, Hutchins declared that "I am resolved myself to become a Spanish Subject."[27]

With his promise to swell the ranks of loyal Spanish subjects in Louisiana with erstwhile American citizens, Morgan began locating a site to establish his settlement in early 1789. Within a few months, the exploratory party of seventy prospective settlers selected a site, developed a town plan, commenced land surveys, and built cabins and a storehouse. Those on the expedition celebrated the region's temperate climate and agricultural potential. Many intended to retrieve their families from the United States for permanent settlement. New Madrid came into existence less than a year after Morgan received permission to settle in Spanish territory.[28]

Morgan believed that New Madrid would have a prominent place in Spain's enduring empire. He identified New Madrid with Spain's broader policy "to cultivate and promote settlements of her own citizens" along the Mississippi River in order to protect New Orleans. As Morgan insisted, "by adopting this policy his Majesty has laid the foundation stone of a lasting empire over the whole country." After all, Morgan predicted, the "good people" of the United States "who wish to form a respectable settlement within his Majesty's territory, and to become his subjects" would do so without hesitation. And from Morgan's perspective, the colonization policy authorized by the Spanish Crown would, if fully implemented in Louisiana, secure the allegiance of American settlers in exchange for economic opportunity and a responsive, protective local government. Under such circumstances, the "upper settlements," New Madrid first among them, would flourish.[29]

Morgan predicted steady population growth at New Madrid. Members of the exploratory party who found the region suitable could receive 320 acres apiece provided they actually settled in the colony within six months—thus deterring absentee land speculators—and swore an oath of allegiance to the Spanish king and his successors. Morgan suggested a modest charge for these plots that could be collected at a later date after the colony was established. Morgan privileged the surveyors in his pay and a few key leaders of the party with first choice of land in the town of New Madrid and agricultural land in the surrounding countryside. These select few could receive up to forty square miles, a vast holding they could distribute to their associates as they saw fit. Morgan thus proposed an organized system of land allocation that privileged initial supporters of the colony but opened the door to a regular influx of American emigrants. He expected the colony to have an initial population of 300 families before eventually acquiring 1,000 families annually. The first 600 people to obtain land in New Madrid or its hinterlands would receive it for a nominal fee after residing in the colony for a year. Subsequent arrivals would purchase land in New Madrid at market value. Newcomers were encouraged to bring families but allowed to bring servants and slaves. Morgan insisted that New Madrid would grow at virtually no cost to Spain because the colonists were responsible for surveying, settling, and daily governance. Morgan expressed great confidence that his proposal for New Madrid "would secure and perpetuate the peace and tranquility of his Majesty's government, and western dominions." With New Madrid's success, "the immense tract of his Majesty's waste lands in America will be a Peruvian mine to him." With a kind of colonial alchemy, Morgan promised to turn vacant land into royal silver and American citizens into imperial subjects.[30]

To bring forth this transformation of place and people, Morgan left few details of New Madrid's establishment to chance. In order to create a local government that could command new allegiances, Morgan outlined the workings of his proposed settlement in a detailed series of "fundamental stipulations for the government and happiness of all who shall become subjects of Spain, and shall reside in this Territory." Morgan's proposal was a fundamentally royalist document. Morgan selected King Street as the name for New Madrid's main thoroughfare from the town center to the Mississippi River. Such naming practices were common in eighteenth-century colonial towns as reminders of royal sovereignty used to foment patriotic affection for a distant monarch. Whereas republicans in places such as Boston and other towns in the United States rejected their colonial past by extirpating royalist symbols from public life, Morgan stamped New Madrid with a conspicuous emblem of the Spanish monarch's sovereignty over the settlement. Morgan's desire to robe New Madrid in loyalty to the Spanish Crown extended to the name that he and the exploratory party chose for their settlement. In selecting the appellation "New Madrid," they meant "to show our determined resolution to become subjects of the King, and our respect and attachment to the Nation." Morgan's proposal for establishing and governing New Madrid revealed a series of choices all intended to demonstrate that the colony would become home to a settler population expatriated from the United States and eager to become Spanish subjects with both loyalty and gratitude to the king.[31]

News about Morgan's proposal for New Madrid spread throughout the United States in time to concern prominent Americans. James Madison obtained a copy of Morgan's invitation while in New York as a member of a Congress that he helped create but that lacked a legislative quorum. Morgan's proposal for a government of his own creation alarmed Madison as "the most authentic & precise evidence of the Spanish project that has come to my knowledge." Madison feared that once Americans became "Spanish Subjects" at New Madrid—that is, people entitled to "certain immunities as free men" but "under Spanish laws"—they would fulfill their new civic obligations as "instruments of Spanish policy." Arthur St. Clair agreed with Madison, but from the presumption that American citizens had little devotion to the nation that the Constitution supposedly conjured into existence. According to this view, western inhabitants, especially Kentuckians, were not allegiant to the new federal government, but they also lacked sentimental attachment to their places of birth, thus without the affections that nationalist boosters believed were necessary to bind disparate citizens to the stronger federal union. Instead, St. Clair disparaged western Americans as unreliable world citizens, as a population eager to accept Morgan's invitation because "they have no country, and indeed that attachment to the *natale solum* that has been so powerful and active a principle in other countries is very little felt in America." The rise of a New Madrid at Columbia's expense would belie nationalist claims that the Constitution could secure the allegiance of American citizens or protect the union's territorial empire any more effectively than the Articles of Confederation that it replaced.[32]

The Constitution created a new federal government for the United States that inherited the problems of colonial administration from the Confederation Congress. American emigrants settled in Spanish Louisiana starting in the 1780s only for emigration from the United States to increase once the states ratified the Constitution. Shortly after 1788, American emigrants also quit the United States for British North America. In both instances, American emigrants responded to colonization policies created by Spanish and British authorities. Empire's architects in the United States quickly realized that the republic must create colonization policies of its own. Early in his presidency, George Washington argued that the federal government must curtail Native land claims, secure private property rights for white settlers, foster local governments, and prepare for the creation of new states within the union. With these steps, the federal government encouraged American citizens to exercise emigration right citizenship within the United States instead of leaving for allegiance to Spain or Great Britain. Distinguishing the harm caused by American citizens expatriating themselves to North America's other imperial powers from the national good created when American citizens emigrated within the United States, Washington described the latter as one in which populations "only go from one part of the building to another; but in the former, they quit the house altogether." Washington's architectural metaphor provided a succinct expression of how Americans more broadly understood the boundaries of their territorial empire.[33]

The United States could secure its borders only by encouraging its citizens to stay. Otherwise, US sovereignty would fall short of the republic's territorial claims. Only a weak government could not exercise uniform power throughout the territory within its borders. Envisioning the United States as a house that inhabitants entered and left at will—as opposed to a prison or a feudal kingdom—affirmed that republican citizenship rested on consent. However, the house metaphor also revealed why the nation's empire would always remain vulnerable to collapse. If Americans found reasons to transfer their allegiance from the United States to other governments, Virginia politician John Dawson feared the beginning of "a remarkable era in the American history, as a door will be open'd through which the United States will loose [*sic*] many thousands of her best citizens." As American observers of the borderlands recognized, the doors on the federal house were already open, indeed forced ajar by the unmovable stop of emigrant rights without which consent was meaningless.[34]

Balancing the right of American citizens to become Spanish and eventually British subjects against the United States' need to keep its citizens from leaving posed a problem that James Madison explored in great detail. Madison was a congressman from Virginia and close presidential advisor when Spain introduced its colonization policy for Louisiana, so he was in a position to influence the federal government's response as citizens from the various states began to leave the republic. Madison approached developments at the borderlands from a broader interest in the economics and politics of migration, a subject he explored in a forceful defense of the freedom of emigration that he published in the *National Gazette* in 1791. In the essay "Population and Emigration," Madison argued that population growth often surpassed nature's capacity to sustain life. In places where people reproduced themselves into crowded accumulations beyond which sustenance and shelter were unobtainable, people succumbed to starvation and disease or resorted to infanticide and warfare. Whether one was afflicted or the afflicter, Madison argued that in most instances bleak forces culled excess population. Emigration was the exception. When the population in one location grew so dense that acquiring life's basic necessities became arduous or even impossible, the excess "overflows, by emigration." According to Madison, emigration occurred according to predictable laws, a sort of fluid mechanics of human mobility with "the course of emigrations being always from places where living is more difficult, to places where it is less difficult." From this perspective, free movement was an unalloyed good. It served "the general interests of humanity" because "the happiness of the emigrant is promoted by the change." Indeed, under most circumstances, Madison argued, "no populous nation has reason to restrain the emigration of its people." Rather, "every nation is impelled by humanity as well as required by the principles of liberty to allow the free exercise of this right." Thus as a matter of right and morality, Madison believed in freedom of emigration. As a matter of national interests, Madison was less certain if emigration allowed expatriation. This is not because the United States lacked demographic pressures of its own. Indeed, such pressures drove emigration from crowded seaboard states to borderlands regions such as Vermont and Kentucky. But according to Madison's calculations, even though some states lost citizens while others gained them, or families grew larger in some regions while shrinking in others, the net increase "added to the citizens of the United States." However, emigration beyond the nation's borders confounded Madison's patriotic arithmetic.[35]

Throughout the 1790s, Congress attempted to keep its citizens by admitting new states to the union. Between 1791 and 1796, Vermont, Kentucky, and Tennessee entered the union. Although shaped by particular political histories of white settlement and Indigenous dispossession, each of these states entered the union under what functioned as a federal emigration policy created by Congress to prevent the United States from losing citizens to its imperial rivals. The admission of new states during the 1790s was the relatively weak federal government's best option for exercising territorial sovereignty. With citizens ready to expatriate themselves for allegiance elsewhere in North America, the federal government attempted to retain its citizens by enlarging the national house, to use Washington's metaphor. Arthur St. Clair explained the logic of the federal government's emigration policy in an argument for Kentucky statehood. "The People would derive Security, at the same time that they saw and felt that the Government of the Union was not a mere shadow: their progeny would grow up in habits of Obedience and Respect—they would learn to reverence the Government; and the Countless multitudes which will be produced in that vast Region would become the Nerves and Sinews of the Union," St. Clair predicted. With state representation, the United States could secure settler allegiance through immediate obedience to the federal government and patriotic affection for the union across generations.[36]

The federal government implemented its emigration policy most directly in the Northwest Territory. The same year that Governor Esteban Miró reformed Natchez's colonial government, the Confederation Congress adopted the Northwest Ordinance that created the Northwest Territory. Under a colonial administrative system that oversaw the surveying, sale, and settlement of the territory, Congress anticipated turning dispossessed Indigenous land into a public domain. Once the Constitution replaced the Articles of Confederation, the new federal government assumed authority over the Northwest Territory, with Arthur St. Clair as the territory's first governor. The Northwest Ordinance anticipated a growing population of white emigrant families from other parts of the United States settled in agrarian townships with clear title to property. The settlers would initially live under the jurisdiction of territorial governments before quickly becoming citizens of new states admitted to the union on equal terms with existing states. Promoters of this colonial system for the Northwest Territory argued that it provided a more efficient process for selling public land to fund the federal government because it offered white men a reliable pathway to full citizenship through property ownership. The Northwest Territory would thus capture the spirit of emigration sweeping the western United States by securing the allegiance of citizens who might otherwise consider becoming Spanish or eventually British subjects.[37]

However, settlement of the Northwest Territory proceeded slowly. Congress delegated authority for surveying and settling the Northwest Territory to the Ohio Company, a private entity with speculator interests. Moreover, the Algonquin confederacy resisted further encroachment on its lands, which the federal government was powerless to open by force. According to a 1790 census taken by Winthrop Sargent, a leader of the Ohio Company, only 4,280 white settlers populated the Northwest Territory. So after three years of direct colonial governance, the Northwest Territory languished with a population not significantly larger than Natchez's population in 1788. As each power competed to harness emigrant rights for its own imperial ends, American settlers displayed no clear preference for remaining citizens over becoming subjects. Instead, Spain's ability to settle and secure the allegiance of American emigrants rivaled that of the United States. Growing communities populated by slave-owning planters who chose to cast aside their American citizenship for land in Spanish territory proved as much.[38]

ALTHOUGH IT CREATED a stronger federal union, the Constitution reaffirmed emigrant rights among the privileges of citizenship. In this regard, the Constitution was no more likely to secure personal allegiance to the United States than the Articles of Confederation. White men exercised their emigration right citizenship under the Articles of Confederation and would continue to do so under the Constitution. The population of the United States after 1788 thus remained one of potential emigrants who might choose to expatriate themselves for other allegiances. Looking across North America from his vantage point as president in New York, George Washington described "two channels open to draw off the inhabitants of the United States." Indeed, Washington continued, "it is a fact that the British, and Spanish nations, have land in the neighbourhood of the territory of the United States; and experience has taught us, that our citizens are settling," and because the "wealth, strength and dignity of a power, consists in any measure, in the number of subjects, these drains must be viewed as highly detrimental to the union, by the patriot and politician." Against an ineluctable spirit of emigration, Washington argued that the federal government must find ways to dam the channels that carried its citizens beyond the United States.[39]

A Baltimore traveler through the Ohio and Mississippi Valleys witnessed the movement of people firsthand. Overawed by the large settler population moving about American territory west of the Appalachians, the traveler from Baltimore reported to eastern newspapers that emigration flowing from the Atlantic states "must afford ample matter, to the philosopher and the patriot, for reflection, and an exertion of their best policy to retain amongst you the invaluable citizens you are daily losing." Into the 1790s, emigration control became a priority of the federal government's efforts to preserve and govern its territorial empire under new powers created by the Constitution. However, in the same decade, North America's other imperial powers pursued settlement policies that challenged the United States' ability to limit emigration beyond its borders.[40]

CHAPTER THREE

Human Ramparts

Ezekiel Forman flourished as a Spanish subject. The Pennsylvanian quit the United States for the Natchez District in 1790. Located on the Mississippi River in the Spanish colony of Louisiana, Natchez was part of New Orleans's commercial hinterlands. Spanish colonists at Natchez used enslaved labor to grow tobacco for sale in Atlantic markets. Forman was one of Natchez's most prosperous inhabitants when he died in 1795. Forman traded his citizenship in the republic for allegiance to the Spanish Crown under a colonization policy created by Spanish officials in the late 1780s. By offering American emigrants free land and royal protection in exchange for their loyalty, Spanish officials hoped to increase the economic value of the colony and protect it from Spain's imperial rivals, Indigenous and European alike. By claiming his emigrant rights to leave the United States for Spanish allegiance, Forman participated in a much larger imperial contest for North America. He joined thousands of people in the Mississippi Valley expected by a Spanish official in St. Louis to build a "human rampart a thousand times more powerful than the one formed by the sharp points of the steepest rocks."[1]

Great Britain invited American citizens such as Jonathan Sawyer to build its human ramparts in North America. Sawyer quit his country in December 1794. He traveled northward from his native Champlain, New York, along the shore of Lake Champlain and then the banks of the Richelieu River until he arrived in St. Johns, Lower Canada, a commercial and administrative center for those who governed British North America. Sawyer identified himself to colonial authorities in St. Johns as a farmer who entered the province with the "intention to become a British Subject if Permitted."[2]

Freeman and Sawyer joined many American men who quit the United States during the 1790s in order to claim the privileges of emigration right citizenship elsewhere. These men who chose to become subjects of the Spanish and British Empires typically brought personal property and household dependents, including their families and sometimes the people they enslaved. Between 1782 and 1792, emigration from the United States helped increase Louisiana's population from approximately 20,000 to 45,000 Spanish subjects. In Lower and Upper Canada, American emigrants eventually comprised a population of 50,000 British subjects. A common set of emigrant rights under the law of nations to move and choose allegiance enabled American men to expatriate themselves from the United States in pursuit of inexpensive land and commercial gain. In return, emigrant rights defined imperial space. During John Pope's travels down the Mississippi River in the early 1790s, he noted the place along his voyage "which his Catholic Majesty limits as his Boundary, and below which, his Vicegerents say, that Citizens of the *United States* shall not inhabit, unless they throw themselves under the Laws, Banners, and Protection of the King of *Spain*." Soon along the way, Pope encountered a residence "occupied by a family of *New-Yorkers*." This family's choice to quit the United States produced Spanish sovereignty at its borders. John Pope witnessed the construction of human ramparts along a relatively narrow stretch of the Mississippi River, but it was a process repeated in places throughout the 1790s. The exercise of emigration right citizenship created North America's borderlands by braiding settler interests with imperial ambitions.[3]

THE UNITED STATES contained a population of individuals free to leave and expatriate themselves, but Spain needed to attract them in order to build human ramparts of any strength. To this end, Governor Esteban Miró put Spanish legal customs in the service of a colonization policy supported by the twin pillars of emigrant rights: cosmopolitanism and the law of nations. Notions of political belonging that developed in Spanish America rested on personal choice, permanent settlement, and local attachments as the basis of legitimate community. Miró rejected the assumption that only settlers immersed since birth in Spanish culture should populate Louisiana for a view that settlers from virtually anywhere could adopt Spanish culture and values. Miró's settlement plan assumed that people could lessen their allegiance to one place in exchange for stronger allegiance to another. Miró accepted this assumption because most American emigrants would likely hold Protestant religious beliefs. Miró's plan departed significantly from other Spanish colonization proposals for its embrace of expansive religious toleration. According to his policy, Protestant emigrants from the United States could worship in private with the expectation that Irish Catholic priests would bring about a generational change of faith by educating the emigrants' children to become devout Catholics. Indeed, Miró expected that American settlers would adopt Spanish cultural ways and Catholicism with long residence in Louisiana or across the generations. Influential law of nations theorists gave reason to believe that American emigrants would transform themselves into Spanish subjects following their adoption of new political allegiances. As Emer de Vattel predicted, "A man's obligations to his natural country may, however, change, lessen, or entirely vanish, according as he shall have quitted it lawfully, and with good reason, in order to choose another." Miró described his colonization plan as a way "of cementing the affections of the new colonists to the Spanish government, and of succeeding in obtaining that the second generation, not knowing any other government, will have the affection which birth in a country will engender, and, lastly, that they may embrace the religion of the Sovereign, which is the principal thing." Confident in its cosmopolitan ethics and guided by the law of nations, Miró's colonization policy assumed that the United States was a vast reserve of potential Spanish subjects.[4]

To secure the settlers' loyalty to Spain and not just their immediate communities, Miró promised that the Spanish Crown would "favor and protect them." Emigrants would be free to transport and market their produce throughout Louisiana, including, most importantly, in New Orleans. Indeed, Miró promised the newcomers that upon settlement in Louisiana "they shall enjoy the same franchises & privileges as the other subjects of his most catholic Majesty." So in addition to the economic benefits of the Spanish Empire, Americans who became Spanish subjects received political and civic rights. To receive the protections, rights, and privileges of a Spanish subject, American emigrants were required to follow a simple legal process. Upon arrival, American citizens publicly swore an oath of allegiance to the Spanish Crown and promised to defend the colony against invasion. Miró's invitation stated unequivocally that before receiving property and trade privileges in Louisiana, American citizens must become Spanish subjects with loyalty and allegiance to the Spanish Crown above all other sovereigns.[5]

Although Miró's invitation opened all of Spain's territory in the Mississippi Valley to American emigrants, he encouraged residency at Natchez, which was situated along a low river bank and adjacent steep hills. Visitors arriving at Natchez by water ascended a narrow road through the settlement until they reached the fort and governor's home on a point overlooking the Mississippi. With about one hundred homes, some near the river and others climbing the hillside and beyond, Natchez was the "Metropolis of the District" according to John Pope, a visitor from the United States in 1791. Homes and public buildings in Natchez had a uniform appearance as many were built from timber frames daubed with a mixture of mud and Spanish moss, which draped the oak and walnut trees common to the region. Natchez's agricultural hinterlands had a reputation for fertile soil that produced tobacco esteemed for its quality.[6]

With an existing population of American emigrants, Natchez could incorporate recent emigrants from the United States to bolster its strategic and economic value to the Spanish Empire while concentrating the newcomers for easier imperial supervision and administration. To further such ends, in 1789 the Spanish Crown elevated Natchez's status. It appointed a governor and military commandant for the district, and it established a cabildo, a council of Natchez planters to address local political and legal matters. Natchez's first governor, Manuel Gayoso de Lemos, supported American emigration and spoke fluent English. An observer in the United States speculated that Miró selected Lemos to signal his ambitious plan to swell the district's population with American emigrants. Otherwise, why would Spanish authorities elevate "a man who from his character and abilities should never have accepted the appointment if their only object had been the government of the subjects they now have in that country"? By 1789, Spanish colonial officials thus built the institutions of local government at Natchez to both monitor and secure the allegiance of the enlarged American emigrant population they expected in the settlement. Natchez's tobacco economy also flourished in the late 1780s, another source of appeal to potential American emigrants.[7]

As the reasons to become a Spanish subject mounted, the number of arrivals from the United States increased. Families with livestock and enslaved people traveled overland from the United States. Emigrants in even larger numbers sailed down the Mississippi on "Kentucky boats," long, narrow flat-bottomed vessels intended for a single downstream voyage. These "floating houses," as some described them, were difficult to navigate on the Ohio's and Mississippi's rapid currents, so they had high sides to keep possessions and people from toppling off the heavily laden decks. Goods and livestock filled the open deck while passengers, usually two large families, clustered under a rude shelter. By way of land and water, Natchez's American-born population swelled. Emigrants typically arrived in the spring and early summer after river ice melted in the North but before water levels dropped in the summer. Carlos de Grand Pré, the military commander at Natchez, witnessed American emigration firsthand. He compiled detailed reports of American traffic through the district. Grand Pré distinguished between Americans who entered Spanish territory for trade and those who intended to settle at Natchez. For the latter group, Grand Pré recorded their place of origin, family size, and property, including enslaved people. The reports from Natchez provide a detailed census of American citizens who became Spanish subjects.[8]

Once they arrived at Natchez, American emigrants had several ways to demonstrate their intent to settle permanently and to prove their prospective loyalty. In a few instances, American emigrants announced their intentions. John Gaskins assured Governor Miró that he expected "to remain for the rest

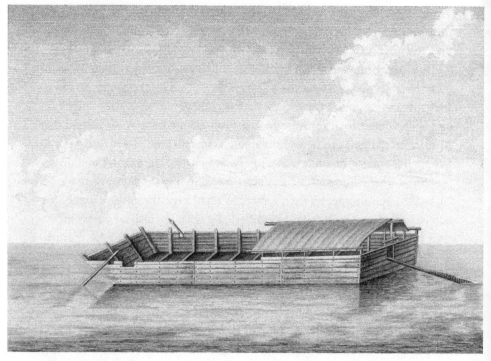

"Sketch of a Flat Bottom Boat," from Georges-Henri-Victor Collot, *Voyage dans l'Amérique Septentrionale* (Paris: A. Bertrand, 1826). Library of Congress, Geography and Map Division, Louisiana: European Explorations and the Louisiana Purchase.

of his Days" in Natchez, where he settled with his wife and three children. Robert Stark, an emigrant settler in Louisiana seeking a passport for travel to the United States, testified that he arrived in Spanish territory in 1791 "with no other intention but to establish a settlement for myself and my Family." Swearing an oath of allegiance to Spain was another way for emigrants from the United States to demonstrate their willingness to become loyal subjects. Each of Grand Pré's reports on American arrivals at Natchez listed the names of Americans who pledged their allegiance to Spain. Of course, settlers seeking land and commercial privileges in Louisiana were unlikely to present themselves as anything but people eager to become loyal subjects for life. The oath of allegiance invited deception as well. According to the recollections of some Americans engaged in the Mississippi trade, oath-taking was a hollow ritual. Charles Wilkins frequently sailed between Pittsburg and New Orleans. Wilkins observed that the owners and crews of American riverboats pledged their allegiance to Spain to evade high import duties imposed on American shipping. If Americans persuaded Spanish officials of their sincere intention to settle in Louisiana, they received passports for unrestrained navigation on the Mississippi and the privileges of preferential commercial policy reserved for Spanish subjects. Once they had offloaded their goods in Spanish markets, Americans such as Wilkins would simply return to the United States leaving their promises of loyalty behind them. The transformation of American citizens into Spanish subjects thus only began with declarations of intent to settle in Spanish territory and oaths of allegiance to the Crown. Colonial officials in Louisiana looked for other indications that American emigrants were genuinely interested in becoming Spanish subjects.[9]

An emigrant's standing and conduct in the United States provided such evidence. Henry Hunter settled in Natchez in 1792. He duly swore his allegiance to Spain upon arriving in Louisiana. Local Spanish officials noted with approval his service as an officer in the American army during the Revolutionary War. Moreover, he possessed needed skills. Hunter's military experience and abilities thus confirmed that he was "a person of worth and special talent in mechanical work." Furthermore, he arrived at Natchez as part of a contingent of American settlers equally worthy of joining Spanish society, all of whom, according to the Natchez official, were "persons of honorable conduct and masters of useful trades." By using Hunter's standing as a virtuous and productive citizen in the republic as evidence for his potential to become a loyal subject, Spanish officials revealed the extent to which allegiance and birthplace were attenuated in Louisiana. Hunter's capacity for civic belonging was portable to nearly anywhere rather than fixed to a particular community, culture, political system, or nation. The same cosmopolitan ethics that underpinned Hunter's freedom to leave the United States thus became a measure that officials used to determine the authenticity of his desire to adopt Spanish allegiance at Natchez.[10]

Although the lives that emigrants willfully left behind in the United States provided strong evidence of their potential loyalty, so did the people whom they forced to come with them to Natchez. Grand Pré listed many Americans who pledged their allegiance to Spain in the company of family and enslaved laborers. Henry Hunter arrived in Natchez with his wife, seven children, and fifteen slaves. In addition to Robert Stark's wife and children, he also stated that he "came to this Government with a tolerable good force of negroes." John Williams of South Carolina settled in the Natchez District with twenty-five enslaved people. These Americans would not have emigrated from the United States with a domestic entourage if they intended to return. Apart from demonstrating their genuine desire to settle in Spanish territory, American men had strong incentives to emigrate from the United States with their families and enslaved laborers. William Martin from the Tennessee region of North Carolina received a passport from Governor Miró that allowed him to bring his family and property free of duties provided he took the oath of allegiance to the Spanish Crown. In exchange, Martin would receive land to match the number of laborers he brought to the territory. Miró hoped that Martin's example would initiate a larger emigration from western North Carolina. "Everyone ought to be acquainted that the familys who chuse to come down for the same purpose, and in like terms will be admitted with the same privileges," Miró declared. From the perspective of the colonial officials they encountered and in their own experiences, newcomers hastened their expatriation from the United States by arriving at Natchez with families and enslaved laborers.[11]

Two prominent Americans in Natchez exemplify this path to obtaining the privileges of emigration right citizenship. Virginian Peter Bryan Bruin arrived in the Natchez District in 1788 with his wife, three children, and twenty enslaved people. A veteran of the Revolutionary War against Great Britain, he intended to settle in Spanish Louisiana for better access to land and commerce. Indeed, Bruin promised to help populate Louisiana by leading thousands of American citizens to the province who were eager to become Spanish subjects. Although Bruin never commenced a significant emigration from the United States to Louisiana, he became a prosperous tobacco planter in Natchez. He eventually became an alcalde in the district, thereby serving as a local legal official in the Spanish Empire. By establishing a permanent settlement in Natchez and entrance into the colonial bureaucracy, Peter Bryan Bruin, the erstwhile American citizen, rose to local prominence as a loyal Spanish subject. Pennsylvanian Ezekiel Forman arrived in Natchez in 1790 with an especially large contingent of family members and human property. Forman settled in Spanish territory after his brother received a land grant on his behalf from Diego de Gardoqui, Spain's foreign minister to the United States. In addition to his wife and four children, Forman forced sixty-seven enslaved people owned by his brother to emigrate with him. Samuel Forman joined the small fleet that carried his uncle's family and enslaved property to Natchez. The younger Forman decided not to become a Spanish subject, so Ezekiel Forman accompanied his nephew to New Orleans to begin his return voyage to the United States. During their stay in the colonial capital, the Formans gained an audience with Governor Miró, which Samuel attributed to his uncle's "high standing" because he settled under Spanish allegiance "with so large a number of people." His uncle's rapid rise to prominence in the colony continued unabated. Forman established Wilderness

Creek, a 500-acre plantation on St. Catherines Creek near the center of Natchez, which eventually yielded nearly 500 tons of tobacco per year. By all accounts, Forman remained a loyal Spanish subject for the rest of his life. Spanish law enabled him to extract labor from his slaves and access to Atlantic markets for the large tobacco crop they cultivated. He amassed a genteel life at Wilderness Creek through his control of human labor and land. Forman traveled through Natchez on a carriage and owned a well-appointed library by the time he died a Spanish subject in 1795.[12]

Emigrants from the United States also populated New Madrid. Although George Morgan never returned after his first and only visit to the region, the original settlers and later arrivals fulfilled his expatriate aspirations. Among the first American emigrants who settled in New Madrid in 1789 and 1790, several remained in the colony almost a decade later according to a Spanish census from 1797. Azor Reese typified the Americans who settled in New Madrid. Reese emigrated from Kentucky with a family, evidence of his good character, and sincere intentions. Members of Reese's extended family emigrated with him. Reese's name appeared on a 1789 petition of New Madrid settlers seeking support from the commandant of Upper Louisiana, Manuel Perez, in their efforts to send a delegate from New Madrid to the United States in order to dispel negative rumors about the settlement. Only by correcting false impressions about New Madrid, the petitioners argued, could they fulfill their "most ardent Wishes to forward & promote the Immediate Settlement of This Country with our Friends and Neighbours resident in The United States of America."[13]

In addition to encouraging other citizens to exercise their emigrant rights in favor of Spanish allegiance, Reese and the early settlers in New Madrid publicly swore their allegiance to the Spanish Crown. The oath of allegiance sworn by Reese and other settlers at New Madrid pledged their "faith, vassalage, and loyalty to His Catholic Majesty." In exchange for protection from a royal government, the settlers promised to obey and uphold local laws in pursuit of "the general welfare of Spain, and the particular welfare of this province," which included military defense if necessary. The oath intimated that settlers at New Madrid would most likely find themselves threatened by the militaries of North American powers from "the upper part of the river, or by way of the interior overland." When Reese and other Americans took the oath, they publicly accepted the obligations and privileges of Spanish subjects, which conceivably included taking up arms against citizens of their former nation. The oath also affirmed prevailing ideas about allegiance, specifically the power of consent. When Reese and others took the oath, they

"Plan of the Fort of New Madrid," from Georges-Henri-Victor Collot, *Voyage dans l'Amérique Septentrionale* (Paris: A. Bertrand, 1826). Library of Congress, Geography and Map Division, Louisiana: European Explorations and the Louisiana Purchase.

not only became allegiant to a new political community, they exercised their "free and voluntary will" to live in obedience to the Spanish king's laws. The oath thus included contractual assumptions about relations of allegiance then sweeping the revolutionary Atlantic world and fundamental for people who possessed emigrant rights to move freely and adopt new loyalties as they saw fit.[14]

By the mid-1790s, Reese's choice to become a Spanish subject in New Madrid served him well. He owned five enslaved laborers, livestock, and land that yielded a sizeable corn crop. Reese and other expatriated Americans including Elisha Jackson and David Gray also served as witnesses when new arrivals from the United States took the oath of allegiance. In this way, settlers such as Reese not only secured the benefits of Spanish colonization policy for themselves, but they also became agents of this policy essential to establishing Spain's actual sovereignty over remote settlements. The legal transformation of American citizens into Spanish subjects at places such as New Madrid could not occur without emigrants such as Reese acting to implement Spanish policy.[15]

Into the 1790s, emigrants who arrived with Reese or soon thereafter prospered as Spanish subjects in New Madrid. Moses Lunsford owned a herd of forty cows and cultivated a large corn crop. Richard Jones Waters was a physician from Maryland who pledged his allegiance to Spain in 1790. By 1797, Waters owned three enslaved people, one hundred cattle, and land that yielded the settlement's largest corn crop. Later arrivals continued to prosper in New Madrid by controlling family labor, human property, and land. By 1797, George Ruddle's family included six children, and he owned five enslaved people who worked his land to produce a sizeable corn crop. Ultimately, American emigrants constituted a majority of New Madrid's population in 1797.[16]

Natchez and New Madrid developed within a common transnational legal culture created by American settlers and Spanish officials who shared an understanding of emigrant rights. Spanish officials welcomed the arrival of Americans such as Ezekiel Forman and Peter Bryan Bruin at Natchez or Azor Reese and George Ruddle at New Madrid because their standing as family patriarchs and property owners vouched for their stable character. Bringing their families and enslaved laborers to Louisiana diminished the likelihood of their return to the United States, which demonstrated their intent to settle permanently. The rationale for this position was evident in a list of instructions for admitting emigrants provided to Spanish commandants at posts such as New Madrid in 1799. Single emigrants without farming skills or "property in negroes or merchandize," or money to purchase either, were required to reside in the settlement for four years on "good behavior in some honorable and useful employment" before obtaining land. Such an emigrant could receive land after only two years if he married the daughter of "some respectable farmer" who found "him industrious and steady." Passing through probationary subjecthood required a steady increase in personal reputation within the community.[17]

Emigrants with families and enslaved people arrived with a reputation for good subjecthood in place. Indeed, Spanish officials affixed a substantial land value of fifty acres for every child and twenty acres for every enslaved person an emigrant brought to Louisiana. Although the 1799 instructions introduced restrictive residency requirements, it rested on assumptions about emigrant rights and character common to Spain's colonization policies from the late 1780s onward. Once settled on land in Louisiana, emigrant patriarchs' private interests in protecting their families and extracting labor from enslaved people complemented Spain's imperial priorities for the region, thus binding American settlers to the Spanish Crown in a reciprocal exchange of allegiance for protection. As indications of potential loyalty, men who arrived with families and enslaved laborers at places such as Natchez and New Madrid had dependents who effectively served as human passports, embodied testimony of their reliability and respect similar in purpose to the era's early paper passports.

By emigrating from the United States to Spanish territory and swearing allegiance to the Spanish Crown, the American settlers expatriated themselves according to every measure recognizable in the eighteenth century. The law of nations included norms that braided settlement to allegiance. Emer de Vattel identified two types of settlement, "natural" and "acquired." Each type of settlement indicated "a fixed residence in any place with an intention of always staying there." Vattel distinguished a natural settlement as "that which we acquire at birth" from an acquired settlement as "that where we settle by our own choice." Every choice Americans made at Natchez or New Madrid—from arriving in the settlements, swearing allegiance to Spain, and establishing a permanent residence—constituted their "express declaration" of "fixing" themselves to Louisiana. As such, the emigrants also chose to expatriate themselves from the United States. The law of nations considered men who emigrated with families and property as clearly intending to change allegiance from one sovereign to another. Vattel specified "families and property" in his definition of emigration while Samuel von Pufendorf argued that a man renounced his allegiance to the government he left behind once he "voluntarily removes into another, and settles himself and his Effects and the hopes of his fortune there." Men with the wealth and power to possess human passports thus had a particular claim to emigrant rights backed by the normative authority of the law of nations.[18]

In addition to the law of nations, numerous American residents at Natchez and New Madrid left states that recognized emigrant rights. Forman's native Pennsylvania recognized the right to emigration in its Declaration of Rights. According to Virginia law, those who left the state for Louisiana such as Peter Bryan Bruin or Ephraim Hubbard—who settled at Natchez in 1790 with his wife, nine children, and ten enslaved people—had expatriated themselves in no uncertain terms. Indeed, politicians in Virginia broadened the state's already permissive expatriation law at nearly the same moment that Spain closed the Mississippi to American navigation and Miró announced his colonization policy. According to the revised 1784 expatriation statute, Virginians preserved their "natural right, which all men have of relinquishing the country, in which birth, or other accident may have thrown them, and, seeking subsistence and happiness wheresoever they may be able, or may hope to find them." Yet the revised law lifted the provision that required a public declaration in Virginia of a citizen's intent to expatriate. Rather, Virginians expatriated themselves if they "entered into the service" of a state at peace with Virginia and the United States, as in the case of Peter Bryan Bruin, or by "any act whereby he shall become a subject or citizen of such state," as did settlers such as Hubbard and numerous others who abided Louisiana's settlement procedures. Kentucky was another source of significant emigration to Louisiana. As Virginia's westernmost county until it achieved statehood in 1792, Kentucky was subject to Virginia's expansive expatriation statute. Moreover, when Kentucky politicians adopted laws for the new state, they incorporated Virginia's expatriation statute. George Ruddle emigrated from Kentucky in 1795, thus expatriating himself from American to Spanish allegiance when he settled in New Madrid.[19]

Spanish officials in Louisiana also recognized American settlers as Spanish subjects. In 1790, local Choctaw chiefs held that an agreement between them and the Spanish to keep the region free of American incursions authorized them to order the evacuation of Americans at two Natchez settlements. The settlers replied to Choctaw demands by asserting their standing as Spanish subjects. Grand Pré reiterated this point in a letter to the Choctaw leadership. According to Grand Pré, "All settlers established throughout this district of Natchez, even though previously of various origins, such as English, Americans, and French, have become naturalized Spaniards and subjects of our great Emperor." As such, protections from the Spanish Crown secured the

Natchez settlers in their property and residences. To mistreat the settlers as American citizens "would disturb their well-being and tranquility," Grand Pré further announced, thus the Choctaw should remember "that to make the slightest exaction on one of these settlers is to make it on a Spaniard." This diplomatic episode not only revealed a shared understanding among Natchez settlers and Spanish colonial officials about the legal status of American emigrants in Louisiana, but it also revealed Native nations' lasting power over settler allegiances. As one emigrant from the Tennessee region explained to Governor Miró in 1789, soon after the United States ratified its new and supposedly more powerful Constitution, white settlers in the region were largely defenseless against the Cherokee and Creek. "The United States afford us not protection," the correspondent explained. "Unprotected, we are to be obedient to the New Congress of the United States: but we cannot but wish for a more interesting Connection." Indeed, across the Mississippi Valley Americans chose to cast their allegiance to the sovereign power most capable of protecting their persons and property from Indigenous nations.[20]

Ultimately, settlements such as Natchez and New Madrid were outposts of Spanish sovereignty created by the convergence of disparate legal developments. People who settled in Louisiana from places such as Virginia, Pennsylvania, and eventually Kentucky exercised their emigrant rights to free movement and expatriation codified in the laws of those states. Spain adopted a colonization policy for Louisiana that provided newcomers with legal procedures to complete their expatriation from the United States by obtaining the privileges of emigration right citizenship once they settled in the colony. Prospective settlers in the United States as well as Spanish colonial officials in Louisiana recognized together that political allegiance was transferable, which resulted in growing populations at Natchez and New Madrid of erstwhile American citizens who by all accounts expected to remain loyal Spanish subjects forevermore.

Throughout the 1790s, newspapers in the United States documented the growth of American emigrant communities under Spanish allegiance. Reprinted letters from visitors to the western United States and Spanish Louisiana described American emigration with awe and enthusiasm. The account of a traveler from Baltimore to New Orleans that appeared in a South Carolina newspaper described sharing his journey with "an incredible number of emigrants" flooding west from the Atlantic states. He attributed mass emigration to reasons easily recognizable to readers familiar with emigrant rights claims under the law of nations, treaties, and state citizenship statutes. Some were "removing from necessity, and others from the natural and commendable desire of making a more comfortable and certain provision for their children." Regardless of individual motivations, the emigrants described in this account were bound for places such as Natchez, where they seemed certain to improve their fortunes. According to a description by a Natchez visitor to a friend in Philadelphia published in a Pennsylvania newspaper, Natchez was "an English settlement subject to the Spaniards" notable for its mild climate, teeming forests and waterways, fecund soil, and thriving live-stock. Most inhabitants were Virginians who had expatriated themselves to Spanish allegiance in accord with the citizenship laws in the American state they left behind. With their emigration they transplanted the Chesapeake's tobacco agriculture and slave labor system to Natchez. Ownership of land and humans allowed the American emigrants to recreate the Chesapeake's genteel culture as well. The visitor met prosperous and healthy local planters who showed their hospitality by sharing fine wine. Waves of American emi-gration might have brought detached wonderment to observers in the United States, but it could clearly bring standing to the white men who entered the flow.[21]

Emigration promised prosperity and power, but the men who found it ap-pealing seemed like exactly those whom the United States should strive to retain. The traveler from Baltimore noted that the emigrants he encountered were nearly all upstanding citizens rather than the "idle and worthless." An account from North Carolina eventually published in a Massachusetts news-paper provided evidence that American emigrants left the United States al-ready men of independent standing. As such, this article condemned the Spanish policy of "offering the most alluring encouragements to American settlers for removing themselves, families, and properties into the dominions of Spain." Arthur St. Clair, governor of the Northwest Territory, elucidated what might have been suggested by "properties." By outlawing slavery in the Northwest Territory, the US Congress unintentionally turned adjacent Span-ish territory in Upper Louisiana into a shelter for American enslavers who feared losing control of their human property. St. Clair thus warned that "many respectable Inhabitants" sought "refuge on the opposite Shore and became Subjects of Spain" in order to secure their wealth in enslaved labor. The emigrants whom Spanish officials desired were thus the very citizens the United States could least afford to lose.[22]

Glowing accounts of emigrant life at Natchez and emigrant opportunity in Louisiana cast doubt on the privileged status of republican citizenship. The Natchez visitor in the early 1790s noted the tradeoffs of changing allegiance from republican Virginia to monarchical Spain by observing that settlers "pay no taxes of any kind, and, independent of their having no share in government, are a very free people." From this account, American readers might conclude that republican citizenship was no better than subjecthood if one could still prosper as a slave-owning, landed patriarch by emigrating from the United States. Other accounts of Natchez declared that citizenship in the United States was inferior to subjecthood in Louisiana where liberty was more robust. Citizenship in the United States often meant submission to the republic's wealthy landowners, a condition of dependence foreign to Natchez "where the people may live free as nature, which is before them, where every sensation, favorable to happiness, may be indulged." However, arguments that American independence required citizens eager to stay in the United States dismissed the right of landless citizens to leave for places such as Natchez. This view expected a landless citizen to plant himself in American soil for a greater patriotic good, and "regardless of his own happiness and welfare, should resign himself, with serene stupidity, to the tender mercies of every wealthy lord and master who chooses to command him." To this critic, republican citizenship offered a meaningless pretense of self-government for those in the United States unable to obtain landed independence. Accounts of life in Natchez identified deficient state and federal governments in the United States incapable of securing the permanent allegiance or the full liberty of its citizens. Should such strong rebukes of domestic politics prove persuasive, dispatches from Natchez might become compelling invitations for American citizens to expatriate themselves.[23]

During the 1790s it seemed clear that Spain's success at building human ramparts threatened the United States as both powers competed to secure the allegiance of settler populations. A proposal from Alexander Fowler suggested confidence that American citizens would continue to find Spanish allegiance appealing well into the future. In 1791, Fowler circulated a proposal in the United States for New Andalusia, an emigrant settlement on the Meramec River, which flowed into the Mississippi just south of St. Louis. Fowler emulated George Morgan's plans for New Madrid. Fowler named his settlement in homage to a historically significant region of Spain, and he extolled the character of Spain's King Charles IV. He was an "enlightened" and "munificent" king, Fowler declared, a sovereign only concerned with encouraging his subjects' happiness so they and his dominions would prosper together.[24]

Although Fowler was a former British officer resident in Philadelphia, he appealed to the emigrant rights valued by his American audience. Fowler promised Americans that they could become Spanish subjects at New Andalusia without giving up the privileges and liberties that supposedly made republican citizenship meaningful. He explained the relationship between the king and prospective subjects at New Andalusia as one that rested firmly on volitional allegiance. As Fowler proclaimed, the Spanish monarch "gives everything and demands nothing but ALLEGIANCE, for which he grants PROTECTION, a reciprocal tie between the governor and governed." If citizens from the United States expatriated themselves for allegiance to Spain, they would thus preserve their liberty and improve their fortunes.[25]

This possibility conflicted with the assumptions of their recent revolution against royal government but one Fowler promised to Americans who settled in New Andalusia. Emigrants in New Andalusia would receive free land from the Spanish king along with relief from all taxes and excises. In the early 1790s, opposition to the federal government's excise tax on whiskey riled places such as western Pennsylvania, so Fowler almost certainly emphasized "No Taxes! No Excise!" in hopes of encouraging discontented Americans to settle at New Andalusia. In an announcement published in a Pennsylvania newspaper, Fowler assured prospective New Andalusia settlers that they could keep servants and enslaved laborers, another liberty dear to his American audience. Indeed, like elsewhere in Louisiana, slaves and servants, along with families, were human passports that testified to a man's character and intent to settle. They also allowed men to obtain more land, for Fowler promised settlers would receive up to 1,000 acres "in proportion to his strength," by which he meant dependent human labor including children, servants, and enslaved people. Pennsylvania passed a gradual abolition law in 1780, so slavery was on its slow demise in the state. Becoming Spanish subjects would allow slave-owning citizens to avoid the eventual loss of human property. Fowler presented New Andalusia as a seamless weaving of American emigrant interests with Spain's established colonial policy for Louisiana, but his settlement never came into existence.[26]

Fowler proposed New Andalusia just as the Spanish Crown imposed administrative changes on Louisiana. The new officials in charge of the colony rejected the notion that inviting American emigrants advanced Spain's imperial interests. In 1792, the Barón de Carondelet replaced Esteban Miró as governor of Louisiana and West Florida. A military officer and seasoned colonial administrator in North America, Carondelet shared the suspicion of many in his era that frequent mobility revealed fickle allegiances because any person unable to stay in one place for long was also incapable of developing lasting ties to a government. Carondelet disparaged American emigrants as a people "accustomed to changing their place of residence as easily as they changed their shirts." Moreover, emigrants who did not form genuine loyalty for the

Spanish government could not be trusted to respect royal authority in Louisiana. Reports from people familiar with American emigrants confirmed the governor's position. Although Barthelemi Tardiveau represented western American and French interests before Congress, he was nonetheless suspicious of concentrated American settlements. When together in large numbers, Tardiveau observed in a letter to Carondelet, Americans craved power and local self-government. "Isolated among strangers and especially separated from one another, they are as docile and as submissive to authority as those who boast less of their independence," Tardiveau explained, but together in even a small group "they become dangerous; soon they want to run things." From the beginning of his governorship, Carondelet thus proved far more distrustful of American emigrants than his predecessor.[27]

Once Carondelet became governor, he adopted a limited colonization policy for Louisiana. American emigrants already settled in Louisiana could remain, and many prospered under Carondelet, but the governor discouraged new arrivals from the United States in favor of European Catholics. Fowler's frustrated ambitions for New Andalusia illustrated Carondelet's new priorities. The governor had several reasons for overturning his predecessor's promises to Fowler. He insisted that Americans already near the proposed site of New Andalusia were occupying land not open to settlement while threatening to organize themselves in ways that would subvert royal authority. To stop this problem, he encouraged Indigenous forces to harass the American emigrants until they returned to the United States. Although Carondelet granted Fowler land in Upper Louisiana, he insisted that only European settlers could join him. Carondelet also responded to mounting protests from officials within the US government against efforts by Spanish officials to "encourage the emigration of their citizens." Whereas Miró believed that peace between Spain and the United States must be enforced with human ramparts built by expatriated Americans, Carondelet reached the opposite conclusion that Spain's North American colonies were more secure without American emigrants. The failure of New Andalusia in 1792 thus marked a turning point in Spain's colonial policy for North America away from employing emigrant rights for imperial ends. However, when Spanish colonial authorities in New Orleans concluded that American emigrants imperiled their empire, British colonial authorities in Quebec City viewed American emigration with promise.[28]

THE REVOLUTIONARY WAR brought significant demographic changes to the Champlain Valley. The conflict's end in 1783 pushed most of the Abenaki from their hunting grounds in the northern valley to settlements north of the St. Lawrence River. A new international border divided the Abenaki's former territory. The province of Quebec in British North America lay to the north and the Vermont Republic to the south. New Englanders populated the region on the heels of Abenaki removal. Many of the new settlers arrived from more densely populated parts of southern New England seeking land in the Champlain Valley, thereby continuing a period of migration beginning after the French and Indian War that extended the limits of colonial settlement ever northward toward Quebec. Moreover, British defeat in 1783 created political refugees. Loyalists kept their allegiance to the British monarch and sought his protection in the secure dominions of British North America. Lake Champlain became an essential water route for Loyalists entering Quebec. According to colonial officials, nearly 5,000 Loyalists resided in Quebec in 1784. The British government took steps to settle the Loyalists in places that fit with larger imperial aims, but some created unauthorized settlements near the border with Vermont and New Hampshire, especially around Missisquoi Bay, a part of Lake Champlain that balloons into Quebec, in an under populated region eventually known as the Eastern Townships.[29]

Under the Constitutional Act of 1791, Parliament divided Quebec into two new colonies, Upper and Lower Canada. Parliament put each province under the administration of a lieutenant-governor, an appointed executive council, a legislative council—the colonial parliament's upper house—and a popularly elected legislative assembly. Although each colony received representative governments organized in a similar fashion, officials in London and Quebec City expected the colonies to differ. Upper Canada was designed as a haven for Loyalist refugees forced to leave the United States after 1783. By the early 1790s, American Loyalists populated settlements that they formed in the region west of the Ottawa River that became southern Ontario. In legal, civic, and cultural terms, Upper Canada was expected to be fully British, with strong support for the Anglican Church and all property owned in free and common socage, which meant that the land could be bought and sold by other loyal subjects. Lower Canada was conceived as a preserve for the cultural and social ways of the French-speaking majority of the St. Lawrence Valley. The Catholic Church remained established and seigneurial land titles remained in place. The reorganization of Quebec thus originated in efforts by imperial officials in London to secure the loyalty of Britain's remaining North American provinces through measures suitable to the distinct ethnic communities already settled in the colonies.[30]

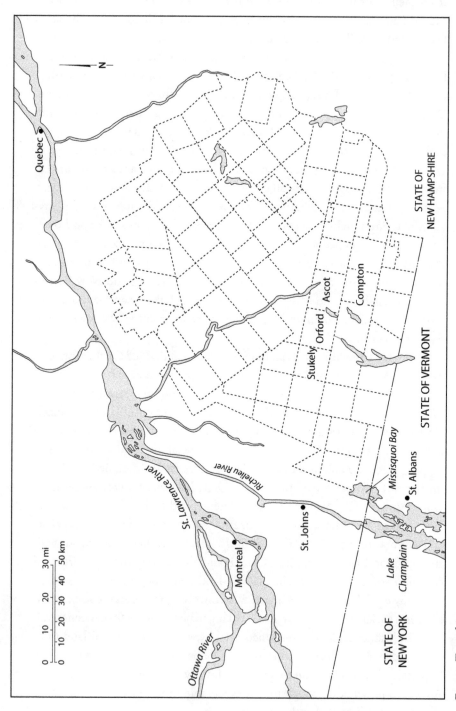

Eastern Townships

However, the Constitutional Act also included provisions that anticipated the arrival of new settlers to British North America. Lord Dorchester assumed executive power over Upper and Lower Canada in 1791. London instructed him to regularize land transactions and limit excessive landholdings in order to prevent speculation and accelerate settlement in both provinces. To meet these demands, Dorchester introduced free and common socage land ownership in all new settlements created in Lower Canada. Aligning property laws in certain parts of Lower Canada with those in Upper Canada made the provinces equally enticing to prospective settlers. Parliament instructed Dorchester to ensure the settlers' willingness to become loyal subjects of Great Britain by requiring land applicants in either colony to swear an oath of allegiance to the Crown and to declare their recognition of the king in Parliament "as the Supreme Legislature of this Province." However, nothing in Dorchester's instructions suggested that settlement was limited to natural-born subjects or people of previous loyalty to the Crown. Rather, Parliament required Dorchester to consider as prospective settlers "all and every Person and Persons who shall apply for any Grant or Grants of Land" and who "shall previous to their obtaining the same, make it appear that they are in a condition to cultivate and improve the same." Dorchester thus changed property laws in Lower Canada to accommodate prospective emigrants from places outside the British Empire. Such expectations were fulfilled in subsequent decades.[31]

The Constitutional Act initiated a period of American emigration northward that lasted until the War of 1812. Upper Canada eventually became the primary destination for American emigrants and the province with the largest population born in the United States. Just before the War of 1812, nearly 80 percent of Upper Canada's 60,000 to 75,000 inhabitants had been born in the United States or were their descendants. However, Lower Canada was the first destination for American emigrants after 1791, partly because of its proximity to New England. Two regions of Lower Canada became especially popular with settlers from the United States, the Ottawa Valley, and, more importantly, a region adjacent to the United States eventually known as the Eastern Townships. By the early 1800s, the Eastern Townships had a population of 8,300 American emigrants.[32]

Since the Eastern Townships came into existence after 1791 under colonial authority created by the Constitutional Act, existing British notions of imperial governance from earlier in the century hardly influenced settlement in this region. If Upper Canada remained a province shaped by the collective settlement of Loyalist refugees, the exercise of individual emigrant rights shaped settlement in Lower Canada. Indeed, formation of the Eastern Township ships reflected Great Britain's efforts to bolster its North American empire in much the same way that Spanish officials tried in places such as Natchez and New Madrid. In both regions, colonial authorities adopted settlement policies compatible with emigrant rights claims under the law of nations. By inviting American citizens to expatriate themselves for lives as loyal subjects in the Eastern Townships, this region, more than any other in British North America, exemplified Great Britain's efforts during the 1790s to build human ramparts at the borders of empire.

Lieutenant-Governor Alured Clarke was the architect responsible for building Great Britain's human ramparts in Lower Canada. In early 1792, Clarke, in consultation with the Executive Council, took steps to create townships in the Crown's "Waste lands." As the Executive Council advised Clarke in February, "it is expedient to make His Majesty's most gracious intentions for the Population, Strength and Prosperity of the Province, immediately and generally known" by circulating a printed proclamation outlining general terms for obtaining land. Shortly thereafter, the *Quebec Gazette* printed a proclamation, "To such as are desirous to settle on the Lands of the Crown in the Province of Lower Canada," similar to Esteban Miró's 1789 invitation for American emigrants to settle in Louisiana. This announcement included stipulations regarding the amount of land available to individual petitioners, a general application procedure, the Crown's control of certain natural resources in the territory, and the reservation of land for support of the Protestant clergy. Clarke's proclamation summarized the basic procedure for obtaining land in the Eastern Townships. The government first required petitioners to demonstrate their sincere desire to settle by swearing the proscribed oath of allegiance and declaring the monarch's sovereignty over Lower Canada. After this initial step, petitioners would receive a warrant of survey to establish the legal boundaries of a new township within six months of their application. Thereafter, the petitioners would receive a patent from the government in Quebec City securing their land title.[33]

Colonial officials encouraged the orderly pursuit of township lands. Under a "leader-and-associate" system, a leader recruited prospective settlers, or associates, and applied for land on their behalf. The leader initiated and shepherded the petition through the government bureaucracy, hired and oversaw surveyors, and paid all required settlement fees. Although the associates were occasionally expected to help defray some of the leader's costs in obtaining land, they always promised to deed significant land shares to the leader in exchange for his work. The government intended to grant groups of leaders and associates entire townships, so each associate could receive 1,200 acres, with 1,000 acres reserved for the leader. The leader would use some of his massive holdings for himself while selling others for profit. This system appealed to colonial officials in Lower Canada for the same reasons that Spanish colonial officials in Louisiana adopted settlement policies of their own. Attracting American emigrants of means and the ability to arrive on their own transferred the costs of surveying, settling, and administering new townships from the government to the settlers.[34]

Officials in Quebec City adopted a colonization policy enticing to American citizens, especially New Englanders. The leader-and-associate system was a familiar method of land allocation throughout New England. Indeed, the federal government of the United States had adopted a leader-and-associate system for the Northwest Territory in its effort to secure the same type of settlers that officials in Lower Canada sought for the Eastern Townships. Moreover, New Englanders, like citizens throughout the United States, claimed emigrant rights as fundamental individual liberties in a republic. Indeed, Vermont enshrined emigrant rights in its laws. Vermont experienced fundamental constitutional changes at the same time as Quebec. In 1791, the United States admitted Vermont to the union, and in 1793 Vermont legislators adopted a new state constitution based heavily on the Vermont Republic's 1777 constitution. The latter document recognized fundamental rights to emigration and expatriation in language from the law of nations and according to notions of republican consent. According to Article 17, "All people have a natural and inherent right to emigrate from one State to another, that will receive them . . . whenever they think that thereby they can promote their own happiness." The 1793 constitution was less verbose but no less categorical. According to Article 19, "All people have a natural and inherent right to emigrate from one state to another that will receive them." Emigrant rights under state laws such as Vermont's ultimately proved no less crucial than Governor Clarke's settlement plans in establishing the Eastern Townships.[35]

Without these separate but complementary legal regimes that entitled free men to change their political allegiance and to move throughout international jurisdictions at will, populating regions such as the Eastern Townships would have proved daunting. British colonial officials in Lower Canada thus had reason to expect that New England, and Vermont in particular, contained a ready population of potential subjects just as Spanish officials in Louisiana had reason to assume the same of American citizens in the Ohio Valley, especially Kentucky. By inviting citizens from states such as Vermont to exercise their emigrant rights for inexpensive land as British subjects, colonial officials in Lower Canada hoped to quickly and efficiently populate the Eastern Townships with expatriated Americans.

Citizens of the United States expressed significant interest in Lower Canada lands that matched government anticipation for the Eastern Townships. As of 1793, 256 leaders petitioned for over 150 townships on behalf of nearly 10,000 associates. The vast majority of leaders and associates were citizens in the United States. Moreover, roughly 157 leaders and associates received government assurances to townships between 1792 and 1793, primarily in the form of survey warrants. New England newspapers in the same period— especially in Vermont, New Hampshire, and, occasionally, Connecticut— regularly announced the meetings of leaders and associates. Individual emigrants from the United States also appeared before colonial officials to proclaim their preference for British allegiance. "I propose to remain in the said province of Lower Canada," Joseph Bigelow of Massachusetts testified, "and to become a subject of the British Government." Ezekiel Roberts, a Connecticut native, declared much the same, for "he intends to remain in this province and to become a Subject of the British government." These declarations and many others amount to a substantial list of citizens from the United States willing to expatriate themselves for a new life in Lower Canada. By the early 1790s, officials in Lower Canada had seemingly created a simple and effective policy for populating the Eastern Townships with loyal emigrants from the United States. Moving forward, however, the policy proved anything but simple or altogether effective.[36]

Problems beset government plans for colonizing the Eastern Townships from the outset. Some reflected competing political interests in the provincial government while others emerged from the nature of the leader-and-associate system. Until 1796, there was confusion among government officials and petitioners regarding the size of land grants and the fees required to complete land transactions. Moreover, members of the Executive Council found this confusion favorable. Many were land speculators who wanted Eastern Township lands for themselves or their patrons among the mercantile elite in Quebec City and Montreal. This put the Executive Council at odds with the lieutenant-governor, which slowed the land-granting process, as did the council's efforts to actively impede settlement in the Eastern Townships. Moreover, the leader-and-associate system encouraged fraud as leaders occasionally submitted spurious lists of associates and potential settlers. Legal settlement of the Eastern Townships was ultimately quite protracted. Between 1792 and 1800, the government granted only six townships. According to the government's own estimation in 1800, it had at its disposal about 150 townships totaling 10 million acres, but only 35 townships "are in contemplation to be granted on the original Terms proposed in the year 1792." Only fifty leaders of the original petitioners assured land in the early 1790s eventually received land patents for their associates, but nearly a decade later in 1802 after accruing significant debt. As a result, absentee landownership increased in the Eastern Townships, development stagnated, squatting became more common, and the original petitioners who sincerely wanted to settle the Eastern Townships faced a long and uncertain wait for land grants.[37]

The Land Committee quickly recognized that the delays experienced by township applicants posed significant problems for the future of Lower Canada. The Land Committee advised Clarke to appoint additional surveyors for the Eastern Townships in order to meet the demand of applicants from "the late colonies" in New England and New York that had "obtained the Desired Assurance of Grants of the Waste Lands of the Crown." These prospective emigrants "have gone back to those Countries and their return may be soon expected with many Hundreds of Industrious men who as they say anxiously wish to be admitted as British Subjects, nothing doubting but they may immediately take possession of the Lots they have been made to expect." The Land Committee also dashed expectations that land applicants might tolerate delays in the land-granting process out of lingering loyalty to the Crown. It warned that American emigrants would "return from whence they came" if the government frustrated their hopes for land. This concern lent urgency to the Land Committee's counsel, for "in the humble opinion of this Committee every possible means should be used to prevent this threatened evil—a check of this nature given to the present spirit of emigration into the Canadas would deprive this Province of an opportunity of increasing the population of the Country and of adding to its Wealth by the ingress of skillful, Industrious Farmers in great numbers." Feckless colonial administrators would thus prevent Great Britain from building its human ramparts in Lower Canada if American citizens lost incentives to expatriate themselves.[38]

Samuel Willard was the type of American citizen whom authorities in Lower Canada expected to emigrate from the United States but feared losing to bureaucratic malfeasance. Although born in Massachusetts in 1766, by the early 1790s Willard resided in northern Vermont with his extended family. Soon after they became citizens of the United States with Vermont's admission to statehood, Willard and the other men in his family considered becoming British subjects in Lower Canada. In response to Lieutenant-Governor Clarke's February 1792 proclamation, they petitioned for 60,000 acres in Orford and Stukely townships. Willard was an active participant in his family's efforts to secure Canadian lands. In 1793, he visited Lower Canada to assess the quality of available land on behalf of the prospective settlers. Should available land in the Eastern Townships meet "my expectations there is no doubt but we Shall move on to it Soon as we can dispose of our property" in Vermont, Willard explained. The available land impressed Willard. Following his visit, he sold his Petersham property in anticipation of quitting the United States. However, the situation was "circumstantial in Quebec" regarding the government's true commitment to the land applicants, so Willard decided not to emigrate until "such time as the mode of settlement is Determined in Canada." English traveler Isaac Weld observed other American citizens hesitant to exercise their emigrant rights on a trip through Lower Canada in the 1790s. According to Weld, "There are numbers who come yearly into the country to 'explore it,' that return back solely because they cannot get lands with an indisputable title."[39]

Some of the first prospective American settlers in the Eastern Townships had no choice but to return to the United States because the colonial government failed to provide a way for them to become British subjects. Colonial officials put men such as Willard who wanted to emigrate in a confused legal status under British law. The colonial government issued warrants of survey that indicated that applicants would eventually acquire the land provided they had taken steps to settle in Lower Canada, such as assessing land quality and selling property in the United States, and they were willing to swear their allegiance to the Crown. Still, officials in Lower Canada created no local legal procedures or appointed no officers to accept oaths, thus emigrants from the United States had no way to complete their expatriation. Without the status of British subjects, landownership in Lower Canada was illegal. One potential emigrant described the difference between Americans who acquired subject status and those who did not as "legal settlers" rather than "intruders." Making it possible for American emigrants to expatriate themselves was essential to officials in Lower Canada who wanted to populate the Eastern Townships.[40]

In 1794, Lower Canada's Executive Council appointed oath commissioners, which finally made it possible for land applicants to transfer their allegiance to the Crown. The oath commissioners were responsible for judging the character of prospective settlers and then administering the oath and declaration to individuals deemed suitable for the colony. In a public notice that outlined the responsibilities of oath commissioners, the Executive Council announced "that prior to the issuing of any Grant of Land, enquiry should be made into the Principles and Character of such Persons as may be desirous of becoming Settlers in this Province, before they be admitted to take the Oaths and subscribe the Declaration" required by the Crown. The commissioners received instructions to collect personal information about all leaders and associates who had received warrants of survey as of 1794 or expected to receive warrants thereafter. Prospective settlers were required to supply the names of all leaders and associates, where they resided, and which township or place where they intended to settle. Commissioners would forward lists with this information to the Executive Council, which would then authorize the commissioners to administer the oath and declaration to approved leaders and associates. Approved settlers were also expected to provide the commissioners and the Executive Council with a more detailed profile of the age, occupation, sex, religious denomination, and overall number of settlers authorized for a given township. The Executive Committee assigned commissioners to specific locations that indicated their expectations for significant emigration from the United States. Of the original fourteen commissioners, six were assigned to the main water routes connecting the Champlain and St. Lawrence Valleys. Four of the six commissioners were concentrated at Missisquoi Bay.[41]

With the commissioners appointed, earnest land seekers took careful steps to secure proof of their good character. The *Rutland Herald*, a Vermont newspaper, explained that potential emigrants must be prepared "to procure a Certificate from an authorized Justice of the Peace, within the state where such Person lives, that he is an honest, industrious Person, and peaceable inhabitant." Oath commissioners directly counseled Samuel Willard, now a principal leader for the Stukley associates and an agent for the Orford associates, "that every man who comes forward as a settler must produce a certificate from a magistrate that he is a man of good moral character and will be likely to make a good inhabitant." Hopeful emigrants took this requirement seriously. A group of sixteen associates for Orford or Stukely from Amherst, Massachusetts, received a general character reference from Simeon Strong, a local justice of the peace, who confirmed "that all the persons whose names are contained in the foregoing List, are persons of fair character, and are reputed to be honest and useful members of society." Applicants for Olney Township from the Connecticut River towns in northern Vermont and New Hampshire went even further to secure personal character references from local justices of the peace. Edwin Buckman knew from an eighteen-year acquaintance and "considerable dealing" with prospective emigrant Azariah Webb that the Revolutionary War veteran from Lancaster, New Hampshire, was "a very honest industrious man and good Citerson." A group of Olney associates from Grafton, New Hampshire, and Bradford, Vermont, were mostly worthies from each town's legal, mercantile, and landed establishment. Fellow associate William Tarlton described them as "good Citzens & loyal Subjects, to the Laws & Regulations of their respective States to which they belong." Tarlton then secured his own character reference from a justice of the peace unaffiliated with the Olney applicants who described him as "a worthy good citizen of" New Hampshire. Their reputations in the communities they planned to leave behind thus provided emigrants with an important measure of personal character.[42]

A man's local reputation for good citizenship in the United States provided a reliable indication of his potential to become a loyal British subject in Lower Canada because a common notion of allegiance prevailed in both places. Although subject and citizen were fundamentally different forms of legal status, settlers in the Eastern Townships expected to trade one for the other with relative ease because on a regional level, political belonging in northern New England and southern Lower Canada was determined less by municipal laws of civic membership and more by the privileges and obligations of emigrant rights under the law of nations. Allegiance in this region did not create obligations to birthplace, communal ties, or to one sovereign over another. Instead, allegiance was portable to the extent that a person of demonstrated respectability in one place could be expected to behave the same elsewhere. By this standard, meeting the conditions of citizenship in a particular location entitled individuals to claim the privileges of emigration right citizenship anywhere.

When American citizens received character references as evidence of their potential loyalty, they subjected themselves to the authority of New England justices of peace and Lower Canadian oath commissioners. Despite testimony that they could become loyal British subjects, oath commissioners rejected the Olney and Suffolk petitioners' land request, thereby denying their emigrant rights claims as well. The Orford and Stukely petitioners were more successful. Commissioners at Missisquoi Bay confirmed the good character of the respective leaders and associates for Orford and Stukely. According to Samuel Willard, acting as agent for the Orford applicants, they "are recommended by the land commissioners at Missisquoi Bay as good and wholesome Inhabitants for the Township of Orford." The commissioners declared that the Stukely applicants "have been recommended to us by good principal characters from the place of their abode—We therefore recommend them and have reason to believe they will make good Subjects." In the end, nearly eighty associates seeking land in the two townships received permission to swear the oath of allegiance. As suggested by the various fortunes of land applicants, local legal officials in the United States and Lower Canada exercised considerable power to interpret and implement emigrant rights under the law of nations, albeit with a decided preference for their exercise.[43]

However, some observers in Lower Canada were skeptical about the emigrants who chose to expatriate themselves from the United States. "Like all money-making emigrants," observed American visitor Charles Stewart, expatriated settlers from his country "accommodate their political complexion, to that of the multitude, by whom they are surrounded; and so well do they compare with the cameleon." Canadian writers were especially critical of the American propensity to expatriate because it threatened their claims to land in the province of their ancestors. Articles in *Le Canadien*, the principal Canadian journal in Lower Canada, described American emigrants as a shiftless and immoral population, a people for whom "the ties of blood are of absolutely no account." From both perspectives, American settlers were effectively subversive citizens of the world who found traditional sources of personal and social identity—birthplace, family, cultural inheritance—worthless. Such views suggested that character references from the places they left behind were irrelevant indicators of the settlers' potential to become loyal subjects because individuals who emigrated were incapable of developing sincere civic attachments to any place.[44]

Prospective settlers in the Eastern Townships ultimately had good reason to prove that they would become loyal, worthy subjects. Of course, leaders described their associates as nothing but ideal potential subjects. Samuel Willard received reports from family members who testified to the good character of the associates retained by the Orford and Stukely leaders. One correspondent described them as "good members of society" and "many of them will carry considerable property." Another boasted to Willard that "innumerable advantages will result with a new settlement by having its first Inhabitants a peaceable industrious and enterprising people." Willard's correspondents measured character by those attributes—some wealth and a capacity for labor—necessary for reducing forests to private property put to agricultural production within an orderly community. Land petitions from Upper Canada suggest that similar notions prevailed in that colony. John Eaton announced to local officials his intent "to come forward with Provisions, Farming Utensils &c. to commence a Settler." In addition to bringing personal property, Eaton emigrated with his wife and nine children, a family that included five sons "able to bear Arms." Caleb Piper, another Upper Canada petitioner, emigrated with livestock, farming tools, and a family that included his wife and eleven children.[45]

Land petitioners in both Canadian colonies not only boasted of their potential to become loyal, useful subjects, they also demonstrated their intent to settle permanently by emigrating with property and families. Large families necessary for agricultural labor provided evidence for the standing of American men eager to become British subjects just as enslaved people did for the American men who became Spanish subjects in Louisiana. American emigrants thus brought human passports of their own to Canada that complemented the character references they received from the communities they left behind. With evidence of their good character in the references from the communities they intended to leave and embodied in the families they controlled, American emigrants demonstrated an authentic desire to expatriate themselves from the United States for settlement as subjects within the British Empire.

The appointment of oath commissioners promised that Americans could finally pursue their interest in Canadian lands by giving them the opportunity to profess their allegiance to Great Britain. Although an administrative choice by authorities in Lower Canada, it nevertheless facilitated the exercise of emigrant rights by braiding settlers' personal economic interests with Great Britain's imperial ambitions in North America. Once prospective settlers proved their good character and received permission to swear their allegiance to the Crown, the Crown's representatives in Lower Canada would hopefully grant them the land they had requested. With the land-granting system apparently operative, land applicants in the United States prepared for imminent emigration and expatriation. Leader Reuben Tuller of St. Albans, Vermont, placed an announcement in the *Rutland Herald* to remind the men who signed his petition that they "must hold themselves in readiness to take the oath of allegiance, and to go on the Lands when chartered." English traveler Isaac Weld visited Lower Canada in the mid-1790s and expressed optimism about the colony's potential to populate the Eastern Townships with expatriated Americans such as Tuller. "It is not probable that these people, if they had a clear title to their lands, would return back to the United States," especially not those "who have voluntarily quitted the country . . . whilst self-interest, which led them originally to come to Canada, operated in favour of their remaining there. It was the prospect of getting land on advantageous terms, which induced them to emigrate; land is still a cheaper article in Canada than in the United States," Weld predicted. However, authorities in Lower Canada took actions that jeopardized Weld's predictions and the hope of prospective subjects such as Tuller.[46]

Lieutenant-Governor Clarke gave American applicants with warrants of survey less than one year to demonstrate their good character and to appear in person before oath commissioners to swear allegiance to the Crown. Applicants who failed to meet this deadline relinquished all land claims in the Eastern Townships. The government announced that it would begin considering new applications in place of the voided warrants. In response to the government's demand, Samuel Willard received a panicked report from another leader of the Orford and Stukley associates that "it will be impossible to forward all the associates to take the Oath immediately" even though the "settlers are good members of society" with every intention to remove themselves and their "considerable property" to Lower Canada. Nevertheless, the Land Committee declared the original warrants of survey for Orford and Stukely void and the townships open to new petitioners. The Land Committee reasoned that Willard, as an agent for the associates and other leaders, could not secure legal land patents for the people he represented. As "subjects of the United States," all associates must appear in person to swear the oath of allegiance and take the declaration, the Land Committee insisted. Willard could not swear an oath or pronounce a declaration on behalf of other leaders or applicants. Although some of the Orford and Stukely leaders asserted their unwavering loyalty to Great Britain during the late revolution, colonial officials in Lower Canada were unmoved. The laws of settlement for the Eastern Townships required applicants from the United States to relinquish their citizenship through emigration or forgo the prospect of land patents in Lower Canada.[47]

Frustrated settlers accused Lower Canada's lieutenant governor of undermining their emigrant rights. American men would choose British allegiance only with confidence that their expatriation would bring them secure land titles and political status meaningful enough to protect their interests. Without gaining the privileges and obligations of British subjects, expatriation was not only a bad bargain for emigrants but would also undermine Britain's imperial ambitions. Asa Porter threatened as much in a letter to the Land Committee vouching for the integrity of the original Orford and Stukely applicants. They had every reason to expect that the provincial government would honor its pledge to grant land patents, Porter argued. Otherwise, Porter warned, "it is my candid opinion that if persons of this description are disappointed they will be extensively influential in discouraging people of property and the better sort of settlers from coming into this province."[48]

Indeed, men who claimed emigrant rights gained privileges that were ideally suited to navigating the legal uncertainties created by Lower Canada's fickle land bureaucracy. American emigrants considered themselves free to move about with little regard for borders and to expatriate themselves at will when opportunities became available to change allegiance. This prepared them to wait for officials in Lower Canada to complete land transactions while considering other places to pursue their interests. Writing from Vermont, Samuel Willard announced his "wish to remove from this place and should be as well pleased with going to Canada as any other place—Provided I can do it on as good terms." Shortly thereafter, Willard quit Vermont to settle in Stukely. Luke Knowlton, Willard's father-in-law and a leader of the Orford associates, believed Willard's emigration helped his group's land claims because it allowed him to adopt a new legal status in the empire. As Knowlton assured Willard, "by your going into the province, in person and becoming an actual subject (or more democratically a citizen) ... the concern fondly hope that their capitations and solicitations no longer become the sport of governmental intrigues or delays." According to this view, Willard gained rights to township land and the expectation of a responsive colonial government by choosing to become an actual settler. His emigrant rights purchased settlement rights in Lower Canada.[49]

Leaders for Orford and Stukely, along with their supporters in Lower Canada, successfully lobbied colonial officials in Quebec City. In early 1796, the Land Committee partially acquiesced by allowing the applicants to survey 400 acres in each of the two townships. Although this fell short of their original request, and it did not grant them patent to the land, the government overturned its earlier declaration that Orford and Stukely were vacant. With this decision, the government gave the leaders and associates for both townships reasons to pursue emigration right citizenship in Lower Canada with renewed confidence, nevertheless their grants remained incomplete throughout the late 1790s.[50]

DURING THE EARLY 1790S, Spanish and British officials developed similar colonization policies to build human ramparts for the protection of their North American empires. Each power directed settlement to regions with defensive and commercial potential. For the Spanish this meant encouraging emigrants to settle Natchez and New Madrid in Louisiana whereas the British invited emigrants to the Eastern Townships of Lower Canada. Emigrant rights to free movement and expatriation under the law of nations provided the essential legal and political underpinning for Spain's and Britain's colonization policies. In both instances, local colonial officials created procedures that enabled settlers to exercise their emigrant rights with evidence of good character from the places they quit along with swearing oaths of allegiance to their new sovereigns. These procedures privileged certain characteristics and

qualities in potential subjects. Spain's colonization policy created a preference for white men who emigrated in possession of enslaved people in numbers large enough to labor in a growing tobacco economy. Great Britain's
colonization policy created an alternative human passport regime for the
Eastern Townships. Reducing the region's dense hardwood forests to farms
with eventual commercial value required white men with substantial family
labor to clear and cultivate the land.

In their pursuit of human ramparts, colonial administrators in Louisiana
and Lower Canada competed for the allegiance of the same settler population that officials in the United States hoped to contain within the Northwest
Territory. Thousands of American citizens responded by deciding to expatriate themselves from the United States rather than emigrating within it. Although Spain and Great Britain introduced colonization policies to create
subjects out of American citizens, local Spanish and British officials implemented the policies in ways that reinforced the boundaries of citizenship in
the United States. Colonization policies adopted outside the United States
denied emigrant rights of free movement and expatriation to all but the white
men within the United States who already claimed these rights for themselves. The choices that American citizens made in North America's borderlands thus shaped debates over citizenship rights in places far from the
republic's margins. In courtrooms and the burgeoning partisan press of
the 1790s, the emigrant rights claims that allowed political belonging across
borders also came to define the conditions of citizenship within the republic's borders.

CHAPTER FOUR

Human Balloons

In 1797, Virginia congressman William Giles asserted that the right to expatriation "was the foundation of our Revolution." Although a view shared by many in the United States, by the late 1790s it was not a position free of controversy. Giles's remarks were part of a contentious debate in Congress over a proposed federal law regarding expatriation. Federal officials outside of Congress and within the federal courts also considered the legal limits of emigrant rights. Similar debates about the limits and rights of citizens to expatriate themselves also appeared in the press. In every instance, these debates concerned a citizen's legal relationship to the United States and with the world beyond its borders. Without establishing this relationship, one observer held that an expatriated American was akin to a "human balloon, detached and buoyant in the political atmosphere, gazed at wherever he passes, and settled wherever he touches." This depiction of expatriates as unmoored wonders, but subversive nonetheless, reveals why many in the United States found it critical to establish the legitimate balance between emigration control and emigrant rights. The specter of expatriated Americans thus haunted considerations of citizenship and sovereignty in the United States during the 1790s, but for good reason.[1]

In this decade, when several thousand citizens quit the United States for allegiance to Spain and Great Britain, the French Republic also sought the allegiance of American citizens for reasons of its own. In response, legal and popular opinion in the United States diverged with those who emphasized citizenship's birthright obligations as opposed to those who emphasized citizenship's emigrant right privileges. The former position rested on a limited right to expatriation as opposed to the latter position's assumption of a mostly limitless right to expatriation. Nevertheless, both views reinforced the unstable terms of citizenship in the United States by defining who belonged as those with a lawful right to leave. The reality of American citizens expatriating themselves by land and by sea during the 1790s caused the first sustained controversies over emigrant rights in the United States. These controversies unfolded in the courts, the partisan press, and Congress in ways that clarified the terms of emigration right citizenship.

However, legislators, jurists, and partisans were not free to decide the limits of emigration right citizenship on their own. Instead, legal authority over the freedom of citizens to leave and expatriate themselves was constrained by the choices of American citizens in distant borderlands, whether in North America's imperial borderlands or the maritime borderlands of the revolutionary Atlantic world. This became evident in the adoption and enforcement of treaties intended to govern life in Natchez and the Eastern Townships. Both agreements originated in the foreign policy concerns created by the French Revolution. Yet, in each instance, the United States and other nations reached agreements that accommodated the notion of emigration right citizenship already exercised by local settler populations.

AT WAR WITH nearly all of Europe's monarchs by early 1793, France sought assistance from the United States, a sister republic and presumed ally. To secure American support, France dispatched Edmond Charles Genet on an ambitious diplomatic mission to the United States. Citizen Genet's government in Paris expected him to negotiate a new treaty to reaffirm the defensive alliance first established in 1778 while also bolstering commercial ties between the two republics. Genet also sought permission for French privateers to use American ports to outfit and arm their vessels to attack British shipping in the western Atlantic. He envisioned US territory as the staging ground for fomenting rebellions against British authority in Canada and Spanish authority in Florida and Louisiana. Finally, Genet expected to recruit US citizens for his operations on the seas and in North America. Upon disembarking in Charleston, Genet pursued his charge with unwavering zeal that received a checkered reception in the United States. He received an enthusiastic welcome in Charleston. South Carolina governor William Moultrie sanctioned Genet's plans while the townspeople celebrated his arrival. Charleston quickly became a haven for French privateers and a staging ground for the invasion of Spanish Florida and Louisiana. Genet's overland journey from Charleston to Philadelphia brought him before adoring crowds at nearly every stop along the way. However, federal officials in Philadelphia proved less sanguine about Genet's mission.[2]

France's declaration of war against several European powers convinced leaders of the US government to preserve its neutrality or risk its ruin. The United States' peace treaties with France and several of France's enemies, including Great Britain and the Netherlands, were compacts that demanded impartiality. Not only were states expected to honor treaties and national friendship under the law of nations, so were their citizens or subjects. John

Jay combined his diplomatic and legal expertise to explain the obligations of American citizens. The Constitution's foundation in popular sovereignty meant that "every citizen is party to" the republic's treaties. The "virtuous citizen" must, Jay argued, "concur in observing and executing them with honour and good faith." Diplomatic accords along with the norms of international law thus invested American citizenship with obligations to the larger world.[3]

The United States' ability to remain neutral proved precarious without guarantees that its citizens would behave virtuously at home as well as within the community of nations. Indeed, only a few weeks after Genet arrived in the United States but before the breadth of his mission became evident, the federal government took steps to prevent its citizens from embroiling the nation in international conflicts. President George Washington, under advice from his cabinet, issued a neutrality proclamation. Washington's proclamation pledged before the world that the United States would "with sincerity and good faith adopt and pursue a conduct friendly and impartial toward the belligerent Powers" while threatening federal prosecution for citizens that violated it. Within a year, Congress further enforced Washington's neutrality proclamation with a law that prohibited US citizens from joining or providing any support for a foreign army or navy. This law applied to citizens within US territory and those who went "beyond the limits or jurisdiction of the United States with intent to be enlisted or entered in the service of any foreign prince or state." Under the 1794 law, both offenses were punishable by fines and imprisonment. The presidential neutrality proclamation reminded American citizens of their duties under the law of nations while the 1794 law punished American citizens who failed to honor their obligations.[4]

Ultimately, Genet's diplomatic mission precipitated a conflict between the rights and duties of American citizenship that remained unresolved throughout the 1790s. The United States government attempted to solve this problem by bolstering its neutral standing in the world against claims by American citizens that their right to expatriation outweighed their duty to help enforce treaties. Genet asserted the priority of rights over duties when he protested to Secretary of State Thomas Jefferson that he gave military commissions only to those "brave republicans of South-Carolina, whose intention appeared to me to be to expatriate themselves." At least some South Carolinians agreed with the French diplomat. Revelers at a meeting of Charleston's Palmetto Society celebrated the advance of French revolutionary principles across the globe with their toast to the "right of expatriation to all those who wish to quit our country." Attorney Alexander Moultrie claimed this right for his client

Stephen Drayton, a secretary to the South Carolina governor who worked to recruit volunteers for Genet's proposed invasion of Spanish territory. When the South Carolina House of Representatives charged Drayton for conspiring with Genet contrary to federal law, Moultrie asked, "Have not the citizens a right to expatriate themselves; And when out of the limits of this state on such footing, have they not a right to act under the authority of any government they chuse?" Critics of the federal government's neutrality policy thus argued that it imposed undue legal restraints on its citizens' emigrant rights.[5]

Americans opposed to Genet's behavior welcomed any policy that curtailed emigrant rights. Several leading citizens of Somerset and Middlesex Counties in New Jersey, led by New Brunswick mayor John Bayard, issued a series of resolutions reprimanding Genet but defending Washington's leadership in upholding their nation's neutrality. They proclaimed that "no citizen, under the pretended right of expatriating himself at pleasure can legally" join a privateer to engage in hostilities against nations at peace with the United States. To allow such actions, the resolution continued, invited armed retaliation because "the whole community is liable to be involved for the crime of one." Another observer condemned Genet's threat in pithier terms, for he had "transubstantiated treason into expatriation, and revealed the mystery that a nation might be neutral and all her citizens at the same time engaged in acts of hostility."[6]

Condemnation notwithstanding, American citizens partook of Genet's revolutionary communion rite. During a 1793 visit to Richmond, Virginia, Edmund Randolph, the United States attorney general, learned "that an inhabitant of this place expatriated himself, while Mr Genet was here and immediately took the oath of a French citizen before him." Apparently, local officials took no steps to prevent this act of expatriation, which revealed the unsettling potential of Genet's mission. Anywhere Genet set foot became an enclave of French sovereignty within the United States. These outposts of the French republic would disappear without Genet present while the population of newly created French citizens remained. The prospect of American citizens expatriating themselves from the United States without emigrating nullified the Washington administration's neutrality policy and compromised national sovereignty. A sailor from Salem, Massachusetts, gave the federal government an opportunity to bolster both.[7]

Gideon Henfield was a crewman on the French privateer *Citoyen Genet*, a vessel the French minister commissioned in Charleston. While cruising the Delaware River, the *Citoyen Genet* captured the *William*, a Scottish merchant ship. Prize master Henfield brought the ship to port in Philadelphia. Authorities arrested Henfield for violating the neutrality proclamation. Washington's administration tested the legal standing of his proclamation by orchestrating a federal case against Henfield in the United States Circuit Court of Pennsylvania. United States District Attorney William Rawle and United States Attorney General Edmund Randolph prosecuted Henfield. Genet hired Philadelphia lawyers Peter Stephen Du Ponceau, Jared Ingersoll, and Jonathan Dickinson Sargent to defend Henfield.[8]

The court's central question concerned Henfield's citizenship when he enlisted on the *Citoyen Genet*. Henfield's defense attorneys argued that his "natural right of emigration" absolved him from laws that only applied to US citizens. Rawle and Randolph admitted that emigration was a fundamental right, as did the presiding judge James Wilson in his charge to the grand jury. However, Henfield's actions were so hazardous that his individual right to abandon citizenship in the United States required restraint for the security and liberty of remaining citizens. Rawle and Randolph explained to the grand jury that Henfield could not expatriate himself amid a conflict that he intended to join, or perhaps to cover hostilities that he already perpetrated, without violating the basic principle of republican society that citizens are only equal when all obey the law. "That equality is destroyed if one man with impunity may involve three millions in war," argued Rawle and Randolph. Besides, Henfield's guilt was obvious since he provided no evidence of genuine expatriation—that "he has renounced his own country, and has been received and domiciliated by the other"—before he became a belligerent. By all accounts, argued the government's lawyers, Henfield's American citizenship never ceased. "Is not the defendant's family still at Massachusetts? Is he not still upon the roll of their citizens; were his family in want, would they not be entitled public relief?" they asked rhetorically. The grand jury exonerated Henfield because he expressed contrition for unwittingly violating the neutrality proclamation, not because it accepted the defense's position on the right to expatriation.[9]

Henfield's trial sparked debate over expatriation's legal standing in the United States separate from the jury's actual reasoning for its verdict. One observer believed the jury acquitted Henfield because his American citizenship vanished the moment he accepted a French commission, and no law, domestic or international, could prohibit free individuals "from quitting their native country when they please, and from becoming citizens of any foreign country, where to inclination or accident may happen to lead them." James Monroe agreed with this view in a letter to Thomas Jefferson. The US senator for Virginia and eventual minister to France considered a right to expatriation part of citizenship rights "construed more freely" since the Revolution, so that "the mere act of accepting a commission in a foreign service be deemed such if the party pleases." Supporters of the Henfield verdict thought laws, residence, or family ties could not determine national allegiance without undermining a citizen's freedom to choose allegiance on his own. On the contrary, a critic of the verdict maintained that "Citizen Henfield" gladly adopted the novel doctrine of expatriation imported by Genet, for he was part of a "faction of desperadoes, who are ready to fight under any banner against government in every form." John Adams grumbled that the Henfield verdict was a result of "several thoughtless Articles" in various state constitutions "about quitting the Country," which a foolish jury "construed to render all our Treaties nugatory, and authorize our People individually to go to War when they please and with whom they please." The conclusion of Henfield's trial thus seemed like the vindication of a natural right or the advance of a dangerous doctrine.[10]

Whereas Gideon Henfield concluded his trial an apostate to the French Revolution, William Talbot, a sea captain from Norfolk, Virginia, maintained his faith throughout trials of his own. In November 1793, Talbot steered his schooner *Fairplay* into the Chesapeake Bay bound for the Caribbean. Like countless other sailors on Atlantic waters, Talbot's voyage occurred in a hostile world. European monarchs defended their kingdoms against French revolutionaries in conflicts that reached the shores of continents and islands in the Western Hemisphere. Talbot set course for Guadeloupe, a sugar-growing slave colony in the French West Indies. In the years preceding Talbot's voyage, republicans had seized control of the island from royalist stalwarts, and the enslaved rebelled in an effort to claim the rights of man as their own. Guadeloupe was an island rife with shifting allegiances and expansive ideas about liberty when Talbot dropped anchor at Pointe-à-Pitre. Talbot's destination suited him well. Only weeks after departing Virginia, Talbot underwent a remarkable political transformation. By December's end, Talbot renounced his allegiance to the United States in exchange for French citizenship. He devoted himself and his vessel, renamed *L'Ami de la Pont-a-Petre*, to the French Republic.[11]

With the authority of a French commission, Talbot and the crew of *L'Ami de la Pont-a-Petre* captured the *Magdalena*, a Dutch merchant ship, near Cuba in 1794. Once aboard, Talbot discovered that it was under the command of Edward Ballard, a citizen of Virginia who had seized it the day before. According to later testimony, Talbot considered Ballard's actions illegal because the United States was at peace with the Netherlands, so Talbot claimed the *Magdalena* as his rightful prize. Talbot ordered the *Magdalena* to Charleston.

Ballard and his crew accompanied Talbot and the captured Dutch ship to port. Lawyers for Captain Joost Jansen and the *Magdalena*'s owners sued Talbot and Ballard for restitution of their clients' property. Jansen's lawyers maintained that Ballard and Talbot together captured the *Magdalena* while still citizens of the United States, aboard ships that were owned and outfitted by the same, on a cruise that had commenced in Charleston. The lawyers accused Ballard and Talbot of fraudulent collusion to attack foreign shipping in violation of Washington's neutrality proclamation and the country's treaty obligations to the Netherlands. On behalf of himself, the other sailors, and the owners of *L'Ami de la Pont-a-Petre*, Talbot contested the charges against him by submitting proof that he was a naturalized French citizen with a commission from officials in Guadeloupe to cruise against enemy shipping.[12]

Under the law of maritime prizes, jurisdiction to determine rightful ownership of the *Magdalena* belonged to the United States District Court for South Carolina. Presiding district judge Thomas Bee believed the case had broad implications, for it involved "the law of nations, the faith of treaties, the rights of sovereignty and neutrality, the private rights of individuals, and the honour and justice of the United States." Although Bee refused to acknowledge that Talbot had expatriated himself under Virginia law, he nevertheless asserted a right to expatriation under US law. The nation's naturalization law recognized the doctrine of expatriation explicitly, and even Washington's neutrality proclamation recognized it tacitly. Bee thus did not deny Talbot's right to expatriation. However, he had no right, the judge asserted, "in his new character, to injure the country of his first and native allegiance, by open violation of her treaties with friendly powers" lest he face prosecution if he returned to the United States. Ultimately, Bee ruled against Talbot because the judge concluded that he abused his emigrant rights, especially in light of evidence that he and Ballard, an American citizen, colluded to plunder the maritime commerce of countries at peace with the United States. A circuit court upheld Bee's ruling, which Talbot appealed to the United States Supreme Court.[13]

Lawyers for both sides debated the privileges and obligations that belonged to citizens exercising their emigration right citizenship in distant places. Jansen's lawyers argued that obligations curtailed privileges. They distinguished a right to "lawful expatriation," which required a person to emigrate from the United States with an expressed desire to expatriate and proof of "joining himself to another state," from Talbot's "pretended expatriation" as "merely a colour to the general scheme of plunder and depredation." Talbot thus violated recognized legal restraints "on this loco-motive right," Jansen's lawyers argued, as "it shall not be exercised either in contravention of a national compact . . . or to the injury of the emigrant's country." Jansen's lawyers urged the justices to reject Talbot's appeal or risk conjuring "a political monster" with "all the citizens of a country at war, though the country itself at peace."[14]

Talbot's lawyers Alexander J. Dallas, Du Ponceau, and Ingersoll argued that emigrant rights were natural rights "antecedent and superior to the law of society." It would be absurd for individuals to enter a social contract and form a government to protect their liberty and private interests only to yield their privilege of seeking happiness and security elsewhere. Governments could not regulate emigration because the emigrant's "private motives of interest, or of pleasure, do not affect the community; and it is of no importance to what country he goes." In this view, a citizen's obligation to the state consisted only of obeying its municipal laws while living within its jurisdiction, but "once he has expatriated himself, the state is no longer interested, no longer responsible for his conduct; the ligature, which bound them is severed, and can never again be united, without their mutual consent." According to Talbot's lawyers, a citizen completed his expatriation through "the act of swearing allegiance to another sovereign," which "is unequivocal and conclusive; extinguishing, at once, the claims of the deserted, and creating the right of the adopted, country." Talbot's lawyers concluded that his obligations to the United States ceased once he pledged allegiance to France.[15]

The Supreme Court upheld the lower court rulings against Talbot but not before the justices attempted to establish the conditions of lawful expatriation. The justices concluded that Talbot's status as a French citizen was dubious while conclusive evidence existed that he and Ballard colluded to violate the law of nations and neutrality. Nevertheless, the justices shared the emerging legal consensus in the United States that emigrant rights, particularly freedom of expatriation, were fundamental to full citizenship in a republic. With the existence of the right beyond dispute, the justices instead debated "the proper manner of executing this right," as Justice James Iredell announced in his opinion. For Iredell, citizens were free to exercise their right to expatriation "with no other limitation than such as the public safety or interest requires, to which all private rights ought and must forever give way." Overall, Iredell and the other justices agreed with Jansen's lawyers that obligations to the larger community governed a citizen's emigrant rights.[16]

The justices suggested that lawful expatriation occurred when a citizen completely and permanently removed himself from his community. By the permanence standard, oaths of allegiance alone were nothing more than hollow utterances before agents of foreign governments on distant shores or far at sea. An oath of allegiance, or a military commission, might begin a citizen's expatriation from the United States, but it could only be completed elsewhere. Authentic expatriation demanded evidence of stronger commitments to a sovereign power other than the United States. Justice William Cushing stipulated that genuine acts of expatriation required "the emigrant's actual removal, with his family and effects, into another country." Justice William Paterson agreed, noting that when an American citizen brought "his fortune, and family" to settle under another government, he thus intended "an entire departure from the United States." The justices suggested a standard for the legitimate exercise of emigration right citizenship, one that reserved this privilege for men who could already claim full citizenship in the United States—that is, men with enough wealth and standing to create independent households. Should such men emigrate with their property and families, they completely severed themselves from the communities they left behind, which, in turn, freed these communities from responsibility for their actions beyond American borders. Taken together, the justices attempted to uphold expatriation as a fundamental right shorn of its most subversive consequences.[17]

Although courts in the United States during the 1790s decided the expatriation cases without any consideration of North America's borderlands, they nevertheless established legal standards for the exercise of emigration right citizenship that affirmed understandings of allegiance already common in the borderlands. Outside of the federal courts, Americans expressed more contentious understandings of their emigrant rights. Clashing opinions about the freedom to quit the United States that appeared in newspaper polemics and congressional debates produced two competing concepts of citizenship. Each contained distinct claims about allegiance, patriotism, and personal character. Protagonists in the expatriation debates of the 1790s defined these elements of citizenship in ways that both unleashed and restrained the emigrant rights of free men to leave the republic.

Writers defending a robust right to expatriation understood allegiance in purely contractual terms. Citizens who obeyed their nation's laws should expect the state to protect them in return. However, citizens were also free to seek protection from other sovereigns by transferring allegiance from one nation to the next. Should such individuals seek to expatriate themselves from a nation where they had lived in good legal standing, then no restraints should be placed on their right to leave. In return, the nation they departed lost all claims to their obedience. A citizen was free, one proponent argued, to "alienate himself at all times of tranquility; and when he has voluntarily cut the ligature, he is then exonerated from the original covenant." Another writer explained the terms for maintaining and terminating the relationship between citizens and governments in more detail. A citizen's obligations are "daily discharged by his supporting a uniformly irreproachable conduct—his account current with society is thus daily balanced—the society reaps daily the benefits of his industry, and is bound in return daily to afford him, in common with his neighbours, the same protection against injury, or redress for violence." However, when a citizen "deliberately quits a society without having transgressed its laws, his subjection to them ceases, and his connection with it, in the aggregate, is dissolved." This view that citizens were entitled to constantly renew the social contract with their government did away with any meaningful notion of tacit consent—the theoretical foundation necessary for a durable citizenship in one political community enacted throughout a lifetime.[18]

A notion of allegiance governed only by express consent created a portable form of citizenship amenable to frequent and easy changes. This understanding of allegiance held that loyalty oaths to new sovereigns or commissions in foreign militaries enabled American citizens to expatriate themselves regardless of their settlement. According to this view, citizens completed their expatriation from the United States once they publicly professed allegiance to a new sovereign. However, the contributor to an Albany, New York, newspaper in 1797 dismissed those who believed that "any man, by mumbling hocus pocus, ceases to be an American, and to be bound by the laws as a citizen." Indeed, critics rejected a right to expatriation because it encouraged fickle national allegiances rather than binding expressions of political consent. A right to expatriation was part of a "new fangled system" within which "you may be a citizen of America today, a subject of England to morrow, and a citizen of France on the day following," another critic argued, "for a man now a days, has only to will it to be a citizen of any country he pleases, and he is one." Uriah Tracy, a Federalist congressman from Connecticut, derided expatriates for assuming that changing their citizenship was no more significant than "pulling off a pair of mittens."[19]

A notion of allegiance that allowed for constant renewal and frequent changes rendered patriotism irrelevant. Writers who defended the right to expatriation dismissed patriotism as the "prejudice, or enthusiasm" of a people that roused irrational nostalgia for "the spot which gave them birth." The right to expatriate suited those unmoved by patriotic nostalgia. Indeed for some individuals, another writer observed, "accidents of nature may cast one in his nativity, on any peculiar spot, where his will is not consenting." Upon maturity, "he is not obliged to reside in his native country, unless he choses [*sic*]: he is at liberty to chose the spot of his own happiness." None of these writers suggested that American emigrants would never form patriotic attachments to their adopted countries, but rather they argued patriotism should not restrain citizens from exercising their right to expatriation. By granting individuals the right to conclude their citizenship at will, critics of the right to expatriation feared that its proponents ignored how a person's place of birth, inherited culture, and traditional institutions cultivated patriotic affections that created unshakeable citizenship obligations. "Supposing a man may throw away his Americanism, as he would his old shoes, why do we prate about love of country," asked one incredulous writer.[20]

Stripping patriotism from allegiance led defenders of emigrant rights to celebrate limitless freedom of movement because the absence of which amounted to enslavement. Writers from states with the largest populations of enslaved people developed this argument most forcefully. According to US senator Charles Pinckney, an American citizen "can have no idea of being confined to one country, or one allegiance, if he thinks proper to change them," Pinckney argued, because he possessed the "right of living where he thinks proper; instead of being fixed to one spot, of becoming, if he pleases, a citizen of the world." "Aristogiton," writing from Richmond, Virginia, insisted that American citizens must have a right to expatriation or else they were enslaved by an "accident of birth," thus shackled by the political choices of their ancestors with a force no less powerful than the subjugated status forced on enslaved people at birth. Proponents of a right to expatriation during the 1790s reinforced it as the privilege of white men capable of choosing world citizenship, the opposite of enslavement or other forms of dependency. From this perspective, full citizenship in the United States only belonged to white men with untrammeled rights to quit the country whenever they saw fit.[21]

Such a notion of citizenship threatened to collapse the United States from within according to critics who feared that expatriates wreaked havoc in the nations they left behind. Expatriation was a "palpably absurd" doctrine, one critic declared. Unless citizens and their government shared mutual obligations, there was "no ligament to connect society together: all social compact must of necessity be dissolved and nations be converted into a heterogeneous mass of individuals, each putting on and putting off his relationship to Government, according to his own whim and caprice, with a certainty of entailing upon the country all the horrors of direful anarchy and endless confusion."

Equally alarmist, another writer insisted that Americans who accepted emigrant rights to renounce the United States and their freedom "to chuse any other or no nation" should then expect the countryside swarming with "hosts of expatriated individuals, perhaps in arms too, composing no society, nor forming a nation." The very cosmopolitanism that defenders of a right to expatriation counted among the privileges of citizenship for white men appeared to create stateless rogues. Critics concluded that virtuous citizenship could not accommodate emigrant rights, so they described expatriates as people outside the racialized boundaries that reserved full civic belonging for white men. Expatriates destabilized the racial and gender order that undergirded American citizenship; they were, in Uriah Tracy's words, "a kind of political mulatto, without real attachment for any government."[22]

Two conflicting concepts of citizenship emerged from the expatriation polemics of the 1790s. The proponents of expatriation rights unmoored citizenship from a binding preference for a particular state or place so that unrestrained emigration became the most important exercise of self-governance. Taking the law of nation's doctrine of "acquired settlement" as its starting point, expatriation culminated the exercise of emigration right citizenship, which undermined notions of birthright citizenship coalescing at the same time. Emigration right and birthright citizenship each reserved full civic belonging for white men but with different normative values attached to nativity. Critics of expatriation rights insisted that citizenship was inseparable from the obligations created by birth in a particular state or place. By turning to the press instead of the state to enforce their concept of birthright citizenship, opponents of emigrant rights effectively developed a form of perpetual allegiance compatible with republicanism. Although federal and state governments could not prevent their citizens from leaving, a nationalist print culture devoted to instilling patriotism could achieve the same ends. Patriotic citizens would never choose to leave the United States, so those who chose otherwise, or even considered the option, must lack the moral and ethical qualities necessary for virtuous citizenship. For Americans in the 1790s who found it incomprehensible that their fellow citizens might hold other countries in such high regard, they disparaged those who quit the United States. Citizens "not satisfied with the liberty and equality enjoyed in the United States, may avail themselves of the benefits to be derived from expatriation" if another country might "claim a preference in the opinion of those grumblers," scorned one critic of expatriation. Ultimately, patriots remained but malcontents moved elsewhere under this perpetual allegiance of the willing.[23]

By the late 1790s, evidence suggested popular sentiment in the United States favored a notion of citizenship that included emigrant rights to free movement and expatriation. Congressman William Smith, a South Carolina Federalist, believed that "it was the general opinion of the citizens of this country that they had the right to expatriate themselves." Smith's Federalist colleague Samuel Sitgreaves of Pennsylvania conceded that the federal judiciary and the executive branch indirectly recognized the existence of expatriation rights in the Henfield and Talbot cases, so he believed that it was impossible for Congress "to say the right did not exist." The federal government's implicit recognition of expatriation rights lagged behind popular opinion, which suggested that Congress should act to align federal law with common assumptions about citizenship. Jurists and politicians argued for a federal expatriation statute as a legislative remedy to reconcile this disconnect. Supreme Court justices in the *Talbot* case argued in favor of a federal expatriation statute to clarify the right under US law. Justice William Paterson summarized this common view among them. Several states preserved English common law, so also possibly the doctrine of perpetual allegiance, and Paterson recognized that such a statute would provide clear guidance to the courts. According to Paterson, a law determining "the manner, in which expatriation may be effected, would obviate doubts, render the subject notorious and easy of apprehension, and furnish the rule of civil conduct on a very interesting point." Justice James Iredell suggested Virginia's expatriation law might provide a model for federal legislators.[24]

In 1797, the House of Representatives debated a bill that included provisions for a federal expatriation statute similar to the Virginia law. The bill's proponents argued that it accommodated the federal government's neutrality policy with a unilateral right to expatriation. It would have therefore protected a citizen's right to expatriation in ways that safeguarded society. Under this bill, citizens of the United States exposed themselves to fines or imprisonment once they left the country to enter a foreign nation's army or navy. However, the bill provided an exception to this law for Americans who expatriated themselves. In order to make this law enforceable, the bill outlined the "mode in which a citizen may dissolve the ties of citizenship, and become an alien." Under the proposed federal law, any citizen, by birth or naturalization, who emigrated beyond the nation's borders after he "absolutely and entirely renounces all allegiance and fidelity to the United Sates, and to every of them" would "be considered expatriated, and forever thereafter shall be deemed an alien, in like manner and to all intents as if he had never been a citizen." Congress allowed citizens to renounce their allegiance either in writing or by spoken testimony, before two witnesses, and confirmed and recorded by a state, federal, or territorial judge in the Northwest Territory. In one regard, this was a gradual expatriation since any former citizen who entered foreign service less than a year after formally quitting the nation could still be prosecuted as a US citizen under the law. In all other ways, however, the law was absolute, for it prohibited expatriates from becoming US citizens ever again.[25]

The expatriation bill proved controversial because it gave Congress the power to determine which notion of citizenship would prevail in the United States, a form of emigration right citizenship with limitless freedom of expatriation or a form of birthright citizenship that curtailed expatriation. Critics of the bill, primarily Federalists, rehearsed the dangers that expatriation posed to any nation that condoned it. Samuel Sewall of Massachusetts argued that no civil society could permit its citizens "at their will, and without any pretence, to say they would be no longer subject to the Government." Allowing so would invite "insult to our courts and country" at a "moment of danger." Sewall and other Federalists such as Connecticut's Joshua Coit opposed codifying the right of expatriation in federal law. The bill's supporters, typically Republicans, reiterated expatriation's standing as a fundamental natural right. Thomas Claiborne, a Virginia Republican, denied that citizens had special obligations to their country. Rather, political allegiance was akin to freedom of conscience in matters of religion in that conclusions about patriotism and faith were fundamentally private decisions beyond state coercion. Thus according to Claiborne, "It was no more binding for citizens born in the United States to continue citizens of the United States, than it was for a Roman Catholic or Protestant to continue of that opinion when he arrived at years of maturity, and could judge for himself." Claiborne voted in favor of keeping the expatriation provision in the bill because it recognized one of the American people's basic revolutionary freedoms. The bill's opponents voted to suspend further debate, which killed the bill.[26]

Although federal lawmakers failed to codify an expatriation process for American citizens, the bill assumed that lawful expatriation required permanent residence outside the United States. In this regard, the House of Representatives reiterated the standard for determining when citizens had rightfully relinquished their former allegiances that the federal courts had established in earlier expatriation cases. Whereas the courts ruled that citizens proved their intent to expatriate themselves from the United States by emigrating with their families and property, the failed House bill assumed as much by requiring former American citizens to reside in their adopted countries for at least a year before waging war on their behalf.

Together, the courts and Congress during the 1790s defined a standard of lawful expatriation for US citizens that privileged emigration within North America over emigration beyond the continent's shores. Congressmen from both parties emphasized this distinction in debates over the expatriation bill. Massachusetts Federalist Harrison Gray Otis believed the bill would only restrain the constitutional rights of "persons expatriating themselves, and engaging in the service of foreign countries," not "persons emigrating into the Spanish or English territories." This distinction conceded to the reality that a significant population of American citizens had already adopted allegiance to Spain or Great Britain. Pennsylvania Republican Albert Gallatin predicted that developments at the republic's borders would ultimately settle expatriation debates in the United States because "ten to twelve thousand of our citizens had gone to Canada, and upwards of five thousand beyond the Mississippi." Although some of these emigrants remained property owners in the United States, Gallatin noted, others had expatriated themselves by becoming "citizens under another Government." The thousands of American emigrants already settled under Spanish and British sovereignty effectively produced a national right to expatriation that the courts and Congress had no choice but to accept.[27]

Moreover, the federal government's acquiescence to expatriation rights produced in the borderlands influenced its foreign policy toward imperial rivals in North America. In 1795, the United States ratified the Jay Treaty with Great Britain. A year later, the United States entered the Treaty of San Lorenzo del Escorial with Spain. Ratification of these treaties continued efforts by Great Britain, Spain, and the United States to maintain their respective human ramparts in North America amid an unstable international order caused by the French Revolution. Each agreement included provisions regarding territorial sovereignty and commerce that were unenforceable without satisfying the interests, thus securing the allegiance, of American emigrants settled in places such as the Eastern Townships and Natchez.

THE JAY TREATY addressed grievances between the United States and Great Britain stemming from the conclusion of the Revolutionary War. These concerned boundary issues and the presence of British forts on US territory in North America, prewar debts to British merchants, British naval seizures of American merchant ships, and the United States' trading rights as a neutral power. The final treaty resolved some of these issues outright but left others to the judgment of mutual arbitration commissions. On the subject of commerce and neutrality, the countries granted each other most favored nation status, and US merchants gained access to the East Indies and—with tonnage restrictions on their ships—to the West Indies. However, the British refused to recognize a principle of free trade held dear by many Americans that "free ships make free goods." Although the United States remained neutral in Europe's wars, under the Jay Treaty American merchants were unable to trade an array of goods the British government declared contraband of war. The Jay agreement provoked intense, strongly partisan protests in the United States with the trade provisions sparking the most rabid public outcry. Republicans condemned Jay and his Federalist supporters for shackling the US economy to the whims of a British master. Federalists, on the contrary, argued that the treaty was essential to the country's commercial security in a world dominated by British naval power. It seemed better to tie the nation's commerce to the stable British Empire than to the tumultuous French Republic.[28]

The treaty relied in part on regulating emigrant rights in order to fulfill its agreements. Article III allowed US citizens, British subjects, and Native people engaged in commerce to freely pass back and forth across the border separating the United States and British North America. However, Article XXI denied emigrant rights in another context by making it illegal for citizens or subjects of the two nations to attack each other under commissions or instructions from a "foreign prince or state." Furthermore, citizens or subjects could be prosecuted for piracy if they obtained a commission or letters of marque from a state at war with either signatory to the treaty. This article fit with the principle of perpetual allegiance under British common law. It also corresponded with the neutrality doctrine first adopted by the United States in 1793 and codified in the 1794 neutrality act.[29]

The prosecution of Connecticut sailor Isaac Williams revealed how the Jay Treaty qualified the rights of American citizens to expatriate themselves. According to federal charges brought against him in 1799, Williams had attacked British vessels in 1797 while cruising with a French commission. Authorities arrested Williams when he visited Connecticut and charged him with violating the United States' neutrality laws and its recent treaty with Great Britain. Williams's case came before the US Circuit Court in Connecticut. Williams's lawyer argued that his actions were those of an authentic expatriate, not a violator of the Jay Treaty. Williams testified that he had resided in French dominions for all but six months over the previous seven years. Moreover, he had lived the last three years on Guadeloupe and "has made that place his fixed habitation, without any design of again returning to the United States for permanent residence." Oliver Ellsworth, the judge in Williams's case, maintained that citizens could not unilaterally renounce their allegiance "without the consent or default of the community," rejecting Williams's defense. The jury agreed with Judge Ellsworth and found Williams guilty. If Williams, like many other New Englanders, had quit Connecticut for Lower Canada in 1792 instead of residing on Guadeloupe, Article III would have likely protected him from prosecution. Ultimately, the Jay Treaty further limited emigrant rights at sea while accommodating overland emigrant rights within North America.[30]

The Jay Treaty was thus a boon for citizens and subjects in places such as the Champlain Valley, especially for citizens willing to become subjects in locations such as the Eastern Townships. The treaty accelerated trade between northern New England and Montreal with a notable rise in the value of pot and pearl ash, byproducts of the forest clearing necessary to create new settlements. Commerce on Lake Champlain also grew, and landowners near trade routes could hope for increased property values. A few years after the treaty ratification, John C. Ogden aimed to acquaint readers in the United States "with those, who are now connected with us by Treaties, as well as a Similarity of Laws and Customs" now that "Peace, Commerce, and Emigrations are extending our Connections." To prospective settlers in the Eastern Townships, benefits of the Jay Treaty became apparent immediately once news of its ratification reached this region. In a letter to Samuel Willard, Luke Knowlton praised the treaty for its potential to improve their fortunes as both New Englanders and hopeful property owners in the Eastern Townships. Knowlton believed the treaty was certain "to establish a lasting friendship and intercourse between the two provinces." He boasted that "our wilderness in Canada will soon be covered with inhabitants and become fruitful fields."[31]

After 1795, land petitioners in the Eastern Townships sought ways to perfect their land titles and complete their expatriation from the United States with renewed urgency. The principal leaders for the Eastern Townships land applicants, Willard first among them, formed the Missisquoi Bay committee in 1797 to lobby the governor on behalf of applicants for thirty townships. The original members created a standing committee with rules requiring a three-member quorum empowered "to call meetings and do any other business as to them may appear beneficial to the Concerned." In addition to Willard, Jesse Pennoyer and Gilbert Hyatt also played prominent roles in the committee. Like Willard, Pennoyer and Hyatt were born in the British colonies just before tensions emerged with Parliament. Pennoyer joined a New York regiment of the Continental Army to fight against the British Crown before settling in Canada in the late 1780s. Pennoyer worked as a royal surveyor throughout Quebec but, after 1792, his work focused on the area

This watercolor from 1827 depicts life in the Eastern Townships after several decades of settlement in the region. Joseph Bouchette, *Kilborn's Mills, Stanstead, QC, 1827*, McCord Stewart Museum, gift of David Ross McCord.

around Missisquoi Bay. He became a leader for Compton Township and was appointed one of the first commissioners at Missisquoi Bay. Hyatt was part of a Loyalist family in Vermont and fought in a Loyal unit during the war. Following the peace, he migrated with others to the northern reaches of Lake Champlain in Quebec where they settled without permission from colonial officials. They remained in this region illegally until Lieutenant-Governor Clarke's proclamation opened the wastelands to settlement, at which time Hyatt petitioned for Ascot Township. Despite different past allegiances, Willard, Pennoyer, Hyatt, and other prominent figures on the Missisquoi Bay committee were all frustrated land applicants.[32]

This shared experience reflected a legal status that committee members held in common. When Lieutenant-Governor Clarke opened the Eastern Townships to settlement, his proclamation expressed no preference for Loyalists but rather declared all applicants aliens for the purpose of obtaining land—thus, the universal requirement that all petitioners swear an oath of allegiance to the Crown and declare royal sovereignty over Lower Canada. Because a government policy turned the men who joined the Missisquoi Bay committee into internal aliens regardless of their legal status in the past, emigrant rights provided a powerful legal position for challenging the deficiencies of land allocation in Lower Canada. The committee acted first by drafting a memorial and petition addressed to Robert Prescott, governor-in-chief of Upper and Lower Canada. Petitioners requested Governor Prescott honor their original warrants of survey by granting them final patent to their townships. They devised this request as an expression of their emigrant rights, of their freedom to settle and grant allegiance at will.

Perhaps most importantly, petitioners sought land in the Eastern Townships by choice rather than necessity or chance. The memorialists described themselves as representatives for "several Thousands of industrious and well respected Farmers." Regarding their past allegiances, the petitioners and those they represented included people consistently loyal during the Revolution who "have ever since the conclusion of the War entertained an earnest desire of settling again under his Majesty's Government." Moreover, there were "a Considerable number likewise of those who had departed from their allegiance to his Majesty during the time of the" American Revolution but who "became afterwards convinced that they had from mistaken principles and have long entertained the same wishes as the former." However, a shortage of oath commissioners and the Executive Council's failure to finalize land transactions frustrated their choice to become full subjects even though many had demonstrated their intent to do so. They came "forward to take the Oaths to his Majesty and to make beginnings on the land they had Petitioned for" after having already "disposed of their property in the States." Delays created hardship for the applicants who could not afford to stay in Lower Canada until they received their grants, thus forcing them to emigrate once again. Some chose the republic over the empire by returning to northern Vermont in hope that the government would eventually approve their claims. Others simply went to new settlements in New York. Regardless, the petitioners pleaded, there were many worthy settlers forced to "remain for a time in a Country in which his Majesty's national sceptre ceased to sway." When promises of potential loyalty failed to secure land titles, the Missisquoi Bay committee recounted the contributions they had already made to Lower Canada's development. According to the Missisquoi Bay committee, the Crown's wastelands were in a "state of nature" as of 1792 until "his Majesty's faithful Farmers from the States" received the government's assurances to the land and exerted considerable labor and money to build roads, mills, and farms. Not only did the settlers have the potential to become loyal subjects under law, they had already demonstrated their mettle as good emigrants.[33]

Seeking land in Lower Canada under a settlement policy that colonial officials failed to implement, applicants for Compton Township experienced the denial of their emigrant rights as commonly understood in the United States. Led by men who had fought to overthrow the British Empire in North America in a rebellion for emigrant rights, they argued that government delays created economic hardship and diminished their political standing in ways that undermined their freedom to move and expatriate themselves. After the Land Committee favorably responded to a petition from the Compton leaders, many associates made "serious preparations for going on to the land—they accordingly purchased Mill Irons, and made other costly arrangements in order to be ready to go on at the shortest notice." Many also "disavowed their allegiance in the Country from whence they came and removed within the limits of this Province—have since taken the Oaths of Allegiance to His Majesty and have been wasting at great expence ever since." The Compton petitioners had thus expatriated themselves according to standards articulated in American legal opinions and familiar to the law of nations. They indicated their intent to settle permanently in Lower Canada, and they proclaimed the end of their citizenship in the United States. In exchange, and as American critics of emigrant rights would have warned, the Compton applicants expatriated themselves without securing allegiance to a new government and the protection it provided. Because of the legal void created by the British colonial government's unfulfilled promises to land, a Compton applicant thus found himself in what Congressman William Vans Murray characterized as an "unnatural state" that existed "between the allegiance and country he has just disowned, and the allegiance and country to which he may intend to pledge himself." By exercising what they believed were their inherent rights to expatriate themselves, the Compton applicants behaved according to their understanding of themselves as free men whose race, standing, and rights should bring them full civic belonging under any sovereign where they chose to settle. Instead, the Compton applicants became the political mulattoes denigrated in the United States because they lost their claims to white manhood and propertied citizenship once they chose to leave behind their place of prior allegiances.[34]

Samuel Willard acted on his own during the late 1790s to complete his expatriation from the United States. To this end, Willard secured evidence of his good character in 1799 and again in early 1800. In both instances, oath commissioners at Missisquoi Bay declared that Willard should be allowed to swear his allegiance to Great Britain in order to become a landowner in Lower Canada. He was, in the words of one certificate, "a loyal, good, and deserving Subject," who, as explained in the other certificate, had "at all times shewn himself to be warmly attached to British Government." These descriptions of Willard's affection for Great Britain came nearly a decade after starting his land pursuits in Lower Canada. In both documents, the primary evidence for Willard's loyalty was his move to Sheldon, Vermont, in 1794 with his family and possessions in tow. Willard's potential to become a good British subject had nothing to do with his birth in the empire in 1766 or his family's Loyalist leanings. Rather, it rested on his standing as a man of good character in possession of human passports, a standing only available to men with property and families. Willard thus demonstrated his potential to become a good British subject by taking steps to emigrate and eventually expatriate himself from the United States.[35]

The ambitions of Americans such as Willard and those who formed the Missisquoi Bay committee to become landowning subjects in the distant reaches of the British Empire ultimately required lobbyists in London. In the summer of 1799, Samuel Gale sailed to London with Governor Prescott. Gale was the governor's private secretary and an early advocate of American emigration. He used his audience with Prescott to persuade the governor to help him put the land claims of the Orford and Stukely applicants, in addition to the interests of other township applicants, before the king and his ministers. Over the course of a year beginning in fall 1799, Gale circulated a petition that reiterated the applicants' central grievance, first expressed in the Missisquoi Bay resolves. They were sincere emigrants—"faithful old subjects," as Gale preferred—who had diligently pursued township land at great financial and physical hardship despite government proclamations that were difficult if not impossible to obey, bureaucratic delays, and opposition from speculator interests in Montreal and Quebec. Gale first petitioned Prescott in London and then placed his request before the highest levels of imperial government, the Privy Council and the Board of Trade and Plantations. In each instance, Gale pleaded with officials in London to overrule local authorities in Lower Canada. Persistent lobbying in Lower Canada and London ultimately proved successful. At the end of 1799, Governor Prescott officially granted Willard one-half of Stukely Township. By fall of 1800, the Land Committee of the Executive Council for Lower Canada confirmed and issued Willard's patent. After nearly a decade, Willard and the associates he represented became landowners in Lower Canada, culminating their transformation from citizens of the United States to subjects of the British Empire.[36]

Soon after Willard finally received a land title in Stukely, he also gained certain privileges and responsibilities of an imperial subject. The colonial government appointed him justice of the peace in 1803, and by 1807 he had become a commissioner authorized to administer oaths of allegiance. Even though Willard assumed a subject's privileges in Lower Canada, the financial hardship caused by the delays in receiving his patent left him in chronic debt for the rest of his life. Willard's subject status was ultimately precarious due to the threat of financial ruin, an outcome he hoped to avoid by realizing the economic potential of his Canadian land.[37]

With land patents secured by the early 1800s, leaders such as Samuel Willard worked to attract emigrant settlers. Land advertisements published frequently in New England newspapers described Lower Canada as a province where diligent settlers could easily realize their fortunes. In a series of announcements printed in 1802 for Orford and Stukely land, Willard and John Holbrook offered "men of industry" in the United States "the Surest way of getting Rich." They described their grants in the two townships as part of a region "now settling very fast from New England." Emigrants from the United States could obtain land at low cost or on credit provided they settled and cleared their land. Moreover, the townships were close to Montreal, a growing market center "where ships float of almost any size" and trade occurred with "no taxes nor duties to swallow the earnings of settlers," they added. Oliver Barker of Compton Township had several thousand acres for sale in Lower Canada. Barker was especially interested in attracting "the enterprising and industrious farmers" of New Hampshire and Vermont. To entice them, Barker lauded Lower Canada's natural, political, and economic advantages. The region's prospects were even brighter should its population increase, Barker continued, as "the present rapid emigration of Farmers and Mechanics from the New England States bids fair to convert it soon into a very populous and wealthy country." Ultimately, Barker boasted that in Lower Canada "the rights and privileges of the subject are happily secured by a free, wise and beneficent government." Lower Canada's bounty was available to New Englanders who abandoned their citizenship in the United States for lives as prosperous British subjects.[38]

Much like the glowing accounts of emigrant life at Natchez that appeared in US newspapers during the early 1790s, Lower Canada offered monarchy rather than a republic as the government where white men could obtain full civic standing. Indeed, by 1803, 8,300 people had emigrated from the United States for settlements in the Eastern Townships. The Jay Treaty created a legal logic in the Champlain Valley borderlands that privileged emigration and expatriation from the United States as the basis of society, politics, and the economy. By the early 1800s, American citizens could settle in Lower

Canada without doubts that the colonial government would prevent them from expatriating themselves. Colonial officials in Lower Canada encouraged commercial development in the colony by allowing American emigrants to obtain property and local political privileges.

Observers in the United States seemed willing to surrender American citizens to British subjecthood in order to secure larger economic benefits from an alliance with Great Britain. The Treaty of San Lorenzo created an alternative legal logic in the lower Mississippi Valley. In places such as the Natchez District, the United States and Spain competed with each other under the terms of the treaty to secure and control the allegiance of the region's propertied slave owners. This context of uncertain sovereignty invited uncertain allegiances within the American emigrant settlements at Natchez. In order to protect their land and maintain control over their enslaved property, Natchez planters claimed emigrant rights to make a diplomatic accord decided far from Louisiana serve their local interests.

Spain and the United States entered the Treaty of San Lorenzo del Escorial in 1795. Thomas Pinckney led negotiations for the United States, where the agreement was known as Pinckney's Treaty. Spain sought a peaceful relationship with the United States, so it agreed to open the Mississippi and New Orleans to American trade. Spain also surrendered its claims to territory east of the Mississippi River north of the thirty-first parallel. This meant that the Natchez District now fell within US territory along with Creek, Choctaw, and Chickasaw lands. The territory south of this revised boundary remained the Spanish provinces of East and West Florida. Spain also remained in possession of its vast Louisiana province west of the Mississippi. Although the two powers signed the treaty in 1795, it did not go into effect until 1798 after survey parties from both signatories mapped the boundary and Spanish colonial officials in New Orleans surrendered key forts along the Mississippi, the installation at Natchez principal among them. The treaty's protracted enforcement created uncertainty in various ways. US officials eventually arrived in the region to find themselves in jurisdictional conflicts with Spanish officials already in the district. The precise border separating US territory from Spanish territory remained unmapped. However, amid this uncertainty created by the Treaty of San Lorenzo, the legal status of Natchez's inhabitants remained beyond dispute.[39]

Officials from both governments, along with the settlers themselves, agreed that inhabitants of the Natchez District were Spanish subjects. This recognition influenced negotiations between Spanish and US officials at Natchez. It also influenced interactions between local residents and colonial

representatives from both governments. Manuel Gayoso de Lemos was Natchez's governor when diplomats signed the treaty. Although he was promoted
to governor of Louisiana and West Florida within a few years, he was the
highest ranking Spanish colonial official in Natchez when word of the treaty
first reached the local population. During the protracted enforcement of the
treaty, Lemos insisted on Spain's complete sovereignty over the Natchez District until it was officially transferred to the United States. To Lemos, this
meant Spain was obligated to protect its subjects in the district just as subjects were obligated to remain loyal to the Spanish Crown. In a 1797 proclamation to the Natchez settlers, Lemos expressed his trust "that no person will
deviate from the principles of adhesion to our government" while ensuring
the Crown would protect them by securing "the real property of the inhabitants." The Barón de Carondelet, governor-general of Louisiana, reiterated
this expectation in a proclamation of his own. Suggesting a much longer history of loyal subjects and responsive government at Natchez, Carondelet
hoped that during a moment of uncertainty the inhabitants "will behave with
the same tranquility, and entertain the same affection" they had frequently
exhibited. Spain should expect such expressions of "national gratitude,"
Carondelet continued, because "it has been as at so much pains and expense,
to form and protect" Natchez. Spanish colonial officials had little choice but
to insist on unwavering loyalty from the Natchez settlers, yet the settlers also
had good reasons to affirm their allegiance to Spain.[40]

For the district's inhabitants, many of whom had expatriated themselves
from the United States by settling in Natchez with their families and the people
they enslaved, the prospect of losing Spanish allegiance proved disconcerting.
Changing sovereignty put land titles into question because the treaty did not
address existing property claims and the new international border was undeter-
mined. This situation raised local concerns that Lemos intended to allay with
his proclamation. At least some Natchez planters expressed concerns in the language of gracious Spanish subjects. Natchez planters who lived on Bayou Sarah
praised Lemos's "wise, Vigilant and Mild administration" under which they had
flourished since leaving the United States. Lemos's regard for the petitioners'
well-being filled them with "obedience to the Laws of, & our unalterable fidelity
to our beloved Sovereign." Petitioners acknowledged their uncertainty about
which "side of the line our fate may place us," so they hoped their manifest allegiance to Spain would impel Spanish officials to guarantee their land claims
should their settlement fall within US territory.[41]

The Natchez planters certainly displayed their familiarity with customs of
deference and effacement necessary to successful political demands in a

colony governed by a king. Nevertheless, there is no reason to suggest the planters viewed themselves as anything but loyal Spanish subjects. According to the laws of the United States regarding expatriation, the international law of emigrant rights, and Spain's colonization policy, the Natchez planters were Spanish subjects. Moreover, because the petitioners were seeking to protect property they had received from the Spanish Crown, they likely settled in Natchez long before they had any indication that the United States would acquire the region. Perhaps Henry Hunter typified the views of the Bayou Sarah petitioners. An American officer in the Revolutionary War, he arrived in Natchez in 1792 with his wife, seven children, and fifteen enslaved people. Hunter, and likely the other petitioners, quit the United States to live the rest of their days as Spanish subjects. The Natchez planters thus navigated uncertainty created by diplomatic wrangling not with an eye toward reclaiming the lost privileges of republican citizenship in the United States but rather to protect their gains as loyal Spanish subjects.[42]

American officials at Natchez also recognized that local settlers were legally Spanish subjects but found it difficult to gauge their genuine loyalty. Government surveyor Andrew Ellicott and a small military contingent were among the first US officials in Natchez after diplomats signed the Treaty of San Lorenzo. Ellicott and a Spanish counterpart were expected to identify and map the new border separating US and Spanish territory. Like all government surveyors, Ellicott used his Gunter's chain and compass to create bounded national space. Whether dispossessing Indigenous people of their land or implementing treaty provisions, the surveyor's technical skills might transform some people already on the land into outsiders while elevating others from aliens to citizens. Soldiers enforced and protected the transformations of land and people wrought by the surveyor's steady measurements. Thus by making the Natchez District legible to the federal government in Philadelphia, Ellicott and his accompanying soldiers were charged with building a new section of America's human ramparts. The US officials at Natchez held the nationalist assumption that the republic's strength and future greatness rested on human ramparts that kept citizens loyal to the nation and unwilling to exercise their emigrant rights for allegiances elsewhere. The character and the legal standing of the Natchez planters were thus matters of concern to Ellicott and the army officers deployed to the district.

From a legal perspective, the Natchez planters were aliens to the United States, but Ellicott believed their desire to regain US citizenship revealed national sentiments. Ellicott consistently described local planters as men "in favor of becoming citizens of the United States" even while noting as an aside that the same men were once US citizens. Ellicott's observations suggested a view of birthright patriotism familiar from expatriation debates in the United States that affection for one's birthplace remained fixed even after one emigrated and pledged allegiance to another government. Ellicott assumed that outward signs of loyalty and civic standing in Spanish Louisiana did not align with a majority of the Natchez planters' genuine patriotic sentiments. Isaac Guion, a US Army officer who occupied Natchez, succinctly expressed this view in a passing reference to Stephen Minor as "an American (at heart)," reflecting his nationalist aspirations for Minor more than an accurate description of Minor's actions. The Pennsylvanian Minor fought against the British in the Revolutionary War before settling in Natchez, where he owned significant property, became a captain in the colonial militia, and eventually became the interim Spanish governor of Natchez. Minor ultimately represented Spanish interests during the local implementation of the treaty. By all accounts, Minor was a loyal Spanish subject before 1795, and he remained so even after it became clear the Natchez District would become part of the United States. Nevertheless, Ellicott and Guion assured themselves that Americans might change residence and allegiance without necessarily losing patriotic affections for the United States.[43]

As local implementation of the treaty stalled and uncertainty mounted, Ellicott turned this assumption about settler allegiance against Spanish authority over Natchez. Many planters appealed to him for passports to return to the United States until the region was securely under its sovereignty. One such petitioner was Narsworthy Hunter, a Virginia emigrant who obtained land in Natchez and served in the local militia. Hunter represented other settlers, many of whom were Revolutionary War veterans, seeking passports for "a change of situations by withdrawing to the United States." Ellicott noted that Hunter, a person he considered a Spanish subject in the service of the Spanish Crown, and petitioners like him wanted to expatriate themselves once again, but in this instance from Spanish to US allegiance. Ellicott encouraged this choice just as a rumor spread that Spanish authorities might refuse passports to the Natchez planters inclined to leave. For the settlers who did not depart Natchez but hoped for support from the US government in expressing their discontent with the Spanish government, Ellicott advised them that "it would be necessary that the United States should have some evidence of their having made an election in their favor." Several planters followed Ellicott's guidance by attaching their names to a declaration announcing themselves citizens of the United States.[44]

Stephen Minor depicted in his Spanish military uniform, a visible sign of his expatriation from the United States. Oil on canvas, attributed to William Edward West, *Stephen "Don Esteban" Minor* (New Orleans, LA, ca. 1809). Image courtesy of the Museum of the American Revolution.

Ellicott endorsed this declaration as a justifiable response to Spain's delay in implementing the treaty, which thereby denied the settlers a government that protected their interests. Drawing from familiar emigrant rights assumptions, Ellicott noted that free people had wide latitude to take actions "which will ultimately secure their felicity." In the situation before him at Natchez, "the people conceived themselves citizens of the United States," and "they had a right to conceive themselves so." When explaining developments at Natchez in his official correspondence to Lemos, Ellicott imbued his remarks with appeals to the pursuits of happiness along with a right to expatriation. However, Ellicott's private recollections reveal he attempted to evade international law by fomenting local opposition to Spanish officials "without committing our government." Ellicott thus upheld a right to expatriation and the principles of consensual allegiance to hasten Spain's surrender of Natchez.[45]

Spanish officials detected Ellicott's subterfuge. Lemos accused Ellicott of distorting the rights accorded to Spanish subjects by defending a right to expatriation without any consideration for its exercise. Lemos declared that all Spanish subjects enjoyed free movement throughout Spain's dominions and were at liberty to emigrate whenever they desired. Natchez planters were thus free to expatriate themselves from Spanish allegiance out of choice or necessity, benefiting from a "privilege" in which "consists the greatest liberty of a Spaniard." By denying that Natchez planters enjoyed this privilege, Ellicott invited them to claim US citizenship without leaving Natchez even though Lemos insisted that signatories to the declaration "are actually under oath of allegiance to his Majesty, and under whose dominion and protection they have lived, and enjoyed the benefit thereof." Lemos accused the settlers in question of fomenting insurrection against Spain while accusing Ellicott, who had behaved much like an American Genet, of creating a population of internal enemies beholden to a foreign power. In both instances, Lemos argued that Ellicott and the rebellious planters undermined Spanish sovereignty over the region by manipulating a right to expatriation under international law.[46]

While sovereignty over Natchez was uncertain, a right to expatriation proved essential to government officials and local planters. US officials endorsed an expansive right to expatriation in order to weaken Spanish authority and hasten their possession of the territory. It also provided a legal procedure to rapidly incorporate the local population into the United States. Just as the planters had chosen to quit the United States for life as Spanish subjects in Natchez, they could choose to return their allegiance to the United States. Spanish officials expected the Natchez planters who had expatriated themselves to Spanish allegiance to remain loyal until Spain officially surrendered its sovereignty over the region. The planter population clearly included some individuals ready to attach themselves to the United States without delay and others committed to fulfilling their civic obligations to Spain.

The various options for allegiance at Natchez disappeared in 1798 with the election of leading Natchez settlers to a local committee that assumed governing responsibilities over the district. With the support of Spanish and US officials, formation of this committee transferred sovereignty over the district from Spain to the United States, thus officially implementing the Treaty of San Lorenzo on the ground. In the committee's first public statement, members declared that the Treaty of San Lorenzo transformed the Natchez planters into citizens of the United States. Ellicott viewed the election of this committee as a definitive event, for "it put the finishing stroke to the Spanish authority, and jurisdiction in the district." Indeed, by 1798 Spain evacuated its posts in the transferred territory, thus installing the Natchez District firmly in the United States' human ramparts. Once the United States possessed the Natchez District, the region's new colonial officials faced the familiar challenge of making sure the region served American interests.[47]

Confirming a loyal citizenry was the first requirement. Andrew Ellicott thought the composition of the committee elected to assume authority over Natchez provided reason for optimism. According to Ellicott, nearly all of those elected "were decidedly republican, and firmly attached to the government of the United States." Frederick Kimball was the only exception. His "sentiments were doubtful," Ellicott reported, but he lived in territory that remained under Spanish control. Perhaps some combination of residence "below the line" and genuine loyalty to Spain raised Ellicott's suspicion of Kimball. However, Ellicott soon left Natchez to complete his boundary survey, and governing the territory became the responsibility of a larger cadre of officials who did not share Ellicott's early faith in the planters' allegiance.[48]

Soon after Congress created the Mississippi Territory in 1798, local law enforcement officers required Natchez inhabitants to swear an oath of allegiance to the United States, announcing their loyalty to the United States and their obligation to defend the Constitution. Henry Hunter, who only a few years before had pledged his loyalty and devotion to the Spanish king, was among the many Natchez settlers who pledged his allegiance to the United States in 1798. When put in the context of Congress's recent naturalization acts, which proscribed similar oaths for naturalizing foreigners, albeit with the additional requirement to abjure previous allegiances, the US government did not quite view the Natchez population as aliens within its territory, but it did not view them as birthright citizens either. When viewed within the terms of American expatriation debates of the 1790s, a person such as Hunter was either a man of dubious character who wore his allegiance lightly or a virtuous man always obedient to the laws that governed him. Critics of emigrant rights warned that their exercise would create such ambiguity with baleful consequences for individuals and societies. The oath requirement thus seemed intended to avoid such consequences. It served as a public statement of American loyalty from a newly acquired population that doubled as an impromptu procedure for reversing earlier acts of expatriation in the absence of formal legal mechanisms for returning citizenship to individuals who had cast it aside. Nevertheless, even if Natchez settlers announced their allegiance to the United States, regained their citizenship, and lived as loyal Americans, the US government had very little power to guarantee the territory's citizens would remain attached to the republic.[49]

Keeping citizens of the Mississippi Territory from expatriating themselves once again concerned US officials immediately after their nation gained control of the region. After all, members of the elected committee to implement US governance at Natchez, such as Peter Bryan Bruin, along with many in the planter population at large, had lived and prospered as Spanish subjects for nearly a decade. If the US government could not ensure the same prosperity, then the Natchez inhabitants might look to Spanish territory west of the Mississippi or south of the new border in West Florida. Despite Ellicott's sanguine description of strong republican sentiments at Natchez, he also realized "the danger of losing a number of our citizens, who would be induced to settle in the Spanish territory" if land in the Mississippi Territory remained difficult to obtain.[50]

The creation of a responsive territorial government provided a possible solution. As Secretary of State Timothy Pickering advised in a letter to Winthrop Sargent, the first governor of the Mississippi Territory, the planters expected "the most prudent and conciliatory administration of the new government to fix their attachment to the United States." Admonitions such as Pickering's did not guarantee that federal and territorial governments would address what proved to be planters' most pressing concern in the first decade of US control. The territory was a confusion of land claims, some from the British and others from the Spanish, which current holders wanted the US government to confirm. Moreover, other territorial citizens settled on land without titles but hoped that their labor to clear and cultivate it would allow them to eventually own it through the right of preemption. Until territorial government was stable and land title secure, recourse to expatriation threatened to depopulate and thereby weaken the Mississippi Territory.[51]

Spanish officials confirmed the necessity of a circumspect approach to American settlements in the Mississippi Territory. After the Spanish evacuated its fort at Natchez, it promptly established Concordia directly across the Mississippi. Josef Vidal, Concordia's commander, had a clear sense of life in Natchez along with larger problems created by the new border with the United States. He viewed the United States as an expanded but weak state. The federal government seemed disinterested in controlling its wayward citizens but unable to provide for its obedient population. The presence of a feckless and indolent neighbor posed both dangers and opportunities for Spain, Vidal argued. Lawless Americans in the Mississippi Territory crossed into Spanish domains "to commit disorders, robbery, and rapine," Vidal reported, actions that the US government ignored or proved too "weak in the execution of its laws" to stop. According to Vidal, Americans covered for their lawless behavior by insisting that international borders could not restrain them. They were wedded to the view that "the greatest thing on which they base their liberty is in saying that they are free to go wherever they please."[52]

Vidal suggested a familiar solution to curtailing the depredations of Americans who claimed a criminal right to free movement. He called for populating the west bank of the Mississippi with a denser network of loyal families who would protect their land and thereby the empire's interests. Bolstering Spain's human ramparts in this way, Vidal argued, would "lock the doors which are open from the territory of Mississippi to our posts on this side of the river." The indolence of the US government offered opportunities to achieve this end, Vidal believed. He was familiar with the same discontented American population that caused consternation for officials in the United States. If Vidal's superiors invited the unhappy Americans at Natchez to settle in Spanish territory, he guaranteed "that more than two hundred respected families will emigrate."[53]

Territorial citizens recognized this when they threatened to leave for Spanish territory. In 1803, citizens of the Mississippi Territory petitioned Congress for free land. This unusual request of the federal government reflected what the petitioners described as Mississippi's unique circumstances among US territories. It was far from most states of the union, and it was adjacent to powerful Indigenous nations and a rival imperial power. Requiring Americans to buy land, as was customary elsewhere, would suppress settlement in this distant territory. Without ready access to free land, the petitioners warned, citizens of Mississippi, especially new arrivals too poor from their journey to return home, will "remove to the adjacent Spanish dominions, where both climate and soil are equally productive as our own; and where the prospect of favorable terms is a flattering incentive." The petitioners even threatened that "many of the former description, already indicate intentions of leaving us." In 1807, William Lattimore wrote to President Thomas Jefferson about the many disappointed land seekers attracted by the allure of Spanish territory where the easy terms for obtaining land "were peculiarly adapted to invite them into that quarter." As a result, Lattimore noted that many "have already emigrated, and are lost, as well to the nation as to the territory." A memorial from 1809 recounted Mississippi citizens preparing to "abandon their Country" for Spanish Florida or Texas.[54]

Jefferson's prediction in the 1790s that expatriating Americans would deliver new territory to the United States now seemed doubtful. From the perspective of people in the Mississippi Territory, its border with Spanish territory leaked citizens. In fact, the accounts from 1807 and 1809 described a loss of citizens whom the United States should want to keep attached to the republic. They were not the rootless people incapable of patriotic sentiments portrayed by critics of the right to expatriation. Rather, they were "real American Citizens well attached" to the government and the administration. Or as Lattimore believed, the citizens who expatriated themselves did so out of necessity, as the right to change allegiance allowed, but they reached this decision only when an ineffective US government forced them "to sacrifice their strong political predilections" and to turn against "the feelings, the habits, and the principles of Americans" by emigrating in pursuit of Spanish land and allegiance. As both the threat and the reality of expatriation from the Mississippi Territory to Spanish Louisiana, Florida, and eventually Texas persisted into the early 1800s, it became clear to American observers that building larger human ramparts for the republic did nothing to lessen the urgency of efforts to keep its citizens from leaving.[55]

BY THE EARLY 1800s, emigrant rights created two distinct border regimes in North America. In the Champlain Valley, white men exercised their freedom to move and choose allegiance to create an agricultural and commercial region that bound together the United States and British North America. The Jay Treaty provided an international legal framework that enabled the exercise of emigrant rights toward agricultural and commercial integration in the Champlain Valley. This development vindicated the position of those in the United States arguing for a notion of citizenship that included a robust right to expatriation during the 1790s. White men in the lower Mississippi Valley also continued to exercise their freedom to move and choose allegiance during the early 1800s. However, the exercise of emigrant rights in this region occurred as part of larger imperial contests over territorial sovereignty. The Treaty of San Lorenzo created an international legal framework for this contest to secure or attract settler allegiance. The constant threat of losing American citizens to Spanish allegiance in the lower Mississippi Valley only confirmed the dire predictions of those in the United States who argued against expansive expatriation rights during the 1790s.

Global conflicts during the early 1800s created new demands for strong national allegiances and equally strong arguments in favor of citizens' rights to decide allegiance for themselves. These conflicts unsettled the North American borderlands, especially once Great Britain expected its emigrant subjects in Canada to defend the empire against the United States. The War of 1812 thus originated in emigrant rights controversies while the exercise of emigration right citizenship in North America contributed to its outcome. Ultimately, the war ended in a victory for those who asserted a limitless right to quit the nation, a victory in popular understanding and law that shaped North America's borderlands for decades to come.

CHAPTER FIVE

The Expatriating Crusade

When searching for words to explain the importance of the War of 1812, John F. Dumoulin, an Irish emigrant lawyer, turned to Charles Churchill, a British poet. As Churchill penned in his poem *Farewell*, "To fix thy love on such a wretched spot/ Because in Lust's wild fever there begot/ Because, thy weight no longer fit to bear/ By chance, not choice, thy mother bore thee there/ Is Folly, which admits not of defence." Dumoulin included these lines of verse in an 1816 pamphlet as a critical "commentary on the boasted natural attachment to place of birth." Writing for an American audience, Dumoulin argued that the War of 1812 cast doubt on patriotism because it demanded political loyalty to a particular place. Free people, Dumoulin argued, were unencumbered by national sympathies as they moved about the world granting their allegiance to the nation of their choice. Although Dumoulin recognized that a right to expatriation remained controversial, developments since the eighteenth century convinced him that "the rising generation" will be the first to free itself from the belief that nationality is fixed at birth.[1]

In concluding that the War of 1812 was a victory for Americans who claimed their right to quit the nation, Dumoulin summarized a view about the emigrant rights of citizenship that prevailed in the United States the decade before the conflict. This position maintained that the freedom to leave the United States entailed a limitless right to expatriation. The proponents of this position argued for it in the courts and in the foreign policy disputes that caused the War of 1812. In places such as the Champlain Valley, where American emigrants armed themselves to defend British North America from the United States, personal decisions in the war's borderlands affirmed claims that the right to expatriation existed without limits. Their actions revealed the implications of US opposition to Great Britain's defense of perpetual allegiance when enforcing its impressment policy. If the United States was free to naturalize British subjects, a consistent emigrant rights position meant that its citizens were equally free to expatriate themselves to British allegiance even during times of war.

For some in the United States, the War of 1812 was a nationalist struggle against Great Britain, one that deepened sentimental ties to the republic by stirring patriotic affections. Those in the United States who believed war with Great

Britain was a battle for emigrant rights arrived at an alternative conclusion. In their view, the war finally settled the emigrant rights debates of the 1790s in favor of a right to expatriation without restraint. In asserting this position, critics accused them of using war with Great Britain to launch an "expatriating crusade."[2]

BY THE EARLY 1800s, approximately 70,000 people had left the United States, choosing to become Spanish subjects in Louisiana or British subjects in Canada. The settlement of US citizens beyond the nation's borders occurred at a moment when American legal theorists subjected the relationship between mobility and national allegiance to renewed scrutiny. In 1803, St. George Tucker published an edition of William Blackstone's *Commentaries on the Laws of England*. Tucker was an eminent law professor at the College of William and Mary and later a federal district judge in Virginia. In *Blackstone's Commentaries*, Tucker interpreted English common law in relationship to legal developments in the United States, and especially Virginia, since the American Revolution. Tucker expected that his edition of *Commentaries* would prove more useful to law students and lawyers in the United States than earlier editions that merely reprinted Blackstone's original volumes. For several decades, Tucker's *Commentaries* was the seminal legal reference work in the United States. Tucker's position on the right to expatriation was authoritative in ways unrivaled by other writers. Using language from Virginia law, Tucker maintained that "emigration" and "expatriation" were synonymous terms for "a natural right which all men have, to relinquish that society in which birth or accident may have thrown them, and seek subsistence and happiness elsewhere." Every nation that allowed its people to leave could not then prohibit their expatriation, Tucker argued.[3]

Over the next decade, Tucker's understanding of expatriation gained broad affirmation in legal and popular opinion. Hugh Henry Brackenridge, a justice on the Pennsylvania Supreme Court, reaffirmed Tucker's position on expatriation in his legal treatise *Law Miscellanies* published in 1814. By 1816, according to a dictionary of American language usage compiled by John Pickering, a prolific Massachusetts linguist and attorney, when his countrymen used the phrase "to expatriate," or the words "expatriated" and "expatriation," they more often meant "throwing off one's allegiance" instead of merely "quitting one's country." Whereas Americans in 1816 might still use the term expatriation as a synonym for "emigration," they grounded both terms in a legal discourse of natural political rights. "The words are but little used in England," Pickering noted. Between 1803 and 1816, Americans thus articulated a more expansive view of the right to expatriation.[4]

During the same period, litigants consistently brought cases concerning the right to expatriation before courts in the United States. Federal courts in the United States heard seven cases between 1803 and 1816 in which judges considered a right to expatriation in their opinions. A majority of the cases dealt with maritime prizes, or captured commercial ships during times of war, while the remaining cases adjudicated inheritance conflicts over property stemming from the American Revolution. Deciding cases of each type required judges to determine the nationality of those involved in the suit, be it the owner of a captured schooner or the person who claimed title to property in the United States.[5]

Although such cases presented court officials with an opportunity to issue definitive rulings about a right to expatriation, they demurred in several instances, especially in cases decided by the Supreme Court or by the court's justices in their capacity on the circuit courts. In the inheritance cases, the justices held that individual states were responsible for determining allegiance. In the more numerous prize cases, the justices relied on the established legal principle of "domicile," which held that a merchant's place of residence rather than birth determined his nationality in commercial matters. John Marshall, the Supreme Court's chief justice, explained that domicile created a "commercial national character" for US citizens who settled permanently in foreign nations with the intention to trade.[6]

Under the domicile doctrine, merchants living abroad were bound by the commercial regulations of the government under which they lived rather than those adopted by the United States. Determining if a merchant's residence abroad entitled him to domicile protections or, at its most duplicitous, merely indicated his efforts to evade US law, thus became the basis for judging if a captured ship and its cargo brought to a US port could be condemned as a lawful maritime prize or if it must be restored to its owner. The justices emphasized that the domicile doctrine only determined nationality in specific commercial circumstances but inferred nothing about a right to expatriation. On "the question of expatriation, founded on the self will of a citizen," Justice Bushrod Washington admitted in his opinion in a prize case before the Pennsylvania Circuit Court, "I must be more enlightened upon this subject than I have yet been, before I can admit, that a citizen of the United States can throw off his allegiance to his country, without some law authorising him to do so." John Marshall held the same reservations when, in an earlier Supreme Court opinion, he declined to state if a US citizen "can divest himself absolutely of that character otherwise than in such manner as may be prescribed by law." The circumspect opinions of Supreme Court justices in the early 1800s suggest broad legal uncertainty about the right to expatriation that is misleading. The opinions of federal district judges, state court judges, and trial lawyers reveal that the right to expatriation was a legal subject that engendered definitive positions on both sides.[7]

The major maritime prize case in the decade before the War of 1812 that dealt extensively with the right to expatriation concerned the nationality of Jared Shattuck. Although born in Connecticut, Shattuck had resided on St. Thomas, a Danish colony, since his youth. In early 1800, Alexander Murray, the captain of a US privateer, captured Shattuck's ship, *The Charming Betsy*, during a voyage in the Caribbean. Once Murray learned that Shattuck was a Connecticut native, he declared *The Charming Betsy* in violation of a recent law passed by Congress prohibiting US citizens from trade with France and brought the vessel to Philadelphia for trial. Murray's rationale for condemning *The Charming Betsy* as a legal prize was not altogether specious. After all, in 1799 Chief Justice Oliver Ellsworth ruled that since elements of the common law persisted in the state, only unusual circumstances freed its citizens from allegiance to Connecticut and, therefore, the United States. The *Williams* case, as it was known, became a legal touchstone during the early 1800s for those in the United States who argued for strict limits on the freedom of expatriation. Whether or not Murray believed that this precedent would persuade officials in Philadelphia to side with him, the US Circuit Court of Pennsylvania heard the case.[8]

Shattuck's lawyers argued for an unlimited right to expatriation. Since the United States invited "all the people of the earth" to become its citizens, its government could not "deny a similar choice to our own citizens." A citizen of the United States had the "right to expatriate himself and become a citizen of any other country which he may prefer," Shattuck's lawyers announced, so long as expatriation occurred "with a *bona fide and honest intention, at a proper time, and in a public manner.*" Shattuck met all three standards. He had lived on St. Thomas since childhood, and since becoming an adult around 1793 he had established and maintained "an actual *bona fide* residence" on the island. He married, became a burgher, purchased land, and owned mercantile ships. Before this, in the late 1780s when Europe and the United States "were in a state of profound peace," he became an apprentice on his way toward entering business on his own at a time when his native country "had no claim to his service." Finally, he expatriated himself in a highly public manner by swearing an oath of allegiance to Denmark. According to Denmark's laws, the same steps were necessary for a foreigner to obtain the rights of commerce under the Danish flag. Nevertheless, Shattuck's lawyers argued, citizens could expatriate themselves without becoming naturalized elsewhere; indeed "a man may become a *citizen of the world*—an alien to all the governments on earth." The right of expatriation thus did not require municipal laws in the United States to authorize its exercise nor did it depend on naturalization laws in other nations to complete it. Rather, the intent, timing, and publicity of a person's expatriation were sufficient to determine that the person exercised this right when laws did not prescribe the "form of expatriation," as was the case at the federal level in the United States and in many states.[9]

Alexander J. Dallas, the US attorney for the Eastern District of Pennsylvania, agreed that a right to expatriation existed and recognized the same standards for determining its exercise. Dallas distinguished expatriation, in which a person ceases to be a citizen, from emigration, "a locomotive right, or a right to change the domicile" in which a person gains trade privileges in another country without losing citizenship in the United States. Dallas argued that Shattuck exercised the latter right, evidence of which was his St. Thomas "burgher's brief." Such briefs were trade licenses that allowed purchasers to conduct commerce under the Danish flag, but they were not evidence of expatriation since they did not require an oath of allegiance or residence on St. Thomas. A St. Thomas burgher was thus not necessarily a Danish subject. Nevertheless, even if the court accepted Shattuck's burgher's brief as evidence of his expatriation, this document proved that he expatriated himself in 1797, a time of growing hostilities between the United States and France when new trade restrictions seemed likely. Therefore, Dallas argued that Shattuck expatriated himself with the duplicitous intent of avoiding likely prohibitions on his livelihood at a moment of deteriorating foreign relations throughout the Atlantic world. *The Charming Betsey* was a legal prize, Dallas concluded.[10]

Richard Peters, the federal district judge for Pennsylvania, not only recognized emigrant rights to free movement but to expatriation as well. The judge found abundant proof that Shattuck exercised this right according to all available evidence. Peters thus concluded that Shattuck was "*bona fide* a Danish adopted subject," which amounted "in my mind, to proof of expatriation." Peters ruled in favor of Jared Shattuck. Murray appealed to the US Supreme Court.[11]

The Supreme Court upheld the lower court's ruling. Now under the guidance of John Marshall, the Supreme Court affirmed that certain conditions existed in which citizens born in the United States might need recourse to legal protections that resembled a right to expatriation. Marshall would not rule on the existence of a natural right to expatriation; he meticulously avoided providing definitive answers to questions about whether or not a citizen "can divest himself of that character otherwise than in such manner as be prescribed by law." Nevertheless, in Marshall's opinion Shattuck "has made himself the subject of a foreign power." Shattuck had lived on St. Thomas, a Danish colony, since at least 1790. He traded as a Danish subject, he owned property and formed a family on the island, and in 1797 he swore an oath of allegiance to the Crown of Denmark. Although Marshall noted that Shattuck might not be entirely immune to legal prosecution in the United States, he clearly could not violate laws prohibiting its citizens from trade with France. For the purposes of commercial regulation, Shattuck was a "Danish burgher," not an American citizen. Indeed, Marshall ruled that Shattuck's experiences "seem completely to establish the principle, that an American citizen may acquire in a foreign country the commercial privileges attached to his domocil." Marshall's ruling set a precedent for the view that domicile, determined by actions that indicated a citizen's permanent residence in a foreign country, effectively made nationality a condition of commercial interests.[12]

The most significant inheritance case of the decade before the War of 1812 reached the Supreme Court on an appeal from the circuit court for the district of New Jersey. The case arose from a dispute starting in 1802 between Daniel Coxe, a New Jersey Loyalist who settled in Great Britain after the Revolutionary War, and his cousin Rebecca Coxe McIlvaine, a citizen of New Jersey. Coxe and McIlvaine held competing claims to an exclusive inheritance of property in New Jersey. The lawyers for both sides rested their arguments on competing notions about limits on a right to expatriation. The defendant's counsel argued that people resident in New Jersey at the time of independence consented to becoming citizens of the state, a status that they could not unilaterally change through subsequent inactions. According to the lawyers, a sort of perpetual allegiance existed under New Jersey law that allowed people born in New Jersey to inherit land even if they supported Great Britain during the Revolutionary War and resided in Great Britain thereafter. McIlvaine's lawyers argued that Coxe could not inherit land in the United States because he was an alien, a status Coxe obtained by choice and was confirmed by common understandings of the right to expatriation.

McIlvaine's lawyers William Tilghman and Jared Ingersoll accepted that emigration entailed a right to expatriation. Tilghman asserted that the Revolutionary War ended with the Treaty of Paris in 1783, and "a new aera began, when every man had a right to leave the country and transfer his allegiance where he pleased." In accord with this new era, neither state constitutions nor the federal Constitution denied the right to expatriation. Indeed, Tilghman noted, the state constitutions of Pennsylvania, Kentucky, and Vermont recognized that the right to expatriation, and Virginia confirmed the right under law. Leading authorities on international and natural law asserted the right to expatriation, and so did American legal theorists such as St. George Tucker and American legal precedent in *Talbot v. Janson* and the Pennsylvania Circuit Court ruling in the *Charming Betsy* case. When situated in the legal context outlined by Tilghman, Coxe's choice to live in England after the war—"openly avowing himself a British subject"—proved that Coxe possessed and exercised a "right of expatriation." If the circumstances did not prove that Coxe had expatriated himself according to every measure of the right, Tilghman emphasized, then "it is impossible that any person ever can."[13]

Ingersoll also concluded that Coxe exercised his right to expatriation by emigrating from the United States and swearing an oath of allegiance to the king of Great Britain. To further bolster his and Tilghman's understanding of expatriation, Ingersoll cited an authority on public law to argue that swearing an oath of allegiance was an individual action "sufficient to sever the strongest connection between the United States and a citizen." Furthermore, Ingersoll argued, their position on expatriation did not come from "the mere whim of modern, fanciful, theoretical writers" but rather described a right that was "as ancient as the society of man." One only needed to consult the Bible, Ingersoll argued, "the most venerable book of antiquity," to "find expatriation practiced, approved, and never restrained." According to McIlvaine's lawyers, Coxe had exercised an ancient natural right that prevented him from inheriting land in the United States.[14]

Daniel Coxe could not have expatriated himself according to William Rawle, the opposing counsel in the case. First and foremost, the New Jersey state constitution adopted the common law, according to which "no man can put off his allegiance." When confronted with this stark legal fact, Tilghman and Ingersoll "piled together a confused and shapeless mass of evidence" to prove that a right of expatriation existed and that Coxe had exercised this right. Rawle argued that the court should reject both claims because they were only plausible if one "confounded expatriation with emigration." Rawle identified numerous ways in which the terms differed from each other. At the most basic distinction, "expatriation dissolves the original obligation of the citizen" whereas, according to Rawle, "emigration only suspends its activity." This explained why every nation throughout history except "the severest despotism" recognized a right to emigration but that a right to expatriation at will was nearly unknown in the annals of law, the Virginia statute notwithstanding. The right to expatriation was thus not a natural right available to all humanity but a novel privilege available to free Virginians because their state alone created a regulation for "defining the evidence and the mode, and de-claring the assent of the government" for acts of expatriation. If a right to ex-patriation is to exist in New Jersey or any other state besides Virginia, then states must adopt laws to establish expatriation by "mutual consent" between individuals and their government. If a right to expatriation exists, "it must be dormant until put into motion by a law." Rawle thus concluded that since Coxe was born "a subject" of New Jersey, "it was not in his power, without the concurrence of New-Jersey, expressed by legislative act, to become an alien." Despite Coxe's settlement in Great Britain, and even his pronounce-ments of allegiance to Great Britain, Rawle argued that Coxe remained a citizen of New Jersey, which entitled him to inherit property in the state.[15]

Rawle also identified the dangers posed by the view that emigration en-tailed expatriation. If leaving the nation of one's birth to settle elsewhere turned citizens into aliens, then emigrants could never return to their home nation with the same legal latitude that authorized their prior departure. In-stead of a sojourning citizen of the United States who near the end of life might "wish to return to the bosom of his surviving friends," the emigrant instead became "a modern citizen of the world—a detached, rotator, irre-sponsible and useless being." Conflating emigration with expatriation also meant that, Rawle warned, "a man may shake off his allegiance one year and put it on again the next; it may go and come as often as whim and caprice shall dictate." The court should not rule in favor of an argument that em-ployed an insidious defense of unregulated expatriation, Rawle concluded. The court ultimately issued a tacit denial of an expansive right to expatriation by deciding in Coxe's favor.[16]

Expatriation cases reached state-level courts in the decade before the War of 1812, although the highest courts in three states failed to produce a consen-sus opinion on the right to expatriation. The Supreme Court of New York avoided "deciding on the general right of expatriation" but in two cases iden-tified personal actions that, in the right circumstances, might attest to a per-son's changed nationality. The first case concerned Thomas Stoughton, a naturalized US citizen resident in New York City who swore an oath of alle-giance to the king of Spain in order to serve as Spain's consul to New York. The court rejected Stoughton's claim of "having devested himself of the character of an American citizen" without leaving the country's territorial limits. The court concluded that a person cannot choose to become an alien under US law without at least changing residence, or, in the court's language, establishing "domicil" in a foreign country. Otherwise, the judges warned, foreign sovereigns would have the power "to naturalize any of our citizens; and in the heart of our country, to detach them from the allegiance they owe to its government."[17]

In an 1806 case, also before the Supreme Court of New York, Nancy Jackson sued Archibald Jackson, both citizens of New York, for alimony under the terms of a divorce granted to her by the Supreme Court of Vermont. Although Nancy Jackson resided in Vermont when she obtained the divorce decree, Harmanus Bleecker, Archibald Jackson's lawyer, argued that the laws of coverture determined that a wife's domicile, or "fixed habitation," was that of her husband's, which "was fixed, and always continued" in New York. Bleecker relied on Vattel's writings to establish that domicile "makes a person a subject or a citizen" so that New York's divorce laws, not Vermont's, governed the Jacksons' marriage. Moreover, citing a standard for determining expatriation developed in *Talbot v. Janson*, Bleecker argued that even if Archibald Jackson had resided in Vermont, he demonstrated no intention of staying there permanently, thus he could not have exchanged citizenship in New York for that in Vermont. Bleecker launched a defense that condoned the view that expatriation can occur if an individual genuinely intends to establish permanent residence in a different jurisdiction. Although this position underwrote expansive claims to a free man's right to change allegiance at will, the law of coverture denied married women the privilege of independent mobility. Judge Ambrose Spencer ruled against Nancy Jackson because her husband's residence determined hers, thus the Vermont divorce decree entitled her to no alimony from her husband, a New York resident.[18]

Alternatively, Virginia's highest court recognized a right to expatriation. In 1811, Nancy Murray, an enslaved woman from Maryland, successfully sued for freedom from her owner Daniel M'Carty in a case decided by the Supreme Court of Appeals of Virginia. Under a 1792 statute to limit slave importations, any enslaved person brought to Virginia and resident in the state for a year became free except for people enslaved by citizens from other states who settled in Virginia and testified under oath that they had no intention of evading the state's nonimportation law or of selling the slaves in their possession. M'Carty was a Virginia native who married into a Maryland family and lived with his in-laws from 1800 to 1804. M'Carty purchased Murray while living in Maryland, and Murray subsequently received permission from M'Carty to move to his family's home in Virginia where she would stay to recover from childbirth. M'Carty and his wife returned to Virginia soon thereafter. After residing in Virginia for a year, Murray sued M'Carty for violating the 1792 law. A state district court in Virginia ruled in favor of M'Carty, so Murray appealed to the Supreme Court of Appeals in Virginia.[19]

The three judges on Virginia's highest court ruled against M'Carty. In their opinion, M'Carty remained a citizen of Virginia during his residency in Maryland, thus he could not legally import slaves. The judges shared their opinions about the right to expatriation in order to explain their conclusion. William H. Cabell accepted the expansive view of expatriation as a natural right entailed by mere emigration with the intention to set aside "the character of a citizen" in one state while providing evidence for membership in another political community. M'Carty's actions gave no evidence that he had "relinquished his citizenship" in Virginia for citizenship in Maryland. After all, M'Carty owned no property in Maryland, he paid no taxes in the state, and he possessed no evident rights and accepted no civic obligations in Maryland. In Cabell's opinion, M'Carty "was 'a mere sojourner in the land,' retaining his character of citizen of Virginia." However, had M'Carty left Virginia with a "fair and *bona fide* intention of quitting it" to become a citizen of another state, he would have expatriated himself even without abiding by Virginia's expatriation law. Only then could he have returned to Virginia with his slaves under the 1792 law. Judge Spencer Roane summarized the central question in the case as determining if M'Carty "had ceased to be a citizen of the commonwealth of Virginia at the time of the importation in question." Roane agreed with Cabell that M'Carty's residence in Maryland did not suggest his full membership in the state. Moreover, the fact that he failed to expatriate himself under Virginia law provided further proof to Roane that M'Carty had never intended to permanently settle in Maryland. Indeed, Roane concluded that citizens of Virginia were obliged to expatriate themselves according to provisions outlined in its expatriation statute in order to avoid litigation and doubt about their actions. After all, Roane believed, the expatriation law was authorized by popular consent in Virginia, and under this law "the exercise of that right . . . is as free as air, and depends upon volition only." Ultimately, Virginia's Supreme Court emancipated Nancy Murray by way of establishing a strong legal precedent that expatriation, even in places where laws existed to govern its exercise, also depended on a person's intentions and actions.[20]

The Supreme Judicial Court of Massachusetts reached a different conclusion in early 1812. Chief Justice Theophilus Parsons held that common law limitations on the right of expatriation persisted under Massachusetts law. According to Parsons, under "the common law no subject can expatriate himself." Massachusetts assumed the allegiance of its inhabitants once it declared independence from Great Britain, so all persons born in Massachusetts before or after July 1776 remained citizens of the commonwealth unless they were "expatriated" by "statute or . . . judgment at law."[21]

In various ways during the early 1800s, federal and state courts established wide latitude for expatriation to occur even without always recognizing it as a natural right and often in the absence of statutes regulating its exercise. This affirmed the view that emigration was tantamount to expatriation. State courts did not have jurisdictional authority over cases concerning international disputes or naturalization, so judges and lawyers in state cases understood the implications of expatriation differently from their peers in the federal courts. In particular, state courts typically considered expatriation as a right exercised not by migrating across the seas but rather by traversing land boundaries separating adjacent jurisdictions. Thus, they viewed it as a right more often exercised by American citizens who left the United States rather than by subjects or citizens of other nations who sought citizenship in the United States. The combined effect of federal and state court rulings during the early 1800s favored emigrant rights to free movement and choice of allegiance for native born and naturalized citizens. The foreign policy implications of this position regarding naturalized citizens caused a decade of conflict between the United States and Great Britain.

With Great Britain and France at war once again in 1803, Britain resumed its naval impressment policy with vigor. This policy forced British subjects to serve in the Royal Navy if commanded into service by a naval officer. Sailors who claimed allegiance to other sovereigns were subject to impressment if naval officers determined they were natural-born subjects of Great Britain. Naturalization in the United States was no protection from impressment, and in many instances the British navy also impressed sailors with birthright citizenship in the United States. Ultimately, the British navy impressed nearly 10,000 citizens of the United States between the early 1790s and 1812.[22]

Naval impressment violated emigrant rights as Americans understood them in the early 1800s. As a form of forced labor, impressment denied freedom of movement. Its legal justification in the common law of perpetual allegiance meant that individuals were not free to choose national allegiances of their own. Debates in the United States over the legality of impressment were thus inseparable from questions about the right to expatriation of naturalized citizens. An anonymous Baltimore pamphlet published in 1806 argued that any sailor who immigrated to the United States acquired citizenship because expatriation was a natural right exercised through individual actions, not statutes. This author concluded "that the circumstance of their emigrating from their own country and domiciliating themselves in ours, is a sufficient, though tacit manifestation of their intention of incorporating themselves with our citizens." Or when viewed from the perspective of a person's home government, according to another pamphleteer, "Continuance within the territorial jurisdiction of a government is the sole criterion of implicit consent to yield civil obedience," so departure "from the territorial jurisdiction of a government, whether the person entered by emigration or birth, equally nullifies implicit consent, and therefore, obligation to obey it." According to Charles Jared Ingersoll, expatriation was a "natural right" that only England denied its subjects.[23]

Great Britain's refusal to recognize emigrant rights also fueled its diplomatic conflicts with the United States during the early 1800s. In 1806, US and British diplomats negotiated a new treaty to update the expiring Jay Treaty. The Monroe-Pinkney Treaty, similar to the earlier agreement, failed to halt or limit Great Britain's impressment policy. Great Britain defended its diplomatic position by asserting the common law by doctrine of perpetual allegiance. President Jefferson rejected the new agreement in 1807 because he believed that it violated the United States' neutral shipping rights and the nation's sovereignty.[24]

Republican foreign policy positions regarding Great Britain caused domestic political disputes in the United States that centered on conflicting views about emigrant rights. Republicans maintained that the United States could not remain sovereign or neutral without recognition of a universal right to expatriation under international law. From a Republican perspective, freedom to change allegiance at will was thus entirely consistent and essential to the United States' foreign policy. A contributor to one newspaper summarized the Republican position in no uncertain terms. "I think we shall be able to prove from the most indisputable authority," the commentator wrote in late 1807, "that every person (not peculiarly bound) has a right to expatriate himself, that our government has an undoubted right to naturalize foreigners, and to employ them without naturalizing them, and by their flag protect them on the high seas from being seized by the government of the country from which they emigrated."[25]

Federalist critics feared that Jefferson and the Congressional Republicans risked war with Great Britain by adopting an embargo policy that assumed a natural right to expatriation. By asserting that a natural right to expatriation nullified Great Britain's municipal law of perpetual allegiance, Federalist critics not only accused the Republicans of holding a position that violated Great Britain's sovereignty, they also claimed that Republican foreign policy misunderstood US law. Federalist critics of Republican foreign policy cited Oliver Ellsworth's opinion in the 1799 *Williams* case, which held that US citizens had no absolute right to expatriate themselves at times of national crisis.

The Republicans' embargo and their position on impressment relied on an exaggerated conception of a free person's right to expatriation. Federalist critics also noted that the Republicans' position on expatriation undercut their foreign policy. "Mr. Jefferson, Mr. Madison, and all the democratic party, have always contended, that a man had an unalienable, indefeasible right to expatriate himself at pleasure—at any moment of his life," observed one critic. Thus, Great Britain could search American ships, and even impress sailors that were born in the United States, if at an earlier time such men had become British subjects by virtue of voluntarily joining the British fleet, which bound them to the law of perpetual allegiance. After all, under the "laws of Congress and admitted practice and principles," free Americans were first and foremost "citizens of the world and may quit their country when they please."[26]

The prospect of war with Great Britain over its impressment policy seemed dangerous to many observers because it wrongly assumed that expatriation was a universal right. Charles Brockden Brown, the early republic's first major novelist, dismissed "the supposed right of expatriation" as a harmful fiction. If "man has a natural right to change his country and his allegiance," Brown argued, then it was only reasonable to conclude that "each individual" was "above the law . . . that each can, at his pleasure, release himself from its authority." The rule of law ceased to exist in such a context, Brown warned. Although some in the United States might embrace the "extravagant theory" of expatriation, Brown argued that other nations would certainly reject it. Since a right to expatriation violated the doctrine of perpetual allegiance, Brown argued that robust claims to defending this right threatened to embroil the United States in endless conflicts with Great Britain. Opponents of Republican foreign policy also accused its supporters of holding an expansive view of the country's naturalization laws, one that actually encouraged undesirable British subjects to expatriate themselves contrary to British law. Many who took "advantage of the premature right to citizenship" obtained "certificates of naturalization by purchase or by perjury, as soon as they fairly get foot on our shores" and promptly thereafter joined the republic's mercantile fleet. Such actions invited regular hostile encounters on the open seas between the British navy and American commercial vessels. "Shall we hazard war for a prescription, which at best is but infamous?" queried this critic.[27]

The United States eventually went to war with Great Britain to uphold the emigrant rights of citizen-sailors. A war in favor of the freedom to move and choose national allegiances seemed worthwhile to many Americans because legal decisions and diplomatic pronouncements affirmed this position. In the decade before the War of 1812, Americans developed their views about the right to expatriation in two realms. Federal and state court decisions reinforced expatriation among the rights of citizens born in the United States. Foreign policy debates insisted that expatriation was a right possessed by naturalized citizens. Both aspects of the decade's expatriation debates converged in the various ways that inhabitants of the Champlain Valley borderlands responded to disputes between Great Britain and the United States.

AS THE NAPOLEONIC WARS intensified, Great Britain and France enacted policies that effectively denied the United States' neutrality rights. Great Britain's efforts to control commerce with Europe proved most onerous in the United States since it affected the nation's significant merchant fleet. President Jefferson's administration and its congressional supporters responded with the Embargo Act of 1807, which prohibited all exports to Great Britain and France, including their colonies. Jefferson believed that the United States' important role in the Atlantic economy as an agricultural and shipping nation gave it leverage to force its more powerful adversaries to respect its neutral standing. Although the Embargo Act affected commercial shipping on Lake Champlain, customs officials in Vermont believed that overland transportation and possibly even lumber rafts were still permissible vehicles for trade with Lower Canada. Congress clarified the matter in 1808 when it adopted a land embargo, which outlawed all forms of cross-border commerce.[28]

Many Vermonters strongly opposed the land embargo, which raised questions about the loyalty of New Englanders near the border with Lower Canada. President Jefferson publicly threatened military force against "sundry persons" near Lake Champlain fomenting "insurrections against the authority of the laws of the United States." Town meetings in Burlington and other Champlain Valley habitations in Vermont issued resolutions condemning the embargo for its threat to their livelihoods and its authors' proclamation for impugning the patriotism of their fellow citizens. Nevertheless, the town resolutions also affirmed rights of independent citizens to resist laws that threatened "themselves and their families" with "ruin and wretchedness." Such a view was intellectually akin to the claim that the right of expatriation meant that allegiance to a state ends when its government ceases to protect its citizens. One satirical objection to the land embargo deployed voluntary allegiance as its punch line. The author described a scheme in which New England farmers drove their hogs within eyesight of the border just as a subject of Lower Canada coincidentally appeared on the other side with corn calling "Pig-Pig-Pig." Of course, the pigs would *voluntarily* place themselves under the government of the tyrant of the ocean" in pursuit of the food. Who then, the author asked, violated the embargo? Was it "the farmer who drove his hogs so near despotism, the swine, who regardless of the blessings of a free country, thus ran over the line, or the Canadian who tempted them to this anti-republican act?" The parable of the expatriating pigs suggested that the embargo was absurdly unenforceable in a region where people claimed emigrant rights to cross borders and change allegiance at will. Over the next few years, the federal government adopted stronger measures to prevent trade with Great Britain and its colonies that Vermonters evaded with great success.[29]

As war with Great Britain seemed more likely, smuggling in the Champlain Valley became a partisan issue but one that reversed the usual positions regarding emigrant rights. Supporters of the embargo and its Republican sponsors castigated the "corrupted citizens, who would willingly sell their country's rights for a piece of British gold" and who "are constantly employed in bringing British goods from the Canadas into the United States." A Federalist critic of the embargo set aside his party's usual objection to expatriation by admitting that Republican foreign policy had so decimated trade and industry in the United States that its citizens had no choice but to leave. While commerce stagnated in the United States, it flourished in Lower Canada, as testified to by "the mechanics, who are thrown out of employment, and, by hundreds, are wandering away into Canada, in quest of the necessaries of life."[30]

Officials in Upper and Lower Canada generally believed that Republican foreign policy redounded to their advantage, but concerns about loyalty at the border still burdened them. The emigrant population of Upper and Lower Canada raised suspicions among colonial officials as diplomatic relations between Great Britain and the United States worsened in 1807. The growing population of the Eastern Townships, which, by 1812, included 18,500 inhabitants born in the United States, seemed especially worrisome because of their proximity and close ties to New England. In 1807, the Executive Council of Lower Canada ordered all "settlers on the New Townships, and all other Persons not Natural born Subjects or who have not become Subjects by Denization or otherwise" to take the oath of allegiance. Those who refused to comply with this order would "be considered as ill disposed to the Government" and forced to "quit the province." The Executive Council appointed Samuel Willard, one of the early emigrants, to administer the oath to all who had not taken it in Stukely and neighboring townships. Willard circulated notice of the government's order and shortly thereafter compiled a list of nearly eighty signatures from men who swore their allegiance to King

George III. In a letter to Herman Ryland, a colonial official, Willard announced with pride that the inhabitants of Stukely and neighboring Ely Township to whom the order applied came "fully forward and took the Oath and at the same time expressed a Uniform willingness to Risk their lives and Properties in defence of their King and Country." Willard thus took great pains to convince authorities in Lower Canada that they could count on the loyalty of expatriated Americans, at least those who resided in his corner of the Eastern Townships.[31]

The relative loyalty of the emigrant population in Lower Canada informed predictions by commentators in the United States about the course of war should their country and Great Britain resort to arms. Newspapers in the United States informed readers about steps the government in Lower Canada took to ensure the loyalty of its inhabitants. These included the requirement for individuals to take the oath of allegiance or face banishment from the province, Lieutenant-Governor James Craig's appeal to the virtues of British laws and institutions for all of the king's subjects in Lower Canada, and his order to the province's militia to "carefully watch over the conduct and language of such strangers as may come among them." From the perspective of observers in the United States, actions by leading officials in Lower Canada suggested "that loyalty in his Majesty's North American dominions wants a spur." Further evidence suggested this was so. In 1807, a Pennsylvania newspaper reported on the arrest and imprisonment of draft resisters in Lower Canada who had "avowed their determination not to serve against the United States." Many of those imprisoned were emigrants from south of the border who certainly learned the error of their choice, according to the editor. They were "citizens of the United States, who removed to Canada under the allurements of great land acquirements, but have since found, that there is some difference, in the security of happiness, between the government of a free republic and that of the colony of a corrupt monarchy." As a result, the newspaper reported, 300 families that "had been seduced into" Lower Canada recently returned to Vermont. A wayward population of expatriated American citizens could thus undermine the security of Lower Canada, or so concluded some editors in the United States.[32]

Such a view was most common in American newspapers that assumed a hostile stance toward Great Britain. Papers of this sort often believed that the United States should not only protect its interests in North America from British incursion, but perhaps the United States should conquer Canada. By 1811, when war with Great Britain seemed imminent, hawkish editors viewed American settlers in Lower and Upper Canada as a population essential to bringing Britain's North American colonies into the United States. A New Jersey editor believed that in sheer numbers alone, "Our Canadian Brethren" were powerful enough to overwhelm British forces in the upper and lower provinces. According to a Vermont editor, "native Americans" in Canada— "old tories and their descendants" notwithstanding—would be reliable allies in the US conquest alongside disgruntled Canadians. Both editors presumed that emigrants from the United States still held deep patriotic affection for their native country. They may have quit the United States, this view held, but sentimental ties to their birthplace disposed them to favor US interests.[33]

Other editors were less certain that Americans in Upper and Lower Canada had abiding love for the United States. In this view, the United States' conquest of Canada would win the support of expatriated Americans only if it satisfied their needs. An especially confident editor believed that the United States would certainly take control of Canada, so support from pragmatic expatriates from the United States seemed reasonable. After all, the editor argued, they were "a mixed multitude having few predilections, except those created by interest, and consequently leaning on the side of America." The *National Intelligencer* took the position that Canada rightfully belonged to the United States. However, if the United States did not act to push Great Britain out, it risked losing its rights to Canada, for the "interior inhabitants," including former US citizens, "will obtain it for themselves, or join the nation in the possession of it." Without immediate action by the United States, an internal rebellion or mass expatriation would forever limit the northern reaches of US sovereignty.[34]

Although the ultimate allegiances of people in the Great Lakes borderlands remained uncertain, Great Britain's impressment policy accelerated conflict between it and the United States in the summer of 1812. Great Britain repealed its Orders in Council, which hampered the free maritime trade of neutral nations and tried to improve trade relations with the United States. However, Great Britain defended the doctrine of perpetual allegiance. War still seemed imminent to Great Britain's critics in the United States since American citizens exposed themselves to impressment the moment they went to sea. The United States thus declared war against Great Britain in June 1812.

Once the War of 1812 began, the American emigrant population of Lower and Upper Canada neither confirmed the fears of local British officials nor fulfilled the hopes of expansionist nationalists in the United States. In the case of Lower Canada, Governor George Prevost issued a series of regulations in July 1812 pertaining to the "American subjects" residing in the colony.

Those who refused to take the oath of allegiance or bear arms were required to leave. Those who wanted to remain in Lower Canada without any threat of expulsion, especially landowners, were required to swear their allegiance and bear arms against the United States if necessary. Samuel Willard was charged with enforcing the government's orders regarding settlers from the United States and also defending the province against possible attack as a townships militiaman. He quickly completed his first charge. In August 1812, Willard boasted that all people required to take the oath of allegiance in his community came forth "with perfect willingness and have taken it without qualification." A pleased Governor Prevost wrote Willard to express his gratitude for the loyalty of township subjects and their willingness to defend Lower Canada against attack from the United States.[35]

However, leading figures in the Eastern Townships, including Willard, opposed a draft. They argued that local men should be exempt from any service beyond local protection since the townships' remoteness and sparse settlement posed significant hardships and danger for the families of men required to serve elsewhere. Willard wrote to military commander Sir John Johnson that the "new settlements" should be exempt from an onerous draft, and then he warned Johnson that "a Many far greater number of the Inhabitants would be lost to the Country by their quitting the Province than would be obtained by the Draft." Ultimately, Willard expressed a commonly held view in the Eastern Townships during the War of 1812. They were quick to identify themselves as loyal subjects but also hesitant to participate in the conflict beyond what was necessary for self-defense. Although they identified as subjects of the British Empire, the settlers' understanding of conditional allegiance limited their commitments to local security. Nevertheless, their exercise of emigration right citizenship secured Great Britain's control of its colonial borders with New England.[36]

Ultimately, colonial officials in Lower Canada recognized emigrant rights to wage Great Britain's war in defense of perpetual allegiance. This inconsistent position on the right to expatriation did not go unnoticed in the United States. To supporters of the war, this was an indictment of its Federalist critics. Citing Prevost's regulations, the *Baltimore Patriot* considered it treasonous "that a party, in the very vitals of our land, should contend for the right of Britain to annul the act of her subject throwing off his allegiance; and yet maintain her right, to protect and employ in arms our countrymen, who have thrown off *their* allegiance!" In condemning the Federalists for their inconsistent position on the right to expatriation, the *Baltimore Patriot* announced what became a central issue of contention within the United States during the War of 1812. The war's critics and its supporters held views about the conflict shaped by competing opinions about the right to expatriation.[37]

THE WAR'S CRITICS in the United States discredited the conflict by denying the right to expatriation. From the perspective of the Federalists that dominated opposition to the war, expatriation was already a limited if not entirely absent right. So long as support for war with Great Britain rested in part on defending a presumed right of expatriation, Federalists believed that war fervor was foolish and the war's aims illegitimate. Federalists used the press, the courts, and eventually state and national legislatures to oppose the war by using familiar arguments against the right of expatriation.

The Federalist press prepared its readers for an intractable and destructive conflict so long as the Republicans steadfastly upheld the right to expatriation. Even though Madison's administration pursued peace almost immediately after Congress declared war, such gestures were meaningless, according to administration critics, since Great Britain would never discuss an armistice that forced it to reject the doctrine of perpetual allegiance. Nevertheless, Madison's administration disregarded "all hazards to enforce the principle, that the citizens or subjects of any nation have the right to expatriate themselves whenever they please." The executive's intransigent position would certainly put the "war upon a footing that cannot fail to render it obnoxious to every man attached to the interest and happiness of his country." So agreed the editor of another Federalist newspaper who identified "War, Taxes, loss of Commerce, National Debt and standing Armies" as the unfortunate costs of the Republican's "expatriating crusade." Federalist critics of expatriation's privileged place in Republican foreign policy ultimately proved sympathetic to Great Britain's national interests. As a country waging defensive war almost continuously since the 1790s, it did not have the luxury of allowing its subjects to abjure their allegiance at will. By demanding that Great Britain accept a position on expatriation peculiar to the United States, Federalist critics feared that Republicans would embroil the United States in a perpetual conflict with Great Britain.[38]

Should the United States enter an era of constant war with Great Britain over disagreements about the right of expatriation, military demands would likely discredit the very right that Republicans hoped to defend with arms. In an 1814 oration delivered and published in Charleston, South Carolina, Joshua W. Toomer argued that debates over the right to expatriation were pedantic exercises of little practical value in a hostile world. Toomer warned that during a national crisis, "especially when the great body of the country stands in need of the contributory aid of every citizen, to throw off one's national character is a desertion of his country—a pusillanimous compliance with selfish and interested dictates, and not the just and honorable exercise of a natural right." To realize the treasonous consequences of unrestrained expatriation, Americans only needed to ponder the war's disastrous progress in the Great Lakes and the West. As Gouverneur Morris reminded the audience of his 1813 July Fourth oration in New York, "If we have a right to abandon our native country and become subjects of another we must have the right to abandon her without assuming a new allegiance. But if all this be so, any number of citizens, in the northern and western parts of our states, may lawfully cast off their allegiance, and either join Great Britain, or declare themselves neutral." The United States might become powerless to effectively wage war if Republican positions on expatriation prevailed.[39]

Without peace in the offing, Federalists went beyond the press and oratory to mitigate the hazards created by Republican foreign policy. In Massachusetts, a state dominated by Federalists and dependent on maritime trade, local politicians had a keen interest in advancing a policy that tolerated Great Britain's claimed powers of impressment. With the Orders of Council overturned by 1813, further hostilities against Great Britain stemmed from nothing more than weak claims about defending American honor, which rested on several dubious legal positions. According to a report issued by the state house of representatives, hawkish writers failed to accept that "all the European Powers as well as the U. States, recognize the principle that their subjects and citizens have no right to expatriate themselves," so "it is manifestly unjust for a neutral power to make war upon one nation in order to compel it to relinquish a principle which is maintained by others." At an Amherst town meeting in western Massachusetts in 1814, the townspeople supported resolutions condemning the war. The resolutions denied the existence of a universal right to expatriation, thereby also rejecting a principal Republican position in favor of the war as an attempt to force Great Britain to change its municipal laws governing allegiance in violation of British sovereignty.[40]

Federalists also argued against the right of expatriation in local courts. In 1813, Federalist judge Luther Martin of Maryland delivered instructions to a newly selected grand jury for Baltimore County. Martin assumed that the jurors were entirely prepared to adjudicate cases involving ordinary crimes. However, the grand jury convened in extraordinary times, Martin noted, during a war that he considered God's punishment for the nation's sins. Is it doubtless that "we are not now suffering in consequence of our iniquities?," Martin questioned the grand jury. Baltimore was one of the republic's major ports, frequented by merchant vessels and privateers certain during wartime to become entangled in conflicts and disputes with the British navy concerning the nationality of their crews. God's judgment created legal problems that members of the jury might be incapable of deciding without Martin's guidance.[41]

Under such circumstances, Martin believed that the grand jury needed a lesson on the law of high treason. Martin stated that high treason was a capital crime in every country because traitors rejected the allegiance they owed to their government. Indeed, it was "a sacred and incontrovertible truth, a truth of which, I cannot doubt," Martin announced, "that no citizen can more rightfully divest himself of his allegiance to his government without its consent than his government can without his consent deprive him of its protection." For Martin, "this truth is founded in the very nature of civil society, and essential to its existence." Thus it was all the more urgent for Martin to warn the grand jurors not to be seduced by a "contrary doctrine" that "is the spawn of Folly and Knavery. . . . We are, indeed," Martin continued, "very gravely told by certain wiseacres, of modern growth, that as it did not depend upon any man's choice whether he should be born in any particular government, he is therefore under no obligation to continue his allegiance to it, any longer than he pleases." According to this subversive notion of consent, children could determine the nature of obedience to their parents "because their parents, in begetting them, were actuated by their own pleasure, without consulting them, whether they chose to be begotten" just as humanity owed no obedience to God because God created humanity "without consent being first obtained or ever asked for."[42]

The members of the grand jury were not interested in a law lesson or a sermon. Among those impaneled in 1813 were the jury foreman Richardson Stuart, a prominent nail maker, and William Pechin, a fervent Republican newspaper editor. Within weeks of receiving Martin's order, Stuart, Pechin, and the other the jurors identified the chief judge's "sentiments and expressions of which they totally disapprove." The grand jurors found Martin's defense of perpetual allegiance most odious since it denied a right to expatriation clearly recognized by the Declaration of Independence, the Constitution, and an earlier opinion from US Supreme Court Justice James Iredell. Moreover, the jurors condemned Martin's position by attributing it to his opinion about the war instead of legal reasoning. The grand jurors concluded "that the promulgation of this novel sentiment, on perpetual allegiance, could only be productive of an effect to lessen the physical force of the nation, in its present belligerent attitude." Martin responded by accusing the jurors of putting their support for the war and their hatred for Great Britain before their duty to interpret the law accurately, for without being blinded by their hatred for Great Britain they would not traffic in "a doctrine, first conceived in the womb, and nurtured by the disciples, of that accursed atheism, which hath long struggled to eradicate every principle of religion and social order." Despite Martin's feverish denunciation, the Baltimore grand jurors represented a broader effort to defend the right of expatriation during the war.[43]

This effort proved most urgent to naturalized citizens. In 1813, English emigrant Alexander B. Johnson published a pseudonymous pamphlet defending a natural right to expatriation that he "dedicated to all the adopted citizens of the United States." Johnson articulated his position through a fictional dialogue between a king who asserted that moral people remained faithful to their country of birth out of patriotic love and his erstwhile subject who rejected uncritical love for country as a prejudice. As the subject declared to his king, "it is no breach of any obligation, and no crime, for a man to leave that country, where, by chance, he commenced his existence; and, at his pleasure, assume a residence in any other that may please him better." During turbulent times, it was necessary for people to support their country of residence, a country they preferred over all others, even if their adopted nation was at war with their country of birth. Johnson thus concluded that opposing one's native country in war provided the strongest evidence that expatriates were virtuous. Johnson concluded that naturalized US citizens obtained their status by exercising a natural right to expatriation that in return created an obligation on their part to promote the national defense of the country they chose as their own. Expatriation was morally defensible only if expatriates acted in the best interests of the nation that adopted them. Johnson sent a copy of his pamphlet to President James Madison because he understood that his position had a potentially large political audience.[44]

As the war progressed, supporters of Republican foreign policy upheld a right to expatriation in more expansive terms in order to challenge Federalist claims that they supported an unnecessary war. George Hay wrote the most unequivocal defense of a natural right to expatriation during the war. Hay was a Virginian by birth, the US attorney for the District of Virginia, and Secretary of State and War James Monroe's son-in-law. His pamphlet surveyed ancient history and recent court opinions, the law of nations and British common law, and the US Constitution and Virginia state statutes to argue that the doctrine of perpetual allegiance was inconsistent with any legal or ethical standard, past or present. Yet Hay did not limit his argument to rejecting British demands to the allegiance of its native-born subjects. In a seamless alignment of political principles, professional training, and personal loyalty, Hay concluded that political allegiance is always temporary and local.

Residence alone, Hay argued, created the reciprocal obligations of allegiance and protection that existed between citizens and governments. Whereas governments could only move when revolutions or conquest reconfigured state boundaries, free people could move about anytime they wished. Free individuals thus chose their political allegiance by choosing where to reside, a right announced in, among many of the sources Hay compiled, the Declaration of Independence. "In this pursuit of happiness," according to Hay's understanding of the Declaration's principles, "every man is at liberty to go, withersoever his judgment, or his hope, or even his caprice may lead him." Even oaths of allegiance were contingent, Hay argued, because they could not "compel a man to remain for ever in a country where he enjoys neither health nor prosperity." A person must merely "be faithful and true while he continues a citizen resident," but once "the residence ceases, the obligation," Hay argued, "ceases also." By elevating residence to the principal marker of nationality, Hay articulated a definition of expatriation radical in its simplicity and capaciousness.[45]

According to Hay, "Expatriation is emigration, with an intention to settle permanently abroad." By exercising the right to expatriation under this definition, a person established residence elsewhere and demonstrated an intent to remain by becoming "a citizen in heart and in sentiment" of that person's adopted country. Once a person demonstrated intent along such lines, "the connexion between the emigrant and his native country is dissolved, so far as that connexion depends on the rights which he held as a citizen." From Hay's perspective, "not a fragment remains" of the rights a person held in the nation the person left behind just as a government cannot demand a fragment of obedience from its former residents. Hay concluded that the US Congress should not act on the subject of expatriation because its status as a natural right guaranteed that it existed before the institution of government, thus any law pertaining to its exercise could only restrain it. Nevertheless, Hay did advise Congress to declare that the US Constitution recognized a natural right to expatriation.[46]

Critics of Hay's pamphlet read it as tainted with partisanship and detrimental to the United States. Writing in 1814 under the pseudonym "Massachusetts Lawyer," arch-Federalist and war opponent John Lowell Jr. railed against the novel "Virginian doctrine" promulgated by Hay. Lowell argued that prevailing legal opinion in his own day and earlier recognized an indisputable right to emigrate and seek naturalization in another country. Nevertheless, emigration did not, Lowell argued, permanently free people from considering the national welfare of the country that they left behind. Emigrants' obligations to the nation of their birth remained with them through an unshakeable "natural allegiance," which most importantly, Lowell argued, "denies to the emigrant the right to turn his arms against his native country, or wholly to throw off those tender, natural ties which every man ought to feel, and which most men do feel." However, according to Hay's topsy-turvy reasoning, the "highest act proving Expatriation is bearing arms against one's own country." Hay's pernicious notion of expatriation subverted those "natural feelings of mankind" that cemented civic life, which were necessary sentiments for people in a nation at war.[47]

Lowell also surmised base partisan ambition behind Hay's elaborate legal arguments. Lowell concluded that Hay intended his pamphlet to boost popular support for the war by establishing that the United States should not seek peace until Great Britain renounced perpetual allegiance. Great Britain would never negotiate peace under such conditions, so he challenged Hay's pamphlet as an effort to provide legal cover for a Republican foreign policy based on perpetual hostilities with Great Britain. Indeed, Lowell believed that Hay wrote the pamphlet at the behest of President Madison to publicize the president's opinions, with Attorney-General Richard Rush's endorsement, and with Secretary of State James Monroe's arrangement for the official US printer in Washington, DC, to publish the pamphlet. As essentially an official government statement, Hay's pamphlet provided "evidence of the determination of our cabinet to persevere in this *War*," and "of its insincerity and hypocrisy in sending out envoys to treat for *Peace*."[48]

As the right to expatriation remained a central issue of the war and a contested partisan issue in the United States, proponents of the right thought it necessary to clarify expatriation's standing under US law. In January 1814, Republican congressman Thomas B. Robertson from Louisiana submitted a resolution for the House to create a committee that would investigate the need for a federal law outlining how citizens could exercise their right to expatriation and possibly drafting a bill to carry forth the committee's conclusions. Robertson insisted that his proposal should cast no doubt on expatriation as a "clear, natural, and inalienable" right, a liberty that "required no legal provision to fortify it, otherwise than by prescribing the manner in which it shall be exercised." For Robertson, if citizens followed an established legal process to expatriate themselves, then their choice to change political allegiance could be proved beyond a reasonable doubt no matter the confusion or vagaries caused by international events.[49]

Debate over Robertson's resolution unfolded along abnormal partisan lines since many congressmen anticipated peace in the near future. Thomas Oakley, a New York Federalist virulently opposed to the war, was incredulous that citizens possessed a right to expatriation, so he argued that Congress should avoid taking a controversial position endorsing the right with peace negations pending. Republican congressmen shared Oakley's trepidation about the resolution's timing even if they accepted a right to expatriation. Tennessee Republican Felix Grundy agreed with the resolution's principles and intent, but he also recognized that it "involved questions of great delicacy as to foreign powers," so he joined Oakley's call to table Robertson's measure. Not even South Carolina Republican John C. Calhoun's unrivaled hostility toward Great Britain prevented him from also opposing Robertson's resolution since "agitating such a subject" seemed imprudent during "a state of war."[50]

Politicians willing to deny rights or bend their principles in the name of national interests before a tumultuous world created the very hazards that his resolution was supposed to mitigate, so Robertson insisted that foreign opinion was irrelevant to a domestic concern such as the right to expatriation. The resolution merely asked, according to Robertson, "whether our citizens, leaving the country, should be enabled to show that they expatriated themselves according to law." Republican supporters of the resolution drew an even sharper distinction between foreign interests and domestic rights. Nathaniel Macon, a North Carolina Republican, argued that a federal law allowing citizens to exercise their right to expatriation was irrelevant to treaty negotiations, otherwise foreign governments might take the opportunity to declare "that the people of this country should not go where they pleased." James Fisk, a Vermont Republican, argued that Robertson's resolution asked the House to "inquire into the propriety of giving to man as much liberty as the God of Heaven gave him at his birth, and does not for a moment depend on the feeling of any foreign nation." Bipartisan pragmatism in foreign affairs prevailed over partisan Republican support for the resolution, thus dooming Robertson's measure.[51]

Nevertheless, debate over the right of US citizens to expatriation commenced once again in early 1814 as the House turned to funding the war before peace was official. The US Treasury Department paid for the War of 1812 primarily by selling long-term bonds. Investors provided a loan to the government in exchange for interest on their purchase. Only Congress possessed the power to borrow money on behalf of the US government, so it was required to adopt legislation that determined the amount and terms of each new loan. Congress passed five loan acts during the war. Although the loan bills concerned routine war-financing matters, a proposal to emit a third loan in early 1814 included a partisan fight over war aims and the right of expatriation.[52]

Robertson introduced his defeated resolution three weeks before the Loan Bill, but the two issues bundled together in the debate over war funding. Robertson favored issuing a new loan, but he also wanted to draw, once again, the House's attention to fundamental matters of right raised by the war. In a speech on the Loan Bill, Robertson lamented that only a few weeks earlier members "from either side of the House rushed forward with eagerness to lay the phantom which their own imaginations had created" regarding his expatriation resolution. Some opposed it because it threatened peace negotiations with Great Britain while others thought, according to Robertson, that it was a subject of little practical concern. A few of his House colleagues argued that his resolution had subversive consequences, for they "deduced from it encouragement to desertion and all kinds of abomination." In reply to his opponents, Robertson reiterated that his resolution concerned the exercise of an uncontroversial natural right, which he defined according to the expansive terms that George Hay proposed in his recently published pamphlet. For Robertson, expatriation simply meant emigration "with an intent to permanently reside elsewhere." Robertson thus found bipartisan objection to his resolution altogether peculiar. The "proposition must indeed have been an anomaly in politics," Robertson quipped, "which united in opposition to it the federalism of Massachusetts and the democracy of Tennessee."[53]

Debates over war funding and military measures provided an opportunity for politicians to debate the merits of expatriation as a referendum on the legitimacy of the conflict. One position challenged the supposition that a consistent understanding of naturalization law required that governments acknowledge a right to expatriation. Naturalization involved "municipal" laws that only protected naturalized US citizens within the country's territorial limits, according to Federalist representatives Daniel Sheffey and Alexander Contee Hanson. Republican representative Langdon Cheeves agreed, and he argued further that a right to expatriation implied "a total release of the subject from his allegiance, as well when without as on his return to the territory of his original sovereign, while naturalization is in its operation only co-extensive with the territory and the extension of the territorial power of the adopted sovereign."[54]

Other representatives argued that the War of 1812 originated in competing views about a right to expatriation, so winning the war meant defending a citizen's freedom to change nationality. As a natural right, individuals maintained the freedom to expatriate regardless of the nation they inhabited.

Tennessee representative Thomas K. Harris defended this position before his constituents when he argued "that in the foundation of society generally, the right of expatriation was not surrendered." Moreover in the United States, the Declaration of Independence enshrined the right to expatriate, for "in the pursuit of this happiness," Harris argued, "man has no bounds but the limits of the world. He may pursue it in whatsoever region, or in whatsoever direction or course his hope, his judgment or his caprice, m[a]y direct him." As Pennsylvania Republican William Findley declared, "I am not conscious of where or when I drew my first breath; my will was not consulted about it, it was not my voluntary act. I was wholly passive in that business. Therefore no moral obligation can arise from it to bind my conscience to perpetual allegiance to that spot of earth." The only legitimate political obligations were those obtained by choice, whether in a person's nation of birth or adoption.[55]

Rather than a recent, subversive principle, American supporters of war against Great Britain argued that a right to expatriation had a deep and varied history that proved its legality. According to William Findley, perpetual allegiance was the radically novel doctrine of the "new school," not expatriation, a principle supported since antiquity. Biblical justifications for expatriation were perhaps more authoritative than appeals to history and international law. Alexander McLeod, a Presbyterian minister in New York, assured the faithful that scripture justified the United States' positions in its war with Great Britain. This included a right to expatriation, for McLeod argued that God created the world for all mankind to seek happiness where they pleased and not to remain bound to the land of their birth. Allegiance, according to McLeod's reading of scripture, did not adhere to the territory governed by a sovereign but in a contractual agreement between a free person and the government under which that person lived. For McLeod, the Bible proved that American Christians could remain equally loyal to their faith and their nation's foreign policy.[56]

In early 1815, the United States and Great Britain signed a peace treaty that failed to address many of the grievances that had caused the war. Impressment became somewhat irrelevant because the Napoleonic Wars also ended in 1815, which diminished Great Britain's need for sailors. Moreover, perpetual allegiance remained a settled doctrine in British common law, which left the right to expatriation in doubt, at least under the Treaty of Ghent. The Federalist press cast the absence of treaty recognition for a right to expatriation as further evidence that the War of 1812 was a colossal failure with Republicans to blame. The lack of diplomatic recognition for a right to expatriation mattered little to Americans who believed the freedom to emigrate also entailed a freedom to expatriate. Their view of emigrant rights gained popular appeal and political support in the years before and during the war. From this perspective, a durable victory over Great Britain demanded that American citizens never retreat from their support for the right of expatriation.

Nevertheless, with a right to expatriation still unsettled in US courts and unrecognized by the Treaty of Ghent, Americans who quit the nation remained in a precarious legal position as did the US government in relationship to other powers. To resolve this matter, Louisiana representative Thomas B. Robertson once again called for a federal law to "provide the manner in which the right of expatriation shall be exercised," which he introduced as a bill in late 1817. Modeled on the Virginia expatriation statute, Robertson's bill presumed that expatriation was a natural right exercised without government restraint. Once a citizen declared in his state's federal district court "that he relinquishes the character of a citizen" and departed the United States, his citizenship in the United States disappeared. Robertson claimed that the procedure outlined in his bill would clarify confusion over emigrant rights reaching back to the 1790s, for it would put "our citizens at perfect liberty to become citizens of what nation they chose, on such terms as that nation should prescribe."[57]

The House debated Robertson's bill in early 1818. The bill's strongest opponents considered the right to expatriation from the perspective of the government. Under this bill, warned Delaware Federalist Louis McLane, "a man throws off his country, with the same facility that he lays aside his coat, and with little more form or solemnity," which "annihilates the authority of the State over the citizen without its interposition, at the mere will and pleasure of the individual." State authority over a citizen's emigrant rights was absent to begin with, argued Georgia Republican Thomas Cobb, a supporter of the bill. It was irrelevant to the United States what its citizens did once they relinquished this status. Instead, Cobb insisted, a person who relinquished US citizenship became "as it were, a citizen of the world," that is, "until he has performed some act by which he becomes a citizen of another Government." McLane and Cobb held familiar positions at the margins of expatriation debates in the United States. Expatriation was the choice of those who carelessly discarded their civic obligations or a right that allowed free men the privileges of statelessness.[58]

Other representatives debated the bill from a conciliatory position. North Carolina Republican Lewis Williams summarized the dispute as one over "the point of time at which the right attaches, and not as to the existence of the right itself." Williams distinguished supporters of the bill who contended "that the right of expatriation attaches to the individual upon his leaving his native country" from the positions of opponents such as himself who believed "the right attaches . . . upon his becoming the citizen or subject of the country to which he may have gone." Virginia Republican James Johnson announced an expansive right to emigration but ultimately agreed with Williams's position. A citizen of the United States possessed a right to expatriation "in the most ample, unlimited, and unlimitable degree," Johnson announced, but "he has exercised this right" only once he "changes permanently his residence, and takes the oath of allegiance to the Government of the country in which he has fixed his permanent residence." The House ultimately rejected the bill, along with a declaratory statement in favor of the right to expatriation. Congress did not again consider a federal right to expatriation until the 1860s, at which point it did so to merely to align the law with emigrant rights claims already established in places distant from Washington, DC.[59]

IN RETROSPECT, THE 1818 DEBATE affirmed a right to expatriation that American citizens had already claimed for themselves starting in the 1780s. Those who became Spanish or British subjects over previous decades did so without assuming that the US government had any authority over their choice. These emigrants did set aside their allegiance to the United States as they would a garment. In their oaths of allegiance to other sovereigns and the formation of permanent settlements outside the United States, Congress found the standards of legal expatriation in 1818.

Indeed, America's war in favor of expatriation had a victory of principles in the Champlain Valley borderlands when subjects in the Eastern Townships prepared to defend the British Empire against attacks from the nation they had left behind. In addition to ratifying emigrant rights claims already established in the borderlands, the 1818 debate ratified a particular view of emigrant rights within the United States. From the early 1800s onward, defenders of the right to expatriation responded to international events and legal questions by insisting that emigration entailed expatriation, that the freedom to leave included an unrestrained freedom to decide allegiance. Although Congress did not establish a federal right to expatriation in 1818, this view of emigrant rights prevailed. It defined Republican foreign policy and legal opinions before and during the War of 1812. Kentucky Republican and future vice president Richard Mentor Johnson described this notion of emigrant rights as an individual "privilege of locomotion," a citizen's natural right "to abandon his permanent residence and citizenship."[60]

The 1818 congressional debate was prospective as well. Nothing indicated that Americans would stop exercising their emigrant rights in the future, thus the call for a federal expatriation law and the dispute surrounding it. Only a few years before, Representative William Gaston understood the right to expatriation among the weighty issues before Congress because Americans frequently quit the United States. "It is a point on which this country, surrounded by foreign territories, into which our citizens are migrating in vast numbers, has a very deep interest to form correct opinions," Gaston concluded. In the House votes on the 1818 expatriation bill, western representatives, especially those from Kentucky, Ohio, and Indiana, supported a right to expatriation by a three-to-one margin, higher than any other region in the United States. Affirming emigrant rights was a popular political position in states closest to North America's contested borderlands because these were rights that citizens in this region already claimed for themselves. After 1818, borderlands remained the places where emigration begat expatriation, where legal and political arguments in favor of unrestrained emigrant rights from previous decades gained authority through common understanding and everyday choices. Thus in the early 1820s, citizens once again quit the United States, this time for allegiance to Mexico.[61]

CHAPTER SIX

Voluntary Mexicans

In early 1830, Asa Brigham quit the United States for Mexico. Brigham was a New Englander who lived for several years in Louisiana before he crossed the Sabine River into Texas. He settled in Brazoria where he followed successful agricultural and commercial pursuits. Brigham had a thriving family, especially measured by the values he had acquired in the southern United States. He gloated over his daughter's marriage to a Virginia planter and beamed when describing his granddaughter. She was not even two years old, yet "she is mistress of all the chickens Pigs, Cats and negroes on the place." Brigham's standing also brought him political power. By 1835 he was the Brazoria alcalde. Brigham signed the Texas Declaration of Independence within a year of his election as alcalde, but early letters to his family in Massachusetts offer no hints to his later life as an insurrectionary. Brigham missed New England, but he had no desire to return. He felt "perfectly satisfied here and have settled for life in this country," he assured his siblings in 1832. Brigham realized that his decision to remain in Texas might perplex his relatives who stayed behind. So he elaborated. "You may ask why we leave the United States of America, for that of the United States of Mexico—in answer, I can only say, that it was through choice, with a view of bettering my fortune, which I consider has been realized."[1]

Brigham explained his motivations for settling in Mexico by answering one of his era's most important questions about the nature of political allegiance. Did a person owe allegiance to a nation for reasons of birth, custom, or culture—was allegiance coercive in one way or another? Or was national allegiance voluntary, an expression of personal choice? Brigham held the latter view. By settling in Texas, Brigham exercised his emigrant rights to free movement and expatriation to become a Mexican citizen. Americans such as Brigham who traded their citizenship in the United States for Mexican citizenship in Texas during the 1820s and 1830s affirmed the previous decades' emigration debates. Their choices secured a right to quit the nation without restraint among the privileges of republican citizenship. American colonists in Texas thus embodied the limits of allegiance to the United States rather than its settler expansionist vanguard. Moreover, the colonization policy that brought Americans to Texas revealed the limits of political allegiance in Mexico. Until 1835, common understandings of emigrant rights provided a source of political and legal cooperation among elite Tejanos, Anglo newcomers, and Mexican officials. However, changing political conditions in Mexico created conflicting ideas about the meaning of voluntary allegiance within that nation as well. Ultimately, the end of shared notions about the virtues of voluntary allegiance unleashed rebellion in northern Mexico.

MEXICO HAD A BORDER PROBLEM during the 1820s. Although it gained independence from Spain in 1821, Mexico inherited the empire's porous northern boundary with the United States. Mexico's territorial integrity was especially compromised in Texas. Native people outnumbered all others in Texas during the 1820s. Sizeable populations of Caddos and Cherokees inhabited both sides of the border and freely crossed between Mexico and the United States, while the Comanches maintained a powerful empire that included Texas and well beyond. When a Mexican official touring the border in 1828 asked a high-ranking Caddo in eastern Texas if he was on Mexican or US territory, the Caddo replied that he was "in his own land, which was nothing else but his." Citizens of the United States also crossed the border into Texas, some with nefarious motivations. James Long's exploits gave Mexican authorities another reason to fret about border security in the North. Long, a planter and physician in Natchez, Mississippi, rejected the terms of the 1819 Adams-Onís Treaty in which the United States recognized Spain's rule over Texas. An angered Long believed that Texas belonged to the United States according to the Louisiana Purchase. On the eve of Mexican independence, Long mobilized his discontent to transform Natchez into a staging ground for two, ultimately failed, military ventures to separate Texas from New Spain. Long was eventually murdered in Mexico City in 1822, but Mexico's efforts to secure its border with the United States were just beginning.[2]

Long's demise often marks a closing chapter in the early history of Anglo-American filibustering. However, contemporary debates in the United States and Mexico surrounding Long's incursions highlight an alternative set of intellectual and political assumptions that shaped life in this borderlands region. In the United States, Long's invasions became part of an ongoing debate over a citizen's emigrant rights. As one of Long's supporters argued in the *Louisiana Advertiser*, "the right of expatriation was an inherent right," and the United States had no authority "to prevent any citizen from removing" to Texas, "nor are his motives in doing so a legitimate subject of inquiry." Authorities in the newly independent Mexican Empire under Agustín de Iturbide responded to Long's second failed invasion in 1821 by creating a Colonization Commission to bring greater order and settlement to Mexico's northern frontier. Efforts to colonize Texas remained an important but controversial feature of Mexican statecraft into the 1830s. As a policy for populating Texas, colonization worked. By 1834, over 20,000 emigrants from the United States settled in Mexican Texas. Many emigrated as families, often with considerable numbers of enslaved people, into a province already inhabited by nearly 3,000 Tejanos and powerful Native nations.[3]

From the perspective of the 1820s, Anglo emigration marked the movement of people who consciously left their country for better opportunities elsewhere. Land in Mexico was comparably less expensive than in the United States and easier to acquire. Financially pressed Americans, especially westerners affected by the Panic of 1819, went to Texas for good reasons. Movement across the border encompassed a change in political status. After all, Anglo settlers became Mexican citizens according to Mexico's colonization and naturalization laws. By trading their US citizenship for Mexican citizenship, Anglo migrants exercised their emigrant rights to free movement and expatriation according to legal and political terms that had been decided by the early 1820s.[4]

Domestic debates in the early nineteenth century over emigrant rights in the United States and over colonization in Mexico shared much in common. Both concerned the nature of an individual's allegiance to the state. American emigration for Texas occurred at the same time that dominant legal and popular opinion in the United States affirmed citizenship rights to expatriation. More importantly, Mexico's colonization laws contained provisions that enabled expatriation. Thus during the 1820s, US and Mexican authorities unintentionally created a shared legal space at their border. Here, Anglo understandings of expatriation overlapped with Mexican colonization policies. Both assumed a concept of political allegiance that was malleable and open to change as individuals saw fit.[5]

Well before Mexican independence in 1821, established legal thought and practice throughout the Spanish American world implied a right to expatriation. According to prevailing legal opinion in early modern Spain, individuals had a natural right to change allegiance at will. This right entailed certain responsibilities. Writing in the eighteenth century, theologian and philosopher Benito Jerónimo Feijóo y Montenegro argued that "people who legitimately emigrate from their country of birth and fix their domicile in another dominion owe the same obligation to the new republic as to the one they had to the republic where they were born." Foreigners became full members of their adopted communities by behaving as "good" emigrants. In practice, individuals who established permanent residence in a new jurisdiction for which they cultivated genuine patriotic sentiments were good emigrants. Obeying local laws, paying taxes, and testimonies of strong moral character were all outward signs of patriotic love. Sufficient patriotic love transformed outsiders into citizens. An absence of patriotic love rendered one a dangerous foreigner who must be excluded from community membership. Authorities in Spanish America addressed the civil status of foreigners within their communities according to local needs, but they also recognized the voluntary basis for allegiance. Spanish concepts of land ownership reinforced Spanish naturalization and citizenship laws by prioritizing settlement and productive usage over investment and speculation. However, colonial authorities could remove residents who did not meet membership standards of a given community. Thus for emigrants and officials alike, choice superseded language, race, culture, or ethnicity in determining membership within Spanish American communities. These considerations determined membership claims for the American citizens who adopted Spanish allegiance in places such as Natchez in the 1780s and 1790s under local settlement proposals. However, Spain codified this principle of choice in the Constitution of Cádiz, which was ratified in 1812. Throughout the entire colonial era in Spanish America, therefore, no concept of perpetual allegiance existed in Spanish law or culture.[6]

The Spanish Empire disintegrated in the early nineteenth century, but the new republics that formed in its place, including Mexico, preserved Spanish concepts of allegiance. The 1824 constitution of the Federal Republic of Central America, for example, granted citizenship to "anyone" born in an American republic who established residence and stated his intention to become a citizen before local authorities. Nothing approximating perpetual allegiance appeared in Mexico's founding documents or its colonization policies. Mexico's federal colonization law of 1824 and the Coahuila and Texas law of 1825 both opened colonization to any foreigner who desired to settle in Mexico. In accord with Spanish understandings of citizenship and naturalization, initial membership stemmed from choice. Nevertheless, interested foreigners needed to demonstrate their commitment to Mexico by exhibiting good intentions and establishing residence. This was especially clear in the Coahuila and Texas statute adopted by officials in Saltillo, the state capital. Article 5 of the 1825 law required that "settlers who present themselves for admission, must prove their Christianity, morality and good habits, by a certificate from the authorities where they formerly resided." Under Article 31, "foreigners who in conformity with this law, have obtained lands, and established themselves in any new settlement, shall be considered from that moment, naturalised in the country." As in the Federal Republic of Central America, the Mexican Republic's naturalization and colonization laws had residency and

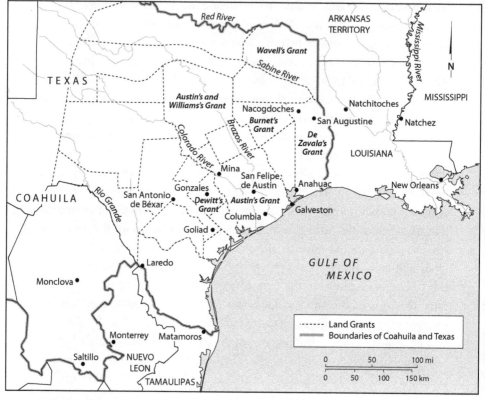

Coahuila and Texas

personal character provisions that mirrored the residency and "good faith" standards used in earlier North American colonization regimes and codified in expatriation statutes in the United States. The colonization proposals developed after Mexican independence were thus intended to exert greater government control over territory near the US border by relying on emigrant rights as a pathway to Mexican citizenship for settlers in the region.[7]

Citizens emigrated from the United States in the wake of larger legal and political developments that cast their settlement in Texas as acts of expatriation. According to pamphleteers during the War of 1812 that asserted a right to expatriation without restraint, American emigrants exercised a natural right. According to political statements that recognized a tacit concept of expatriation—attendant on commerce, changing residence, or as a fact of emigration—and Supreme Court rulings that established economic expatriation, emigration to Texas constituted a desire to expatriate. Yet even stronger evidence suggests a connection between region and support for expatriation. Several states adopted constitutional provisions regarding emigration that implied a right to expatriation. Of the states formed through 1821, the constitutions of only four—Tennessee, Ohio, Illinois, and Maine—did not enumerate a right to emigration. Indeed, by the 1820s, Americans increasingly believed that emigration entailed freedom of movement throughout the world and the natural right to willfully change political allegiance. Emigration was tantamount to expatriation. James Kent reaffirmed this position in *Commentaries on American Law*, his four-volume treatise published between 1826 and 1830. According to Kent, the recognition of emigration as a right in several state constitutions went "far towards a renunciation of the doctrine of the English common law [perpetual allegiance], as being repugnant to the natural liberty of mankind, provided we are to consider emigration and expatriation, as words, intended to be of synonymous import." Most importantly, emigration garnered constitutional mention and protection in nearly every western state formed before 1821, affirming that early nationals with a continental orientation embraced rights to free movement and expatriation. As southern and western states enumerated the right to emigration in their constitutions, they created a legal geography of expatriation that allowed for theoretically easy movement and shifting allegiances. The "privilege of locomotion," as Kentucky representative Richard Mentor Johnson described emigrant rights in the 1818 House debate, authorized travel through this legal landscape that stretched south and west toward Texas. According to a writer in the *Louisiana Advertiser*, "Our laws admit of expatriation." Those Americans "who are willing to exchange their citizenship in the United States for a residence in the province of Texas," and who did so "purely with the view to better their condition," should "expect an honourable or prosperous residence in Texas" obtained "through the peaceful sanction of the constituted authorities of that country."[8]

Anglo colonists in Texas during the 1820s inhabited a legal zone that had been created by more than American laws regarding expatriation. This was a transnational legal zone that extended far across the border into Mexico where the concept of perpetual allegiance was alien to its legal culture. By seeking foreign settlers, Mexican authorities severed assumptions that national citizenship rose from ethnicity, history, or culture. According to colonization's promoters, settlers with vastly different backgrounds and languages could presumably become productive members of Mexican society provided they emigrated with pure motivations to change allegiance. Establishing permanent residency was strong proof of allegiance to Mexico. Mexican authorities in Texas thus recognized that expatriation was a right compatible with

Mexico's colonization laws. The enthusiasm of the Texas booster who wrote in the *Louisiana Advertiser* corresponded with the ambitions of Mexicans who promoted their country's colonization policy.

Nevertheless, the issue of Anglo colonization in Texas divided Mexican opinion along regional lines similar to divisions in the United States caused by debates over expatriation. Support for expatriation generally grew in the United States as one moved farther inland south and west. Mexican concern about Anglo colonization increased as one traveled south from the border toward Mexico City. Moreover, Mexicans brought competing views about allegiance and patriotism to debates over Anglo colonization, views echoed in controversies surrounding emigrant rights in the United States.

The staunchest critics of Anglo colonization were often Mexican officials from the federal government or those with strong nationalist sentiments. Manuel de Mier y Terán fit both of these descriptions. Mier y Terán fought for Mexican independence. He later served in the Mexican Congress and rose to general in the Mexican Army. In 1830 Mier y Terán became commandant general, the top civil and military official, in the Eastern Interior Provinces, which included Coahuila and Texas. In 1828, the Mexican government created a Boundary Commission to map Mexico's border with the United States should the two nations accept the Adams-Onís Treaty. The Boundary Commission was also charged with assessing social, economic, and political conditions at the border. Officials in Mexico City appointed Mier y Terán to head the Boundary Commission's expedition into Texas and to author its report about conditions there. Mier y Terán's observations about Texas in 1828 revealed how authorities in Mexico's central government viewed Anglo colonization, in part because Mier y Terán's standing shaped opinion in the capital.[9]

Mier y Terán was deeply pessimistic about the subject of Anglo colonization. He identified "two classes" of Anglo settlers in Texas. Some were "poor laborers" but "generally industrious and honorable and respect the country." These upright emigrants quit the United States because their meager wealth could still afford them land in Mexico, so Mier y Terán advised Mexican authorities to welcome them. However, Mier y Terán estimated that law-breaking Anglos outnumbered their law-abiding brethren. The other class of Anglos, the "fugitives from the neighboring republic" who were "ready to cross and recross" the border as their criminal activities demanded, threatened Texas's future as a Mexican possession. Mier y Terán observed that even without criminal motivations, many Anglos lacked "respect for borders or boundaries of pure convention, [and] they choose the best land. Nature tells them that [the land] is theirs, because, in effect, everyone can appropriate what does not belong to anyone or what is not claimed by anyone. When the occasion arises, they will claim the irrefutable rights of first possession." Claims to emigrant rights had long entailed squatter's rights, a problem of territorial governance familiar to colonial administrators throughout North America. Thus when assessing the Anglo population in Northern Mexico, Mier y Terán distinguished between virtuous emigrants who left the United States to pursue a better life elsewhere and subversive world citizens without allegiance to any nation.[10]

Other Mexican officials discerned few good qualities in the Anglo settlers. Mexican army officer José María Sánchez, a draftsman for the Boundary Commission, noted that "Americans" occupied nearly all of eastern Texas where they settled "in most cases without the permission of the authorities." Rather, these interlopers took "possession of the sitio that best suits them without either asking leave or going through any formality other than that of building their homes." Even a widely respected and prominent Anglo empresario such as Stephen F. Austin was not above Sánchez's suspicion. He believed that Austin had "lulled the authorities into a sense of security, while he works diligently for his own ends." Although Rafael Antonio Manchola was a Tejano, he was also a career soldier, politician, and son-in-law of prominent Tejano empresario Martín De León, all of which influenced his perception of Anglo colonization. "No faith can be placed in the Anglo-American colonists because they are continually demonstrating that they absolutely refuse to be subordinate, unless they find it convenient to what they want anyway," Manchola warned. Unless forced otherwise, Anglo colonists would follow their own laws, not "the ones they have sworn to obey, these being the laws of our Supreme Government." Thus for Sánchez and Manchola, Anglo settlers in Texas—both illegal and legal—were driven by the same duplicitous motives of mercenary self-interest that critics in the United States attributed to expatriates and proponents of world citizenship.[11]

Critics of Anglo colonization also blamed Tejano culture for Texas's problems. Nearly all of the Boundary Commission's leading members shared Mier y Terán's concern that "Mexican influence" diminished the farther one traveled north into Texas. This reflected the growing population imbalance between Anglos and Tejanos in the region, but it also suggested that Tejano inferiority resulted from their distance from Mexico City, presumptions of their poor education, and their proximity to the United States. As Jean-Louis Berlandier, a French botanist assigned to the expedition, observed, "Trade with the Anglo-Americans, and the blending in to some degree of their customs, make the inhabitants of Texas a little different from the Mexicans of the interior." Tejano "women prefer to dress in the fashion of Louisiana, and by so doing they participate both in the customs of the neighboring nation and of their own." Due to their "education and environment," José María Sánchez claimed that Tejanos were "ignorant not only of the customs of our great cities, but even of the occurrences of our Revolution." Frequent commerce with people from the United States resulted in Tejanos adopting Anglo "customs and habits, and one may say truly that they are not Mexicans except by birth, for they even speak Spanish with marked incorrectness."[12]

Those who criticized conditions in Texas suggested that Tejanos lacked affective sources of patriotic allegiance to Mexico, ties rooted in a common understanding of Mexican history, a shared language, or cultural similarities with the interior. In this view, Texas was a dangerously cosmopolitan region populated by inhabitants whose ethnic and national differences made a single political allegiance or national identity impossible. Tejanos were "in the midst of a great movement of many nations and peoples who are coming to them from all directions," Mier y Terán lamented. How then could Tejanos defend Mexico against Anglo incursions if their own standing as true Mexicans was dubious?[13]

Mexican critics of Anglo colonization addressed this problem by calling for settlers whose patriotism and allegiance seemed fixed. For such observers, authentic patriotism and allegiance required sympathetic attachments to the nation grounded in tradition, culture, and religion. This view informed the critics' proposals for attracting colonists to Texas who possessed the proper character to offset emigration from the United States. Mier y Terán advised federal politicians in Mexico City to support the creation of new Mexican communities in Texas, especially by subsidizing the relocation of citizens from other places in the republic. He argued that people from Yucatán were not only loyal Mexicans but also skilled agriculturalists and navigators who were industrious enough to compete with North Americans in those parts of Texas near its rivers and coast. Much like other efforts in North America to produce sovereignty in the borderlands, the federal government could effectively "counterbalance foreign ways" in Texas by relocating 5,000 Yucatecans to the border. Diplomat and intellectual Simón Tadeo Ortiz de Ayala was an early promoter of colonization in Northern Mexico, and by the late 1820s Texas in particular. Ortiz looked outside Mexico for appropriate settlers. The Mexican government should welcome "industrious and honorable families of different nationalities, habits, and customs" into the republic's northern frontier, Ortiz argued, so long as they were Catholics from "friendly and allied nations or those who have manifested sympathy for our cause and are not located on our boundaries." Ortiz posited that Canary Islanders and the Irish were ideal candidates to balance the influx of American emigrants because they and Mexicans shared a similar history and a common religion. For Mier y Terán and Ortiz, some groups were potentially more allegiant than others, a probability that increased the more a person had in common with native Mexicans.[14]

The reverse was also true, however. Other settlers, especially emigrants from the United States, were likely less allegiant. Mexican observers of Anglo colonization had no reason to believe that Anglos could easily shed patriotism for the United States before settling in Texas. Moreover, Mexican officials developed strategies to limit the influence of Anglos already in Texas by mitigating the intractable influence of previously acquired allegiance. When Stephen F. Austin finally secured a colonization contract from the Mexican government in 1823, the Council of State demanded that Austin's colonists settle far from the border. Otherwise, the council feared, newly arrived Anglos would not sever their prior political allegiance. As the council stated, "If a large population of persons who speak the same language and share the same customs and connections with a neighboring nation should exclusively occupy the same land area . . . they could someday disturb the peace of the Empire." The National Colonization Law of 1824 codified this principle by prohibiting colonists from settling within twenty leagues, or about seventy miles, from an international boundary or within ten leagues of the coast. The council's concern seemed justified later in the 1820s once the American emigrant population increased in Texas, especially near the border, contrary to the law. Ortiz concluded that Mexican authorities should expect Anglos in northern Texas to seek an alliance "with the United States of the North, where a close contact, relationship of blood, the ties of custom, language, religion, national spirit and even other ideals are constantly influencing calculating men, who daily increase the ranks." Ortiz argued that a more extensive government in Texas could encourage, or perhaps force, Anglo loyalty to Mexico.[15]

Tejano elites were less concerned about the prospects of Anglo loyalty because necessity instilled them with concepts of patriotism and allegiance suitable to life in the borderlands. During the 1820s, most important Tejano elites encouraged Anglo colonization to promote Texas's economic growth and to help defend it from powerful Indigenous nations. José Antonio Saucedo, who became Texas's top local official for a time until 1827, provided political support and advice to Stephen F. Austin that proved essential to

Austin's colonization ventures in Mexico. More broadly, prominent Tejanos who organized themselves around the political leadership of José María Viesca, the first governor of Coahuila and Texas, worked to bring cotton agriculture and cotton planters from the United States to Texas. Many Tejano elites thus also proved sympathetic to Anglo demands that slavery remain legal in Coahuila and Texas. Erasmo Seguín lobbied for the interests of Texas's emigrant slaveholders while serving as a Texas delegate to the Mexican Congress.[16]

Anglo emigrants and prominent Tejanos ultimately had compelling security and economic reasons to cooperate in Texas during the 1820s. Texas in the early nineteenth century was subject to a vast empire that Comanches had built and sustained through cultural adaptation and by monopolizing a lucrative livestock trade, primarily in horses. Supporters of Mexico's colonization policy hoped to offset Comanche power, but Anglo colonists settled primarily in east Texas, well beyond Comancheria. Nevertheless, Comanche strength in the region may have actually wed Anglo colonists and Tejanos to the Mexican state. Most colonists in Coahuila and Texas acquired land titles through empresarios, agents who negotiated directly with the state government to form colonies for financial gain. According to the laws of Coahuila and Texas, empresarios were state officials responsible for daily governance in Texas. However, Tejanos and Anglos also shared economic priorities that included access to the United States' developing market economy. Tejanos and Anglos thus pursued their local interests by gravitating toward the nation that could best meet them. Although Texas sat at one of the continent's most clearly defined and recognized international borders, neither Mexico nor the United States fully controlled it. Texas was also a place where Mexican political and legal institutions were strong enough to demand the loyalty of its Euro-American population but also riddled with competing cultural influences that rendered their consent tenuous at best.[17]

In such a world, borderlands people enacted the cosmopolitan ideals that underwrote their emigrant rights claims to regional belonging. These groups fashioned an intellectual middle ground from cosmopolitanism out of necessity rather than deeply shared intellectual commitments. For Mexican authorities and Anglo settlers, cosmopolitanism operated in two ways. First, it allowed individuals to both tolerate, and also elide, fundamental differences of race, ethnicity, religion, and nationality. This aided the colonization process by focusing the attention of both groups on importing seemingly universal political and cultural values into territories with existing complex social relations. Second, it allowed individuals to identify themselves beyond or without national attachments when necessary. This benefited American emigrants the most. It covered any lingering doubts about rights of expatriation by further rendering betrayals of national citizenship virtuous rather than subversive, especially near fluid and contested international boundaries. Although Texas elites did not always hold uniform ambitions, cosmopolitanism advanced important political and cultural efforts to find common cause in attempts to impose order in a region where state authority and economic institutions were in flux.

Cosmopolitan traces appeared in Coahuila and Texas's colonization law. Catholicism was the established religion in the Mexican Republic, and officials expected all colonists to be or become Catholic once they settled in the country. Moreover, Mexican critics of Anglo colonization almost always argued for increased Catholic immigration to Texas as a solution to their concerns. However, the religion clause in Coahuila and Texas's colonization law was actually quite broad. Article 5 stipulated that "settlers who present themselves for admission, must prove their Christianity, morality and good habits, by a certificate from the authorities where they formerly resided." By choosing the word "Christianity" instead of the phrase "Roman Catholicism," members of the state's Colonization Commission eager to attract Anglo settlers intentionally used inclusive language. In an era when distinctions between Catholicism and Protestantism marked fundamental cultural and political fault lines, this was a significant concession to immediate needs over confessional orthodoxy.[18]

It seems that Texas attracted at least some Anglo emigrants who held equally contingent notions of religious identity. One Anglo colonist declared that "for my own part I Care nothing about it know I Can be as good a Christian there as I can here. It is only a name anyhow." Another colonist expressed an even more expansive view. "My Bible teaches but one Religion and I presume a Romans is the same it matters not what names men give it so it is pure and undefiled, whether Roman Methodist Baptist Presbyterian or Catholick; and a liberal minded man can wave on these points for the sake of doing good." Both settlers would have met the religious test outlined in Article 5 of Coahuila and Texas's colonization law even though they did not profess the faith proscribed by the central government in Mexico City.[19]

Stephen F. Austin and Benjamin Milam, two of the most prominent Anglo empresarios during the 1820s, made cosmopolitan choices as well. Austin denigrated Catholicism as superstitious and despotic, yet he tolerated its presence and encouraged his colonists to do the same. Austin eagerly learned Spanish, often referring to himself as Estevan. Of course, these actions enabled Austin to promote the economic growth of his colonies, but Austin filtered his material interests through a cosmopolitan sieve that rendered cultural, political, and even linguistic differences seemingly less different and less threatening. This was no minor change of opinion considering the entrenched anti-Catholicism and anti-Iberian prejudices in Anglo-American thinking. Milam also diminished difference in pursuit of his Texas interests. He converted to Catholicism in his native Kentucky and fought with Mexican armies against Spanish forces in the Mexican Revolution. Milam acquired Mexican citizenship through his military service, and then he obtained a contract to recruit and settle European colonists. Thus for Austin and Milam, cosmopolitanism was the intellectual framework for changing national citizenship.[20]

Tejano and Anglo elites also relied on cosmopolitan principles to promote Texas settlement. José Antonio Saucedo was confident that once Anglo emigrants were "admitted by the Mexican government they will form one single family with the rest of its sons." Regarding colonization in Texas more broadly, Francisco Ruiz of San Antonio quipped, "I cannot help seeing advantages which, to my way of thinking, would result if we admitted honest, hardworking people, regardless of what country they come from . . . even hell itself." At least rhetorically, Saucedo and Ruiz shared a belief that allegiance and patriotism were transferable, a position also advanced by the Galveston Bay and Texas Land Company, which was created and financed by wealthy investors in New York and Boston. The company's recruitment literature traced Mexico's promise to its emergence from "the enthralling yoke of Spanish despotism" into a nation of "free constitutions and of wise laws." Company boosters did not expect the colonists they recruited to transform Texas into an American outpost. Indeed, they warned that independence from Mexico would only harm Texas. Colonists would prosper, according to company literature, because the Mexican government recognized "that the freemen of all countries are patriots wherever their destinies fix or their interest call them."[21]

The most quixotic proposal for settling Texas also advanced the most forceful repudiation of cultural sentiments as the source of patriotism. After founding his experimental community at New Harmony, Indiana, Scottish socialist Robert Owen turned his attention south. In 1828, he lobbied Mexican officials for full control of Texas. In exchange for this authority, Owen promised to create an entirely new society in Texas free from violent revolutions, religious warfare, commercial competition, and economic inequality. According to Owen, a self-described "citizen of the world," this "society is to be formed of individuals of any country, whose minds have been enlightened beyond the prejudices of all local districts."[22]

Lived cosmopolitanism at the border reconciled Mexican colonization policy with US laws of expatriation. "Good faith" was the internationally accepted
standard for expatriation, especially in republics. "Good character," the moral
essence of Hispanic naturalization law, was good faith's measure. Throughout
the 1820s, the Mexican government demanded proof of both. Although plenty
of Anglos ignored the law and settled illegally in Texas, thousands of prospective American colonists readily complied with procedures to prove that they
intended to change their loyalty for honorable reasons. As a result, a shared
acceptance of transferable allegiance eased interactions between Mexican authorities and Anglo migrants at nearly every step of the colonization process,
whether under the Mexican Empire or the republic.

Prospective colonists inquired about the nature of Mexican citizenship
when deciding if they should quit the United States. Managers of the Galveston Bay and Texas Land Company received letters that expressed such interests from several people in New York. Lyman Bostwick claimed that his
family and several others in Livonia, New York, were ready to "emigrate to
that country," but they needed more details about daily life, including an introduction to Mexican law and the presence of the Catholic Church. Nelson
Briant wrote on behalf of several families in Cazenovia, New York, deciding
between the western United States and Texas. These prospective emigrants
sought "some knowledge of the requirements and rights and privileges, civil
and political, of citizenship." Both correspondents clearly wrote for people preparing to exercise their emigrant rights to move where they chose and to expatriate themselves from the United States if necessary. As male householders
with family dependents, they confirmed their intention to establish a permanent settlement elsewhere. Their willingness to change allegiance was a given,
even without a final decision. For these prospective colonists, patriotism was
transferable. Patriotism provided a moral passport to move throughout the
world rather than a testament of their commitment to a specific nation. Only by
assuming that expatriation was a natural right could the prospective colonists
become virtuous citizens of Mexico while still abandoning the United States.[23]

Mexico's national and state colonization laws created formal mechanisms
that enabled emigrants to change their allegiance. Upon arrival in Texas, prospective colonists were supposed to submit evidence of good character, for
themselves and family members, to local colonial officials or the commissioner for a given area. Written testimony from authorities in an emigrant's
native community or that of two witnesses in Texas provided sufficient proof.
This evidence appeared in character certificates, legal documents issued by
the thousands to Texas colonists from the United States and elsewhere.

Character certificates were formulaic documents marked by common rhe-
torical structures. Unsurprisingly, these certificates typically declared that a
prospective colonist was a "man," but also in many instances a "woman," of
"good character," "very good character," or "very good morals and habits." In
Elisha Allen's case, this Louisianan brought proof that he was "a young man of
good morals and industrious habits." Mexican officials took the character certificates seriously as the basis for issuing citizenship permits.[24]

Citizenship permits documented that a prospective colonist swore loyalty
to the Mexican government. As the Nacogdoches alcalde, Encarnacion
Chirino authorized hundreds of citizenship permits for Anglo settlers during
the 1820s, thus finalizing their expatriation process. Virginian John S. Roberts
obtained Mexican citizenship in 1828 after residing in Nacogdoches for two
years, "in which he has justified his good behavior." Jacob Garrett appealed
for citizenship in Nacogdoches in 1827 by stating his desire to "dispose of the
procedures that an adoptive man has to do in this country." As such Garrett
provided evidence documenting that he moved to Texas "with his family
with the intention of settling and to be a citizen of the country" and that he
had obeyed local laws since arriving, "as should all good citizens."[25]

Character certificates and citizenship permits catalog the intent and willingness of thousands of early national Americans to exchange US citizenship
for Mexican citizenship. Of course the banal, formulaic language of these
documents may signify nothing more than self-interested individuals following legal procedures for personal gain. Yet in a culture in which oath-taking
and character were closely linked to Christian teachings about future rewards
and punishments, it should not be assumed that the colonists or the authorities who vouched for them took these certificates lightly. Rather, character
certificates and citizenship permits were essential to a colonization process
that demanded emigrants change their political and religious allegiances.
From an Anglo perspective, these certificates and permits confirmed that
they left the United States in good faith, thus protecting their actions according to the laws of expatriation. Tejano authorities who authorized these documents reaffirmed their relatively open conception of who qualified as a
potential Mexican citizen. These documents added legal authority to the
pragmatic cosmopolitanism that Tejano officials and Anglo settlers shared.
Character certificates and citizenship permits thus approximated actual
moral passports uniquely suited to movement and settlement in the Texas
borderlands.

Individual petitions for Texas land included other attributes that indicated
a person's ability to become a good Mexican citizen. In Eli Russel's petition,

he emphasized his family of four, his arrival to Texas, and his intention "to settle myself permanently" as proof that he satisfied the requirements of the 1825 colonization law. Although unstated, his petition also demonstrated Russel's abidance with the various legal standards for expatriation. Petitions for land in Scottish empresario Arthur Wavell's faltering colony included personal details and standard language. Each petition amounted to a public statement of the petitioner's desire to take the oath of allegiance to Mexico along with confirmation that the petitioner had emigrated from the United States. The petitions also included information about the person's occupation, family, and enslaved property. Jesse Watson emigrated from Kentucky with his family and two enslaved people, while J. L. Phillips quit Alabama with his family and sixty-six enslaved people. As in other borderlands regions, newcomers to Texas sought the privileges of emigration right citizenship on the standing brought by human passports. The reproductive labor of women and the productive labor of enslaved people provided the foundation for these men to become landholding Mexican citizens. Indeed, this was the legal framework for Benjamin Beeson's Mexican citizenship. He and his wife Elizabeth emigrated from the United States in 1823. Five years later he owned a flourishing farm on the Colorado River. According to a Mexican official not sympathetic to Anglo colonization, the Beesons were "very honorable" settlers. More importantly, Elizabeth and the Beesons' teenage daughter spoke "Spanish well enough to be understood in conservation." In every apparent way, the Beesons were ideal Mexican citizens who had fully expatriated themselves from the United States. The exercise of emigration right citizenship in Texas thus reinforced freedom of movement and expatriation as privileges that generally belonged only to free white men.[26]

However, the legal boundaries on emigrant rights were not absolute in Mexican Texas. Harriet H. Wright included herself among the petitioners for land in the Wavell Colony. She was a widow from the Arkansas Territory who intended to settle with her family and an enslaved person. Mary Paxton, a widow from Auburn, Missouri, wrote Stephen F. Austin in 1831 because she had "some idea of moving to your part of the world provided you write me a satisfactory answer" to questions concerning a variety of subjects including soil quality and the legal status of slavery. Both were important to Paxton because she intended to quit the United States with her five children and four enslaved people. Wright and Paxton approached their emigrant rights whereas Keziah Taylor exercised them without question. Taylor was a widowed landowner also from the Arkansas Territory. Early in the 1830s, she stated her intention to leave for the "Spanish country" never to return to the United States. Along with personal property and her children, Taylor quit the United States with an enslaved girl who belonged to the estate of her deceased husband. Taylor's emigration was ultimately an effort to abscond with the enslaved girl who lived in her household but did not belong to her by law. In all three instances, widowhood gave women property rights and authority over children that empowered them to claim emigrant rights as well. Similar to white men, these white women gained emigrant rights by denying the same to enslaved people.[27]

Because of land and dowry disputes involving women in Texas, US courts were forced to consider questions of white women's emigrant rights. Keziah Taylor's emigration became part of the legal record in a property case decided by the Supreme Court of Arkansas in which the judges relied on expatriation law. The Kentucky Court of Appeals addressed the question directly. The first case involved Leah Alsberry. Alsberry and her husband quit the United States for Mexico in 1824. Thomas Alsberry died in 1826 but she remained in Texas until 1836 when she returned to her native Kentucky and filed suit for property that she claimed as part of her dowry. Kentucky courts denied her suit on the assertion that "expatriation may be considered a practical and fundamental doctrine of America." Alsberry's life in Texas proved unequivocally that she had expatriated herself according to all the commonly understood meanings of the term. She moved to Texas when it was a Mexican state, and she voluntarily remained in Texas for several years. Both facts combined suggested to the court that Alsberry intended to reside in Texas permanently since she and her husband had "identified their fortunes with those of that community, and as constituent members of that body politic." Since they had publicly announced their desire to leave Kentucky and then done so with good intentions, the Alsberrys also expatriated themselves according to Kentucky law. Once in Texas they created a permanent residence and established a family. Thomas Alsberry exercised his emigrant rights to settle in Texas and adopt Mexican citizenship, a choice that forever changed his wife's legal status. In the court's words, when a "citizen has, in good faith, abjured his country, and become a subject or citizen of a foreign nation, he should, as to his native government, be considered as denationalized."[28]

The same court ruled in the opposite way in a case involving Martha Moore. Moore settled in Texas in 1838 with her husband, a man who intended "to become permanently a citizen of that Republic, and to renounce his citizenship of the United States." Moore's husband died in 1840 and she returned to Kentucky to live and possess dowry property. Unlike Alsberry, she did not choose to remain an alien to the United States. Martha Moore's choice to live in Kentucky after she became a widow thus convinced the court to rule in her favor. As the court explained in its ruling, "if expatriation be a matter of election, a wife who as in duty bound, has shared the lot of her husband, and abides by his choice during coverture, ought to be allowed upon its termination, to have the privilege of electing for herself, and of fixing, by her election, not only her future, but her past character." Moore's decision to move freely across borders thus forced the Kentucky court to announce the existence and articulate the conditions of white women's emigrant rights. Although limited to a single legal opinion, Martha Moore's case shows that choices taken in Texas during the 1830s could define the limits of citizenship far from the borderlands. Indeed, throughout the 1820s and 1830s events in Texas challenged the limits of emigrant rights in the borderlands and beyond.[29]

AMERICAN COLONIZATION IN TEXAS generated predictions about the future of political power on the US and Mexican border. In 1825, a writer in the *Washington City Gazette* lamented emigration from the United States to Texas, but he noted that expatriation "is one of the fundamental principles of our government." Although the American government could not legally prohibit its people from becoming Mexican citizens in Texas, there was still room for nationalistic optimism. It was possible, the article concluded, "that our citizens will carry with them their love for their country, and thus are in fact preparing gradually, for the certain annexation of Texas to the U. States." In 1829, Mier y Terán also described Anglo designs for Texas. According to the general, "There is no power like that to the north, which by silent means has made conquests of momentous importance. . . . Instead of armies, battles, or invasions—which make a great noise and for the most part are unsuccessful—these men lay hand on means that, if considered one by one, would be rejected as slow, ineffective, and at times palpably absurd. They begin by assuming rights, as in Texas." For both observers, future conflicts at the border would arise from the same sources that created a transnational legal zone in the region. Citizens must quit the United States in order for the United States to eventually gain Texas.[30]

Subsequent events in northern Mexico proved that both of these predictions were prescient in essential ways. Mier y Terán was among the most important Mexican officials who remained doubtful that existing colonization policies had or eventually would secure Mexico's northern provinces within the republic. This pessimism stemmed from mounting evidence that northern Mexicans had tenuous allegiances to the national government.

In the winter of 1826–27, Anglo Americans and their Cherokee allies in east Texas rebelled against Mexican authority. Like many conflicts in colonial

Texas, land was at issue. In November 1826, the state government of Coahuila and Texas revoked a colonization charter it had granted to the region's most influential empresario, Haden Edwards. Government actions infuriated Edwards and his settlers. Moreover, Cherokees in the region faced their own difficulties securing land grants, so they concluded that the government's decision also jeopardized their Texas land claims. On December 21, 1826, Cherokee leaders Richard Fields and John Dunn Hunter joined American emigrants in declaring independence for the Republic of Fredonia. Only a relatively small number of Anglos supported the nascent republic while the Cherokee majority renounced Fields and Dunn's alliance with Hayden Edwards and his brother Benjamin. Nevertheless, the Fredonians had grand ambitions. Fredonia's boundaries would include all of Texas, divided into a northern region allocated to "Red People" and southern region for "White People."[31]

Opponents judged the Fredonians by the standards of legitimate expatriation. A diplomatic mission on behalf of Anglo colonists and the Mexican government traveled to Nacogdoches, Texas, in January 1827. The Fredonians flatly refused the government's amnesty and reiterated their opposition to a tyrannical Mexican government. The rebels' obstinacy was not surprising, the mission reported. "There is scarcely one of the perverse party that has any property; not one slaveholder among them, but many vagabonds and fugitives from justice, who have fled from the United States of the North, and who have so shamefully debased the American character." Without human passports to vouch for their good character, the report suggested, the rebels lacked respectability that came from slave ownership, a value imported from the southern United States, and their behavior seemingly confirmed the fears of expatriation's American critics that lofty ideals about natural rights to move freely throughout the world actually provided cover to criminals. Inhabitants of the DeWitt Colony issued a series of resolutions condemning the Fredonian uprising as the actions of "those of bad character, whom we consider as refugees, and fugitives from justice." They hoped that the Mexican government would not confuse the rebels with the hardworking and "peaceable American emigrants" who had willingly exchanged citizenship in one republic for that in another. Further, the DeWitt colonists reaffirmed "that their great object in leaving their parent country, and migrating hither, was not for the purpose of unsheathing the sword of Insurrection, war, bloodshed, and desolation, but as peaceable and industrious subjects."[32]

By transforming voluntary allegiance from a pragmatic principle into justification for a visionary cause, the Fredonians voided their rights to the body politic. Austin worried that if the Fredonians were not stopped, their actions would mar American character in the eyes of Mexican officials. With such valuable cultural currency at stake, could future emigrants from the North possibly demonstrate their good morals and intentions as the colonization laws required? Austin did not believe so. He labeled the Fredonians "infatuated madmen" set on sowing disorder and violence, and, according to Austin, it was "our duty as Mexicans, to support and defend the government of our adoption."[33]

Although frightening to Anglo elites in Texas, the Fredonian Rebellion proved weak. National troops along with militias from the Austin and DeWitt colonies entered east Texas to forcibly capture the rebellion's leaders, Haden and Benjamin W. Edwards. Both escaped to Louisiana and the uprising ended within a few weeks. Anglo colonists joined Mexican troops to suppress the Fredonian Rebellion because shared ideas of voluntary allegiance provided a legal framework for military cooperation.

The Fredonian Rebellion reflected broader secessionist sentiments and movements in several northern Mexican states. This forced the Mexican Congress to reconsider its colonization program in Texas. In light of worries that American emigration threatened Mexican authority in the North, Congress passed the Law of April 6, 1830. This law, which incorporated recommendations from Mier y Terán, increased the military presence in Texas, both to limit the actions of Anglos and Native Americans but also to ensure effective customs collections. Furthermore, the law prohibited new emigration from the United States and nullified all incomplete empresarario contracts.[34]

Opposition to the Law of April 6, 1830, appeared in several public complaints that Anglos issued to the Mexican government during the 1830s. In many instances, Anglos provided their grievances' moral standing by appealing to their status as emigrants. At an 1832 convention in San Felipe de Austin organized by Anglo communities throughout Texas, delegates petitioned the Mexican Congress that the Law of April 6, 1830, had "entirely paralized the advancement and prosperity of Texas." Petitioners hastened to prove their commitment to Mexico, their adopted nation. They declared that most Anglos in Texas exhibited only "good order and patriotism." Indeed, "there is not an Anglo-American, in Texas, whose heart does not beat high for the prosperity of the Mexican Republic," the petition gushed. The petitioners protested the Law of April 6, 1830, because it implied "a suspicion of our fidelity to the Mexican Constitution." Following an 1832 Anglo uprising at Anahuac against tariff provisions in the April 6, 1830, law, John Austin, the Austin colony's new alcalde, dismissed rumors that his community sought independence from Mexico. "We are Mexicans by adoption, we are the same in heart—and will so remain." According to these public statements, the reforms passed by the increasingly centralist Mexican Congress suggested that American emigrants could not be trusted with citizenship privileges. However, federalists temporarily returned to power, so the Mexican Congress rescinded its ban on emigration from the United States in 1833, a decision overshadowed by a major shift within Mexican politics.[35]

Throughout the early 1830s centralist politicians came to dominate federalist politicians in the Mexican Congress. This shift culminated in 1835 when Congress, with the support of President Antonio López de Santa Anna, introduced a series of centralist constitutional reforms that significantly altered the Constitution of 1824, in particular by proscribing states' rights. This change in Mexico City intensified divisions between Mexico's northern states, especially the federalist stronghold Coahuila and Texas, and its central and southern states. Anglo discontent over colonization policy—as well as disputes regarding tariffs, military establishments in Texas, and their limited local autonomy from Coahuila—merged with efforts by local Mexican officials to defend federalism from what appeared to be an overreaching central government.[36]

Conflicts between federalists and centralists challenged older agreements about the nature of allegiance. Mexican centralists took a cautious view of voluntary allegiance; they were more likely to understand patriotism as a product of common culture. As a result, centralist officials expressed increasingly critical views about Anglo colonization. Although Anglo colonists and Mexican federalists cooperated to challenge centralism, by 1835 Anglo opinion in Texas also fractured over different views of allegiance. Moderate Anglos, eventually labeled "tories" or members of the "peace party," waged the political conflicts of the 1830s according to their standing as loyal Mexican citizens and good emigrants. More radical Anglo colonists also claimed the rights of voluntary allegiance but as rights that only applied to Anglos. Ironically, then, pro-independence Anglos adopted a view of patriotism not unlike their centralist Mexican opponents. Once that occurred, by early 1836, older forms of Tejano-Anglo cooperation became far more difficult in Texas.[37]

As conflict between centralists and federalists accelerated in 1835, appeals to the good character of Anglo emigrants served Anglo colonists as well as Tejano federalist officials. In July 1835, inhabitants of Mina, Texas, issued a proclamation expressing reservations about the Mexican government's recent policies while simultaneously recommitting themselves to the Mexican nation. We "are voluntary citizens of the same Republic; have sworn to support the same Constitution; and are, by inclination and interest, as well as the most solemn obligation, bound to cherish and sustain the liberal and free in-stitutions of this Republic." Coahuila and Texas's staunch federalist governor Agustín Viesca sought Anglo emigrant support by warning that the centralist Mexican government had abandoned the republic's earlier recognition of the right to expatriation for all people and the moral worth of Anglo emigrants in particular. "The party now in power," Viesca direly predicted in 1835, "the same that prohibited the emigration of North American colonists in 1830, has openly declared against all foreigners and secretly favors Spanish policy and Spanish despotism. The law of April 6 is about to be renewed under a still more drastic form." Agreement among elites in Texas that expatriation was a natural right for all thus provided an important intellectual and political ad-hesive in federalist Coahuila and Texas because it bound Anglo colonists and Tejano officials to a shared set of commitments regarding the interests of northern Mexicans.[38]

Questions of allegiance became urgent once more in the summer of 1835. In June, William B. Travis led an armed force that seized the garrison at Anahuac. Direct attacks on Mexican authority that summer compelled many Anglo settlers to publicly reaffirm their loyalty to Mexico. Mexican military officers initially responded to Anahuac by attempting to sort out the loyal colonists from the subversives in their midst. Other Anglos defended Travis and his band. In the aftermath of Anahuac, all sides questioned the Anglo colonists' true allegiances. Critics often cast the loyalties of Travis and those who seized Anahuac in the darkest tones. They were essentially pirates since they had behaved without allegiance to a state or a sovereign.

Many Anglo settlers in the region quickly condemned the attack. Resi-dents of Columbia, Mina, and Gonzales issued separate resolutions that shared much in common. Most importantly, they recognized that proof of their Mexican patriotism required them to remain good emigrants. They had no recourse to cultural or ethnic bonds of allegiance such as Mexican ances-try, birth, language, or even religion. After all, they were voluntary citizens of Mexico. Anglo residents thus disclaimed Travis and his followers by raising the standard of patriotic allegiance that all emigrants valued the most. As ex-pressed by the citizens of Columbia, it was "a strict adherence to the laws and constitution of the land." The people of Mina affirmed a similar view. Accord-ing to one of their resolutions, "we feel an entire confidence in the constitu-tion & laws of our adopted country, & will at all times sustain the legal authorities in the exercise of their constitutional duties." Representatives from San Felipe assured Domingo de Ugartechea, the Mexican commander at Béxar, "that the citizens of Texas generally have become adopted citizens of the Mexican Republic from choice, after a full knowledge of the constitution and laws." On their foundation of sturdy Mexican patriotism, the representatives vowed to fulfill their duties as "Mexican citizens, in the enforcement of the laws and promotion of order, and respect for the government and its agents." On the other hand, Travis and his followers forfeited the possibility of remaining Mexican citizens. They were "foreigners" according to a resolution issued by the people of Columbia.[39]

Mexican authorities also addressed violence at Anahuac by distinguishing between loyal emigrants and subversive outsiders with allegiance to nothing but self-interest. From his perspective in Mexico City, the republic's head of foreign affairs, Manuel Diez de Bonilla, reminded Anglo colonists in Texas to remain good emigrants since they "on adopting this for their country, subjected themselves to the alternations that, respecting the institutions, the majority of the nation may think fit to agree upon." The situation in Texas had greater urgency for Martín Perfecto de Cos, the commanding general of the Eastern Interior Provinces. He issued several statements during the summer of 1835 regarding Anglo actions in Texas. In a private correspondence to Domingo de Ugartechea, Cos explained that his order to disband Anglo militias in Texas targeted "foreigners" with "no property save a gun and no occupation save hunting," not loyal Mexican citizens. Cos reiterated this distinction in a general proclamation to the people of Texas. He warned them to expect a military response if they forgot "their duties to the nation which has adopted them as her children" and pushed "forward with a desire to live at their own option without any subjection to the laws." Those Anglos "who are fauthful to their oaths and to the Laws" were obligated, Cos explained in another statement, to assist the Mexican government in punishing "the faithless adventurers who have nothing to risque in a revolucion." Cos included Travis among the latter category for seeking to mobilize those in Texas "without a home, without moralities or any employment by which to subsist." Claiming to serve the Mexican government, Thomas M. Thompson issued a personal warning to the citizens of Anahuac in July 1835. "Beware!" Thompson exclaimed, "listen not to men who have no home, who have no family who have nothing to loose [sic] in case of civil war and who by merely crossing the Sabine, can put themselves out of the power of the Mexican Nation." Instead, Thompson advised the citizens of Anahuac to remain good emigrants: "Occupy yourselves in your daily avocations for the maintenance of your family, have confidence in the General Government and all will yet be well." In their responses to the uprising at Anahuac, Mexican officials from the nation's capital to its frontier relied on the principle of voluntary allegiance to reassure loyal Anglo settlers and punish the disloyal by treating them as subversive outsiders.[40]

Those involved in the attack on Anahuac disputed how their actions were portrayed by other Anglos and Mexican officials. Mexican authorities arrested and imprisoned Anahuac merchant Andrew Briscoe in 1835 for engaging in illegal trade. The attack on Anahuac bought Briscoe's freedom. This, along with Briscoe's existing opposition to Mexican customs policies in Texas, gave him good reason to seek public vindication for Travis and his supporters. Briscoe took special umbrage at claims by the people of Columbia that Anahuac fell to a band of foreigners. Rather, Briscoe charged in a letter to the Brazoria *Texas Republican* that "some twenty or twenty-five men were present, of whom but two were strangers or foreigners, and they both own land in the country and intend to become citizens." For Briscoe, the two individuals whose loyalty seemed most dubious were on a path to becoming Mexican citizens by taking the essential steps of expatriation that supposedly severed prior national allegiances. Protestations of emigrant loyalty proved equally meaningful to Briscoe and his Anglo opponents. Moreover, Briscoe's position points to a view that became increasingly important among more radical Anglo settlers. Although colonists asserted their loyalty as Mexican citizens, revolutionary action might be necessary to protect their Mexican liberties from centralist corruption.[41]

Indeed throughout late summer 1835, the public and private statements of Anglos stretched the concept of voluntary allegiance to accommodate stronger claims about their rights in Mexico. Yet even then, the colonists' need to prove their good intentions as emigrants, as voluntary Mexicans, tempered their politics. The San Jacinto Resolutions of August 1835 declared that centralists in Mexico City destroyed the republic's social compact. Whether fueled by popular memory of the American Revolution or an education in natural rights political philosophy, the resolutions asserted that Anglo colonists were correct to declare independence from Mexico. The people of San Jacinto demurred, however. Declaring independence would open them to charges of "parricidal ingratitude." Rather, "as adopted citizens, we ought to exercise even our absolute rights with some diffidence, and with a peculiar regard to the moral obligations that may rest upon us." A visit to New Orleans and an audience of US citizens put Stephen F. Austin in an insurrectionary mood befitting his long experience in Mexico. Austin wrote forcefully about his desire to see Texas "Americanized" in a series of letters he sent in August 1835. For Austin, Americanization would occur through increased but legal settlement under Mexican law, not an armed invasion. "A gentle breeze shakes off a

ripe peach," Austin famously quipped. "All that is now wanting is a great immigration of good and efficient families, this fall and winter. Should we get
such an emigration, especially from the western states—all is done—the peach
will be ripe." Revolutionary gales were unnecessary while expatriation remained an option.[42]

When the Consultation finally convened in November 1835, Texas was in
open rebellion against Mexico but far from ready to declare full independence.
The Declaration of the People of Texas, adopted quickly by the Consultation,
betrayed deep political uncertainty about Texas's future. Only a month earlier,
the Mexican Congress had abolished state governments and put governors
under the control of the president. In response to this act, along with previous
grievances, the delegates announced that centralists under López de Santa
Anna had "dissolved the Social Compact" binding Texas to the rest of Mexico.
The people of Texas were thus free to assume their "natural rights" and pro-
ceed collectively however they saw fit. Assertions of emigrant rights became
more powerful amid the deep political uncertainty of the moment.[43]

After they asserted their right to act autonomously, the delegates issued
several resolutions. They embedded the concept of voluntary allegiance in
two of them. The first declared that Texans had armed themselves against the
sitting national government in defense of the liberties granted them by the
Constitution of 1824. Anglos interpreted this provision in a variety of ways
until Texas declared formal independence in March 1836. The delegates also
adopted a resolution designed to gain support for the Texas cause. The declaration made this an official aim of the rebellion by promising to "reward by donations in land, all who volunteer their services in her present struggle, and receive
them as citizens." Under this provision, the revolutionary leadership assumed
naturalization authority but also validated the principle of voluntary allegiance.
The delegates effectively called for emigrants to join the uprising. The declaration's provisions regarding allegiance to the Constitution of 1824 and its call for
volunteers were related efforts to carry forth an emigrant rights rebellion against
Mexican sovereignty. However, these provisions also raised issues that divided
Anglo opinion about the meaning of voluntary allegiance.[44]

By recognizing the Constitution of 1824, the Consultation reiterated the
claim that Anglos were patriotic, voluntary Mexicans. This position appealed
to Anglos who still wanted reconciliation with Mexico by providing an opportunity to form alliances with other Mexicans opposed to centralist policies. In a moment of moderation, Stephen F. Austin argued in December 1835
that Texas colonists should seek alliances with Mexican federalists in defense
of the Constitution of 1824. With this position they could preserve their

standing as loyal but aggrieved citizens rather than belligerents in an independent republic. If independence became the Anglos' only demand, then the centralists could easily place the "Texas war on the footing of a national war against foreigners and adventurers whose object is to dismember the Mexican territory." The Consultation thus set a pragmatic course for its dealings with the Mexican government by recognizing a political conceit essential to notions of voluntary allegiance. Patriotism did not require seemingly immutable ethnic, religious, or cultural qualities; it meant simply obeying the Constitution of 1824.[45]

Loyalty to the Constitution of 1824 persisted into 1836. In January, James Kerr authored a strident statement rejecting calls for independence. His position rested on two claims, one practical and the other moral. In practical terms, Texas could not survive as an independent republic. The financial burdens would be too great, war with Mexico would persist, the economy would suffer, and the nation's overall weakness would expose it to the depredations of foreign powers. In short, Texas needed to remain in Mexico to prosper. Moreover, Kerr argued that Anglo colonists had moral reasons to remain loyal. Anglo colonists had sworn loyalty oaths in order to become Mexican citizens, thereby expatriating themselves from the United States. The current political crisis elevated the colonists' obligations to honor their oaths. A threatened nation needed loyal citizens. Anglo colonists should support their fellow Mexican citizens, the federalist insurgents fighting to defend the Constitution of 1824 in other parts of the republic. Kerr warned Anglos in Texas not "to forget your duty as adopted citizens of Mexico." By abandoning their allegiance to Mexico, "christians and freeman" would treat the Texans "as a people not to be trusted, as having no respect for oaths, or compacts, or honor." Moreover, Kerr advised his fellow colonists that their actions had a global audience. Observers the world over were watching "your movements for the purpose of determining whether or not you have been governed by the selfish desire of promoting your own individual views, and robbing Mexico of her lands; or been influenced by the high, and laudable, and patriotic feelings, inducing a peril of life and property in defence of liberty and the Constitution of 1824." Thus for Kerr, Anglos had no choice but to fulfill their obligations as Mexican citizens. Although some Anglos such as Kerr used the principle of voluntary allegiance in political arguments for continued loyalty to Mexico, others used it to justify more radical steps.[46]

The opinions of Anglo military leaders also divided over differing ideas about the meaning of voluntary allegiance. Francis W. Johnson, the Anglo commander of Béxar, still maintained in early 1836 that the rebellion was a defense of the Constitution of 1824 and Texas's integral place as Mexican province. His call to arms on behalf of the volunteer army drew upon a concept of allegiance predicated on law-abiding citizens and commitment to principles of liberty. Anyone, in Johnson's view, could become a loyal soldier in the struggle to protect the Texans' Mexican liberties. This included Tejanos. As Johnson proclaimed, the people of Texas "invite into their ranks all friends to freedom, of whatever name or nation." The authors of a military report issued only a month earlier viewed the conflict in starkly different terms. Texans were in a battle for independence. After all, "the Mexican people and the Anglo-Americans in Texas never can be one and the same people. A civil compact can never bind together long people who differ so widely in their pursuits, their religion, their Languages and their ideas of civil liberty." From this perspective, patriotic allegiance to the Texas cause could only come from those bound to the Anglo colonists by blood and culture. A group of volunteers from the United States who arrived in February 1836 thus seemed fully justified in demanding local voting rights by "claiming Texas as our adopted country."[47]

Anglos who demanded full Texas independence in early 1836 also recognized the colonists' standing as emigrants. Members of the Committee of Vigilance and Public Safety from San Augustine acknowledged their emigration from the United States under Mexico's colonization laws but attributed their success at building communities in the "uninhabited wilderness" to "individual enterprise, entirely unaided by succors of any kind, from the government." This statement contained no accolades to their adopted country or their duties as voluntary citizens. Rather, the authors indicted the Mexican government for its efforts to abolish slavery and its passage of the Law of April 6, 1830. As a result, "families and nearest ties of kindred and friendship were thus severed." William H. Wharton developed a similar argument in a series of newspaper articles written under the pseudonym "Curtius." He also found the Law of April 6, 1830, highly egregious even though it was consistent with Article 6 of the 1825 Coahuila and Texas colonization law, which reserved the government's prerogative to prohibit future emigrants from settling in the province. By forbidding only "North Americans" entrance into Texas, this law, Wharton exclaimed, "was enough to blast all of our hopes, and dishearten all of our enterprise." The law raised the frightening prospect that the Anglo colonists would "be cut off forever from the society of fathers and friends in the United States of the North." The San Augustine committee and Wharton interpreted the history of Anglo colonization in Texas in such a way to minimize the depth of their obligations as Mexican citizens.[48]

In denying their loyalty to Mexico, the San Augustine committee members and Wharton advanced an idea of patriotic allegiance that differed widely from the views of more moderate Anglos. The San Augustine Address completely elided Mexican Texas's complex politics. It ignored divisions between federalists and centralists as well as reference to the Tejano elites who made Anglo colonization possible during the 1820s. Instead, the authors derided all Mexicans. "The anglo Americans and the Mexicans, if not primitively a different people, habit, education, and religion, have made them essentially so. The two people cannot mingle together." For these reasons, the authors concluded, so "long as the people of Texas belong to the Mexican nation, their interests will be jeopardized, and their prosperity cramped." Wharton agreed, since "none of those ties which are necessary to bind a people together and make them one, existed between the colonists and Mexicans." Among the many intractable differences between the two peoples, several were cultural. Wharton believed that the colonists and Mexicans shared "no identity of pursuits, habits, manners, education, language or religion." The Anglos could not become voluntary Mexicans because respect for the law was a weak cohesive for people divided by vast cultural differences. Members of the San Augustine Committee and Wharton all concluded that Anglos migrated to Texas in order to strengthen the region's connections to the United States. In their estimation, Anglo colonists did not so much quit the United States for Texas as hope to recreate a familiar society there. They wanted to prepare the way for family and friends to follow, thereby populating Texas with like people. Once the Mexican government took steps to deny the colonists' ambitions, independence was their only recourse.[49]

This resulted in the Unanimous Declaration of Independence made by the Delegates of the People of Texas, ratified on March 2, 1836. Indebted heavily to the United States' Declaration of Independence, this was Texas's appeal before world public opinion for acceptance as a sovereign republic in the international order. This document described Anglo Texans as emigrants who adopted Mexican citizenship in good faith only to have the centralist government overturn the political system that protected their rights. Indeed, "the federal republican constitution of their country, which they have sworn to support, no longer has a substantial existence." Events in March 1836 led Anglo supporters of independence to create the Republic of Texas, thereby dissolving their allegiance to Mexico. Anglos opposed to independence eventually acquiesced, but Mexican federalist officials and Tejanos were bitterly divided over Texas secession. Some from both sides eventually allied with the Texas Republic. In a telling shift of allegiance, Francisco Ruiz, the early supporter of Anglo colonization, signed the declaration, becoming one of the prominent Tejanos responsible for creating the

Texas Republic, a testament to the lasting power of pragmatic cosmopolitanism in the borderlands.[50]

ULTIMATELY, THE TEXAS INSURRECTION was deeply rooted in the borderlands' legal culture created by emigrant rights claims. Anglos on both sides of the conflict over Texas independence were emigrants who used this status to shape their arguments. Tejanos, as heirs to Spanish customs of naturalization and early defenders of colonization, brought their own ideas about malleable allegiance to bear on events in the 1830s. Established principles of international law and ideals of world citizenship preceded inchoate sentiments of American nationalism in the origins of the Texas insurrection. Mexico lost a northern province to rebels versed in the moral and political language of changing citizenship. Although they backed their rhetoric with arms, emigrant rights vindicated their conquest. What became known as the Texas Revolution was not, however, a singular event. Political unrest occurred in the British colonies of Upper and Lower Canada during the 1830s. Together, these events gave the appearance of a general emigrant uprising in North America's borderlands.

CHAPTER SEVEN

Lawless Spirits

In January 1838, Kentucky congressman Richard Menefee delivered a lengthy speech at the Capitol warning about the "lawless spirit" that prevailed on the nation's borders. The United States was not, however, threatened by violent outsiders determined to breach its territory. In fact, Menefee's concerns were just the opposite. The nation's enemies were insiders. Citizens of the United States, Menefee believed, posed the gravest threat to border security in North America.[1]

Although the United States was at peace with Mexico and Great Britain in the 1830s, US citizens joined rebellions against each nation, first in Texas in 1835 and two years later in Canada. US citizens who participated in neighboring rebellions raised contentious legal and political questions. From the perspective of Menefee and others like him, volunteers from the United States violated neutrality provisions under national and international law. Their actions threatened to "kindle a war at the two extremities of our overgrown empire," warned a Rhode Island newspaper editor. However, actions that seemed lawless by the diplomatic standards of the day seemed entirely lawful when judged by an equally strong legal standard. As recognized by Menefee's fellow Kentuckian, Senator Henry Clay, US citizens were obligated to obey the laws of their nation, but they might also "choose to renounce their citizenship and enter into the concerns of foreign states." In other words, a right to expatriation without restraint allowed US citizens to join rebellions at their borders. According to this view, officials in the United States could not prohibit citizens from joining foreign rebellions because free people were entitled to grant their loyalty to any power they chose. A claim to what some identified as "insurgents' rights" militarized established emigrant rights to free movement and expatriation.[2]

Emigrant rights had defined life in the North American borderlands since the 1780s. These rights underpinned the colonization policies created by Spain in the lower Mississippi Valley, by British colonial officials for Lower and Upper Canada in 1791, and by the Republic of Mexico for Texas in 1824. These policies attracted settlers from the United States, where legal and popular opinion strongly favored robust rights to free movement and expatriation. The Texas and Canadian rebellions thus occurred in regions shaped for years by a widely shared belief in a free person's emigrant rights. American volunteers for each conflict and those who supported them justified their participation as the exercise of emigration right citizenship. Over the course of the rebellions, a person's relative right to change political allegiance shaped how various government officials, observers, and insurgents approached armed political revolutions in North America.

IN EARLY 1836, large numbers of volunteers from the United States entered Texas to join the rebellion against Mexico. Most of the volunteers answered a request for foreign support from the Consultation, a quasi-sovereign body that in the autumn of 1835 assumed the powers of a provisional government for Texas. During the Texas rebellion, over 3,500 men fought on the Texas side. Of this total force, nearly 1,000 were US volunteers. Anglo-Texans comprised the majority of the remaining forces along with roughly 138 Tejanos, who fought primarily under Tejano officers such as Juan N. Seguín. The vast majority of Anglos and Tejanos avoided participating in the conflict altogether. The composition of Texas's revolutionary army highlights the far-reaching consequences of the Consultation's decision to offer citizenship to foreign volunteers. Despite the provision's universal language, the majority of volunteers came from the United States, ultimately comprising 40 percent of the total fighting force. Moreover, an additional 34 percent of the Texan army had arrived in Texas no more than five years earlier.[3]

The relative newcomers and the American volunteers who comprised such a large proportion of the fighting force exercised a strong influence over changing ideas of allegiance as the war progressed. For many Anglos who fought in the Texas insurgency, a notion that they were voluntary Mexicans had a weak to nonexistent hold on their understanding of the larger conflict. As the new volunteers declared in February, they were voluntary Texans instead. George C. Childress's opinions suggest how volunteer Texans understood the cause they joined. Childress visited Texas for the first time in late 1834 and only returned in December 1835. For him, any idea that Mexico was the colonists' adopted country seemed meaningless. Texas colonists should have declared their independence from the outset rather than maintaining their loyalty. As Childress explained to Sam Houston, "The contest for the Constitution of 1824 was, you know, but a mere *pretence* from the beginning," part of a deeply misguided hope for assistance from other parts of Mexico where the inhabitants "are but a semi-civilized set, unfit to be free and incapable of self government." For a voluntary Texan, patriotism meant allegiance to people with ties of blood and culture to the United States, not support for a vanished political ideal such as loyalty to the Constitution of 1824.[4]

North America, ca. 1835

Anglos began to seek support in the United States even before the Consultation convened. In late October 1835, Richard R. Royall issued what might be called an emigrant's lament in pursuit of American support for a quasi-independent Texas. "We have wandered where danger and tyranny threaten us," pleaded Royall. Although Anglo colonists had "expatriated themselves from their native country, torn themselves from connexions dear, given up the conveniences and luxuries of life, and encountered for years back toils and dangers and privations of every sort," the centralist government of Mexico abolished the Constitution of 1824 that had secured their liberties as Mexican citizens. Royall reminded citizens of the United States that "you are united to us by all the sacred ties that can bind one people to another . . . we are alients to you only in country; our principles both moral and political are the same—our interest is one, and we require and ask your aid." Views such as Royall's became more pronounced once volunteers from the United States began arriving in response to the Consultation's call for outside support.[5]

The Consultation appointed a diplomatic mission to the United States to stoke support for Texas. The delegation consisted of William H. Wharton, Branch T. Archer, and Texas's most prominent Anglo emigrant, Stephen F. Austin. The Texas diplomats left for the United States in late December 1835 and remained there until June 1836. During their six-month mission, they stopped in major western cities including New Orleans, Louisville, Nashville, and Cincinnati. They also fanned north and south along the East Coast. Austin drummed the Texas cause from Baltimore to New York. Archer sought support in Richmond, Virginia. Wharton remained in Washington, DC, to measure official opinion about events in Texas. The Consultation instructed the diplomats to muster money and men—by contracting loans, accepting donations, and recruiting volunteers. Texas's diplomatic delegation had limited success, yet enthusiasm for Texas in the United States made their work less onerous.[6]

Observers in the United States quickly learned about growing political unrest in Texas. Segments of the population just as quickly organized public meetings, donated money, and formed volunteer units who set off for Texas. The Texas diplomats attended these meetings whenever possible. New Orleans and Mobile, Alabama, hosted the earliest and some of the largest public gatherings. Texas boosters in the rest of the nation followed suit. Texas volunteers eventually organized themselves throughout the South and West, and as far north as New York and Boston. In an article for the New York press, a writer using the pseudonym "Citizen of New Orleans" explained the background and aims of the public meeting in his city. Although the American colonists had "expatriated themselves to better their condition, and secure a patrimony for their children," recent developments in Mexican politics threatened to destroy the liberties that colonists had once enjoyed. At such a dire moment in Texas, efforts to "prevent United States citizens from volunteering to assist their brethren and blood" were "Anti-American." Americans could not ignore the Texans' plight. According to a somewhat exaggerated New York newspaper report from the autumn of 1835, a "very considerable number of men are leaving various parts of our country for Texas, taking with them the arms and munitions necessary for war. Some hundreds will leave the Atlantic coast within ten days, and a still greater number will probably go from the West."[7]

Despite passionate popular support, the Texas diplomats and the organizers of public meetings engaged in a legally dubious pursuit. Under an 1818 law adopted by the US Congress, it was illegal for citizens in the United States to volunteer or recruit for military service against a foreign power at peace with the United States; to set out on military expeditions from US territory; or to organize or provide support to any entity or group at war with a peaceful nation. Foreigners were also prohibited from recruiting US citizens for conflicts against peaceful nations. In 1835, Mexico and the United States were at peace, as recently affirmed in the 1828 Treaty of Limits. Under this agreement, the two republics confirmed the location of their international border as that set by the United States and Spain in 1819. Providing material support to the rebellious Texans potentially violated domestic and international law.[8]

Officials in the United States and Mexico responded to Texas enthusiasm in the United States by stressing its illegality. Strong public support for the Texas rebellion in New Orleans prompted US Secretary of State John Forsyth's instructions to Henry Carleton, the US attorney for the Eastern District of Louisiana. Should the Texas conflict intensify, Forsyth predicted, "some of our citizens may, form their connexion with the settlers there, and from their love of enterprise and desire of change, be induced to forget their duty to their own Government and its obligations to foreign Powers." According to Forsyth, the 1818 law required all US citizens to "abstain, under every temptation, from intermeddling with the domestic disputes of other nations." Forsyth ordered Carleton to prosecute any citizen who violated their nation's treaty with Mexico by going to Texas with arms or otherwise supporting the rebellion. Louisiana governor Edward D. White issued a public proclamation in November declaring that any US citizen who crossed into Mexico to aid the rebellion invited prosecution for violating the 1818 congressional act.[9]

Officials in Mexico City protested that the Texas insurgency already violated US and international law. José María Ortiz Monasterio, Mexico's foreign minister, wrote to Forsyth that the Texas uprising would not have erupted without moral, military, and financial support from sympathizers in New Orleans. Indeed Monasterio claimed that foreign influence fomented Anglo disloyalty: "The Mexican colonists—for they are so and can be nothing else, since they have renounced their original nationality—would never dare to violate so openly their duties towards their adopted country, had they not the assurance that prompt and efficacious succors would be given them along their frontiers." Texas supporters in New Orleans ignored the basic legal fact that Anglo-Texans had expatriated themselves, that they were no longer citizens of the United States, Monasterio argued. Moreover, he accused the Texas supporters in New Orleans of merely claiming cultural allegiance to their supposed brethren in Texas in order to justify self-serving interference in Mexico's domestic affairs. Those in New Orleans sought "to give a color of American nationality to what is in fact a mere speculation of different adventurers of all kinds."[10]

By December 1835, centralist Mexican officials adopted strong measures against anybody from the United States who entered Mexico to join the rebellion in Texas. Secretary of War José María Tornel described such people as "speculators and adventurers" whose incursions into Mexico violated US laws. Tornel believed that American officials condemned the actions of individuals who entered Mexico illegally and would prosecute them if possible. There was precedent for this view. When armed citizens from the United States attempted to foment rebellion in Texas years earlier, dominant opinion in Washington, DC, held that such individuals "forfeit the distinction of citizens"; indeed "they denationalize themselves" by taking arms against a government at peace with the United States. Yet Tornel also advised Mexican authorities to take action. The government must, Tornel declared, treat and punish all foreigners who enter Mexico "armed and for the purpose of attacking our territory . . . as pirates, since they are not subjects of any nation at war with the republic nor do they militate under any recognized flag." From Tornel's point of view, volunteers from the United States were stateless rogues without emigrant rights protections.[11]

The national governments of the United States and Mexico converged on the opinion that Anglo colonists had expatriated themselves thereby becoming Mexican citizens. This was a useful diplomatic position for both sides. It allowed officials in both countries to treat the Texas rebellion as a civil war. Federal officials in the United States could thus justify their country's neutrality. After all, by recognizing the legality of expatriation, they expected Anglo settlers in Mexico to behave as patriotic citizens who obeyed the laws of their adopted country. Those who did not should expect the Mexican government to punish them. The Mexican government also expected Anglo colonists to behave like law-abiding adopted citizens. By characterizing the rebellion as a combination of Anglo settlers stirred to disloyalty by meddlers from the United States, Mexican officials felt confident that they could treat rebellious Anglo colonists appropriately while still expecting the US government to respect Mexico's national sovereignty in its efforts to crush a domestic uprising.

Popular opinion in the United States was divided over the legality of supporting the Texas insurgents. Critics of assistance largely agreed that aid to the Texas rebels in money, munitions, or volunteers violated international and domestic laws. Editors at two New England newspapers criticized resolutions in favor of the Texas revolutionaries adopted at the large public meeting in New Orleans. The editor of the *Connecticut Courant* reprinted parts of the 1818 congressional act that Texas volunteers and supporters supposedly violated. The editor of the *Farmer's Cabinet* in Amherst, New Hampshire, warned readers about the suspect motivations of their fellow citizens eager to volunteer under the mantle of shared political principles and lofty rights. "They are not all Lafeyettes who are such outwardly and professedly," concluded the *Cabinet's* cynical editor. An article in the *New York Advertiser* described the Anglo Texans' legal status in terms very similar to those used by Montaserio. They should not expect support from the United States because they had severed their claims to protection by becoming Mexican citizens. "Those inhabitants of Texas were once citizens of this country, voluntarily withdrew from their place, and put themselves under foreign jurisdiction. On them, of course, the consequences will fall, let them be favorable or otherwise." American critics of involvement in Texas affairs thus put their understanding of emigrant rights at the center of their arguments. These rights created an absolute change to the legal status of Anglo colonists—they had become Mexican citizens—so the people of the United States had no obligation to help them. Patriotic sympathy for the perceived sufferings of erstwhile countrymen was undeniable, but the law of nations was absolute. The first should be recognized but the latter could not be violated.[12]

In light of official and popular condemnations, some individuals otherwise eager to volunteer in Texas hesitated from concerns about violating the law. New Yorker H. Meigs wrote favorably to Stephen F. Austin about armed resistance against the Mexican government. Yet he declined to become directly involved. "By the Law of Nations, by Treaty with Mexico we cannot yet interfere," Meigs lamented. Near the rebellion's end, Stuart Perry of New Orleans celebrated growing popular opinion in favor of the Texas cause in the United States, but, he admitted, "There has been much apathy and enmity here—people were afraid of prosecutions by the U. States." The Texas Declaration of Independence did not remove reservations about volunteering in Texas, especially if the US government did not recognize the new republic. As George C. Childress explained to David Burnet in a letter from Nashville, "Many persons, who now feel scruples about volunteering to take part in the internal conflicts of a foreign country, would freely do so if the independence of the party with which they sympathize was recognized by the Government of their own."[13]

Texas supporters in the United States sought ways to provide assistance without violating the law. To some extent this was a moot concern by November 1835. That month judges in the US District Court for the Southern District of New York ruled that pro-Texas meetings and volunteer efforts organized in New York City did not violate the 1818 law. Yet Texas supporters in the United States still pursued their ambitions cautiously. The concept of voluntary allegiance provided them legal cover. It allowed them to honor patriotic sympathy with Anglo-Texans while opening a legal detour around the congressional act of 1818 and the United States' treaty obligations with Mexico. A writer in the New York press supported the rebellion and encouraged US citizens to participate. Indeed, it was "natural that the resistance of the settlers should be supported and maintained by thousands, not by the Government of the United States, but by thousands of individual American citizens." Declared a contributor to another paper, "It would be a lasting stigma upon the US to suffer the tyrant Santa Anna to overrun with slaughter and ruin their brethren in Texas." However, this author clarified the nature of US support: "We do not mean that the Government need interfere—but volunteers!—volunteers! shoulder your rifles and march to Texas!" The *New Orleans Bee* called for "emigrant volunteers." In each of these instances, Texas supporters suggested an answer to legal doubts about volunteering. As free individuals, they could move about as they pleased; as "emigrants" they exercised their rights to change citizenship and allegiance. Since the United States was and would likely remain at peace with Mexico, volunteers to the Texas cause had good reason to claim emigrant rights in their favor. If individuals chose to join the Texas fight and did so by abandoning their US citizenship, then they were no longer open to charges of violating US law.[14]

Proposals adopted during public meetings for Texas suggested that American volunteers exercised their right to expatriation by joining the Texas uprising. At the large New Orleans gathering, participants resolved to "aid and support" the Texas rebels "by every means in our power, consistent with duties we owe to our own government, to save them from the tyrant's military rule." Supporters in Nashville issued a public call for volunteers. However they noted that the "government of the U. States, as a government, is prohibited by the laws and policy of nations, from interfering in the internal conflicts of a foreign country, whatever be the merits of the controversy. If, therefore, they [Texans] are to receive any assistance from the people of the United States, it must be from them as individuals." American citizens could thus abide by US law but still join the Texas war so long as they proceeded to Mexico and chose to grant their allegiance to Texas's provisional government once they left the United States.[15]

Although the Texas insurgency effectively ended following General Antonio López de Santa Anna's defeat at the Battle of San Jacinto, support for the Texas cause remained strong in parts of the United States. In June 1836 a group of Nashville citizens petitioned Congress to recognize Texas independence. Regardless of congressional action, Texas "will draw from these States the means of conquering her enemy," the petitioners declared. This included money, arms, and, most importantly, volunteers. As the petitioners asserted, "Every man in the Union has the undoubted right to emigrate to Texas if he chooses." This was especially important since the petitioners believed the situation in Texas remained dire. They accused the Mexican government of "savage cruelty" for its military actions at the Alamo and Goliad. In the wake of these events, "treaties are as cobwebs in the way of the torrent of popular opinion and will." The conflict in Texas was supported in the United States "as if the war had been our own. . . . Our people felt all legal and moral obligations cancelled, and viewed the Mexicans as they did pirates on the seas—enemies to all mankind."[16]

Volunteers to Texas promised to expatriate themselves before joining the rebellion. L. R. Kenny of New Orleans provided Sydney S. Callender, a printer and occasional editor of the *Lafayette Gazette*, a letter of introduction to Stephen F. Austin. Kenny assured Austin of Callender's mettle. "Sympathizing in your Cause," Kenny announced, "he has determined to make Texas his adopted Country and to fight in her defence." On a single January day in 1836, over seventy volunteers from the United States swore an oath before Nacogdoches judge John Forbes that effectively dissolved citizenship in, and allegiance to, the United States, at least according to common understandings of the right to expatriation. Those who took the oath swore, in part, to "bear true allegiance to the provisional Government of Texas, or any future Government that may be hereafter declared."[17]

The revolutionary leadership in Texas adopted policies that enabled volunteers to expatriate themselves. Sam Houston, as the commanding general of the Texas revolutionary army, quickly incorporated a notion of voluntary allegiance into his orders for recruiting volunteers. Houston reminded his recruiting officer Amasa Turner to "advise that all forces designed for Texas associate as emigrants." In another instance Houston ordered a Texas agent to visit New Orleans with the goal of "recruiting 'Emigrants' for Texas." So it is unsurprising that authorities in Nacogdoches were well prepared to administer mass oaths of allegiance in early 1836. A month earlier, Houston had sent

Captain Isaac W. Burton to the Sabine region to establish a "recruiting station." Houston supplied Burton, and presumably Nacogdoches officials as well, with blank enlistment forms to greet all volunteers who crossed into Texas. The enlistment forms contained the oath of allegiance, thus transforming these documents into citizenship papers and evidence of naturalization. Under this system, volunteers were considered "emigrants" to avoid prosecution in the United States, but they participated in a process of expatriation recognized by various American laws since the late eighteenth century.[18]

As it transitioned from war to peace, the Republic of Texas incorporated emigrant rights into its own policy for populating the nation. The republic's constitution codified the freedom to move and choose allegiance as citizenship rights exclusive to white newcomers. Section 6 of the general provisions offered citizenship to any "free white" person who settled in Texas, established permanent residence and their good character, and swore a loyalty oath to the constitution and the republic. The constitution allowed emigrants from the United States to bring enslaved people into Texas, but free persons of "African descent, either in whole or in part," could emigrate to Texas only under special permission from Congress. Authorities in the Republic of Texas thus embraced voluntary citizenship as a principle to attract settlers provided they had the racial, and presumably, cultural qualities necessary for loyalty. When Asa Brigham, now treasurer of the Texas Republic, wrote his sister in Massachusetts in 1837, he boasted that "emigration flows in rapidly, the country is improving beyond account." Tejanos had good reason to remain skeptical about that aspect of Texas's revolutionary settlement celebrated by Brigham. In addition to the ordinary Tejanos who fought during the rebellion, prominent Tejanos José Antonio Navarro and Francisco Ruiz signed the Texas Declaration of Independence and were later elected to Congress. Tejanos participated in the rebellion but were also recognized as citizens of the republic after independence. Nevertheless, the voluntary Texans described in Brigham's letter were helping to create a society in which the terms of patriotic allegiance would prove far more racially exclusive than what had existed in Texas during the Mexican period.[19]

Although the US government did not take forceful action to prevent its citizens from joining the Texas rebellion, those who did remained in legal limbo until March 1837. President Andrew Jackson finally recognized Texas independence just before departing the White House. Joining the Texas insurgency remained legally dubious while the province's revolutionary government lacked genuine authority to naturalize foreign volunteers. Once an outside power recognized the Texas republic, volunteers legally completed their expatriation since international law transformed foreign invaders into citizens of a new sovereign nation. Military victory combined with US recognition of Texas independence allowed previously suspect activities to appear completely legal in retrospect. The lawless invasion of a sovereign nation at peace with the United States suddenly became legal precedent for American citizens to exercise their insurgents' rights elsewhere. Events in Canada soon proved how perilous this precedent would be.

TOWARD THE END OF 1837, separate political reform movements in Lower and Upper Canada erupted into a general rebellion against British colonial power in North America. Each insurrection originated in opposition to the oligarchic political culture that prevailed in both provinces. During the 1830s, political authority and economic power in Lower and Upper Canada—especially over land—resided largely with executive officials and their influential supporters who were constitutionally protected against popular oversight. The *Parti Patriote* led reform efforts in Lower Canada and the Reform Party did the same in Upper Canada. Frustrated by political obstruction in the provinces and London, radical factions in each party adopted violent measures in late 1837, first in Lower Canada and shortly thereafter in Upper Canada. Rebels in Lower Canada were mostly Francophone Canadians from Montreal's rural hinterlands joined by a smaller portion of the province's Anglophone population. Louis-Joseph Papineau and Wolfred Nelson were among the most prominent rebel leaders in Lower Canada. Before the rebellion, both men were members of Lower Canada's popularly elected Legislative Assembly from the *Parti Patriote*. In November 1837, *Patriote* forces briefly seized three towns before British regulars defeated the insurgent forces in a bloody counteroffensive. Rebels in Upper Canada launched their uprising in early December. Firebrand editor and former member of Upper Canada's Legislative Assembly William Lyon Mackenzie led a failed assault on Toronto. Farther west in the London District of Upper Canada, local physician and politician Charles Duncombe raised and led an armed force that intended to march on Toronto to reinforce Mackenzie. Duncombe's defeat combined with opposition to his plans from Loyalist militia ended the so-called Western Rising soon after it began.[20]

During the early 1830s, reform opinion was strong in regions of both provinces settled by emigrants from the United States. Reform positions appealed to these populations who considered themselves loyal subjects because they addressed issues such as land distribution, economic development, and local political representation. Without these entitlements, settlers felt deprived of the government's full protection and benefits, exactly what they expected in return for trading their allegiance in the United States for allegiance to the British Crown. In 1834, Massachusetts native Marcus Child, an elected representative of the Eastern Townships, argued that his constituents held legitimate reform opinions because "this is the land of our adoption and choice, and as properly ours as though it were the land of our birth; its chartered rights are ours." Most settlers in Lower Canada's Eastern Townships refused to address their grievances by joining the rebellion in November 1837, choosing instead to adopt a stance of local vigilance to protect their communities against possible *Patriote* incursions from New England and New York. Emigrant communities in Upper Canada resorted to violence.[21]

Subjects born in the United States were prominent in the rebellion's initial phase in Upper Canada. Samuel Lount, one of Mackenzie's lieutenants in the attempted Toronto raid, emigrated with his family from Pennsylvania to Upper Canada in 1811. Charles Duncombe, leader of the Western Rising, was a Connecticut native who settled in Upper Canada in 1824. Most of the rebellious western townships that supported Duncombe were populated by subjects born in the United States or their children. Of the rebels and their accomplices whose backgrounds are known, at least 25 percent of Duncombe's armed followers and 50 percent of those who provided material aid were born in the United States. Many others who joined Duncombe or aided his forces likely had ancestry in the United States. Duncombe and his followers with roots in the United States were not relative newcomers to Upper Canada who might be expected to harbor republican political sympathies anathema to life in a British colony. On the contrary, rebels born in the United States had resided for an average of twenty years in Upper Canada, where they owned property, voted in provincial elections, and some held elected office. By every standard, Lount, Duncombe, and the lesser-known Upper Canadian insurgents with origins in the United States acted in late 1837 according to their expatriate's expectations. They owed loyalty to their adopted country only so long as their government upheld the basic contractual agreement that tied all free people to the state—allegiance demanded protection of life and livelihoods. If a government's policies failed to protect its people, the people were free to reconstitute the terms of their allegiance.[22]

Colonial officials in Upper Canada viewed the insurgents as anything but principled emigrants. A government report on the political climate of each district in Upper Canada concluded that "immigration from the United States was too freely encouraged" in the London District, Duncombe's stronghold, and that "the whole body of inhabitants of that class are found to be republican, and revolutionary in their sentiments and wishes." Robert Baldwin Sullivan, a member of the Executive Council, a powerful advisory body to Upper Canada's lieutenant-governor, believed that the province's significant American emigrant population "never had as a body any active principle of loyalty or attachment to England." George Arthur, Upper Canada's lieutenant-governor, refused to trust the province's population of emigrants from the United States, for he viewed them as almost entirely responsible for the colony's political turmoil. "With regard to the cause of Rebellion in this Province, it is easily accounted for," Arthur declared with certainty. "In the first place a great number of American Citizens were injudiciously invited to settled [sic] in the fertile soil of Canada and having wormed themselves into very fair possessions avowing a temporary allegiance, they soon began with their accumulated wealth to desire democratic institutions." Such internal enemies deserved harsh treatment. The provincial government executed Lount as a traitor. Many captured insurgents from the Western Rising were also tried and convicted of treason, but none were executed.[23]

Prominent rebel leaders from Lower and Upper Canada fled to the United States. Papineau and other *Patriote* leaders went to Vermont and New York. Mackenize retreated to Buffalo, New York, and Duncombe to Detroit. Popular support for the Canadian Rebellion ran high in border communities from Vermont to Michigan. Beginning in December 1837, citizens held a series of public meetings organized in towns and cities from Burlington to Detroit to offer sympathy to the rebel cause in Canada and assistance to refugee insurgents in their midst. Participants in most of these meetings were careful to assist the rebellion in ways that also upheld their obligations to US neutrality. Others, however, hatched more aggressive plans to involve American citizens in Canadian affairs. By escaping to the United States and regrouping near the border with assistance from local citizens, the exiled Canadian insurgents thus transformed a domestic rebellion into an international conflict.

Activities in Buffalo, New York, first demonstrated the Canadian Rebellion's full international consequences. Beginning in early December 1837, Buffalo resident Thomas Jefferson Sutherland appealed for volunteers to join the Canadian insurgency even before Mackenzie launched his attack on Toronto. Sutherland was a Marine Corps veteran, journalist, and an occasional lawyer who regaled audiences with invented tales of revolutionary glory in South America under the command of Simón Bolívar. Sutherland visited Toronto just before Mackenzie's offensive and probably offered the Upper Canadian rebel his support, but he did not openly begin recruiting volunteers to fight in Canada until he returned to Buffalo and Mackenzie had arrived seeking refuge. Mackenize, Sutherland, and other leading supporters of the Canadian Rebellion in Buffalo recruited Rensselaer Van Rensselaer, part of a prominent New York family, to lead an expedition to seize Canadian territory. Once they occupied Canadian territory, the invaders would regroup themselves into a "Patriot" army commanded by Van Rensselaer for the purpose of launching an offensive against the colonial government in Upper Canada. On December 15, 1837, Van Rensselaer, Sutherland, and a small volunteer force armed themselves with stolen government weapons before crossing the Niagara River's treacherous waters for Navy Island, a spot of British territory just above the falls. Mackenzie arrived on Navy Island soon thereafter, and the occupying force eventually grew to 450 men.[24]

Navy Island became home to the Republic of Upper Canada. Mackenzie announced the creation of this new republic and the terms of its provisional government in a proclamation published soon after Patriot forces occupied the island. According to the proclamation, Mackenzie held temporary executive power. Once established, the government would rest on popular sovereignty, religious liberty, and free trade. Mackenzie also outlined the myriad sufferings of Upper Canadians under British domination in order to both rally greater support within Upper Canada and to justify rebellion before world opinion. The revolution would not succeed without soldiers, so Mackenzie promised 300 acres "of the best public lands" to "any volunteer, who shall assist personally in bringing to a conclusion the glorious struggle" then underway in Upper Canada. Mackenzie envisioned an independent nation for Upper Canadians but not exclusively so, for its fruits were available to the "worthy men of all nations" who settled there. Mackenzie ultimately rejected any notion that patriotic citizenship in the Republic of Upper Canada stemmed from birth on a common soil or from a shared culture. Choice was the operating principle behind his call for volunteers and the basis for membership in the society they would create if victorious.[25]

Emigrant rights were essential to establishing the republic that Mackenzie willed into existence on Navy Island. Sutherland argued that he was free to cast his allegiance to rebel forces on the island because the "institutions and laws" of the United States "leave the individual citizen free to go from the country and unite himself in arms with any people to whom his likes or interests may direct him; and with them carry on war against any other nation or people." Daniel Heustis, of Watertown, New York, described the moment in January 1838 that he quit his business to devote himself "to the cause of Canadian liberty." Although he arrived in Buffalo too late for action on Navy Island, he served as captain of Patriot forces until British forces defeated the insurrection later in the year. According to Heustis, "Our citizens who passed over the line, and took sides with Canadians on their own soil" behaved lawfully because they "had the legal right to do so."[26]

Positions such as Sutherland's and Heustis's depended on the assertion that the provisional government of the Republic of Upper Canada was a legitimate sovereign. Edward Alexander Theller, a naturalized citizen from Pennsylvania, argued that the forces on Navy Island were part of a movement with all of the trappings of a sovereign power. It had a provisional government with executive authority, a military commanded by officers, a proposed currency, established communication networks, and a national flag that Canadian authorities inadvertently legitimized when they negotiated with insurgents early in the rebellion. The provisional government of the Republic of Upper Canada transformed Navy Island into the seat of a sovereign power that absolved all who pledged their service of legal culpability. Navy Island provided Mackenize and the rebel leadership a place to "raise their country's banner on Canadian soil, where they could regularly enrol and discipline the volunteers who might come to them." Theller accepted his commission as an officer in the "Canadian revolutionary service" in just such a fashion so as to avoid implicating the US government or to "infringe its neutral and amicable relations." Theller and the other citizens from the United States eager to join the insurgency thus agreed to "cross the river unorganized, although equipt, and join the Canadian force already in the field."[27]

Insurgent forces ultimately occupied Navy Island for less than a month. A combined force of Loyalist militia and British regulars bombarded the insurgents into retreat and also destroyed the American steamboat *Caroline*, an important supply ship that ferried arms, men, and supplies from the United States to the rebel stronghold. British forces seized the *Caroline* in American waters before setting it ablaze to drift downstream and over the falls. The so-called *Caroline* Affair strained diplomatic relations between Great Britain and the United States. British authorities justified destruction of the *Caroline* as a necessary act of national self-defense against lawless actors in a region where the United States seemed powerless. More belligerent voices in the United States, especially coming from areas near Canada, viewed British actions as a violation of their nation's territorial sovereignty that deserved diplomatic recourse and possibly military retaliation. The *Caroline* Affair was a volatile moment that put the United States and Great Britain at risk of war. However, the British party that destroyed the *Caroline* acted with some precedent under international law, and both sides seemed eager to find a diplomatic solution. The insurgent occupation of Navy Island, albeit short-lived, raised legal questions about the roles of foreign fighters that seemed more intractable to many British and US officials than did the destruction of the *Caroline*, especially as the Canadian Rebellion stretched into 1838.[28]

The actions of Canadian rebels and their American supporters enflamed the entire Great Lakes region in 1838. Organized into secret societies with elaborate membership rituals and local lodges in many northern states, the "Patriot Hunters" divided themselves into eastern and western forces to attack Lower and Upper Canada. They also proclaimed the creation of the Republic of Canada at a convention in Cleveland that extended the claims of sovereign power first announced by Mackenzie on Navy Island. For a time, the armed insurgents largely erased the border separating British North America from the United States. They moved freely throughout the Great Lakes region at the risk of embroiling the United States and Great Britain in another North American war. Following several largely unsuccessful raids on both provinces, armies on both sides of the border effectively defeated the Patriot Hunters by late 1838. However, in order for authorities in the Canadian provinces and the United States to weaken the Patriot Hunters, they first had to address the fact that US citizens were responsible for most of the Patriot actions, especially in Upper Canada as the conflict grew throughout 1838. The role of American volunteers in the Canadian Rebellion thus proved to be a constant source of debate and government concern in the United States and British North America for the duration of the conflict.[29]

Opinion in the United States was sharply divided over the rights of citizens to join the Canadian Rebellion. Supporters of the Navy Island invasion claimed Mackenzie's Republic of Upper Canada was truly an independent state. If authorities in North America and beyond accepted this assertion, the forces that occupied the island would gain significant legal cover. For one, the insurgents could define themselves as legitimate belligerents entitled to enter treaties with foreign powers, thereby gaining recognition under international law. Asserting their independence also allowed the insurgents to seek trade and support from neutral powers, most immediately the United States.

Established free trade doctrine under international law allowed nations to enter commercial relations against the enemies of their allies. In such a situation, the United States was a neutral power with no special obligation to Great Britain above and beyond its obligations to the Republic of Upper Canada. From this perspective, the *Caroline* incident was especially egregious. For even if all of the accusations by Canadian authorities about the *Caroline*'s activities were true, that it "was the property and in the service of the 'Republic of Navy Island'" as a US newspaper described the case, then "by the laws of nations the British had no right to pursue her into a neutral port." A group of citizens from Niagara County, New York, raised a similar consideration in their memorial to Congress. The signatories to this memorial recognized that British officials were authorized to seize contraband goods aboard the *Caroline*; however, they protested that its destruction violated the United States' free trade privileges and its territorial sovereignty. The petition maintained that the occupying force on Navy Island was sovereign. They left the United States as American citizens, without a doubt, but, like foreign fighters in previous rebellions, they went to Navy Island on their own accord and "*there* enlisted under the Patriot banner." The memorialists thus assumed that there was a semblance of independent authority on Navy Island equipped to accept the allegiance of volunteers from the United States and, as a result, the United States was a neutral power in its relationship with them.[30]

Supporters of the Canadian Rebellion also argued that neutral obligations between nations had no authority over individual actions. According to one legal opinion, "Every man may shoulder his musket alone, expatriate himself, and go into the service of any body of men or of any nation he pleases. He may embark in the Quixotic enterprises of any part of the world he may choose. It is his right, if he pleases to exercise it." International laws "allow men to interfere privately in any national quarrels," another supporter of the Canadian Rebellion argued, as did emigrant rights to free movement and expatriation under US laws, which allowed "any American citizen to leave his own country and join any other, at any time, and for any or no cause, or any purpose." As a result, "such men cease to be American citizens, and become Canadian insurgents."[31]

Officials on both sides of the border rejected this view for its threat to the international order. South Carolina representative Francis Pickens argued that the United States would suffer grave consequences by yielding power over its citizens who made questionable claims about their rights to join foreign conflicts. "If we cannot restrain the lawlessness of our citizens under fear of encroaching upon their liberty," Pickens argued, "we will be thrown out of the pale of nations, and the people of this Confederacy will be made what France was under the reign of Robespierre and Danton, a nation of public robbers and murderers, defying the laws of God and man." A government that seemed unable or unwilling to control the actions of its citizens betrayed its obligations to the international order. Even more harmful to national interests, only weak states seemed unable to police violence at their borders. If "our citizens engage without restraint in military enterprises, against the peace of other governments, we shall be considered and treated, and justly too, as a nation of pirates," warned Supreme Court Justice John McLean in his charge to an Ohio circuit court grand jury regarding neutrality law. A newspaper editor feared that by failing to enforce its neutrality laws, "the United States will become a by-word among the nations for bad faith, and for want of moral power, or of physical inability to exert it," since the government would do nothing to stop "the laws of this land" from being "trampled upon with impunity by hordes of desperate and unprincipled adventurers." Upholding US neutrality became a central foreign policy concern for many American observers of Canadian affairs.[32]

To officials in Upper Canada, the occupation of Navy Island reflected an ominous mood among the people of northern New York. George Rykert, a member of Upper Canada's Legislative Assembly from the Niagara region who had emigrated to the province from western New York as a teenager, was aghast at the lawlessness of his native country. Despite New York governor William Marcy's neutrality proclamation and the orders by Secretary of State John Forsyth for federal district attorneys to prosecute neutrality violations, the rebellion's American supporters stole weapons from local arsenals, acquired ammunition, and openly recruited volunteers to reinforce the insurgents on Navy Island. Such actions occurred near Buffalo but farther inland as well. So much for "the pride and glory of their boasted republican institutions," Rykert mocked, since US "authorities are completely powerless" to overturn "mob law."[33]

Visitors to New York returned to Upper Canada with more alarming testimony that popular sentiment for the rebellion existed far from the front in Buffalo. Thomas Moxey, a Stamford innkeeper, testified that citizens from throughout New York were "openly aiding, abetting and assisting the rebels on Navy Island," in addition to the fifty to one hundred volunteers who daily enlisted in Van Rensselaer's service. According to a confidential report from another informant, "The people of the towns of the interior are making common cause with the rebels" to such an extent that women incited their husbands and sons to join the fight and one woman even spent her days casting bullets for the insurgent forces. Such information from Buffalo and its hinterlands confirmed Lieutenant-Governor of Upper Canada Francis Bond Head's opinion that US officials must take forceful measures. In a letter to Henry Fox, Great Britain's ambassador in Washington, DC, Head stated bluntly that "the United States' Government must either put down this aggression by force, or be held responsible for the consequences." The Navy Island occupation exposed the United States' weakness at its Canadian border that, whether real or feigned, demanded government action to avoid war.[34]

The US government responded to the international insurgency on the nation's northern border from a relatively weak legal position. Federal officials at the border along with the governors of Vermont and New York proved unable to discourage hostile movements from the United States into Lower and Upper Canada. Even once President Van Buren embodied the state militias under the command of US Army General Winfield Scott, the federal government's powers remained uncertain. Secretary of State John Poinsett informed General Scott that he must rely on gravitas instead of the law to uphold US neutrality at the border. Beyond the authority of Scott's personality, existing US laws granted the executive no authority to restrain people under its jurisdiction from entering foreign territory adjacent to the United States with hostile intentions against neighboring governments. Moreover, popular opinion was so hostile to British authorities in Upper and Lower Canada that Poinsett advised Scott to remind the governors of Vermont and New York of "the propriety of selecting troops from a portion of the state distant from the theatre of action." By early 1838, government officials recognized that US neutrality laws were useless for controlling American participation in foreign conflicts at its borders instead of across the seas.[35]

The US government took two important steps to restrain its citizens from attempting to join the Canadian Rebellion. In early January 1838, President Martin Van Buren issued a presidential neutrality proclamation reminding American citizens that international and US law prevented them from joining the "civil war" then underway in Canada. Citizens who violated their neutral obligations faced prosecution in US courts, Van Buren warned. Moreover, the president prepared American-born insurgents who escaped the law for an uncertain fate across the border. All "who shall compromit the neutrality of this government by interfering in an unlawful manner with the affairs of the neighboring British provinces," Van Buren continued, "will receive no aid or countenance from their government into whatever difficulties they may be thrown." Also in early 1838, the senate introduced an updated neutrality law to display the US government's strength and its good faith to the international order.[36]

The Canadian Rebellion exposed deficiencies in US neutrality law when nothing but a porous land border—that citizens and subjects had crossed freely for decades—separated a population sympathetic to the insurrection from centers of British colonial power. As recognized by a Vermont newspaper commentator who valued respect for his nation's neutrality laws, the government could probably do little to effectively stop an American volunteer who was determined to make the conflict "a personal matter and go into the province to their aid." The federal government's best option was thus to disavow those citizens who joined the insurgency by taking earnest legal steps to prosecute them.[37]

Congress initially relied on the 1818 neutrality law to prosecute Canadian volunteers. However, this law was adopted primarily to stop citizens from joining foreign conflicts some distance from the nation's borders. The amended 1818 law would specifically address the unique problems posed by rebellions at the nation's borders. Pennsylvania senator and future president James Buchanan explained the rationale for updating the 1818 law. The earlier statute was sufficient at a moment when the most pressing issues of neutrality concerned potential US involvement in conflicts that occurred on distant shores over questions of free maritime trade. The Canadian Rebellion posed unique problems of geographic proximity. As Buchannan explained, "We have three neighbors on our frontiers, Canada, Texas, and Mexico; and the duties of good neighborhood required something from us in relation to them than could be strictly demanded under the law of nations." Such duties put the United States under a heavy burden to prevent its citizens from abetting or committing acts of violence just beyond its borders. "It is against all reason and justice," Buchannan continued, "that in case of a sudden commotion in a neighboring country along our frontiers, the citizens of the United States should be permitted to take part with the insurgents, by furnishing them with vessels, arms, and munitions of war, for the express purpose of aiding and assisting in such hostilities." Buchannan warned that if the federal government did not prevent such actions, "we would make ourselves parties to every intestine commotion which might arise in the states and colonies along our frontier."[38]

The updated neutrality law of 1838 preserved the crime of joining or organizing a military expedition on US soil against a nation at peace with the United States original to the 1818 statute. The new law also granted the federal government power to seize armaments and vessels when agents at the border had probable cause to believe that they were intended for insurgents. The owners could reclaim their property only after posting bond as security that they had no intention of joining the rebellion. Although the updated law targeted populations in the Great Lakes borderlands, the law applied to "any military expedition or enterprise against the territory or dominions of any foreign prince or state, or of any colony, district or people conterminous with the United States." As Maryland representative Benjamin Howard noted, the United States' government and its people had unique duties to respect the territorial sovereignty of "coterminous countries" since they were "separated from us by an imaginary line." Americans debated the updated neutrality law in Congress and the press well into 1838.[39]

Many American citizens in the northern borderlands opposed the amended neutrality law. Communities from Burlington, Vermont, to Cleveland, Ohio, petitioned Congress with the reasons why the law violated the emigrant rights of US citizens. As asserted by petitioners from Erie County, New York, "The right of any citizen to abandon his country and go abroad . . . or to attach himself to the armies of any nation not at war with his own, your memorialists contend, cannot be questioned." The neutrality law notwithstanding, "this is an inalienable right and cannot be taken from him," the Erie County citizens protested. More generally, citizens from Tuscarawas County in northeastern Ohio accused federal officials of using the neutrality law to harass citizens for "exercising the unalienable right of American Freeman, in peaceably leaving, or coming into the United States." The amended neutrality law also exposed Congress's partiality according to a common protest in the petitions. Citizens in Franklin County, Vermont, criticized the neutrality act because it denied Americans the right "to remove at pleasure with their effects." However, by imposing these restrictions only on inhabitants of northern border states, Congress created "odious distinctions" among the citizenry of the United States. Rather, for the law to be legitimate it should "have been general in its operation and have provided for the safety of the dominions of Spain and other foreign powers, as well as for the preservation of the provinces of Great Britain alone."[40]

The Navy Island occupation was an altogether different and more urgent matter for authorities in Upper Canada. They described invaders from the United States using various terms including "brigand" and "banditti." In other words, the invaders were effectively land pirates, allegiant to no state so not entitled to legal due process. Under the "doctrine of outlawry," an established principle of international law, officials could execute such characters on the spot where they were captured, and indeed certain authorities in Upper Canada believed hostile invaders should meet this fate. Upper Canadian justice Archibald McLean argued that an armed invader from the United States, a nation at peace with Great Britain, violated international law so was "liable to be dealt with according to the will and pleasure of his Captors." No protests for leniency were tenable if such a person "were summarily punished with death" since he had placed "himself out of the protection of all Law." Other officials in Upper Canada worried that enforcing the outlawry doctrine in a borderlands region characterized by frequent and easy movement across international boundaries might exacerbate rather than lessen Patriot enthusiasm.

Besides, other authorities in the province turned to an alternative legal doctrine known as "local allegiance," which held that any person who entered the Crown's dominions was under its protection, so that person owed the Crown their allegiance until they left. Under this doctrine, invaders need not be natural-born or naturalized subjects of Great Britain to face capital charges of treason. Local allegiance remained a questionable doctrine in Upper Canada since legal opinion differed over the applicability of treason, a crime reserved for subjects or at least individuals resident in the province for a time, not simply invaders.[41]

Upper Canadian officials sought a path between the perils of enforcing the outlawry doctrine and the uncertainty of local allegiance by adopting the Lawless Aggressions Act in January 1838. This law created the felony of lawless aggression, which allowed local courts and courts-martial to try captured invaders from the United States for a capital offense akin to treason. John Beverly Robinson, chief justice of Upper Canada, explained the rationale for the Lawless Aggressions Act as one to place American citizens who joined the insurgency "on the same footing in respect to trial and punishment, as the rebels with whom they might be associated."[42]

Although occurring independent of each other, political actions on both sides of the border in early 1838 effectively stripped invaders from the United States of any citizenship protections they might claim in their defense. Michigan Senator John Norvell recognized this result in his commentary on the case of Edward Alexander Theller, a naturalized US citizen tried for treason in Upper Canada. Norvell argued that "by engaging in a foreign civil war in a country with which the United States were at peace," Theller "had in so doing expatriated himself from his adopted country, and thereby forfeited all the protection which he might otherwise claim from its constitution and its laws." Other commentators in the United States believed the same held true for native-born volunteers. A New Hampshire newspaper editor summarized the implications of government policies on both sides of the border. Much "like the Texan volunteers," the Americans who joined Mackenzie on Navy Island "are no longer American citizens, and must meet the consequences of their own rash act."[43]

Indeed, observers in the United States viewed the insurrections in Upper and Lower Canada against the backdrop of recent events in Texas. Publications within the United States condemned American insurgents in Canada. Belligerents at the Canadian border threatened "the same violence done to good faith and national honor that was shown in the affairs of Texas and Mexico," lamented one newspaper. Massachusetts senator John Davis argued that "if similar lawless proceedings had not been encouraged at one extremity of the union, they would not have been exhibited so soon and so boldly as at this moment on the northern frontier." On the contrary, South Carolina representative Waddy Thompson thought recent events in Texas and Canada revealed a basic truth that the federal government was largely powerless to prevent its citizens from joining rebellions in neighboring nations. No laws existed, Thomspon argued, that "could forbid a man's expatriating himself, and going to reside in Texas," and arriving armed and intent on "volunteering in the service of another nation." The US government was equally weak at its border with Lower and Upper Canada.[44]

Others in the United States denied the similarity of conditions at the nation's northern and southern borders. Tennessee congressman Ebenezer Shields distinguished between lawful Texas volunteers and their lawless imitators to the north. Shields asserted that "not one man out of fifty of those who had gone from the United States, and entered into the struggle for Texas independence, had gone there without a bona fide purpose of remaining in Texas as a citizen of that republic." "These people," Shields concluded in reference to the Texas volunteers, had thus "expatriated themselves, and chosen Texas as their future country," which they had every right to defend with arms. In comparison, Shields dismissed the Patriot volunteers in Canada as nothing more than the perpetrators of an illegal invasion. After all, the Republic of Canada never received international recognition. This made all the difference for many observers in the United States who insisted that conflicts in Lower and Upper Canada remained domestic insurrections, not genuine revolutions. Unlike the recently created Latin American republics and even the Texas republic, the Republic of Canada was not admitted "into the family of nations." Volunteers could not become legitimate combatants armed in defense of their adopted country because the Republic of Canada had no recognized standing as a state, so it also lacked authority to naturalize expatriates. As one observer described the status of the rebels on Navy Island, "It is perfectly obvious that this temporary change of residence does not affect their nationality," so they were "lawless banditti," not legitimate revolutionaries.[45]

Recent events in Texas demonstrated to British officials why they should take a guarded approach toward the United States while keeping the Canadian rebels from achieving legal standing under international law. Indeed, the Lawless Aggressions Act was a response to the clear example of the Texas Revolution. By ensuring that the Canadian rebels and the volunteers from the United States who supported them remained criminals rather than legally recognized belligerents, British officials hoped to prevent Upper Canada from becoming an independent republic like Texas before it. Henry Fox, the British ambassador in Washington, DC, believed the updated neutrality bill could go far toward stopping American volunteers from joining the conflict if the authorities "honestly carried it into execution." However, Fox also cautioned that enforcement was difficult since the American population along the border was overwhelmingly lawless. "The President has not more power of controlling these piratical communities," Fox commented, "than the Sultan at Constantinople has generally had over the States of Tripoli and Algiers." For this reason, Fox noted in a later report to authorities in Upper Canada, US neutrality could become a hostile position. If American invaders ever received popular support from Canadian colonists, then the US government, and perhaps governments elsewhere, could view the conflict quite differently. Under the terms of international law, interested outside governments would have the excuse "of dignifying the contest with name of civil war." In such a scenario, Fox was certain that the US government would assume "a high and offensive tone of neutrality" thus allowing it to legally support those fighting against British colonial authority by elevating "the combined armament of rebels and brigands to the rank of a lawful belligerent." Lieutenant-Governor Arthur agreed with Fox's assessment. In light of the failed Prescott raid in November 1838, Arthur confidently stated, "I have no doubt the American Govt. intended on this occasion to make another Texas affair of it but they have been disappointed in this."[46]

Texas provided a mixed legacy for Patriots from the United States. In many instances, they cited Texas volunteers as precedent for their actions. After all, Heustis noted, "When Texas rebelled against the government of Mexico, thousands of American citizens crossed the lines, and assisted in achieving her independence." Citizens had the same emigrant rights to join the rebellions in Canada, Heustis believed, which was a popular opinion in the northern United States. Citizens of Montpelier, Vermont, held a local convention in "relation to Canadian affairs" in 1839. Among their resolutions was an appeal to a consistent understanding of emigrant rights, a position that gave men in the northern United States the same choices as American men elsewhere. As the resolution stated, "We hold all persons who supported the cause of Texas, and oppose the cause of Canada, to be enemies of northern interests, northern institutions and northern men." However, the Canadian volunteers also recognized fundamental limitations on their insurgents' rights not shared by the Texas volunteers. Despite fighting, as many believed, for a more noble political cause not tied to slavery's expansion, the failure to establish independent republics in Upper and Lower Canada denied them the legal cover of emigrant rights claims. Without a new government to accept their allegiance, they were "branded as foreign assassins, free-booters, pirates, brigands and bucaneers, Yankee cutthroats, &c., and go down to posterity with the reputation of Bedouin Arabs" rather than heroes in the advance of global republicanism. Canadian rebels thus believed that Texas insurgents fought for malicious ends, but only their success influenced how the world viewed their actions in hindsight.[47]

Citizens of the United States who joined the failed Canadian Rebellion ultimately found themselves in a far more precarious legal standing than the Texas volunteers. In large part this difference reflected a greater willingness by officials in the United States and Canada to prosecute US citizens who became Canadian insurgents. Thomas Jefferson Sutherland, Rensselaer Van Rensselaer, and Edward Alexander Theller were among the more prominent participants in the Canadian Rebellion charged with violating US neutrality law. However, most cases in the United States ended similar to Theller's in which juries found the accused not guilty. As Theller described his trial in a federal district court in Detroit, the jury acquitted him in mere minutes since they agreed that he "had joined the patriot force when in British waters, and beyond the jurisdiction of the United States," which, Theller added, "I had a perfect right and liberty to do."[48]

Citizens of the United States captured in Upper Canada often faired much worse than their countrymen tried in American courts. Although the Lawless Aggressions Act was supposed to provide legal clarity for prosecuting captured insurgents from the United States, military officers in the field continued to apply other legal standards throughout the rebellion, and court officials occasionally acted according to legal reasoning of their own. Windsor militia colonel John Prince applied the outlawry doctrine to five captured "Brigands and Pirates" who invaded Sandwich, Upper Canada, from Detroit. All were "shot upon the spot," in Prince's words, an order with popular support in Sandwich. A resolution from residents of Sandwich warned future insurgents from the United States that, if captured, "certain, instant, and inevitable death at our hands will be their Fate, without any recognition of them as Prisoners of War or as any other sort of prisoners." Pennsylvanian James Morreau was apprehended after leading an unsuccessful raid on Short Hills, Upper Canada. A Niagara jury found Morreau guilty of treason under the doctrine of local allegiance, and he was duly executed. Captured insurgents from the United States who escaped execution still faced what they argued were illegal trials in which the combined legal effects of policies adopted by officials in the United States and Upper Canada rendered them stateless. Two cases illustrate the degree to which captured insurgents in Upper Canada lost state protection of any sort, all the more revealing because one involved a person naturalized in the United States and the other case a person born there.[49]

Based in Detroit, Edward Alexander Theller was a leading figure among the western Patriots. He participated in a failed attack on Fort Amherstburg, Upper Canada, an important royal military installation on the Detroit River. Theller and other Patriots were captured and brought to Toronto where authorities tried them for treason. Henry Sherwood, the Crown lawyer in the trial, argued that the case against Theller was beyond reproach according to the doctrine of perpetual allegiance. After all, Theller was born a British subject in Ireland even though in the 1820s he immigrated to North America, where he lived in both Lower Canada and the United States. Theller insisted that he had expatriated himself to become a citizen of the United States, thus he was not open to charges of treason against the Crown. His right to expatriation trumped any claims of perpetual allegiance, Theller declared, "because man, as a free agent, has a right to domicile himself in any country in the world to which he fancies it his advantage to emigrate, so long as he consents to observe and respect the laws of that country which he may select to reside in." Theller even suggested that he had expatriated himself once again by casting his allegiance to the "independent provisional government of Canada" and fighting under its flag, "an acknowledged flag against her majesty's dominions . . . planted on the soil of Canada by Canadians themselves, at Navy Island."[50]

Christopher Hagerman, the attorney general of Upper Canada, was not persuaded. Hagerman found Theller's appeal to the natural right of expatriation and his claim that the forces on Navy Island were legitimate belligerents under international law thin cover for deeply subversive actions. Hagerman labeled Theller "a brigand, a murderer, a pirate, a robber, a Yankee, an inhuman monster" who cast his lot with "lawless republicans, actuated by the passions of the Jacobins of France." Under their influence, Theller violated his native loyalty to the Crown. Only a guilty verdict, Hagerman warned, would send a clear message to others who might emulate Theller "that the people of her majesty's provinces would not submit to have their property wrested from them, nor their wives and daughters given as a prey to the lust of the brigands." Although the jury spared Theller's life, contrary to Hagerman's recommendation, he received a life sentence in Australia.[51]

Theller escaped from prison in Quebec and fled to the United States before his sentence was executed, but not before he petitioned the US government to intervene on his behalf as an American citizen. Theller's appeal failed, despite popular support in the United States for his cause, because his actions violated Van Buren's neutrality proclamation. Theller condemned this proclamation for violating his right to expatriation no less than the charges against him for treason in Upper Canada. According to Theller, US law allowed any American citizen "if he so wished, to expatriate himself; to leave this country and go to any other he liked" to "join any other at any time, and for any purpose he may think proper, or see fit." Theller insisted that policies in Upper Canada and the United States effectively nullified a right that all free people supposedly possessed, especially US citizens. The right to expatriation, Theller argued, "although bound with the stars and stripes, carr[ies]no shield against British construction of man's natural right to choose his own home, and adopt his own country. These boasted privileges of American law sound well in theory, and work well in peace," but "little practical blessing is conferred in times of commotion and war." Theller was ultimately tried for violating US neutrality law.[52]

Robert Marsh was captured in Sandwich, Upper Canada, after joining a doomed invasion organized in Detroit. A few years earlier, in 1833, Marsh had emigrated from the United States to Upper Canada, living first in St. Catharines and then Chippewa, a town on the western bank of the Niagara River. Much of Marsh's family also resided in Upper Canada. Despite every outward indication that Marsh had exercised his emigrant rights for life as a British subject, at his trial Marsh rejected accusations by Crown lawyers that he was a rebel, replying that "I owe the Queen no allegiance, consequently am not a rebel, as you term me." However, the United States refused to recognize him as a citizen. Indeed, Marsh believed that President Van Buren and the US government betrayed him and those who shared his principles. Prospective volunteers who might have joined the Canadian Rebellion decided not to risk prosecution or lost respectability once "Matty" decreed "that all engaged in the Patriot cause were blacklegs, horse thieves, &c. &c." The details of Van Buren's decree were also well known in Upper Canada. On Marsh's march to jail, someone in a crowd of onlookers in Windsor jeered that he was a criminal according to what "your good President says in a late proclamation." For all of his revolutionary ambition, Marsh eventually found himself in a Toronto prison with fetid living conditions where inmates survived on a steady diet of bullock's head soup, a dish prepared with the animal's eyes, teeth, and brains intact and simmered in a broth that Marsh described as thick with fur and rodent feces. And this was before Marsh served seven years in Van Diemen's Land, a British penal colony in present-day Tasmania.[53]

British authorities in Upper Canada eventually "transported" nearly one hundred US citizens to hard labor in the antipodes. This fate stands in stark contrast to that of the Americans who exercised their insurgents' rights in the Texas Revolution. Rather than participants in what seems in hindsight like the United States' inevitable expansion, the northern insurgents were obscure casualties of a stillborn rebellion.

THOSE WHO JOINED the borderlands rebellions of the 1830s claimed emigrant rights to justify their armed attempts to overthrow established state power. In each instance, the same rights claims provided the basis for new assertions of state power. Government officials responded to these insurrections—as did opinion shapers and armed volunteers—by accepting that political allegiance in the North American borderlands was fundamentally contingent—that is, both transferable and probationary. Despite originating in a common legal culture, the rebellions had widely different outcomes. American insurgents secured emigration right citizenship in Texas, which enabled them to establish a sovereign republic on territory they had seized from Mexico. American insurgents failed to exercise emigration right citizenship in Upper or Lower Canada, which prevented them from establishing a Republic of Canada.

The power of emigrant rights to create borderlands places during the 1830s would seem most evident in Texas. Moreover, the particular relationship between emigrant rights claims and race in the Texas insurrection became more pronounced in subsequent decades. White men asserted their freedom to move freely throughout the world, claim sovereignty in land, and extend racial slavery in contests over territory within the United States and in filibustering expeditions throughout the Western Hemisphere. Ultimately, however, the Texas insurrection merely reinforced with arms the racial and gender privileges considered the basis of emigrant rights since their advent in the eighteenth century.

On the contrary, the failed Canadian insurrections unleashed an unforeseen expansion in emigrant rights claims. Nearly 1,000 Black men joined the colonial militia to successfully defend British North America against republicanism. The vast majority of these men were born into enslavement or nominal freedom in the United States until becoming part of a growing Black population that quit the United States to claim the rights and privileges of British subjects. The failure of rebellions in Lower and Upper Canada thus transformed the Great Lakes borderlands into the region where the freedoms to move and choose allegiance gained their most consequential expression in the decades after 1838.[54]

CHAPTER EIGHT

My Bones Are a Property Bequeathed to Me

In early 1846, Lewis Richardson stood before an audience of Black and white townspeople in Amherstburg, a community in Canada West on the Detroit River near its mouth at Lake Erie. To those crowded into Union Chapel, Richardson embodied the slaveholder's republic visible just across the river. In his remarks, Richardson recounted the brutality he suffered while enslaved to Henry Clay, the powerful US senator for Kentucky. Richardson explained to his audience that the daily violence he suffered at Ashland, Clay's Kentucky plantation, "caused me to flee from under the American eagle, and take shelter under the British crown." As the audience cheered Richardson's successful escape to British sovereignty, he mocked the man who once enslaved him. "I now feel as independent as ever Henry Clay felt when he was running for the White House," yet "he was running for slavery, and I for liberty." Clay's highest ambitions constantly failed whereas Richardson's succeeded. "Thanks be to God that I am elected to Canada," Richardson exalted. Henry Bibb, a man who also escaped enslavement in Kentucky for a life in Detroit and eventually Canada West, attended Richardson's lecture. Bibb captured the significance of Richardson's "election" in remarks of his own. He welcomed Richardson to his new life, for "the very moment you set your foot on British soil" you are "no longer three-fifths of a man" but rather entitled "to all the privileges and immunities of a citizen of Canada."[1]

Richardson's defiant speech expressed a revolution in Black rights led by the self-emancipated and the nominally free. Crossing the border into British North America activated Richardson's emigrant rights to free movement and expatriation, rights denied to Black people by governments and courts in the United States. Once Black emigrants settled in communities such as Amherstburg, British imperial laws and provincial statutes recognized them as royal subjects, a basis for freedom and personhood nearly unimaginable in the United States. For Thomas H. Jones, the revolution was visceral. He escaped enslavement to live in Salem, Massachusetts, before leaving once again to settle in British North America, where "I now feel that my bones are a property bequeathed to me for my own use." Black people such as Richardson, Bibb, and Jones pursued the promises of emigration right citizenship beyond the borders of the United States, but their departure also shaped Black political life in the nation they departed.[2]

In the decades before the Civil War, Black Americans insisted that they possessed citizenship rights equal to those of white Americans. Republican citizenship included emigrant rights, so Black Americans asserted their freedom to quit the United States or remain in the nation of their birth. Indeed, Black Americans judged all proposals intended to improve their lives in freedom, or those who sought freedom for their enslaved brethren, with the assumption that they were a people with rights to move and choose their national allegiances. For a significant number of Black Americans, this choice meant remaining in the United States to claim the privileges of birthright citizenship. Yet many Black Americans chose to leave the United States for allegiances elsewhere. By exercising their freedom to move and expatriate, Black emigrants claimed equality for themselves. In their thousands of individual choices, they also realized the possibility of full Black citizenship in the United States.[3]

The Great Lakes borderlands, more than anywhere else in North America, became the region where Black people asserted their emigrant rights with the most determination. Several developments starting in the 1830s made this possible. In 1833, Great Britain abolished slavery in its empire, thus making British North America a place for Black Americans to exercise emigration right citizenship after the law took effect in 1834. The failure of the Canadian Rebellions of 1837–38 preserved royal sovereignty in British North America by keeping the provinces free of republicanism and its easy accommodation with slavery. By 1860, over 20,000 Black people, many enslaved but more of whom were free, claimed their emigrant rights to leave the United States for Canada West. On the contrary, the Texas insurrection created a new slaveholder's republic in North America, one that dramatically foreclosed opportunities for Black emigration southward from the United States. Black emigrants who still settled in Mexico obtained a tenuous freedom.[4]

The Black Americans who quit the United States ultimately redefined emigrant rights. Since their advent in the eighteenth century, emigrant rights reinforced white claims to place and belonging according to both law and custom. Black Americans divorced emigrant rights from the racial order these rights had often reinforced. In exercising their freedom to move and expatriate themselves from all authority in the United States, they asserted their standing as persons entitled to belonging anywhere they chose.

BLACK AMERICANS CONSIDERED quitting the United States from the moment the nation was formed. Beginning in the 1780s, Black residents of northern port cities formed civic associations to challenge slavery and defend their communities' interests. These associations considered the possibility of living in Sierra Leone or in self-created settlements in the western territories of the United States. Moreover, in the late 1810s, Black communities in the United States also sent visitors to Haiti and formed Haitian emigration societies. Ultimately during the 1820s, up to 13,000 Black people emigrated from the United States for land and new allegiances in the Republic of Haiti. By 1830, Black Americans surveyed an expansive geography of potential freedom both within and beyond the United States.[5]

While Black people organized to decide where to emigrate, prominent white Americans devised Black emigration plans of their own. Formed in 1816, the American Colonization Society (ACS) gained support from leading politicians in federal and state governments, prominent jurists, and ministers dedicated to religious reform. This coalition believed that a colony in West Africa would allow manumitted slaves and free Black people a place to live as independent landowners on terms of equality impossible in the United States. The founders of the ACS also had a missionary purpose, hoping that Black Protestant settlers would Christianize the Indigenous people of West Africa. Although white supporters of colonization opposed slavery, they did not believe manumission could occur without removing once enslaved people from North America. The ACS established Liberia in 1822 to realize their ambitions. Over subsequent decades, state colonization societies also established colonies in West Africa. By 1860, Liberia received nearly 11,000 Black colonists from the United States.[6]

None of the proposals for Black settlement escaped controversy. Black abolitionists held competing views about the value of emigration. Opponents of emigration concluded that any departure of free Black people from the United States only strengthened slavery by diminishing the population most likely to seek its abolition. Proponents of emigration argued that without equality of citizenship in the United States, free Black people were unlikely to gain enough substantive legal or political power to effectively challenge slavery, so removing themselves to places where such power seemed obtainable was, ultimately, the best antislavery option before them. Nevertheless, nearly every prominent Black civic and religious leader rejected the ACS, thus turning Black opinion in the North against Liberia. Black-led opposition to the ACS also convinced some white abolitionists, William Lloyd Garrison among the most influential, to oppose African colonization as well. In an era when the federal government instituted new policies to dispossess and remove Indigenous people from their land, outmoded notions of expatriation as a term that described forced migration and denationalization

This image illustrates the abolitionist argument that Liberian colonization deprived Black people of their emigrant rights. From the 1839 *American Anti-Slavery Almanac* (New York: American Anti-Slavery Society, 1838), Library Company of Philadelphia.

seemed relevant once again. Abolitionists adopted this view by rejecting Liberian colonization in favor of "emancipation without expatriation." If the colonization movement created circumstances that coerced Black people to leave the United States for Liberia rather than letting them decide for themselves, then it denied freedom to the people it purported to elevate.[7]

Abolitionists thus challenged the colonization movement by turning emigrant rights reasoning against it. Voluntary emigration was impossible under the terms of freedom endorsed by the colonization movement. The *Anti-Slavery Reporter* argued that the colonization movement offered "*freedom,* on condition that freedom of choice shall *not exist*; that the person made *free,* shall not remain where he *chooses,* and reside where he *pleases.*" Genuine freedom for Black people meant they could choose for themselves to either quit the United States or remain where they were born. "The power of locomotion was given to be used at will," William Lloyd Garrison announced in *Thoughts on African Colonization,* yet the oppressive conditions of Black life in the United States—their denial of "equal rights and privileges with other citizens" and the "incorrigible hate and prejudice" they experienced—deprived them of meaningful choice. Unlike white citizens who were "free as the birds in choosing the time when, the mode how, and the place where they shall migrate," Black inhabitants of the United States were forced to "choose between exilement and perpetual degradation," Garrison argued. Without the existence of choice, emancipation did not amount to freedom, "for if a man is free, he must be free to stay in the land of his birth," according to the *Anti-Slavery Record,* a newspaper published by the American Anti-Slavery Society.[8]

Insistence that Black people must possess full emigrant rights equal to those of white citizens remained central to abolitionist opposition to colonization through the 1850s. In 1855, prominent Black abolitionist and Chicago civil rights activist Henry O. Wagoner protested the Illinois governor's support for colonization with an argument honed over previous decades. Emigrant rights to free movement and settlement anywhere in the world provided a powerful justification for Black people to remain and enjoy citizenship rights in the United States. Asserting Black claims to the cosmopolitanism that white citizens took for granted, Wagoner announced that "God has given this whole earth as the habitation of the whole human race, and as part of the human race, I claim that we have a *natural right* to live anywhere on God's beautiful earth." For Wagoner, this meant Black people were equally free to live where they were born or in a place elsewhere of their choosing. Many abolitionist critics of colonization ultimately accepted emigrant rights reasoning because it reinforced their claims to Black birthright citizenship in the United States.[9]

Although abolitionists rejected colonization as the forced removal of an entire population from the United States based on racial prejudice, Black Americans were careful to reserve an individual right to free movement and expatriation for themselves. Condemning Liberian colonization was thus often paired with defending personal emigrant rights. Participants at a meeting of the free Black community of Butler County, Ohio, included this viewpoint in a set of public resolutions. "That while we are in favor of a free-will emigration to countries where larger liberties await us," the attendees rejected schemes to force their community to settle in Africa. The American and Foreign Anti-Slavery Society, one of two national abolitionist organizations in the United States, denounced colonization as "coercive expatriation" but asserted the rights of "colored citizens" of the United States to quit the nation for any "portion of the globe, as their enterprise, business, or inclination, may lead them in common with other citizens." By preserving their individual right to leave, Black Americans insisted that they knew how best to improve their lives.[10]

The pursuit of Black emigrant rights challenged decades of law and custom. Freedom of mobility and expatriation had been considered strictly privileges of white male citizenship since the eighteenth century. Black activists reckoned with this association in their work to dislodge emigrant rights from presumptions of whiteness. The *North Star*, Frederick Douglass's abolitionist newspaper, recognized conventional arguments for emigrant rights as a kind of "sophistry" that was "not designed to aggrandize any but the descendants of European nations." This reasoning assigned every racial group but white people to a particular part of the world; thus, for example, "Africa is the country for Africans" and "the East Indies the place for the Malays," but "any place the white man chooses to go, HIS country!" This account cast the freedom to move and choose allegiance as a thinly disguised legal pretense for Europeans to conquer the world and dispossess other people of their land. Nevertheless, an article published in another issue of the *North Star* suggested that emigrant rights might be redeemable. After all, "it is right that every one should go where he thinks fit; but it is wrong that he should be subjected to any undue influence in the formation of his opinion."[11]

The *North Star* articles expressed a broader moral ambivalence toward Black emigration. In publishing these articles, Frederick Douglass worried that Black people possessed emigrant rights as a condition of their humanity, but at what cost to the abolitionist movement in the United States or perhaps to people elsewhere in the world? Other Black writers had no such reservations. Henry Bibb insisted "that the world is the colored man's home, and that any attempt on the part of human legislation to restrict his boundary, or to circumscribe his field of locomotion, is a gross violation of the fundamental principles of right and justice." Bibb claimed cosmopolitan freedoms for all Black people to pursue their interests anywhere across the globe. Asserting that the privileges of world citizenship belonged to all humanity meant that race could not determine a person's freedom to move and choose allegiance. Bibb and other Black proponents of emigrant rights formed their views in response to the worsening conditions of Black life in the United States during the early 1800s.[12]

Northern states gradually abolished slavery, and Congress outlawed enslavement in the Northwest Territory. Nevertheless, legal freedom did not amount to equal citizenship for Black inhabitants of northern states. By 1840, Black men lost their right to vote in places such as Connecticut, New Jersey, and Pennsylvania, where state legislatures adopted statutes and constitutions limiting suffrage to white men. The New York legislature subjected Black voters to higher property requirements than white voters. Moreover, no state that entered the union after 1820 allowed Black men to vote. Legislatures in the states created from the Northwest Territory often prohibited Black suffrage by adopting restrictive "black laws." State black laws required Black inhabitants to pay onerous fees to register their presence and to receive residency certificates in the counties where they lived. Black residents were also required to secure a $500 bond from at least two local freeholders as a guarantee of their "good behavior" and in anticipation of poor relief the county may have to spend on their behalf. Moreover, black laws allowed for racial discrimination in public education, denied militia and jury service to Black men, and prohibited Black people from testifying in court against white people. In 1839, abolitionist and judge William Jay singled out Ohio's black laws for depriving Black people of their "right of locomotion," which thereby deprived them of full citizenship. In subsequent decades, northern states and territories adopted even stricter limits on Black migration. Illinois, Iowa, Indiana, and the Oregon Territory banned Black settlement altogether. By 1850, denying Black emigrant rights became the basis for denying Black citizenship throughout most northern states.[13]

Legislators in southern states also enacted laws that imposed strict limits on freedom of movement for the region's Black inhabitants. A majority of the southern Black population was enslaved so subject to slave codes that restrained and monitored their movement. Southern state legislatures tightened constraints on slave mobility by raising legal barriers to manumission. Reducing the number of free Black people in the South reduced the number of people who might claim freedom of movement for themselves. By the 1850s all but three slave states outlawed manumission or forced manumitted people to leave the state where they obtained their freedom. In either scenario, Black people were not free to move as they saw fit.[14]

Yet even when manumission was permissible, legal doubts remained about enslaved people's capacity to decide for themselves where to settle. Georgia slaver George M. Waters manumitted certain slaves in his will with the expectation that they "may select their residence out of the State of Georgia, and in any part of the world." Following his death, some of Waters's heirs contested his will "because the election is given to the slaves to choose where they will go; and that they are incapable of making this choice." Chattel property could not possess emigrant rights, argued lawyers for the aggrieved heirs. The Supreme Court of Georgia rejected this argument, but such opinions do not indicate a larger recognition of free Black mobility rights in the South. Southern state legislatures subjected free Black inhabitants to residency requirements and freedom certificates to police their movement. Free Blacks in the South were unable to challenge laws dictating the terms of their mobility because southern state legislatures also prohibited Black suffrage and equal standing in the courts. Finally, several southern states banned free Black settlement from elsewhere. Ultimately, southern state legislators, like their northern counterparts, realized that denying meaningful Black emigrant rights was essential to denying Black citizenship, a necessary conclusion for legislators most concerned with protecting slavery and bolstering white supremacy.[15]

Federal law also denied Black emigrant rights. In 1850, Congress adopted the Fugitive Slave Act, which empowered federal officials to apprehend suspected runaway slaves and decide if they must be returned to owners in the South. The law required northern citizens to help federal officials capture and remand suspected runaways. As a result, after 1850, Black mobility anywhere in the country became subject to greater legal surveillance and intrusion.

Opponents of the Fugitive Slave Act repudiated the law by articulating emigrant rights claims that were more expansive than any considered before 1850. Nowhere was the radical potential of unfettered freedom of movement and expatriation more evident than in the insistence that even enslaved people possessed emigrant rights. According to New Haven minister and antislavery editor Leonard Bacon, one could find an enslaved person's right to escape enslavement under either "natural or international law." An enslaved person thus possessed the same right of "expatriating himself and seeking a new home under other institutions" that "our government, and, and, and even our existence as a people, is founded," Bacon argued. In an antislavery lecture in Boston, Horace Mann included the right to expatriation among the civil liberties possessed by all people including those enslaved. Enslaved people claimed their civil liberties by escaping to freedom and defending their liberty with violence if necessary, for "if resisted, in fleeing from bondage, he that was held had the right to use force as far as was necessary, even to the slaughter of him who opposed."[16]

Arguments for enslaved people's emigrant rights recognized their personhood contrary to the foundational legal principles of slavery. In 1860, a South Carolina appeals court outlined the unsettling implications of this view for any claim to property rights in people. To assert the emigrant rights of enslaved people meant they could choose freedom for themselves by simply "breathing the atmosphere" of a place where slavery was illegal, a place the fugitives could then adopt as their "native domocil—as their birth-place as persons, contradistinguished from chattels." Whereas slavery's defenders in the 1850s presumed no place in the United States allowed enslaved people to shed their degraded status, the emigrant rights challenge to the Fugitive Slave Act created the opposite presumption. Enslaved people everywhere in the United States were potentially free.[17]

The abolitionists' legal basis for their expansive view that mobility promised freedom for all fit with American responses to massive global migration during the 1850s. Between 1850 and 1860, over 2.5 million migrants settled in the United States. This emigration, mostly from Europe, came to signify flight from despotic governments, especially for those aligned with the Democratic Party, so abolitionists drew comparisons to the status of enslaved people under the Fugitive Slave Act. "Civil despots" elsewhere were no different from American slaveholders, according to an 1851 article in the *National Era*, because both denied "their subjects the right of voluntary expatriation." However, this article anticipated the federal government's inconsistent treatment of enslaved runaways in the United States compared to migrants from Europe when the author asked a question with an obvious answer: If Congress required American citizens to help "deliver up to one class of despots their fugitives, are we not equally bound to deliver up to another class their runaways too?" This inconsistency became more obvious later in the 1850s, which abolitionist proponents of enslaved emigrant rights again turned to their advantage.[18]

Seeking to bolster protections abroad for the country's burgeoning population of naturalized citizens, Secretary of State Lewis Cass announced what became the Buchanan administration's unyielding recognition of the right to expatriation in an 1859 circular letter to its diplomats. "The right of expatriation cannot at this day be doubted or denied in the United States" because, Cass informed diplomats abroad, "the idea has been repudiated ever since the origin of our Government, that a man is bound to remain for ever in the country of his birth, and that he has no right to exercise his free will and consult his own happiness by selecting a new home." Once the liberating power of expatriation became a central foreign policy assertion of the Democratic Party, abolitionists took notice. An article in the *Independent*, the antislavery newspaper most committed to constructing a basis for enslaved emigrant rights, insisted that nothing distinguished European emigrants from the millions of enslaved people in the United States for whom the "right of expatriation—the right of exercising their own free wills and selecting new homes—is utterly denied" under a legal system beholden to enslavers. This inconsistency reinforced the abolitionist truth that the US government defended citizenship rights until the point that doing so threatened the property rights of enslavers.[19]

However, this inconsistency was peculiar to the United States. The *Independent* also noted that it was "well known that a certain class of the subjects of our Government are constantly expatriating themselves beyond the jurisdiction, which they find as oppressive to them as any jurisdiction" that European migrants fled for citizenship in the United States. Evidence for this appeared in the actions of every enslaved person who "has taken an opportunity of improving his condition by a voluntary removal to Canada, and has become a naturalized subject of her Britannic Majesty" after deciding that "the condition of slavery, to which he was subjected, [is] disagreeable to him, and inconsistent with his pursuit of happiness." The enslaved person who "renounced and abjured all allegiance to any other power or jurisdiction than that of the country which he has chosen and of the Queen whose loyal subject he has sworn to be" had thus exercised emigrant rights to free movement and expatriation that were no less legitimate nor legally binding outside the United States than the rights European emigrants exercised within the United States.[20]

These legal arguments gained meaning through the actions of enslaved people, such as those in Detroit on a December morning in 1854. With the sun just visible, a group of sixteen—mostly women and children—passed through town and boarded the ferry for Canada West. Whereas they were once considered "chattels" in Covington, Kentucky, they became "subjects of the British Crown" after "renouncing their claim to protection under the 'glorious stars and stripes,'" according to the *Detroit Tribune*. The group's short trip across the Detroit River brought them from the republic that denied their liberty to a royal colony that recognized their legal personhood.[21]

Enslaved people from the United States realized their emigrant rights in Canada West at the same time that many free Blacks in the North claimed these rights for themselves. James Theodore Holly, a boot maker in Burlington, Vermont, outlined the options before his people in the starkest terms. "Our oppression having now reached its culminating point," Holly wrote in 1851, "when the only alternatives left to us to choose are, everlasting slavery, expatriation, or annihilation." If lived experience alone did not suggest the correct choice for Black Americans, Holly also looked to lessons from the past. "History attests," Holly insisted, "that emigration and settlement beyond the operation of political disabilities are the great means, by which an oppressed people become renovated. It is the regenerative power of baptism, politically, to a denationalized people." British North America was the place of Black political rebirth, Holly concluded.[22]

The same year that Holly implored his people to abandon the United States, a group of free Black people exercised their emigrant rights before congregating in the Niagara District of Canada West, a region on the wide peninsula between Lakes Ontario and Erie. Although this group left the United States to escape the oppression of the Fugitive Slave Act, they petitioned the US Congress for its repeal so they could return to their birthplace with confidence that the laws would protect their persons and their property. The group identified themselves in the petition as "temporary residents" of Canada West, thus suggesting they were reluctant emigrants, but their demands of Congress revealed that they understood themselves in complete possession of emigrant rights, as individuals free to move and cast allegiance as they saw fit. Although grateful for the government in Canada West that allowed them to "dwell in peace and quietude under the mild and benignant sway of Queen Victoria's scepter," they had also never "forfeited the protection" of the US government. The petitioners informed Congress that they would decide which government deserved their allegiance. They preferred to live in the United States but would choose Canada West if the government of their birthplace failed to meet their expectations. Holly and the Niagara petitioners shared a common understanding of their emigrant rights in 1851. They assumed the power to decide their allegiance rather than surrendering that power to any government. As the 1850s progressed, those Black Americans who were determined to decide their allegiance chose British North America with less reluctance as their lives became more untenable in the United States.[23]

BRITISH NORTH AMERICA in the decade of sustained Black emigration consisted of several Crown colonies and vast territories administered by the Hudson's Bay Company, the most powerful fur trade monopoly on the continent. Although the colonies and territories of British North America were different in culture, commerce, and origins, they were part of a global empire that abolished slavery in 1833. Once the law took effect in 1834, British North America became a place where Black abolitionists believed they could exercise their claims to emigration right citizenship. The colony of Upper Canada became the primary destination for Black emigrants from the United States during the 1830s. Black subjects helped defeat the Rebellions of 1837–38 in Upper Canada. Supporters in the United States viewed them as republican revolutions in favor of white men's emigrant rights to move and decide allegiance, so their failure bolstered the appeal of Upper Canada to Black Americans as a place where monarchy and abolition prevailed. Following the rebellions, Parliament created the Province of Canada by merging Lower and Upper Canada into a single colony in 1841. What had been separate colonies since 1791 became the administrative districts of Canada East and Canada West under the provincial authority of a governor general and a bicameral legislature.[24]

With passage of the Fugitive Slave Act, more places in British North America seemed preferable to nearly any place in the United States for many Black Americans. Proximity often dictated the options for Black emigrants seeking lives under British sovereignty. Black New Englanders could choose to settle in Nova Scotia, where Black communities had existed since the Revolutionary War. On the Pacific Coast, Parliament created the Colony of Vancouver Island in 1849, which eventually attracted several hundred Black emigrants from California.[25]

Although a relatively wealthy Black community of professionals and civic institutions formed in San Francisco and Sacramento, Black Californians suffered from daily legal discrimination and racial prejudice. Writing for a Victoria newspaper in 1859, John Moore, a minister and leader of the Black community in San Francisco, cited racial discrimination as the main reason that he and the other "Colored Emigrants" quit the United States for Vancouver Island. Moore used the language of emigrant respectability that long distinguished legitimate claims to free movement and expatriation from instances of shiftless sojourning. He insisted that Black emigrants intended to settle permanently in a place where they expected "to enjoy those common social rights that civilized, enlightened, and well regulated communities guarantee to all their members." Black emigrants proved their intent and demonstrated good character by bringing their families and enough wealth to purchase the land they lived on, Moore noted. Black emigrants thus arrived on Vancouver Island in possession of the moral and human passports that eased the exercise of emigration right citizenship in borderlands regions throughout North America. As Moore concluded, using the language of emigrant rights, "We have come to this country to make it the land of our adoption for ourselves and our children." Despite racism in Victoria, most Black emigrants from California remained there through the 1860s.[26]

Canada East was another possible destination for Black emigrants from the United States. The Eastern Townships in particular seemed like an ideal place for Black settlement because it was a borderlands region shaped since the 1790s by the laws and expectations of emigration right citizenship. Nevertheless, few Black people chose settlements there. John W. Lewis spent considerable time in the Eastern Townships during the 1850s as a traveling agent for *Frederick Douglass' Paper*. Although a free Black man resident in St. Albans, Vermont, Lewis wrote to Douglass "that I always feel a peculiar sensation in crossing the line between the two countries," not because "I feel myself any more of a man when I get into Canada, yet I am in a place where the rights of men are more respected." Still, Lewis observed differences between the Eastern Townships and other regions of British North America that mattered to Black emigrants. "The fact is," Lewis noted, "Canadians, in the border towns, on the part near the United States, have become so Americanized and Yankeeized, they do not manifest that noble spirit of philanthropy in all respects, that is seen and felt in the Western townships." In Lewis's estimation, racism in the Eastern Townships limited emigrant rights to white men despite colonial laws and abolitionist arguments recognizing the freedom of Black people to move and choose allegiances. The Black population of Canada East thus remained relatively small even in 1860 after a decade of significant Black emigration from the United States.[27]

Although anywhere in British North America seemed preferable to Black emigrants from the United States after 1850, a majority continued to choose Canada West. Indeed, in the autumn of 1850 alone, approximately 3,000 Black emigrants left the United States for British North America, with a majority crossing the Niagara and Detroit Rivers to settle in Canada West. Writing in 1854, Black abolitionist Wesley W. Tate attributed the steady growth of the Black population in British North America to the Fugitive Slave Act. For all of this law's many evils, it had nevertheless "done good, in pushing colored emigration into Canada" by rousing more Black people than ever before to quit the "so-called free states" for lives in an actual "free country under the protection of the British flag." By 1860, a majority of the Black population in British North America lived in Canada West.[28]

Activists in Canada West responded to the arrival of Black newcomers without delay. Black and white abolitionists formed the Anti-Slavery Society of Canada during a public meeting at Toronto's city hall in early 1851. In the following years, the Anti-Slavery Society of Canada (ASC) sponsored abolitionist lectures and activities, corresponded with abolitionists elsewhere, gained crucial assistance from a ladies' association, and spread its reach with the formation of local auxiliaries throughout Canada West. Although motivated by opposition to the Fugitive Slave Act, the founders of the ASC shared two broad aims. First, they wanted to associate themselves with the international abolitionist movement in order to help end slavery in the United States. The founders also hoped to end slavery in the United States "by manifesting

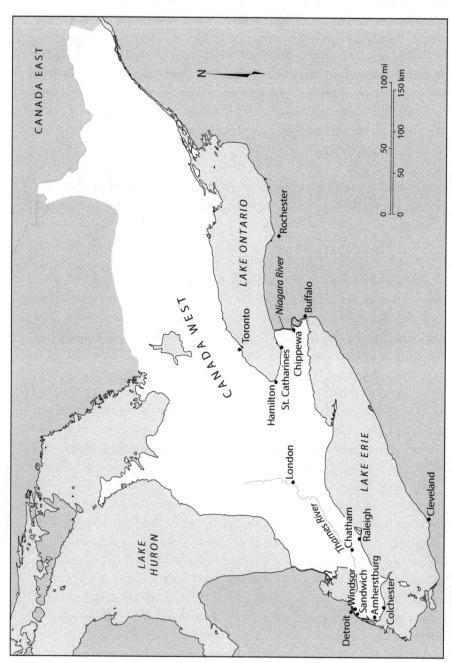

Canada West

sympathy with the houseless and homeless victims of slavery flying to our soil." Responsibility for the latter went primarily to the Ladies Association for the Relief of Destitute Colored Fugitives. Annual reports detail the work of these abolitionist women to meet the immediate needs of Black newcomers to Canada West and to help them flourish in the colony, primarily through education and landownership. Although the ASC touted British North America as a place of Black equality, its white members rarely considered Black settlers in Canada West except as refugees or fugitives. Essentially, the ASC emphasized its work creating conditions for personal independence over concerns with helping Black settlers know and exercise their full rights as subjects.[29]

Black members of the ASC put equal importance on meeting material needs and assistance with becoming subjects. Henry Bibb exemplified this view. Bibb lived in Sandwich, Canada West, after fleeing enslavement in Kentucky and a decade's residence in Detroit. Bibb supported the ASC as the vice president responsible for the Sandwich auxiliary. However, Bibb's activism was not limited to the ASC. In 1851, Bibb called a large meeting of Black abolitionists in Toronto. The North American Convention of Colored Freeman included delegates from Canada West and a few cities in the upper United States. This gathering also endorsed the common view that landownership was essential to Black independence in British North America. However, a majority of the delegates also approved a resolution encouraging Black emigration from the United States as essential to abolitionist goals and the realization of Black freedom, both for those enslaved and those subject to racial discrimination in northern states. "An Address to the Colored Inhabitants of North America," a summary of the convention proceedings coauthored by Bibb, extolled Canada West as a place where "here, and here only, we participate in all the rights and privileges which other men enjoy." From their perspective, Canada West was not merely a haven of last resort for Black people fleeing enslavement or the prospect of recapture in the United States, contrary to the prevailing view of the ASC. Instead, it was a place where Black people decided for themselves to claim the full rights of British subjects. Bibb's organizational work in the early 1850s thus helped introduce the emigrant rights legal claims of abolitionists in the United States to antislavery activists in British North America.[30]

Apart from organizing public meetings, Bibb worked to create institutions to further his view of emigrant rights abolitionism. In the fall of 1850, Bibb and other Black residents of Sandwich organized the Fugitive's Union Society. The resolutions creating this society announced the founders' intention to help Black newcomers become independent landowners with an expectation that they would also become royal subjects. As one resolution declared, "we duly appreciate the high privileges which we freely enjoy in this land of equal rights," a sentiment which they intended to share with the Black people they assisted in order for them to "discharge the duty of good, peaceable, loyal subjects to her Majesty—the Queen of Great Britain." This society developed into the Refugee Home Society (RHS), an organization funded by white abolitionists in Detroit but directed from Windsor, Canada West, by Bibb and his wife Mary Bibb. The RHS purchased land near Windsor for resale to Black settlers on easy terms so they could become independent property owners soon after their arrival. The RHS also supported the formation of schools and churches for the Black settlers. The Bibbs started *Voice of the Fugitive*, a newspaper for the growing Black community in Canada West that promoted the RHS and, of equal importance, insisted its readers do everything necessary to become full British subjects.[31]

The organizational and editorial work of Henry and Mary Bibb helped transform the Detroit River borderlands into a region of Black emigrant activism. In 1853, leading figures from this region called a General Convention for the Improvement of the Colored Inhabitants of Canada. They met in Amherstburg, a town at the endpoint of a common Underground Railroad route and a center of Black emigrant life on the Detroit River. Black residents comprised 25 percent of Amherstburg's population in the 1850s. William Wells Brown, the prominent Black American abolitionist, visited Amherstburg in 1861. He described the town's location in a fertile region with many Black property owners and farmers of some renown, at least as measured by the prize-winning crops they displayed at local agricultural fairs. Thomas Buckner's one-hundred-pound squash caught Wells's attention. In addition to his farming accomplishments, Buckner was active in Black public life. In 1851 he voiced his support for the North American convention, and the Amherstburg convention appointed him to a local committee. More unsettling to racial hierarchies familiar to Brown, successful Black carpenter William Lyons employed and bossed six white laborers.[32]

At this place of visible Black independence and accomplishment, delegates to the 1853 convention issued a forceful call for Black emigration from the United States. Emigration was the only way for Black people "to secure their elevation and development" because they would never have authentic economic, educational, and religious opportunities in the United States. In their resolutions, delegates claimed the benefits of their own expatriation from the United States by affirming their obligations and privileges as loyal

British subjects. They announced their readiness to defend their "adopted country" and implored all Black emigrants to swear the oath of allegiance to the Crown without haste. As subjects, the delegates declared their commitment to protecting "all the rights and immunities which the British Constitution guarantees to every man, without respect to clime, sect or party against all unjust prejudices that may show itself in Canada against the colored man."[33]

The delegates compared their public standing as full British subjects to the conditions of Black life in the United States. This took the form of a *Report on Emigration* commissioned by the delegates. Beneath its innocuous title, the report's authors, principally Black abolitionist and *Voice of the Fugitive* correspondent James T. Holly, insisted that their people in the United States would forever remain "oppressed and denationalized" without strong action. Free Black people suffered "systematic" legal discrimination under a "well digested and long pursued course of oppression" commenced in 1787 at the Constitutional Convention. The same was true for Black people subject to enslavement. In both instances, Black people in the United States owed "that Government no allegiance, but interminable hatred." Their hope for freedom and citizenship rested on a choice, the authors concluded, between "Revolution or Emigration." Although "the boldest and probably the most glorious alternative," revolution was impractical compared to emigration. The report considered various destinations in the Western Hemisphere that Black emigrants might choose but argued that Canada West offered the most promise. The Amherstburg convention contributed to a perception of Canada West as the only place where enslaved and free Black people should expect full legal personhood.[34]

Mary Ann Shadd did more to promote, and in ways confirm, this view than any other Black writer in the 1850s. Shadd belonged to a family of free Black abolitionists from Delaware who settled in Canada West in 1851. Shadd was a free but also unmarried Black woman. This status allowed her to exercise the privileges of emigrant rights to a degree unavailable to women whose husbands or enslavers denied their freedom to move and to adopt national allegiances. This position certainly informed Shadd's unqualified endorsement of Canada West as the Black emigrants' destination of choice. Shadd outlined her views in *A Plea for Emigration; or, Notes of Canada West*, a pamphlet she published in 1852. Although Shadd extolled Canada West as a place of freedom from enslavement, her anticipated audience was free Black readers in the United States. These people, "always free" as Shadd described them, were now eager to quit the United States with passage of the Fugitive Slave

Law. Shadd wrote to guide their choice of British North America, and Canada West in particular, a province she believed was unique for its combination of fertile climate, available land, and political and civic rights for Black subjects. For Shadd, prospective emigrants should not consider material subsistence separate from their legal standing when deciding where to settle. As Shadd described this relationship, "Lands out of the United States, on this continent, should have no local value, if the questions of personal freedom and political rights were left out of the subject." Black emigrants should only consider settlement where "a permanent nationality is included in the prospect of becoming purchasers and settlers." Canada West promised both because of its abundant land and laws that granted Black emigrants, in the language of the law, the "full 'privileges of British birth in the Province.'"[35]

A Plea for Emigration furthered the abolitionist insistence that emigrant rights were not constrained by race. Relying on justifications for free movement and expatriation commonplace since the eighteenth century, Shadd believed that accidents of birth could not bind Black people to the country that oppressed them. Moreover, Shadd encouraged Black people to decide for themselves where they were most likely to flourish. In this way, Shadd adhered to a cosmopolitan perspective that no nation was inherently superior to another. Instead, Black emigrants must have confidence that adopting new allegiances will improve their lives. Shadd thus drew an invidious comparison between Canada West and nations such as Mexico. "People who love liberty do not emigrate to weak governments to embroil themselves in their quarrels with stronger ones," Shadd stated, "but to strong ones, to add to their strength and better their own condition." By this measure, Shadd concluded that Black Americans should consider adopting new allegiances in Canada West before anyplace else.[36]

Encouraging Black people to quit the United States for Canada West became the focus of Shadd's work editing the *Provincial Freeman*, a newspaper she established in 1853. She published the newspaper until 1859 at various locations in Canada West starting in Windsor before Toronto and, finally, Chatham. Shadd contributed articles to the *Provincial Freeman* but she also held nearly complete editorial control over the newspaper, giving her power to shape the public sphere unusual for nineteenth-century women. Shadd concerned much of the *Provincial Freeman* with instructing Black emigrants in how to obtain and defend their rights and privileges as subjects guaranteed by British law. This work, as Shadd understood it, demanded a capacious editorial view. The *Provincial Freeman* reported on an array of subjects relevant to emigrant life, from how and where to buy land in Canada West to matters of education and religion, provincial politics, and Black public life in British North America. Shadd and her *Provincial Freeman* became the leading advocate of Black emigrant rights and the concerns of Black subjects in Canada West following the demise of Henry and Mary Bibb's *Voice of the Fugitive* in 1853 and Henry Bibb's death a year later. The privileges of emigration right citizenship in Canada West promised in the pages of the *Provincial Freeman* captured the attention of Black readers in the United States.[37]

Correspondents from the United States described varying degrees of enthusiasm for emigration and organized emigration activism in Black communities. A visitor to Buffalo estimated that a majority of the city's Black residents were "silently in favor of Emigration" but hesitant to share their views because prominent New York abolitionists opposed it. Nevertheless, some of these people "will yet leave for Canada, and whose departure from their land of their birth, should shame the American profession of equality." On the contrary, forthright endorsements of emigration shaped Black public life in Brooklyn, New York. Frustrated by barriers to landownership and complacent community leaders, "many respectable and intelligent colored men" were, according to a regular Brooklyn correspondent, "looking Canadaward," and doubtless within a year "you will have an extensive emigration of that class from this state." The same Black men of means and standing held a public meeting at Brooklyn's Granada Hall to create a Canadian Emigration Society to inform and organize the growing number of local Black families who chose to leave the United States. The attendees appointed Francis Champion as chairman and J. N. Still as secretary, but they voted to indefinitely postpone forming a permanent society. Nevertheless, the Brooklyn correspondent, likely Still, boasted that steps toward an organized emigration movement among free Black people of standing revealed that "a great revolution has taken place in public sentiment" marked by "the universal disposition of our people to leave the States for Canada—the place of their own choosing."[38]

This revolution was visible in Canada West. An observer in Windsor reported to the *Provincial Freeman* that over sixty Black people arrived from the United States in one week alone in 1854, the vast majority of whom were "free emigrants," primarily from Indiana and Pennsylvania, rather than self-emancipated fugitives from enslavement. Ephraim Waterford was likely among this group. Waterford owned a forty-acre farm in Indiana when the state legislature adopted a new law that made it illegal for Black men to devise real estate. Without full control of his property, Waterford could only claim partial citizenship, a status that soured his view on the United States. As

Waterford decided, "if that was a republican government" that stripped him of his property rights and full citizenship, then "I would try a monarchical one." He and a group of thirty to forty Black adults and children quit the United States for Canada West in 1854. Within two years, Waterford owned 200 acres in Colchester, an agricultural community near the shores of Lake Erie, with five already fenced and put to corn cultivation. The correspondent who likely saw Waterford and his family pass through Windsor predicted that they were "but the advance guard of a 'crowd,' most of whom have pockets well lined." The *Provincial Freeman* celebrated the increased number of Black arrivals from this "class which before this year has been small," that is, "free persons" in family groups, often with their furniture in tow, and with enough money to buy homes and property.[39]

Drawing attention to the relative wealth and family status of recent Black arrivals confirmed their good character and potential to become loyal subjects. Under the law, legitimate emigrant rights to move and choose allegiance belonged to people who could prove their intention to quit one sovereignty for another. According to borderlands interpretations of the law, this proof was long considered evident in visible wealth and human passports in the form of household dependents. Every instance of people such as Ephraim Waterford expatriating himself from the United States thus gave emigration's Black advocates reason to urge the same choice on others like him.

The advent of a national emigration movement in the United States reflected the push by activists to make emigration a respectable option for Black people of means and standing. To this end, a National Emigration Convention of Colored People gathered in Cleveland in 1854 and again in 1856. The organizers and attendees at the first gathering were Black proponents of emigration, men and women mostly from northern states and some from Canada West, including Mary Bibb. Over three days, attendees considered ways to support emigration within Black communities, to obtain and share information about the best settlement options for Black emigrants, and to encourage publications favorable to their movement.[40]

Martin R. Delany, a physician and abolitionist editor from Pittsburgh, emerged from the convention he helped organize as the most prominent Black emigration activist in the United States. He delivered the convention's keynote address, "The Political Destiny of the Colored Race on the American Continent," which summarized his argument for Black emigrant rights in *The Condition, Elevation, Emigration, and Destiny of the Colored People of the United States*, published in 1852. Although it appeared in print the same year as Shadd's *Plea for Emigration*, Delany's perspective was decidedly more cosmopolitan in its ethics and assumptions about Black life outside the United States. Delany insisted that "the world belongs to mankind—his common Father created it for his common good," an inheritance that gave Black people equal freedom with all humans to move and settle as they pleased. Delany asserted Black emigrant rights with familiar arguments for the virtues of adopted allegiance and portable patriotism, virtues in opposition to any notion of birthright obligation to one privileged nation above others. Although Black people were free to "go when we will, and where we may," Delany realized that they might have some patriotic affection for the United States that emigration would not diminish so much as direct elsewhere, for "we shall love the country none the less that receives us as her adopted children." Fugitives from enslavement were best to consider Canada West, but Delany advised free Blacks to choose Nicaragua or New Granada, republics formed in Central America and northern South America, which he touted as places that offered Black people citizenship and political power along with treaty protections from Great Britain. Regardless of where they settled, Black emigrants left the United States with "but one object—to become elevated men and women, worthy of freedom—the worthy citizens of an adopted country."[41]

The organized emigration movement in the United States captured the attention of Black activists elsewhere, including Mary Ann Shadd. She publicized the 1856 convention in the *Provincial Freeman*. In promoting the convention, Shadd criticized Black abolitionists in the United States who opposed emigration for condemning their people to suffer while striving to achieve even gradual improvements to their condition. The National Emigration Convention promised an alternative. "Go to the Cleveland Convention," Shadd implored her readers in the United States, "and determine to remove to a country or to countries, where you may have equal political rights, and thus be *elevated* at *once*." By the time the second convention gathered in Cleveland, the movement's leading voice in the United States made the choice that Shadd recommended to all Black Americans. In 1855, Delany assessed the conditions of Black life in the United States in his role as president of a national board of commissioners created at the 1854 convention. Published as the "Political Aspect of the Colored People of the United States," Delany adopted a more sanguine view of Black settlement in Canada West, noting that "our people are flocking into this beautiful country, and substantially settling themselves down by becoming possessors of the soil, as loyal British subjects." Delany still believed that Black people possessed emigrant rights to move and belong anywhere in the world, but in 1856 he decided to exercise his emigrant rights for settlement in Chatham, Canada West. Delany's choice in 1856 was that of the thousands of other Black emigrants from the United States in the 1850s.[42]

Chatham's streets and its surrounding countryside bustled with Black life in the 1850s. Black physicians, including Delany, lived in the town. Black artisans and mechanics, including several cordwainers, carpenters, and an accomplished gunsmith, serviced local needs, several from shops in brick buildings prominently located on King Street adjacent to the Thames River. The publishing office of the *Provincial Freeman* was located on the same street. Black men owned property in the town. They also owned large farms in Chatham's hinterlands, all the more noteworthy to William Wells Brown because these "several splendid farms" were "owned and paid for by men once held in slavery." Chatham's Black residents worshiped in Methodist and Baptist churches and formed a separate school for their children after white residents prevented them from attending the local common school. Shadd taught in this school in addition to publishing the *Provincial Freeman*. Chatham's location on the Thames River and along the Great Western Railway connected its residents and the goods they produced to Detroit and to Canada West's other growing towns and cities. Chatham thus proved quite appealing to Black emigrants from the United States during the 1850s. "Here, indeed, more fully than anywhere else, the traveler realizes the extent of the American exodus," claimed Benjamin Drew, a white abolitionist from Massachusetts who visited Chatham in the 1850s. Drew estimated that Black residents comprised 50 percent of the population in Chatham and its agricultural periphery, an estimate that matches William Wells Brown's impression that "every other person whom I met was colored." Chatham in the 1850s was thus a place of Black self-reliance rooted in visible networks of social, commercial, and intellectual exchange, but it was far from a community unto itself.[43]

Black emigrants from the United States settled in several communities similar to Chatham. Apart from Toronto, most Black emigrants lived in the southernmost townships of Canada West. The region closest to the United States, it stretched from St. Catharines near the Niagara River to Windsor and Sandwich on the Detroit River. Windsor was the gateway to westernmost townships in the region with sizeable Black populations, including those such as Chatham, Amherstburg, and Colchester. East toward St. Catharines, Black emigrant communities existed in London and Hamilton. Colonial officials had opened this entire region to settlement decades earlier with a series of treaties that dispossessed Mississauga and Wyandot of waterways and land that belonged to them since the early eighteenth century. In Canada West, as with elsewhere in North America, people exercised their emigrant rights in response to the presence or loss of Indigenous power. Despite the forced transformation of Indigenous land into Crown property, settler populations were relatively sparse in the southwestern townships of Canada West. By 1850, less than 20 percent of the land in much of this region was occupied and farmed unlike in the densely settled and more expensive townships on the north shore of Lake Ontario, including Toronto. Thus for reasons of proximity to the United States and access to relatively low cost land, Black emigrants concentrated in communities such as Chatham and the surrounding farming districts.[44]

With their arrival and settlement, Black emigrants shaped life in this region of Canada West. They pursued livelihoods, formed families, and established institutions including schools, churches, and associations, or sought access to those they could share with their white neighbors. Black emigrants established themselves within a provincial legal system that prohibited racial discrimination in voting and office holding, in jury service and court testimony, and in access to public and private services. Although white racism worked to limit these rights, Black emigrants responded in various ways to secure equal protection before the law, especially in their communities where recent political reforms transferred local legislative and administrative authority from courts to elected county or township councils. Black emigrants used both to embody their standing as rights-bearing British subjects. Black settlers shared their legal reasoning and political views with Benjamin Drew during his tour of Canada West. "What circumstances have led them to prefer a monarchy to a *republic*?" Drew queried. Black settlers responded with a variety of answers all informed by their understanding of international law and the rights it gave them to move freely in pursuit of allegiances of their own choosing. The region of Black settlement in Canada West was thus much more than a collection of places where Black people created communities. It was here that Black emigrants became British subjects, a legal status both meaningful in their private lives and essential to their public aspirations, thus finally realizing the promise of emigration right citizenship that they first claimed by leaving the United States.[45]

Merely setting foot in British North America entitled Black emigrants to the protections that subjects expected. Black emigrants realized this sense of instant subjecthood waiting just across the border, according to Samuel Ringgold Ward, especially for people escaping enslavement. The moment they reached British North America, "that 'leap' transforms him from a marketable chattel to a free man." Ward had already leapt for freedom several times in his life before becoming a forceful advocate for Black emigrant rights in

Canada West. Born to enslaved parents who escaped Maryland when he was a toddler, Ward eventually became an abolitionist editor and minister in up-state New York. He arrived in Toronto in 1851 to evade prosecution in Syracuse for assisting fugitive slaves. Once in Canada West, Ward aligned himself with Shadd and the editorial positions of the *Provincial Freeman*, which he occasionally co-edited and tirelessly supported. Throughout the 1850s, Ward reiterated his view on the consequential personal effects of Black emigration. Canada West, Ward insisted, "offers and secures to the American slave the moment he arrives here, Freedom—British Freedom—impartial Freedom." Alexander Hemsley experienced a sense of sudden change to his status that matched Ward's description. Although emancipated by the Supreme Court of New Jersey in the 1830s, Hemsley considered the threat of illegal re-enslavement real enough that he and his family eventually settled in St. Catharines, where he lived as a Methodist minister. "When I reached English territory," Hemsley explained, "I had a comfort in law—that my shackles were struck off, and that a man was a man by law."[46]

Officials and judges in British North America bolstered this sense among Black emigrants of an immediate expatriation from the authority and laws of the United States once they arrived within British territory. By the late 1840s, interpretations of the Webster-Ashburton Treaty, backed by an extradition statute adopted by the Province of Canada, guaranteed that no former slaves or people accused of fleeing enslavement were extradited to the United States. The convergence of municipal and international law in the Great Lakes borderlands reinforced the emigrant rights claims that Black Americans brought with them from the United States. The Province of Canada's extradition law facilitated the exercise of Black emigration right citizenship in fact. However, Black emigrants turned to the province's naturalization statutes to exercise their emigration right citizenship with the force of law, which allowed them to live in Canada West not merely as free residents but as rights-bearing British subjects.[47]

The Province of Canada's naturalization statutes secured the freedom of Black emigrants by giving them legal options to complete their expatriation from the United States. In 1849, the Legislative Assembly of Canada enacted a comprehensive naturalization law that "admitted to and confirmed in all the Privileges of British birth" all aliens "with a settled place of abode" and continuous residence in the Province of Canada as of February 10, 1841, when the Act of Union was proclaimed in Montreal, or before that date when Upper and Lower Canada were separate colonies. This law covered all adults, their children, and descendants of deceased aliens. However, to benefit from the

Born in Maryland to enslaved parents, Samuel Ringgold Ward became a prominent advocate for Black emigrant rights in Canada West during the 1850s. Frontis and title page of Samuel Ringgold Ward, *Autobiography of a Fugitive Negro* (London: John Snow, 1855), courtesy of the New York Public Library.

law, men were required to swear an oath of allegiance to the Crown. Going forward, aliens could naturalize themselves after seven years of continuous residence in the province. Once they met the residency requirement, all applicants for naturalization, men and women, were required to swear an oath of residence confirming their intent to make the province their permanent settlement and affirming that they had not lived outside the province during the previous seven years. Men were still required to swear the additional oath of allegiance. Local officials received the oaths, determined their veracity, judged the oath taker's character, and provided residency certificates in return. Unless their residency certificates were contested, individuals filed them with any provincial court to complete the naturalization process and receive a certificate of naturalization. Wives of British subjects were naturalized by virtue of marriage. The statute also clarified that naturalization afforded full property rights.[48]

The Legislative Assembly amended the 1849 law twice during the 1850s, each time to lower the residency requirement. The first change in 1854 lowered the requirement from seven to five years, and then, in 1858, from five to three years. The 1849 law and its subsequent amendments applied to "every Alien." Alexander Hamilton captured not only the broad reach of the province's naturalization law but also its significance to the lives Black emigrants created for themselves in Canada West. Hamilton quit slavery and the United States in 1834 when he left St. Louis for London, where he owned significant real estate by the 1850s. His legal status complemented his standing as a property owner in descriptions of himself. "I am naturalized here," Hamilton announced in 1856, "and have all the rights and privileges of a British subject." Thus not only did the Province of Canada's naturalization law increasingly favor emigrant rights during the 1850s, it did so without racial or status distinctions.[49]

Potential Black emigrants were likely more familiar with naturalization law in the United States, which, since 1790, limited citizenship to "free white" people. Advocates of Black emigration from the United States thus emphasized the Province of Canada's inclusive naturalization laws. In her *Plea for Emigration*, Mary Ann Shadd explained the privileges possessed by British subjects and the necessary legal procedures Black emigrants should follow to obtain them, even reprinting the oath of allegiance. The *Report on Emigration*, written in 1853 at the request of the delegates to the Amherstburg convention, contrasted the status of a Black person in the United States, where due to racist law and custom he was "rendered an out and out alien on the very soil that gave him birth," against the status of a Black man who chose to quit the United States for Canada West where "his color is no bar to his naturalization." The delegates thus included among their resolutions a recommendation that Black emigrants familiarize themselves with provincial naturalization law in order to take the oath of allegiance so they could become "good loyal subjects" without delay. Writing in the *Provincial Freeman* in 1853, Samuel Ringgold Ward summarized the province's naturalization law to emphasize its power for Black emigrants who chose to use it. It was the legal fulfillment of their pursuit of emigration right citizenship, which culminated in their expatriation from the laws and authority of the United States, for when a Black emigrant "has stood his seven years' probation, and taken the oath of allegiance, Canada secures to him, at home and abroad, in law and equity, all the rights and immunities of a British subject." In emphasizing the details and significance of naturalization law in the Province of Canada, advocates of Black emigration provided potential emigrants a legal primer along with reasons to claim provincial law for themselves.[50]

Although Black emigrants used naturalization law to expatriate themselves from the United States, extended residence empowered them to identify as free

British subjects. "I am a regular Britisher," announced Alexander Hemsley. During his years in St. Catharines, "my American blood has been scourged out of me; I have lost my American tastes; I am an enemy to tyranny." Hemsley's affective expatriation from the United States is reflected in sentiments of other Black emigrants. Family concerns drove Sarah Jackson's determination to settle in a free state with her three children, although she ultimately chose London, Canada West, instead. While the laws of slavery in the United States denied Jackson the rights of legal marriage, her experience as the primary caregiver for her children seems to have created space for her to claim emigrant rights, much as it did for white widows in other borderlands regions. Nevertheless, Jackson chose to quit the United States under unusually little duress for an enslaved mother because the man in Kentucky who enslaved her also let her decide when to leave his home. Nevertheless, only a week's residence in London relieved Jackson. With the possibility of employment, homeownership, and education for her children, Jackson described feeling "better here than I was at home—I feel lighter—the dread is gone." Such experiences of affective expatriation were meaningful in personal ways that shaped private lives. For Dan Joshiah Lockhart, quitting enslavement for life in Canada West meant freedom from outside authority over his family, a feeling of personhood tied to his standing as an independent father and husband. A woman identified only as Christopher Hamilton's wife nevertheless described with confidence the reasons she claimed her emigrant rights. Once she was mortgaged to satisfy the creditors of the family that enslaved her, she "thought it best to come to Canada, and live as I pleased." After fourteen years in London, where she was free to work, think, and move about on her own terms, "I am now my own mistress."[51]

Other Black emigrants found it difficult to establish themselves in Canada West, which made expatriation in any form both incomplete and undesirable. William Johnson, once enslaved in Virginia, preferred life in St. Catharines to that anywhere in the United States, but severe frostbite on his feet left him permanently debilitated. Unable to work and subsisting on the economic margins left Johnson without full claims to subjecthood. Nancy Howard quit her enslavement in Baltimore for freedom in Lynn, Massachusetts. She preferred to remain in Lynn, but she became convinced that the Fugitive Slave Act threatened her liberty, so she quit a life once again, this time settling in St. Catharines. Howard found life difficult in Canada West, especially her inability to find employment. "It is a sin on the slaveholders that I had to leave and come here," Howard lamented. Unlike Black emigrants who experienced elation or independence by leaving the United States, "it has brought me lower to the ground," she regretted.[52]

The personal experiences of affective expatriation from the United States likely informed a newfound sense of British patriotism among Black residents of Canada West. In some instances, they expressed their patriotism in individual terms, as their personal affection for the Crown and their loyalty to Great Britain. Since emigrating from the United States, Samuel Ringgold Ward reported that he and his entire family "have each and severally been, *con amore*, the most loyal and grateful British subjects." Ward confessed an earlier skepticism toward the very notion of patriotism, an incredulity informed by the racism he had experienced in the United States. Nevertheless, Ward celebrated, Canada West "had become to me, in a sense in which no country ever was before, my own, and those people my fellow citizens." Mary Jane Robinson extolled life in Canada West in a letter she wrote to Sarah Ann Harris in New York, from where Robinson had emigrated with her husband in 1854. Robinson encouraged Harris to choose a life in Canada West, where they could live "without the white man's foot on our necks." The freedom Robinson experienced quickly formed patriotic sentiments for the British Crown, which she shared in her advice to Harris. "Away with your King Fillmore," thus mocking the false liberty of republican government in the United States, "I am for Queen Victoria," Robinson proclaimed, "God Save the Queen." Ultimately, Black emigrants claimed a place in Canada West for themselves and their families through personal expressions of British patriotism.[53]

Collective expressions of British patriotism allowed Black settlers to claim their rights to public space. Black residents of Canada West affirmed their standing as loyal subjects at commemorations to mark the abolition of slavery in the British Empire. Celebrated annually on August 1, this day of Black independence held particular significance for emigrants from a nation where enslavement had only become more entrenched since the 1830s. At an 1854 celebration in Toronto, a large number of participants from the city and its hinterlands gathered for sermons, a procession, and an address to Queen Victoria. They announced their loyalty and gratitude to the queen "on this, the anniversary of our *death* to *Slavery*, and our *birth* to *Freedom*." Although the celebrants understood their personal quest for liberty as part of a hemispheric challenge to slavery, their adulation for the queen also reflected the particular conditions of Black freedom in the Great Lakes borderlands of North America. "What a happy, what a proud reflection it must be to your Majesty," the celebrants exclaimed, "to know that the moment the poor crushed slave sets foot upon any part of your *mighty* dominions, his chains fall from him—he feels himself a man, and can look up." Queen Victoria thus deserved the loyalty and allegiance of all Black residents of Canada West because she reigned over an empire that enabled the exercise of Black emigrant rights even for the most oppressed. British patriotism thus not only provided Black emigrants a path to local belonging in Canada West but a claim to an imperial identity that gave them rights and duties anywhere in the empire.[54]

Although Black emigrants were often eager to announce their British patriotism, they never did so from a position of limitless gratitude. Indeed, the liberty to move and choose allegiance had always presumed a notion of conditional patriotism. Free people chose to remain allegiant to a government and settled under its authority insofar as they received protection and rights in return. In claiming their emigrant rights, Black people also decided the limits of their patriotism. H. Ford Douglas expressed this position in strong terms. Born an enslaved person in Virginia before escaping to build a free life in Cleveland, Douglas was an ardent advocate of emigration in the 1850s as both a participant in the national conventions and an emigrant from the United States. Douglas helped edit the *Provincial Freeman,* in which he published his views. "If rights are the basis of loyalty and obedience to governments, then the path of duty is plain," Douglas informed his readers. "We owe every thing to the country of our adoption and nothing to that miserable, contemptible, despotism the government of the United States," Douglas proclaimed, "who with the cant of liberty, democracy and christianity upon her lips, plunders the black-man's cradle, and sells babies new-born, in the market place for money." With Canada West satisfying every condition of Black patriotism, Black settlers were empowered to demand their full inclusion into provincial society and public life. "Colored men should become as thoroughly British as they can," Douglas insisted. He was not alone in this conclusion. It was central to Mary Ann Shadd's editorial perspective. Samuel Ringgold Ward outlined the full implications of this position. For Ward, "where there are no legal difficulties in the way, as there are not in Canada, there is no reason why we should not buy, build, live, die and be buried, just where other of Her Majesty's subjects live." With a notion of patriotism beyond mere gratitude, Black settlers articulated and asserted their rights as full British subjects.[55]

Their full inclusion in provincial life as rights-bearing subjects rested on property ownership. Access to quality agricultural land was central to Shadd's argument in *Plea,* in "so far as colored people are interested in the subject of emigration to any country, their welfare, in a pecuniary view, is promoted by attention to the quality of the soil." Shadd regaled her readers with the variety of fruits, vegetables, grains, livestock, and wild game one encountered on the province's fertile farms and in its healthy forests. She emphasized that a bushel of wheat, a staple crop in Canada West, weighed significantly more than a bushel grown in the United States, evidence of its superior quality and value. Promoting the agricultural potential of inexpensive land in the western townships of Canada West became a recurring topic of *Provincial Freeman*. Noting the attention within the midwestern press to a recent provincial law allowing newcomers who became actual settlers to purchase and convey land in up to 200-acre allotments for $1.50 an acre, the *Provincial Freeman* advised Black readers to emigrate from the United States before white settlers overwhelmed the land. "Golden opportunities are now before them," the paper advised, "which will not occur again, while they are quietly waiting for better times, in a country where land is high, and everything else in proportion, and which is of the most importance, they are not acknowledged as citizens." A correspondent to the *Provincial Freeman* from Raleigh touted his community for the same reason. Noting the abundance of grain crops and produce that Black settlers cultivated on farms of 50 to 200 acres of inexpensive land with ready access to markets, the correspondent was perplexed that more of his brethren had not quit the United States for Raleigh. Indeed, "it seems strange that thousands who are living on worse lands and under more contemptible laws do not avail themselves of peaceful homesteads."[56]

For those who did avail themselves of land, many acquired holdings of about one hundred acres. This matched the average size of a farm in Canada West during the 1850s, which indicates that Black property owners equaled their white neighbors in landholding. Town real estate also provided land wealth for Black emigrants. Abel B. Jones owned a prominent brick home on a central London street, along with a commercial building and several lots near the freight depot of a major railway. Although Jones was a property owner, a landlord, and a real estate speculator in the 1850s, he started life enslaved in Kentucky before his brother paid to manumit him. Frustrated by his "nominally free" life in a slave state, Jones "wished then to emigrate to some place where I could be really a free man." In accounts of Black people flourishing in Canada West, emigrant rights and property ownership reinforced claims to full freedom and belonging.[57]

Since the advent of emigrant rights claims in the late eighteenth century, people often claimed them by moving about in pursuit of land. They completed their expatriation from prior allegiances with actual settlement and property ownership. The tight legal and customary connection between land and rights could just as easily facilitate personal movement across borders as fix people within a given community. This connection became even more pronounced for Black emigrants because the Province of Canada made nearly every British subject's civil rights, including voting, jury service, and access to schools, dependent on property ownership.

As emigrant populations grew throughout the province and land became increasingly scarce, the provincial legislature adjusted property requirements for voting in 1853, suggesting its intent to govern in favor of emigrant rights much as it did by easing naturalization laws. Under its revised voting statutes, the legislature extended suffrage to male tenants and those lawfully settled on Crown land so long as they were not behind in their rent or payments. The law proved more restrictive in other ways as it included a higher qualification, based on land value or the revenue generated annually on the land, that limited voting to male property owners, tenants, or settlers who occupied land above the valuation threshold set by statute. In this system, local tax assessors determined land values, which in turn provided the basis for local voter registries compiled by other local officials. Moreover, tax assessors not only influenced the pool of eligible voters, local officials used their assessments to create lists of potential jurors. Paying taxes gave Black parents rights to demand a place for their children in public schools. Black people also possessed an unqualified right to testify in court against white people. Nevertheless, local officials in Canada West held significant power to determine who could exercise their civil rights in a given community. A prejudiced tax assessor, or officials responsive to prevailing racism that existed in many parts of Canada West, could deprive Black subjects of their civil rights despite provincial laws that prohibited racial discrimination. Within this context, Black subjects both exercised their civil rights and protected them when challenged by their white neighbors.[58]

Suffrage was a fundamental civil right for Black residents of Canada West. In addition to property qualifications, suffrage was limited to male subjects twenty-one or older. Eligible voters could participate in elections for a variety of councils and local offices at the town, township, and county level. At an 1851 election for town councilors in Sandwich, Henry Bibb's *Voice of the Fugitive* reported with pride "seeing the people of color walk up to the poles and cast their votes for civil officers, &c., unmolested by a rum-sucking mob, as would have been the case just across the river, perhaps in the name of Democracy."[59]

Black voters identified their suffrage rights with an equal sense of personal significance. As a Windsor resident exclaimed in 1855, "We are British subjects, I among others, though once a fugitive, am a voter." William Grose felt much the same. Suffrage was the keystone to a life of freedom and respectability for him and his family in St. Catharines because here "I am a true British subject, and I have a vote every year as much as any other man." Mary Ann

Shadd even devoted a section of her *Plea* to the intricacies of provincial suffrage laws, reproducing text from the relevant statutes. "Colored men comply with these provisions and vote in the administration of affairs," Shadd informed her readers. For those who celebrated Black suffrage or exercised it themselves, it marked the fulfillment of emigration right citizenship, their departure and expatriation from the United States that transformed them into rights-bearing British subjects. Individual voting rights also gave the Black community a collective claim to a fundamental place in the civic life of the province. As the *Provincial Freeman* reminded eligible Black voters before an 1856 election, suffrage made them "a part of the great 'Sovereign of British people.'" With this right, "we are a constituent element in the British Canadian body politic—a kind of *carbon* in the great national atmosphere, without which the three other elements would be inadequate."[60]

This perspective invested hope in the political power of a Black electorate. William P. Newman asserted with confidence that Black voters "will have doubtless the *balance of political power*" in Kent and Essex Counties, thus controlling the political destiny of the westernmost region of the province. Although Black voters never dominated politics in this region, the formation of a Black electorate provided strength to challenge regular attempts by white people to disenfranchise them through violent threats and collective force, or with discriminatory enforcement of tax assessments. The Black electorate also used its power to help defeat politicians who threatened their standing as free British subjects, such as Edwin Larwill, a member of the Legislative Assembly from Kent County. Although a member of the Conservative party, which Black voters often supported, Larwill opposed Black settlement in Canada West and proposed stripping civil rights from the Black subjects already resident. He also mobilized racist opinions of white residents in Chatham to gain popular support for his views. Larwill's position denied the legitimacy of emigrant rights claimed by Black settlers in Canada West including their expectation to live as equal British subjects.[61]

Black opponents responded to Larwill from an emigrant rights perspective. An anti-Larwill article published in the *Provincial Freeman* summarized his position with a question: "Can a nation make, *ex post facto* laws to deprive persons of citizenship, who become subjects according to her *then* established laws, without dishonoring herself?" Should the law allow this, the Province of Canada was no better than the United States as it too would deny full Black rights and eliminate birthright claims to Black children born in the province, thus reducing them to "'exiles upon their native soil'" with little choice but to leave. Larwill thus tested the limits of Black patriotism for their adopted country. Black voters mobilized against Larwill to help defeat him in 1857. Although suffrage gave eligible Black subjects visible political power in Canada West, contests to defend Black civil rights included those they exercised apart from elections.[62]

For many Black subjects, an equal right to testify in court was nearly tantamount in importance to suffrage rights. Unlike in the United States, Black people were not prohibited from testifying against whites. Samuel Ringgold Ward explained this difference by noting that despite the prevalence of racial discrimination in Canada West, Black people have legal recourse and courts will rule against white people in favor of Black rights. "Happily for us," Ward continued, "we have equal laws in our adopted country." Indeed, several Black men quit the United States because they faced discrimination in the courts. Aaron Siddles paid taxes in Indiana but was never secure in his property or his person because he could not testify against the white people who often threatened both. "I removed to Canada, where I would have an equal oath with any man, when any thing occurred; where I would have every right that every man has." Ephraim Casey suffered financial loss because he could not testify under oath against whites, so he "left on principle—on account of the laws." Both men left Indiana, a state with notorious black laws. The expectation of Black subjects to equal treatment in the courts and before public officials was put to the test in various ways. They claimed their full subject rights when seeking redress against white people who denied them access to accommodations such as omnibuses or hotels—and in ways that seemed more urgent, in matters involving education.[63]

The right to a public school education concerned many Black subjects. Education law in Canada West permitted separate schools for white and Black students, which satisfied the racist demands of white parents. Black parents rejected segregated education because the poorly funded schools for their children denied their standing as equal British subjects. Segregated schools proved especially offensive to Black parents because they often cited their right to educate their children as a reason they quit the United States. Henry Johnson was a free Black man born in Pennsylvania before moving to Ohio. Local officials in Ohio prohibited his daughter from attending a public school once she began to excel. At that point, Johnson reflected, "I left the States for Canada, for rights, freedom, and liberty." Such was the protest of an individual from Hamilton who petitioned the Province of Canada's governor on behalf of the town's Black residents. His community paid taxes, but local officials denied their children access to the public schools. The petitioner expressed his community's complaint in a set of emigrant rights expectations.

He, like many in the community, left property in the United States and bought property in Hamilton. They were thus a people of previous means and standing—that is, of good character, who chose to settle in Canada West as loyal British subjects. Indeed, "we left the United States because we were in hopes that prejudice was not in this land" only to experience it for themselves "under the British flag." Without the protection of their adopted sovereign, the petitioner suggested there were limits to Black allegiance. The petition proved effective because local officials eventually desegregated schools in Hamilton.[64]

Nevertheless, school segregation persisted throughout the 1850s in most parts of Canada West. According to William Wells Brown, Toronto and Hamilton were the only exceptions. As the decade progressed, persistent school segregation was a barrier to the equal rights of Black subjects. An 1857 article in the *Provincial Freeman* explained why. Mary Ann Shadd Cary, who had recently married Thomas Cary, authored the article informed by her particular understanding of the relationship between education and the demands Black emigrants should make for full inclusion in their adopted home. Separate schools could never provide what Black children needed most, she argued, which was "a good *British* Education, through instruction to the young by means of British school books, by teachers British at heart." With nearly 40 percent of Canada West's Black population born in the province, many children needed this education. The demand for integrated public schools was thus about the need to create generations of Black subjects loyal to Great Britain. This perspective expressed confidence in Canada West as the best place for Black people to live as free, rights-bearing individuals, a confidence bolstered by deepening pessimism about the prospects for Black life in the United States.[65]

From the perspective of those in Canada West, the *Dred Scott* decision foreclosed the possibility that Black people would ever become full citizens of the United States, so their reasons to stay disappeared as well. Isaac D. Shadd announced this view in a *Provincial Freeman* article he addressed to the "Colored Men of the States," published in the spring of 1857. Shadd queried, "After struggling for years for their political rights ... what eminence in the scale of political equality have they attained?" The US Supreme Court gave the final answer to this question and thereby "prostrated all the past efforts of the colored man." The time had arrived, Shadd argued, for Black people in the United States to finally give up the country for life in the "Canadas," which was not merely a refuge for fugitives but a place where their people had already become "acknowledged British subjects, and those that are not, in due time will be." A correspondent to the *Provincial Freeman* from London was even more scathing. Writing under the pseudonym "Americus," the person viewed the *Dred Scott* decision as the legal culmination of a concerted effort by the federal government in the United States during the 1850s to ensure that "all the descendents of the African race" were "denationalized." For Americus, this was an indictment of the abolitionist movement and Frederick Douglass in particular. By advocating their "stand still" doctrine over an embrace of emigration, leading abolitionists betrayed Black Americans, Americus concluded.[66]

Indeed, the *Dred Scott* decision, which revealed the inefficacy of standstill abolitionism, only confirmed the power of emigrant rights abolitionism. In the wake of *Dred Scott*, the standstill position was a dangerously gradual approach to ending slavery and improving Black life when compared to the immediate effects of emigrant rights claims, its advocates argued. As early as 1851, Thomas Smallwood, a man who quit slavery for Canada in the 1840s, denounced American abolitionists opposed to emigration for supporting a position that offered no protection to Black people, either free or those who escaped enslavement. "Whereas," Smallwood argued, "if they had been encouraged, or even let alone, they would have gone to Canada first, and be now secure in their persons and property as British subjects." For proponents of Black emigrant rights, the *Dred Scott* decision meant that Black subjects in Canada West were the future of abolitionism in North America. H. Ford Douglas proclaimed that Canada West gave Black people Archimedes's power to "turn the world upside down." Indeed, Douglas continued, "We have that spot here in Canada, where all may labor unitely too for the extinction of American slavery." Should they continue to emigrate from the United States, Black subjects, in concert with the power of the British Empire, would push "our fulcrum to raise that bloody system to its very foundation."[67]

THE WORLD THAT SLAVERY made in North America eventually overturned. During the Civil War, enslaved people sought freedom with federal troops. This exercise of enslaved emigrant rights during wartime transformed the conflict from an effort to preserve the union to one against slavery. Once it became a war of abolition, Black Americans had powerful reasons to join. Military service in the Union army became the basis for new citizenship claims in the United States. When the Union defeated the slaveholder's rebellion, Black activists and their white allies pushed Congress to codify Black citizenship in the Constitution.[68]

The Civil War and its aftermath changed the meaning of Black emigrant rights in the Great Lakes borderlands. To the Black subjects of Canada West, the Civil War created unforeseen possibilities. Some returned to the United States to join the war. Others returned after the war ended and Black citizenship seemed secure. However, a vast majority of Canada West's Black subjects apparently stayed in the province. Taken together, these individual choices demonstrated once again that Black people were determined to claim their emigrant rights to move freely and decide their own national allegiances. Moreover, the push for Black emigrant rights from the 1830s onward, and their realization in Canada West, thus prepared the ground for the United States to recognize that all citizens possessed freedom of movement and expatriation.[69]

A World of Emigrants

With the United States fractured by a slaveholder's rebellion in 1862, the future for free Black Americans seemed less certain than ever. After Lewis Henry Douglass surveyed his prospects in the United States, he considered joining a proposed colony in Central America. Although Black settlers would establish this colony for themselves and future generations, President Abraham Lincoln proposed it and he charged Kansas senator Samuel Pomeroy with the responsibility of creating it. Douglass turned to his father, the eminent abolitionist Frederick Douglass, for a letter of introduction to Pomeroy that vouched for his intention to quit the United States. The elder Douglass complied with his son's request, but he repudiated the Central America plan as a new colonization scheme to pressure Black Americans to leave the nation that belonged to them. Despite this disagreement with his son, he reiterated support for an emigrant rights position independent of white authority that Black activists had championed for decades. As Frederick Douglass emphasized, "It is hardly necessary for me to say that against natural, self-moved, spontaneous emigration, where no pressure of legislation or public opinion is exerted to compel it, and colored men are left perfectly free to consult their own interests and inclinations as to where they shall go, and in what lands they shall make their homes, there can be no objection whatever." The colony never came into existence, and Lewis Douglass instead decided to remain in the United States. Following Lincoln's Emancipation Proclamation, he enlisted in the Fifty-Fourth Massachusetts Infantry Regiment, eventually achieving the rank of sergeant major. In various ways, Lewis Douglass's choices in the 1860s marked a turning point in the emigrant rights history of the United States.[1]

Until the middle of the nineteenth century, slave owners claimed that their freedom to move and choose allegiance included the power to force enslaved people to move against their will. This view of enslaver's emigrant rights appeared in secessionist debates following the presidential election of 1860. Florida planter Richard Keith Call viewed northern claims that the federal government should limit slavery's territorial expansion as unconstitutional because "the denial of the government to the master the right to emigrate with his slave to such region would be as wrongful, arbitrary, unjust, and despotic, as the denial of the master's right himself to emigrate without the slave." Call ultimately opposed Florida's secession from the union just as Southern secessionists ultimately turned their attention from defending the individual emigrant rights of enslavers to move freely throughout the United States.[2]

Instead, secession rested on a state's rights justification for collective expatriation. Southern secessionists insisted that citizens owed their allegiance to state governments rather than the federal government, which left white citizens of the states that formed the Confederacy no choice but to withdraw their allegiance from the United States. Secessionists ultimately used claims to collective state expatriation as the basis for Confederate nationalism. With its emphasis on forming a new slaveholder's republic powerful enough to command allegiance and exercise sovereignty, secessionist nationalism proved incompatible with emigrant rights cosmopolitanism. The one instance of collective expatriation accomplished in the United States quickly ended with the victory of Union forces in 1865. Four years later, the US Supreme Court ruled that state secession, as an act of collective expatriation, was unconstitutional. Lewis Douglass thus helped win a war that abolished slavery and, with it, secessionist claims that expatriation was a collective right rather than strictly an individual right.[3]

The abolition of slavery also created new demands for full Black citizenship within the United States, including the emigrant rights that Douglass's father and many other Black Americans insisted they deserved. Frederick Douglass and his son thus helped culminate a much longer history of citizenship. Emigrant rights emerged from the American Revolution to shape life in North America for the next century. During this period, individuals chose to move about the continent and expatriate themselves from one national allegiance to another. More often than not, the continent's various sovereign powers adopted laws to govern their shifting territorial boundaries that accommodated emigrant rights claims because restricting them in these regions seemed largely impossible. In the 1860s, the notion of emigration right citizenship created in North America's borderlands became a pillar of national citizenship in the United States.

Several developments converged in the late 1860s to align federal law with established emigrant rights claims. In 1867, the US Supreme Court recognized a citizenship right to free movement within the United States. The next year, Congress adopted the Expatriation Act of 1868, which declared that expatriation was a natural right of citizenship. Congress addressed the expatriation question in response to international conflicts over the status of naturalized

US citizens abroad, in particular the standing of men who joined the failed Fenian Revolt to liberate Ireland in 1867. At this moment, the histories of American emigration and immigration converged. Although the Supreme Court and Congress acted on legal concerns particular to the 1860s, the justices and politicians arrived at their views long after Americans had decided the meaning of emigrant rights for themselves. In this way, individuals deciding to leave the United States and expatriate themselves in the North American borderlands before the 1860s created a citizenship right that naturalized citizens and their political allies adopted for themselves during the 1860s. Under the federal citizenship regime created by the Fourteenth Amendment, emigrant rights became a privilege of birthright and naturalized citizens.[4]

Furthermore, after 1868 the United States signed a series of naturalization treaties with several nations. These agreements recognized freedom of movement and a right to expatriation between signatory countries. The United States entered such treaties with Mexico and Great Britain. Great Britain also amended its naturalization laws in 1870 to allow its subjects the right of expatriation, thus abolishing the doctrine of perpetual allegiance within the United Kingdom. These developments under international law and within the nationality law of the United Kingdom operated in North America much the same as legal developments within the United States. In each instance, central governments ratified emigrant rights already claimed by mobile populations and accommodated by local officials in various borderlands regions before 1860. By the 1870s, an individual right to free movement and expatriation seemed ascendant in much of the world. This was an illusion.[5]

Instead, developments in the 1870s marked the beginning of new state limits on emigrant rights intended to strengthen the legal bond between territory and citizenship. The naturalization treaties all prioritized state decisions about whom to admit across its borders and who could move freely within them. This change was also evident within the United States when viewed from the perspective of Congress's earliest attempts to adopt a federal expatriation law. In both 1797 and 1818, congressional debates concerned the rights of natural-born citizens of the United States to quit the nation and adopt national allegiances elsewhere. The rights of naturalized citizens abroad were a secondary concern in the earlier debates unlike in 1868 when Congress adopted the Expatriation Act. This change over time marks a shift from viewing expatriation as an individual freedom to adopt new allegiances outside the United States to expatriation as a right subject to considerable state authority within the United States.

In effect, Congress's adoption of the Expatriation Act signaled a transition in the relationship of the United States to the world, a change in which an immigration regime replaced an earlier emigration regime. This transition allowed for restrictive immigration policies beginning with the Chinese Exclusion Act of 1882 and continued with the racial and ethnic quotas created under the Immigration Act of 1924. Although subsequent immigration laws relaxed these restrictions, the United States expanded its police powers over its territorial borders, especially its border with Mexico. The 1924 Immigration Act authorized the formation of the United States Border Patrol, a federal agency with broad law enforcement and surveillance powers. Finally, states throughout the world have adopted passport systems that give them a "monopoly of the 'legitimate means of movement,'" as John C. Torpey argues. The expansion of state power over borders and individual movement combined with renewed political demands to delimit citizenship to territorial boundaries occurred across the globe, which indicates a much broader state preference for immigration control over individual emigrant rights that continues into the twenty-first century.[6]

The sovereign power states claim over borders and human mobility clash with protections for free movement under twentieth-century international law. In 1948, the United Nations adopted the Universal Declaration of Human Rights, which recognizes free movement within nations and a right to emigration under Article 13. Freedom of internal movement and emigration are also included in the International Covenant on Civil and Political Rights, a multilateral treaty adopted in 1966 and eventually ratified by a majority of the world's countries. However, there is no commensurate individual right under international law or enforceable by treaties to enter and remain in a nation of one's choosing. This is a problematic discrepancy that privileges state power over individual rights. The historian Charles Maier summarizes the effects of this discrepancy, "Sovereignty in short implies the authority to exclude but not to confine." Any claim to free movement is weak when governments are left free to decide whom to accept across their borders. Scholars of nation-states and border formation, political theorists, and migrant advocates share concerns about the uneven relationship between state power and personal mobility in the contemporary world.[7]

From their various perspectives, this problem is fundamentally one of citizenship. In particular, nation-states claim a sovereign right to enclose citizenship within their territorial borders with such force that alternative forms of citizenship cannot gain legitimacy. As a result, a world in which states grant or withhold citizenship rights to individuals inside their borders appears self-evident rather than the outcome of a particular history of sovereignty. As an alternative, these scholars explore the histories and possibilities of citizenship as varied or multileveled rather than singular, as having local or decentralized forms along with supranational forms. As Willem Maas argues, "By demonstrating that alternative, nonstate communities or jurisdictions *do* in fact constitute important sources of rights and status, the artificiality and arbitrariness of the sovereign state's monopoly on conferring citizenship becomes clear." Recognizing the baleful consequences for individual rights to free movement posed by dominant notions of state sovereignty, recent citizenship theorists seek to decouple political belonging from territoriality. They have also argued against citizenship laws that close territorial borders to free movement. These writers suggest alternatives to onerous naturalization policies or citizenship by birthplace or parentage alone, all of which privilege state power to determine political belonging by holding accidents of birth as the basis of civic inclusion for some people but not for others. Ayelet Shachar argues for a "*jus nexi*" basis for citizenship that emphasizes "the significance of actual membership in the community, over and above any privileges obtained by inherited entitlement." Jacqueline Stevens contemplates "a world of states without nations, where people belong because of choice, residence, and commitment." From both perspectives, citizenship rights accrue from one's connection to a community and contribution to its welfare above all else, which empowers individuals to choose their state allegiances and to move about in pursuit of them.[8]

Proponents of emigrant rights in the eighteenth and nineteenth centuries understood citizenship in ways that anticipated the arguments of twenty-first-century citizenship theorists. Americans who exercised their emigrant rights created a particular form of citizenship that satisfies the demands of contemporary migration advocates despite historical origins marked by exclusion. Initially, emigration right citizenship reinforced prevailing racial and gendered limits to full political belonging, and those who exercised it often did so to gain membership in political communities that dispossessed Indigenous people of their land. This form of citizenship also contained radical potential, however, as first recognized by Black emigrants from the United States. In its fully realized form, emigration right citizenship insists that all individuals are free to leave any nation, and their decision to leave entails an expectation of rights wherever they decide to settle. Rights to political belonging are thus individual, portable possessions. Emigration right citizenship provides a model for an individual, universal right to stay under international law that makes a complementary and existing right to leave meaningful.

As the twenty-first century advances, meaningful emigrant rights will become indispensable. Climate change combined with population growth are the most pressing among the myriad reasons people throughout the world will need or choose to leave one place for another. A 2020 report from the Institute for Economics and Peace, an Australian nonprofit think tank that assesses global trends, estimated that the effects of climate change on access to water, food supplies, and habitable land could make sustainable life tenuous for over 1 billion people by 2050, forcing many to leave nations or regions susceptible to extreme temperature increases and rising sea levels. The United Nations has already made the implications of climate change central to its policy on global migration along with the human rights concerns raised by people crossing borders. However, the UN also acknowledges that a refugee framework, which has clear legal meaning under international law, confounds efforts to address climate migration. The case for environmental changes in a particular place causing irreparable personal harm is disputed, especially by countries currently less affected by climate change but major contributors to its causes nonetheless. The refugee framework thus lets governments avoid culpability for their contribution to climate change by giving them permission to avoid receiving climate change migrants. This calls for the creation of a new emigration regime for the world.[9]

Indeed, an emigrant rights framework may better hold governments accountable to the individual needs of people seeking to leave uninhabitable places. When human-caused climate change makes a place uninhabitable, it also makes citizenship and legal personhood in that place effectively meaningless. Treating such people as climate refugees reinforces state authority over their movement. From this perspective, people fleeing environmental collapse must hope that a forbearing state will accept them based on a generous interpretation of international law. To view such people as climate emigrants presumes they are individuals with portable rights to civic belonging wherever they choose. Under an emigrant rights framework, people who decide to seek lives in more habitable places are thus free to leave and bring their right to political belonging with them.[10]

Climate change has already put people on the move from parts of Southeast Asia, the Middle East, central Africa, and Central America. More will likely leave from elsewhere by the late twenty-first century, including from the southern tier of the United States as extreme heat makes this region difficult to inhabit. Should this come to pass, the United States may become a nation of emigrants once again. As its citizens seek habitable places to live within its borders or perhaps farther north beyond them, extending the privileges of emigration right citizenship to the entire world's people will prove essential to life within North America. Writing in the early nineteenth century, Thomas Jefferson explained the significance of emigrant rights for a world that seems in formation today, for an individual was free from "any obligation to die by disease or famine in one country, rather than go to another where he can live." Once again, the formerly enslaved perfected the world envisioned by the enslaver. This world, as anticipated in Frederick Douglass's words from the 1860s, sets all individuals "perfectly free to consult their own interests and inclinations as to where they shall go, and in what lands they shall make their homes." The emigrant rights revolution that began in eighteenth-century North America is thus far from over.[11]

Acknowledgments

For a book that insists on the freedom to move where one chooses, it's fitting that this work had its own journey from one place to another. What I intended to write is very different from what I eventually wrote. I have many people and institutions to thank for helping me think in new directions.

Over the years, I was fortunate to present my research for this book at several academic conferences and seminars. Together, the amazing scholars with whom I shared panels, and the engaged audience members who listened to my ideas, helped me find the story I wanted to tell and often challenged me to think critically about how best to tell this story. I owe a collective thank you to everyone who participated in this collaborative intellectual process.

No less important, I received critical financial support from the National Endowment for the Humanities and the American Philosophical Society. These research fellowships allowed me to use archival collections at several locales including the Beinecke Library at Yale University, the American Antiquarian Society, the National Archives in Washington, DC, and the Dolph Briscoe Center for American History at The University of Texas at Austin. Knowledgeable archivists and efficient staff made my days at these institutions both enjoyable and essential to this book.

The University of Texas at Dallas, my institutional home since I began working on this project, helped make it possible for me to finish it. On two separate occasions, Dean Dennis Kratz and later Dean Nils Roemer approved releases from my teaching responsibilities, which allowed me to devote my full attention to writing. UTD is also indirectly responsible for providing the first critical audience for the chapter drafts that became this book. My colleagues and friends in the writing group always asked important questions about my ideas, offered trenchant critiques of my writing, and did both in only the most supportive ways. I'm certain that careful readings by this interdisciplinary group of scholars made this a better book, as I learned so much from their engagement with my work and mine with theirs. For this, my deepest thanks to members past and present: Ashley Barnes, Erin Greer, Charles Hatfield, Annelise Heinz, Natalie Ring, Shilyh Warren, and Dan Wickberg.

I also offer my great thanks to other readers along the way. Ed Countryman provided a lively, engaged, and greatly helpful reading of the entire manuscript informed by his deep understanding of the American Revolution and its aftermath in North America. Jack Little generously shared his expertise on the history of the Eastern Townships by pointing me to relevant archives and responding to my writing about them. Finally, Gabe Loiacono's close reading of the introduction helped me articulate my larger claims.

In August 2019, I started the academic year at the William P. Clements Center for Southwest Studies as the Summerlee/Summerfield Roberts Research Fellow for the Study of Southwestern America. Andy Graybill, the center director, and Neil Foley, its associate director, welcomed me to the Southern Methodist University campus with generosity and enthusiasm for the manuscript I planned to finish that year. Although I only traveled across town for this fellowship, Ruth Ann Elmore, the center's assistant director, treated me as if I'd journeyed much farther. Her kindness gave me a smooth start to center life. Once there, Ruth Ann made sure I knew where to find the office coffee pot. I also joined a cohort of collegial fellows that included Natalie Mendoza, Allison Powers Useche, and Sam Haynes. I owe Sam particular thanks because years before our time together at the Clements Center, he invited me to participate in "Contested Empire: Rethinking the Texas Revolution," a conference at the University of Texas at Arlington that helped shape my early thoughts about this project.

During the initial, uncertain months of the pandemic, in-person center activities ceased for us all, but Andy, Neil, and Ruth Ann did everything possible to recreate what is special about residential fellowships in a world gone remote. One example of this was my fully online, and glitch-free, manuscript workshop. I owe gratitude to the many scholars who read my manuscript and logged into the workshop to discuss my ideas in detail at a time when it was quite easy to decline such acts of scholarly generosity. My thanks go to every participant, including Andy, Neil, my fellow Clements Center fellows, Ben Johnson, James Nichols, Tommy Richards, Jess Roney, and Patrick Troester. I owe additional thanks to Rachel St. John and Rogers Smith. They brought their respective expertise in the histories of North American borderlands and citizenship to their comments during the workshop and the written responses they provided after. Ultimately, I am certain that I wrote a much better book because of this engagement, made possible by support from the Clements Center.

Ben Johnson and Andy Graybill deserve particular thanks for their unwavering support in the years before and after my time at the center. In addition to his eagerness to read drafts and discuss my ideas, Ben invited me as a guest to his National Endowment for the Humanities summer seminar at the Newberry Library titled "Bridging National Borders in North America." More recently, Ben and Andy have championed my work as the series editors for the David J. Weber Series in the New Borderlands History.

At UNC Press, many thanks to Debbie Gershenowitz for moving the manuscript through the review process with all the speed at her command and for securing a pair of readers that any author would envy. My gratitude also goes to other press staff whose work was essential to this book.

From the very beginning, my friends and family have always showed interest in this project. This is true for those who simply asked about my progress to others who did much more. My parents Ray and Sue remain as excited about this book as they were for my very first publication, which signals their loving support for my life and career. I have stacks of notepad pages filled with chapter outlines, research questions, writing goals, and inchoate thoughts related to this book, all of which appear in my wife Ilyssa's handwriting. This archive, accumulated during our family's biannual road trips, is evidence of the boundless love and encouragement that Ilyssa gives me in every part of our lives together. When I began this project, our kids Hazel and Ruben were very young and illiterate. Now that they're a bit older and able to read, they've made clear their intentions to read these acknowledgments first. I could reward their excitement by answering a question they've asked me more than once: Do I have a favorite child? They will have to settle for a dedication instead. To Hazel and Ruben, this book is for you.

Notes

Introduction

1. "For the Time Piece," *Time Piece* (New York), January 24, 1798. There is a growing historiography about the precarious sovereignty of the early United States and efforts to redress this through constitutional means and the law of nations. For a selection of this literature, see David C. Hendrickson, *Peace Pact: The Lost World of the American Founding* (Lawrence: University Press of Kansas, 2003); Daniel M. Golove and Daniel J. Hulsebosch, "A Civilized Nation: The Early American Constitution, the Law of Nations, and the Pursuit of International Recognition," *New York University Law Review* 85 (2010): 101–227; and Eliga H. Gould, *Among the Powers of the Earth: The American Revolution and the Making of a New World Empire* (Cambridge, MA: Harvard University Press, 2012).

2. On Ezkekiel Forman, see Samuel S. Forman, *Narrative of a Journey Down the Ohio and Mississippi in 1789–90*, ed. Lyman Draper (Cincinnati, 1888); and Ruth L. Woodward and Wesley Frank Craven, *Princetonians, 1784–1790: A Biographical Dictionary* (Princeton, NJ: Princeton University Press, 1991), 114; on John Bell, see *Lower Canada, Declaration of Aliens-H-1154*, Image 61, Library and Archives Canada; on Leah Alsberry, see Alsberry v. Hawkins, 39 Ky. 177, 9 Dana 177, 33 Am. Dec. 546 (Ct. App. 1839); and on Isaac Griffin, see Benjamin Drew, *A North-Side View of Slavery* (Boston, 1856), 284–85.

3. Aristide R. Zolberg, "The Exit Revolution," in Nancy L. Green and François Weil, eds., *Citizenship and Those Who Leave: The Politics of Emigration and Expatriation* (Urbana: University of Illinois Press, 2007), 33–60. See also Green, "The Politics of Exit: Reversing the Immigration Paradigm," *Journal of Modern History* 77 (June 2005): 263–89. This scholarship considers the histories of emigration and expatriation rights as originating with the French Revolution and central to the experiences of Europeans.

4. For an overview of immigration to the United States with attention to naturalization, see Aristide R. Zolberg, *A Nation by Design: Immigration Policy in the Fashioning of America* (Cambridge, MA: Harvard University Press, 2008). For the role of federal naturalization policy in nineteenth-century immigration control, see Gerald L. Neuman, "The Lost Century of American Immigration Law (1776–1875)," *Columbia Law Review* 93, no. 8 (1993): 1833–1901.

5. Thomas Lloyd, *The Congressional Register; or, History of the Proceedings and Debates of the First House of Representatives of the United States of America* (New York, 1789), I: 400 and 405. For emigrant population estimates, see David J. Weber, *The Spanish Frontier in North America* (New Haven, CT: Yale University Press, 1992), 281; and Cole Harris, *The Reluctant Land: Society, Space, and Environment in Canada before Confederation* (Vancouver: University of British Columbia Press, 2008), 288 and 309; Hans-Jürgen Grabbe, "European Immigration to the United States in the Early National Period, 1783–1820," *Proceedings of the American Philosophical Society* 133 (1989): 194.

6. James H. Kettner, *The Development of American Citizenship, 1608–1870* (Chapel Hill: The University of North Carolina Press, 1978), 173–209.

7. For histories of citizenship that consider free movement, see Barbara Young Welke, *Law and the Borders of Belonging in the Long Nineteenth Century* (Cambridge: Cambridge University Press, 2010); Kunal M. Parker, *Making Foreigners: Immigration and Citizenship Law in America, 1600–2000* (Cambridge: Cambridge University Press, 2015); Elizabeth Stordeur Pryor, *Colored Travelers: Mobility and the Fight for Citizenship before the Civil War* (Chapel Hill: The University of North Carolina Press, 2016); and Kristin O'Brassill-Kulfan, *Vagrants and Vagabonds: Poverty and Mobility in the Early American Republic* (New York: New York University Press, 2019). For histories of citizenship that consider the right to expatriation, see Kettner, *Development of American Citizenship*; Rogers H. Smith, *Civic Ideals: Conflicting Visions of Citizenship in U.S. History* (New Haven, CT: Yale University Press, 1997); and Douglas Bradburn, *The Citizenship Revolution: Politics and the Creation of the American Union, 1774–1804* (Charlottesville: University of Virginia Press, 2009). Scholarship devoted to the right of expatriation in the United States is relatively sparse except for a few notable works. I-Mien Tsiang, *The Question of Expatriation in America Prior to 1907* (Baltimore: Johns Hopkins Press, 1942) provides a detailed but tightly focused legal and foreign policy history of the right to expatriation. Nancy L. Green, "Expatriation, Expatriates, and Expats: The American Transformation of a Concept," *American Historical Review* 114 (2009): 310–11, views the history of expatriation in the United States before the 1860s as "a form of nation-building," thus a story of immigration and naturalization. Lucy E. Salyer, *Under the Starry Flag: How a Band of Irish Americans Joined the Fenian Revolt and Sparked a Crisis over Citizenship* (Cambridge, MA: Harvard University Press, 2018), is a significant recent book that "seeks to recover the history of the forgotten right of expatriation" by focusing on political, legal, and foreign policy issues concerning the status of naturalized US citizens during the 1860s. The history of emigrant rights that follows complements Salyer's work with a geographic focus on the North American borderlands, a temporal focus on events before the 1860s, and a thematic focus on the right to expatriation of natural-born US citizens.

8. William J. Novak, "The Legal Transformation of Citizenship in Nineteenth-Century America," in Meg Jacobs, William J. Novak, and Julian E. Zelizer, eds., *The Democratic Experiment: New Directions in American Political History* (Princeton, NJ: Princeton University Press, 2003), 85–119. Zolberg, "The Exit Revolution," 54, questions the usefulness of analytic distinctions between internal and external migration. Thomas Jefferson to John F. Dumoulin, May 7, 1816, in *The Papers of Thomas Jefferson, Retirement Series*, vol. 10 (May 1, 1816–January 18, 1817), ed. James P. McClure and J. Jefferson Looney (Princeton, NJ: Princeton University Press, 2004–15), 20; and Drew, *North-Side View*, 284–85. An emigrant rights perspective challenges claims that nation-states began to exercise greater control over the movement of their citizens and solidified their borders to movement in the early nineteenth century. For such claims in the history of citizenship, see John C. Torpey, *The Invention of the Passport: Surveillance, Citizenship and the State*, 2nd ed. (Cambridge: Cambridge University Press, 2018), with his argument for nation-states securing a "monopoly of the legitimate 'means of movement,'" 2; and in borderlands history, see Jeremy Adelman and Stephen Aron, "From Borderlands to Borders: Empires, Nation-States, and the Peoples in between in North American History," *American Historical Review* 104 (1999): 840, with their conclusion that the bordered "states of North America enjoyed unrivaled authority to confer or deny rights to peoples within their borders" while their "ossified borders reduced the freedom to 'exit.'"

9. For the most recent history of citizens leaving the United States for settlements else-where in North America, see Alan Taylor, "Remaking Americans: Louisiana, Upper Canada, and Texas," in Juliana Barr and Edward Countryman, eds., *Contested Spaces of Early America* (Philadelphia: University of Pennsylvania Press, 2014), 208–26. See also Weber, *The Spanish Frontier in North America*, 280–82; Andrés Reséndez, *Changing National Identities at the Frontier: Texas and New Mexico, 1800–1850* (Cambridge: Cambridge University Press, 2005), 15–55; Stephen Aron, *American Confluence: The Missouri Frontier from Borderland to Border State* (Bloomington: Indiana University Press, 2006), 69–105; Kathleen DuVal, *Independence Lost: Lives on the Edge of the American Revolution* (New York: Random House, 2015), 313–24; and Lawrence B. A. Hatter, *Citizens of Convenience: The Imperial Origins of American Nationhood on the U.S.-Canadian Border* (Charlottesville: University of Virginia Press, 2015). On shifts in the language of emigration to immigration, see Mae M. Ngai, "Immigration and Ethnic History," in Eric Foner and Lisa McGirr, eds., *American History Now* (Philadelphia: Temple University Press, 2011), 358–75.

10. On the relationship among emigration, rights, and territorial sovereignty under contemporary international law, see Thomas Kleven, "Why International Law Favors Emigration over Immigration," *University of Miami Inter-American Law Review* 33 (2002): 69–100; and Vincent Chetail, "Sovereignty and Migration in the Doctrine of the Law of Nations: An Intellectual History of Hospitality from Vitoria to Vattel," *European Journal of International Law* 27, no. 4 (November 2016): 901–22. On the history of territory as a concept, see Charles S. Maier, *Once Within Borders: Territories of Power, Wealth, and Belonging since 1500* (Cambridge, MA: Harvard University Press, 2016). On contemporary theories of territory and sovereignty, see Kristine Beurskens and Judith Miggelbrink, "Sovereignty Contested: Theory and Practice in Borderlands," *Geopolitics* 22 (2017): 749–56; and John Agnew, "Sovereignty Regimes: Territoriality and State Authority in Contemporary World Politics," *Annals of the Association of American Geographers* 95 (2005): 437–61.

11. My conception of emigration right citizenship is informed by the scholarship of political theorists critical of border restrictions and concerned with alternatives to birthright citizenship. In particular, see Joseph H. Carens, "Aliens and Citizens: The Case for Open Borders," *Review of Politics* 49 (1987): 251–73; Ayelet Schachar, *The Birthright Lottery: Citizenship and Global Inequality* (Cambridge, MA: Harvard University Press, 2009); Jacqueline Stevens, *States Without Nations: Citizenship for Mortals* (New York: Columbia University Press, 2010); and Willem Maas, ed., *Multilevel Citizenship* (Philadelphia: University of Pennsylvania Press, 2013). For a compelling account of individuals' relationship to state power, see James C. Scott, *The Art of Not Being Governed: An Anarchist History of Upland Southeast Asia* (New Haven, CT: Yale University Press, 2009).

12. On the ways that the law and practices of citizenship created multiple limits to full civic belonging in the early United States, see Welke, *Law and the Borders of Belonging in the Long Nineteenth Century United States*; and Parker, *Making Foreigners*. Laurel Clark Shire, *The Threshold of Manifest Destiny: Gender and National Expansion in Florida* (Philadelphia: University of Pennsylvania Press, 2016), explains the power white men claimed to place through their control of women's physical and reproductive labor. On the Loyalists, see Maya Jasanoff, *Liberty's Exiles: American Loyalists in the Revolutionary World* (New York: Knopf, 2011). The historiography of Indigenous dispossession and removal is vast, but for two recent histories, see Claudio Saunt, *Unworthy Republic: The Dispossession of Native*

Americans and the Road to Indian Territory (New York: W. W. Norton, 2020); and Michael John Witgen, *Seeing Red: Indigenous Land, American Expansion, and the Political Economy of Plunder in North America* (Chapel Hill: The University of North Carolina Press, 2022). The historiography of the slave trades is equally vast, but see Edward E. Baptist, *The Half Has Never Been Told: Slavery and the Making of American Capitalism* (New York: Basic Books, 2016); and Andrés Reséndez, *The Other Slavery: The Uncovered Story of Indian Enslavement in America* (Boston: Houghton, Mifflin, Harcourt, 2016). On the deportation of Irish immigrants, see Hidetaka Hirota, *Expelling the Poor: Atlantic Seaboard States and the Nineteenth-Century Origins of American Immigration Policy* (New York: Oxford University Press, 2017). On the early history of the Mormons, see Benjamin E. Park, *Kingdom of Nauvoo: The Rise and Fall of a Religious Empire on the American Frontier* (New York: Liveright, 2020).

13. "Right of Secession," *New York Observer and Chronicle*, February 16, 1860. For the history of efforts by citizens of the United States to create new sovereign republics in North America or reconfigure national sovereignty in other ways, see Thomas Richards Jr., *Breakaway Americas: The Unmanifest Future of the Jacksonian United States* (Baltimore: Johns Hopkins University Press, 2020); and Rachel St. John, "The Unpredictable America of William Gwin: Expansion, Secession, and the Unstable Borders of Nineteenth-Century North America," *Journal of the Civil War Era* 6 (2016): 56–84.

14. On the analytical power of a comparative borderlands framework, see Benjamin H. Johnson and Andrew R. Graybill, eds., *Bridging National Borders in North America: Transnational and Comparative Histories* (Durham, NC: Duke University Press, 2010). By revealing the ways that North America's borderlands produced legal, political, and intellectual limits to state power, the history of emigrant rights expands the methodological claims of the borderlands critique of national histories outlined by Pekka Hämäläinen and Samuel Truett, "On Borderlands," *Journal of American History* 98 (2011): 358–61; and early "state-centered" approaches critiqued by Michiel Baud and Willem Van Schendel, "Toward a Comparative History of Borderlands," *Journal of World History* 8 (1997): 241.

Chapter One

1. David Ramsay, *A Dissertation on the Manner of Acquiring the Character and Privileges of a Citizen of the United States* (1789), 3–5. See also Arthur H. Shaffer, *To Be an American: David Ramsay and the Making of the American Consciousness* (Columbia: University of South Carolina Press, 1991).

2. Ramsay, *Dissertation*, 5. On volitional allegiance, see James H. Kettner, *The Development of American Citizenship, 1608–1870* (Chapel Hill: The University of North Carolina Press, 1978), 173–209.

3. On perpetual allegiance as it relates to the origins of citizenship, see Kettner, *Development of American Citizenship*, 44–61.

4. On international law, political thought, and constitutionalism in the early United States, see David C. Hendrickson, *Peace Pact: The Lost World of the American Founding* (Lawrence: University Press of Kansas, 2003); David Armitage, *The Declaration of Independence: A Global History* (Cambridge, MA: Harvard University Press, 2007); Daniel M. Golove and Daniel J. Hulsebosch, "A Civilized Nation: The Early American Constitution,

the Law of Nations, and the Pursuit of International Recognition," *New York University Law Review* 85 (2010): 101–227; and Eliga H. Gould, *Among the Powers of the Earth: The American Revolution and the Making of a New World Empire* (Cambridge, MA: Harvard University Press, 2012).

5. Immanuel Kant, "Perpetual Peace: A Philosophical Sketch," in H. S. Reiss, ed., *Kant: Political Writings* (Cambridge: Cambridge University Press, 1991); and Emer de Vattel, *The Law of Nations, Or, Principles of the Law of Nature, Applied to the Conduct and Affairs of Nations and Sovereigns, with Three Early Essays on the Origin and Nature of Natural Law and on Luxury*, ed. Béla Kapossy and Richard Whatmore (Indianapolis: Liberty Fund, 2008), 2:322.

6. Jane McAdam, "An Intellectual History of Freedom of Movement in International Law: The Right to Leave as a Personal Liberty," *Melbourne Journal of International Law* 12, no. 1 (2011): 1–29; and Vincent Chetail, "Sovereignty and Migration in the Doctrine of the Law of Nations: An Intellectual History of Hospitality from Vitoria to Vattel," *European Journal of International Law* 27, no. 4 (2016): 901–22.

7. Jean-Jacques Burlamaqui, *The Principles of Natural and Politic Law*, trans. and ed. Thomas Nugent (Indianapolis: Liberty Fund, 2006), 2:366; Samuel von Pufendorf, *Of the Law of Nature and Nations* (London, 1729), 7:868; and Vattel, *Law of Nations*, 1:223.

8. Vattel, *Law of Nations*, 1:220.

9. Vattel, *Law of Nations*, 1:222 and 221; and Burlamaqui, *Principles of Natural*, 2:119.

10. For a concept of emigrant rights as the basis for belonging within England's early empire, see Dan Hulsebosch, "English Liberties outside England: Floors, Doors, Windows, and Ceilings in the Legal Architecture of Empire," in Lorna Huston, ed., *The Oxford Handbook of English Law and Literature, 1500–1700* (New York: Oxford University Press, 2017), 747–72. On imperial debates over the relationship between migration and rights, see John Phillip Reid, *Constitutional History of the American Revolution: The Authority of Rights* (Madison: University of Wisconsin Press, 1986), 114–31.

11. [John Adams], *Novanglus; or, A History of the Dispute with America, from Its Origin, in 1754, to the Present Time*, no. 7, in C. Bradley Thompson, ed., *The Revolutionary Writings of John Adams* (Indianapolis: Liberty Fund, 2000), 238; and Thomas Jefferson, *A Summary View of the Rights of British America* (Williamsburg, 1774), 5.

12. [Adams], *Novanglus*, 238; and Jefferson, *Summary View*, 5–7.

13. On the Declaration of Independence as an appeal to the international order, see Peter S. Onuf, "A Declaration of Independence for Diplomatic Historians," *Diplomatic History* 22, no. 1 (1998): 71–83; and Armitage, *Declaration of Independence*

14. On runaway enslaved people and loyalism, see Kunal M. Parker, *Making Foreigners: Immigration and Citizenship Law in America, 1600–2000* (Cambridge: Cambridge University Press, 2015); Cassandra Pybus, *Epic Journeys of Freedom: Runaway Slaves of the American Revolution and their Global Quest for Liberty* (Boston: Beacon Press, 2006); and Alan Taylor, *The Internal Enemy: Slavery and War in Virginia, 1772–1832* (New York: W. W. Norton, 2013). On white Loyalists, see Holger Hoock, *Scars of Independence: America's Violent Birth* (New York: Penguin Random House, 2017); and Maya Jasanoff, *Liberty's Exiles: American Loyalists in the Revolutionary World* (New York: Penguin Random House, 2012).

15. "Passport to Comfort Sands, a Member of the Provincial Congress, Who Is about to Make a Journey to and beyond Albany," in vol. 5, Peter Force, ed., *American Archives* (Washington,

DC, 1839), 1480-81; and "Passport for Gerard G. Beekman, a Friend to the Cause of American Liberty, to Go to Bristol, in Pennsylvania," *American Archives*, 5:1415.

16. On the concept of "treaty-worthiness" as a significant reason for the creation of the United States, see Gould, *Among the Powers*. On union as a type of peace treaty, see David C. Hendrickson, *Peace Pact: The Lost World of the American Founding* (Lawrence: University Press of Kansas, 2003).

17. Pufendorf, *The Whole Duty of Man According to the Law of Nature*, trans. Andrew Tooke, ed. Ian Hunter and David Saunders, with Two Discourses and a Commentary by Jean Barbeyrac, trans. David Saunders (Indianapolis: Liberty Fund, 2003), 2:250; and Vattel, *Law of Nations*, 1:224–25.

18. Articles of Confederation, Article III (1781).

19. Articles of Confederation, Article IV (1781). On the Articles of Confederation as a multilateral agreement, see Akhil Reed Amar, *America's Constitution: A Biography* (New York: Random House, 2006), 26–27. See also Hendrickson, *Peace Pact*; and Alison L. La-Croix, *The Ideological Origins of American Federalism* (Cambridge, MA: Harvard University Press, 2010).

20. Gould, *Among the Powers*, 133; William J. Novak, "The Legal Transformation of Citizenship in Nineteenth-Century America," in Meg Jacobs, William J. Novak, and Julian E. Zelizer, eds., *The Democratic Experiment: New Directions in American Political History* (Princeton, NJ: Princeton University Press, 2003), 88–89; and Amar, *America's Constitution*, 252–54.

21. Pennsylvania Constitution (1790); *The Proceedings Relative to Calling the Conventions of 1776 and 1790* (Harrisburg, 1825), 264.

22. "An Act Declaring Who Shall Be Deemed Citizens of this Commonwealth," *Acts Passed at a General Assembly, Begun and Held at the Capitol, in the City of Williamsburg, on Monday the Third Day of May, in the Year of Our Lord One Thousand Seven Hundred and Seventy Nine* (Williamsburg, 1779); "An Act for the Admission of Emigrants, and Declaring Their Rights to Citizenship," *Acts Passed at a General Assembly of the Commonwealth of Virginia. Begun and Held at the Public Buildings in the City of Richmond, on Monday the Twentieth Day of October, in the Year of Our Lord One Thousand Seven Hundred and Eighty-Three* (Richmond, 1783); and "A Bill Declaring Who Shall Be Deemed Citizens of this Commonwealth," *Report of the Committee of Revisors Appointed by the General Assembly of Virginia* (Richmond, 1784), 41–42.

23. Vattel, *Law of Nations*, 1:154; and "A Citizen," *Gazette of the State of Georgia*, December 6, 1788, in Merrill Jensen, ed., *Ratification of the Constitution by the States: Delaware, New Jersey, Georgia, and Connecticut*, vol. 3, *The Documentary History of the Ratification of the Constitution* (Madison: Wisconsin Historical Society Press, 1978), 253.

24. "The Observer, No. 1," *Massachusetts Centinel* (Boston), April 10, 1784.

25. "For the Daily Advertiser," *Daily Advertiser* (New York), April 7, 1787; "New York, Oct. 21," *New Jersey Gazette* (Trenton, NJ), October 30, 1786; and Fougeret de Montbron, *Le Cosmopolite ou le Citoyen du Monde* (London, 1750), quoted in Pauline Kleingeld and Eric Brown, "Cosmopolitanism," *Stanford Encyclopedia of Philosophy* (Winter 2019), ed. Edward N. Zalta, https://plato.stanford.edu/archives/win2019/entries/cosmopolitanism/.

26. "The Buck, Fop, and Quack," *Carlisle Gazette* (Carlisle, PA), November 23, 1791; "New-York, December 22," *Royal Gazette* (New York), December 22, 1781; Jonathan Elliot,

ed., *The Debates in the Several State Conventions on the Adoption of the Federal Constitution* (Philadelphia and Washington, 1845), 5:400. Eighteenth-century understandings of cosmopolitanism were decidedly different from contemporary understandings of cosmopolitanism. The former emphasized universal rights in order to challenge perceived prejudices of all sorts whereas modern understandings focus on cultural pluralism and a fundamental recognition of and respect for difference. On early modern usage, see Thomas J. Schlereth, *The Cosmopolitan Ideal in Enlightenment Thought: Its Form and Function in the Ideas of Franklin, Hume, and Voltaire, 1694–1790* (Notre Dame, IN: University of Notre Dame Press, 1977); on historic tensions within the idea of cosmopolitanism, see Margaret C. Jacob, *Strangers Nowhere in the World: The Rise of Cosmopolitanism in Early Modern Europe* (Philadelphia: University of Pennsylvania Press, 2006); for a philosophical treatment that explores modern understandings of cosmopolitanism, see Kwame Anthony Appiah, *Cosmopolitanism: Ethics in a World of Strangers* (New York: W. W. Norton, 2006).

27. Johann Georg Schlosser, "Politische Fragmente," in *Deutsches Museum*, February 1777, quoted in Kleingeld and Brown, "Cosmopolitanism," *Stanford Encyclopedia of Philosophy* (Summer 2009), ed. Edward N. Zalta, http://plato.stanford.edu/archives/sum2009/entries/cosmopolitanism/; and Jean-Jacques Rousseau, *The Social Contract and Other Later Political Writings*, ed. and trans. Victor Gourevitch (Cambridge: Cambridge University Press, 1997), 158.

28. Vattel, *Law of Nations*, 1:224; and "An Act Declaring Who Shall Be Deemed Citizens of This Commonwealth," *Acts Passed at a General Assembly, Begun and Held at the Capitol, in the City of Williamsburg, on Monday the Third Day of May, in the Year of Our Lord One Thousand Seven Hundred and Seventy Nine* (Williamsburg, 1779).

29. On the relationship between statelessness and cosmopolitanism in histories of citizenship in the United States, see Linda K. Keber, "Toward a History of Statelessness in America," *American Quarterly* 57 (2005): 727–49; and Kerber, "The Stateless as the Citizen's Other: A View from the United States," *American Historical Review* 112 (February 2007): 1–34.

30. James Wilson, "Lectures on Law," in *The Works of the Honourable James Wilson* (Philadelphia, 1804), 1:315.

Chapter Two

1. Stephen Aron, *American Confluence: The Missouri Frontier from Borderland to Border State* (Bloomington: Indiana University Press, 2006), 71–72.

2. "Governour Browne's Reasons, as Presented to the King, for an Immediate Civil Government in the British Dominions Adjoining to the River Mississippi, in North-America," in vol. 2, Peter Force, ed., *American Archives* (Washington, DC: 1839), 994.

3. David J. Weber, *The Spanish Frontier in North America* (New Haven, CT: Yale University Press, 1992), 277–79.

4. Kathleen DuVal, *Independence Lost: Lives on the Edge of the American Revolution* (New York: Random House, 2015), 268–69; and Richard White, *The Middle Ground: Indians, Empires, and Republics in the Great Lakes Region, 1650–1815* (Cambridge: Cambridge University Press, 1991), 416.

5. White, *Middle Ground*, 441 and 434; and Weber, *Spanish Frontier*, 277–79.

6. Paul Frymer, *Building an American Empire: The Era of Territorial and Political Expansion* (Princeton, NJ: Princeton University Press, 2017), 32–71.

7. Alan Taylor, *American Revolutions: A Continental History, 1750–1804* (New York: W. W. Norton, 2016), 344; and Jessica Choppin Roney, "1776, Viewed from the West," *Journal of the Early Republic* 37 (2017): 679.

8. Bethel Saler, *The Settlers' Empire: Colonialism and State Formation in America's Old Northwest* (Philadelphia: University of Pennsylvania Press, 2015), 19. See also Michael Witgen, "A Nation of Settlers: The Early American Republic and the Colonization of the Northwest Territory," *William and Mary Quarterly* 76, no. 3 (2019): 391–98; and Peter Onuf, *Statehood and Union: A History of the Northwest Ordinance* (Bloomington: Indiana University Press, 1987).

9. Hon. Hu. Williamson to Gov. Alex. Martin, November 18, 1782, in Walter Clark, ed., *The State Records of North Carolina* (Goldsboro, NC, 1899), 16:459–60. On Franklin and western state-making movements during the 1780s more broadly, see Roney, "1776," 683 and 685–86.

10. George Washington to George Plater, October 25, 1784, in W. W. Abbott and Dorothy Twohig, eds., *The Papers of George Washington: Confederation Series* (Charlottesville: University of Virginia Press, 1992), 2:108.

11. White, *Middle Ground*, 418–19; George Washington to Benjamin Harrison, October 10, 1784, in Abbott and Twohig, *Papers of George Washington: Confederation Series*, 2:93; and George Washington to François Barbé de Marbois, June 21, 1785, in W. W. Abbott and Dorothy Twohig, eds., *Papers of George Washington: Confederation Series* (Charlottesville: University of Virginia Press, 1995), 3:65.

12. "Call for Election of Delegates to Form a State Convention West of the Ohio River," March 12, 1785, in Archer Butler Hulbert, ed., *Ohio in the Time of the Confederation*, vol. 3, *Marietta College Historical Collections* (Marietta, OH: Marietta Historical Commission, 1918), 98–99.

13. "Petition of Kentuckians for Lands North of Ohio River," in Butler, *Ohio in the Time*, 3:137–44.

14. James E. Lewis, *American Union and the Problem of Neighborhood: The United States and Collapse of Spanish Empire, 1783–1829* (Chapel Hill: The University of North Carolina Press, 1998), 15–17.

15. "Copy of Two Letters from a Gentleman at the Falls of the Ohio, to His Friend in New-England," *Maryland Journal*, July 3, 1787, in *The Documentary History of the Ratification of the Constitution Digital Edition*, ed. John P. Kaminski, Gaspare J. Saladino, Richard Leffler, Charles H. Schoenleber, and Margaret A. Hogan (Charlottesville: University of Virginia Press, 2009). See also for details about letter authorship and circulation.

16. George Washington to Benjamin Harrison, October 10, 1784, in Abbott and Twohig, *Papers of George Washington: Confederation Series*, 2:92–93.

17. For contemporary concerns about the formation of separate confederacies, see "The Idea of Separate Confederacies," in *Documentary History of the Ratification*.

18. George Washington to Benjamin Harrison, October 10, 1784, in Abbott and Twohig, *Papers of George Washington: Confederation Series*, 2:92–93.

19. Gilbert C. Din, "War Clouds on the Mississippi: Spain's 1785 Crisis in West Florida," *Florida Historical Quarterly* (1981): 55; Brandon Layton, "Indian Country to Slave Country:

The Transformation of Natchez during the American Revolution," *Journal of Southern History* 82 (2016): 27–58.

20. Francisco Bouligny to Esteban Miró, August 22, 1785, in Lawrence Kinnaird, ed., *Spain in the Mississippi Valley, 1765–1794*, 3 parts (vols. 2–4), *Annual Report of the American Historical Association for the Year 1945* (Washington, DC: US Government Printing Office, 1946–49), 2:140–42; Gilbert C. Din, "The Immigration Policy of Governor Esteban Miró in Spanish Louisiana," *Southwestern Historical Quarterly* 73 (1969): 158; and Weber, *Spanish Frontier*, 281.

21. "Extract of Letter from a Gentleman on the Mississippi, to a Citizen of This Place, Dated New Orleans, Feb. 11, 1787," *Massachusetts Gazette* (Boston), April 6, 1787.

22. Weber, *Spanish Frontier*, 281.

23. On the possibility of Hispanization, see Din, "The Immigration Policy of Governor Esteban Miró in Spanish Louisiana," 175. For contemporary theories of citizenship that describe growing local connections and residence more than legal forms such as naturalization in forging ties of meaningful civic belonging, see Joseph H. Carens, *The Ethics of Immigration* (Oxford: Oxford University Press, 2013); and Ayelet Shachar, *The Birthright Lottery: Citizenship and Global Inequality* (Cambridge, MA: Harvard University Press, 2009).

24. Arthur St. Clair to George Washington, August 1789, in Dorothy Twohig, ed., *The Papers of George Washington: Presidential Series* (Charlottesville: University of Virginia Press, 1989), 3:585–88.

25. St. Clair to Washington, August 1789, in Twohig, *Papers of George Washington: Presidential Series*, 3:585–87; George Nicholas to James Madison, May 8, 1789, in William T. Hutchinson et al., eds., *The Papers of James Madison, Congressional Series* (Charlottesville: University of Virginia Press, 1979), 12:138–40; George Nicholas to James Madison, November 2, 1789, in Hutchinson et al., *Papers of James Madison, Congressional Series*, 12:442–44.

26. Gilbert C. Din, "Empires Too Far: The Demographic Limitations of Three Imperial Powers in the Eighteenth-Century Mississippi Valley," *Louisiana History* 50 (2009): 282 and 286.

27. Don Diego de Gardoqui to Esteban Miró, October 4, 1788, in Louis Houck, ed., *The Spanish Regime in Missouri*, 2 vols. (New York: Arno Press, 1971), 1:284–85; and Thomas Hutchins to Daniel Clark, December 20, 1788, in Kinnaird, *Spain in the Mississippi Valley*, 2:263–64.

28. Letter from the Exploratory Party at New Madrid to Turnbull and Company at Pittsburgh, April 14, 1789, in Houck, *Spanish Regime in Missouri*, 1:279–83

29. George Morgan to Don Diego de Gardoqui, August 20, 1789, in Houck, *Spanish Regime in Missouri*, 1:291.

30. Morgan to Diego de Gardoqui, August 20, 1789, in Houck, *Spanish Regime in Missouri*, 1:295, 305, 301, 302, and 299.

31. Morgan to Diego de Gardoqui, August 20, 1789, in Houck, *Spanish Regime in Missouri*, 1:302–4, 306, and 297. On royalism's appeal in eighteenth-century British colonies, see Brendan McConville, *The King's Three Faces: The Rise and Fall of Royal America, 1688–1776* (Chapel Hill: The University of North Carolina Press, 2007).

32. James Madison to George Washington, March 26, 1789, in Hutchinson et al., *Papers of James Madison, Congressional Series*, 12:28; James Madison to James Monroe, November 5,

1788, in Hutchinson et al., eds., *The Papers of James Madison, Congressional Series* (Charlottesville: University of Virginia Press, 1977), 11:332–33; and "Governor St. Clair to the Secretary for Foreign Affairs," December 13, 1788, in Clarence Edwin Carter, ed., *The Territory Northwest of the River Ohio*, vol. 2, *The Territorial Papers of the United States* (Washington, DC: US Government Printing Office, 1934), 168–70.

33. George Washington to James Madison, June 12, 1789, in Twohig, *Papers of George Washington: Presidential Series*, 2:479–80.

34. J. Dawson to Governor Beverley Randolph, New York, January 29, 1789, in William M. Palmer, ed., *Calendar of the Virginia State Papers* (Richmond, 1884), 4:554–55.

35. James Madison, "Population and Emigration," in Hutchinson et al., *Papers of James Madison*, 16:117–22; and James Madison, "Notes on Emigration," November 19, 1791, in Hutchinson et al., eds., *The Papers of James Madison, Congressional Series* (Charlottesville: University of Virginia Press, 1989), 16:114.

36. St. Clair to Washington, August, 1789, in Twohig, *Papers of George Washington: Presidential Series*, 3:588.

37. Saler, *Settlers' Empire*, 41–82; and Onuf, *Statehood and Union*, 44–87.

38. "Population of the Northwest Territory," in Julian P. Boyd, ed., *The Papers of Thomas Jefferson: Main Series*, vol. 18 (Princeton, NJ: Princeton University Press, 1971), 217–18.

39. Washington to Madison, June 12, 1789, in Twohig, *Papers of George Washington: Presidential Series*, 2:479–80.

40. "Copy of a Letter from a Gentleman at New Orleans, to His Friend in This Neighbourhood, Dated September—, 1790," *City Gazette* (Charleston, SC), December 14, 1790.

Chapter Three

1. Carlos de Grand Pré to Esteban Miró, April 22, 1790, in Lawrence Kinnaird, ed., *Spain in the Mississippi Valley, 1765–1794*, 3 parts (vols. 2–4), *Annual Report of the American Historical Association for the Year 1945* (Washington, DC: US Government Printing Office, 1946–49), 2:326–27. On Forman's background and life in Natchez, see Ruth L. Woodward and Wesley Frank Craven, *Princetonians, 1784–1790: A Biographical Dictionary* (Princeton, NJ: Princeton University Press, 1991), 114.

2. *Lower Canada, Declaration of Aliens-H-1154*, Image 255, Library and Archives Canada.

3. For population estimates, see David J. Weber, *The Spanish Frontier in North America* (New Haven, CT: Yale University Press, 1992), 281; and Cole Harris, *The Reluctant Land: Society, Space, and Environment in Canada before Confederation* (Vancouver: University of British Columbia Press, 2008), 288 and 309; John Pope, *A Tour Through the Southern and Western Territories of the United States of North-America, the Spanish Dominions on the River Mississippi, and the Floridas, the Countries of the Creek Nations, and Many Uninhabited Parts* (Richmond, VA, 1792), 28. The focus on how the laws and customs of emigrant rights informed imperial considerations and justified personal claims to move and choose allegiance offers an alternative to and complements Alan Taylor, "Remaking Americans: Louisiana, Upper Canada, and Texas," in Juliana Barr and Edward Countryman, eds., *Contested Spaces of Early America* (Philadelphia: University of Pennsylvania Press, 2014), 208–26, which privileges economic demands as central to both imperial interests and the actions of American emigrants. An emigrant rights approach to Spain's colonization policies for Louisiana also

builds on the argument for the plausibility of Spain's intentions in Sylvia L. Hilton, "Loyalty and Patriotism on North American Frontiers: Being and Becoming Spanish in the Mississippi Valley, 1776–1803," in Gene Allen Smith and Sylvia L. Hilton, eds., *Nexus of Empire: Negotiating Loyalty and Identity in the Revolutionary Borderlands, 1760s–1820s* (Gainesville: University Press of Florida, 2010), 8–36.

4. Emer de Vattel, *The Law of Nations, Or, Principles of the Law of Nature, Applied to the Conduct and Affairs of Nations and Sovereigns, with Three Early Essays on the Origin and Nature of Natural Law and on Luxury*, ed. Béla Kapossy and Richard Whitmore (Indianapolis: Liberty Fund, 2008), 1:221; and Protest of Governor Miró against Grant to Col. George Morgan, 1789, in Louis Houck, ed., *The Spanish Regime in Missouri*, 2 vols. (New York: Arno Press, 1971), 1:277. On Miró's view that Spain should adopt a more open colonization policy for West Florida and Louisiana, see Gilbert C. Din, "The Immigration Policy of Governor Esteban Miró in Spanish Louisiana," *Southwestern Historical Quarterly* 73 (1969): 157. On notions of political belonging in Spain and Spanish America, see Tamar Herzog, *Defining Nations: Immigrants and Citizens in Early Modern Spain and Spanish America* (New Haven, CT: Yale University Press, 2003), 66, 163, and 198.

5. Miró's Offer to Western Americans, April 20, 1789, in Kinnaird, *Spain in the Mississippi Valley*, 2:269–70; Hilton, "Loyalty and Patriotism," in Smith and Hilton, *Nexus of Empire*, 8–36.

6. For descriptions of Natchez, see Pope, *A Tour*, 30; and Philip Pittman, *The Present State of the European Settlements on the Mississippi; with a Geographical Description of That River* (London, 1770), 37–39.

7. George Nicholas to James Madison, November 2, 1789, in William T. Hutchinson et al., eds., *The Papers of James Madison, Congressional Series* (Charlottesville: University of Virginia Press, 1979), 12:442–46; Din, "Immigration Policy of Governor," 158; and Weber, *Spanish Frontier*, 281.

8. "Copy of a Letter from a Gentleman at New-Orleans, to His Friends in This Neighbourhood, Dated September—, 1790," *City Gazette* (Charleston, SC), December 14, 1790; and Ellen Eslinger, ed., *Running Mad for Kentucky: Frontier Travel Accounts* (Lexington: University Press of Kentucky, 2004), 14–15.

9. Dorothy Williams Potter, ed., *Passports of Southeastern Pioneers, 1770–1823: Indian, Spanish and other Land Passports for Tennessee, Kentucky, Georgia, Mississippi, Virginia, North and South Carolina* (Baltimore: Gateway Press, Inc., 1982), 14–15, 43, and x.

10. "Report of Americans Arriving at Natchez, April 17, 1792," in Potter, *Passports*, 37.

11. "Report of Americans Arriving at Natchez, July 5, 1788," in Kinnaird, *Spain in the Mississippi Valley*, 2:257; Carlos de Grand Pré to Esteban Miró, March 12, 1790, in Kinnaird, *Spain in the Mississippi Valley*, 2:313; Carlos de Grand Pré to Esteban Miró, April 22, 1790, in Kinnaird, *Spain in the Mississippi Valley*, 2:326–27; and Potter, *Passports*, 19.

12. On Peter Bryan Bruin, see William S. Coker, "The Bruins and the Formulation of Spanish Immigration Policy in the Old Southwest, 1787–88," in John Francis McDermott, ed., *The Spanish in the Mississippi Valley, 1762–1804* (Urbana: University of Illinois Press, 1974), 62–70; Samuel S. Forman, *Narrative of a Journey Down the Ohio and Mississippi in 1789–90*, with memoir and illustrative notes by Lyman Draper (Cincinnati, 1888), 61.

13. People of New Madrid to Manuel Perez, May 30, 1789, in Kinnaird, *Spain in the Mississippi Valley*, 2:274.

14. Pedro Foucher to Esteban Miró, April 15, 1790, in Kinnaird, *Spain in the Mississippi Valley*, 2:325; and Some Persons Who Took the Oath of Allegiance at New Madrid from 1789 to 1796, in Houck, *Spanish Regime in Missouri*, 1:319–21.

15. Statistical Census of New Madrid of 1797, in Houck, *Spanish Regime in Missouri*, 2:393; and Some Oaths of Allegiance Taken at New Madrid from 1793 to 1795, in Houck, *Spanish Regime in Missouri*, 1:334–38; "Providence, August 1," *Newport Herald*, August 6, 1789, included Israel Shreeve's assessment that New Madrid was flood prone.

16. People of New Madrid to Manuel Perez, May 30, 1789, in Kinnaird, *Spain in the Mississippi Valley*, 2:274; Pedro Foucher to Esteban Miró, October 25, 1790, in Kinnaird, *Spain in the Mississippi Valley*, 2:385–86; Statistical Census of New Madrid of 1797, in Houck, *Spanish Regime in Missouri*, 2:393; Louis Houck, *A History of Missouri: From the Earliest Explorations and Settlements until the Admission of the State into the Union* (Chicago: R. R. Donnelley & Sons, 1908), 2:160; Some Oaths of Allegiance Taken at New Madrid from 1793 to 1795, in Houck, *Spanish Regime in Missouri*, 1:337; Statistical Census of New Madrid of 1797, in Houck, *Spanish Regime in Missouri*, 2:395. On the American majority at New Madrid, see Gilbert C. Din, "Empires Too Far: The Demographic Limitations of Three Imperial Powers in the Eighteenth-Century Mississippi Valley," *Louisiana History* 50 (2009): 291.

17. "From the Kentucky Herald," *Albany Centinel*, November 8, 1799.

18. Vattel, *Law of Nations*, 1:220; and Samuel von Pufendorf, *Of the Law of Nature and Nations* (London, 1729), 8:868. On the ways that men's control of women's physical bodies and reproductive systems eased their claims to place and belonging in North American colonial contexts, see Laurel Clark Shire, *The Threshold of Manifest Destiny: Gender and National Expansion in Florida* (Philadelphia: University of Pennsylvania Press, 2016).

19. The Virginia General Assembly recognized and outlined a procedure for exercising a right to expatriation in 1779 in "An Act Declaring Who Shall Be deemed Citizens of This Commonwealth," *Acts Passed at a General Assembly, Begun and Held at the Capitol, in the City of Williamsburg, on Monday the Third Day of May, in the Year of Our Lord One Thousand Seven Hundred and Seventy Nine* (Williamsburg, 1779). In 1783, the Virginia General Assembly adopted "an Act for the Admission of Emigrants, and declaring their Rights to Citizenship" that included an expatriation provision and replaced the 1779 law, *Acts passed at a General Assembly of the Commonwealth of Virginia. Begun and Held at the Public Buildings in the city of Richmond, on Monday the Twentieth Day of October, in the Year of Our Lord One Thousand Seven Hundred and Eighty-Three* (Richmond, 1783); "A Bill Declaring Who Shall Be Deemed Citizens of this Commonwealth," *Report of the Committee of Revisors Appointed by the General Assembly of Virginia* (Richmond, 1784), 41–42; and Carlos de Grand Pré to Esteban Miró, June 10, 1790, in Kinnaird, *Spain in the Mississippi Valley*, 2:350.

20. Carlos de Grand Pré to Esteban Miró, October 2, 1790, in Kinnaird, *Spain in the Mississippi Valley*, 2:380–82; James Robertson to Esteban Miró, September 2, 1789, in Kinnaird, *Spain in the Mississippi Valley*, 2:279–80.

21. "Copy of a Letter from a Gentleman at New-Orleans, to His Friends in This Neighbourhood, Dated September—, 1790," *City Gazette* (Charleston, SC), December 14, 1790; and "Extract of a Letter from a Gentleman in New-Orleans, to His Friend in This City, Dated June 27," *Pennsylvania Mercury*, November 16, 1790.

22. "Copy of a Letter from a Gentleman at New-Orleans, to His Friends in This Neighbourhood, Dated September—, 1790," *City Gazette* (Charleston, SC), December 14, 1790; "United Columbia," *Massachusetts Spy*, March 4, 1790; and Arthur St. Clair to George

Washington, May 1, 1790, in Dorothy Twohig, Mark A. Mastromarino, and Jack D. Warren, eds., *The Papers of George Washington: Presidential Series* (Charlottesville: University of Virginia Press, 1996), 5:373–74.

23. "Extract of a Letter from a Gentleman in New-Orleans, to His Friend in This City, Dated June 27," *Pennsylvania Mercury*, November 16, 1790; and "Philadelphia, December 4," *Independent Gazetter* (Philadelphia, PA), December 4, 1790.

24. "Proposal for New Andalusia," in Kinnaird, *Spain in the Mississippi Valley*, 3:46–50.

25. "Proposal for New Andalusia," in Kinnaird, *Spain in the Mississippi Valley*, 3:46–50. On volitional allegiance, see James H. Kettner, The Development of American Citizenship, 1608–1870 (Chapel Hill: The University of North Carolina Press, 1978), 173–209.

26. "Proposal for New Andalusia," in Kinnaird, *Spain in the Mississippi Valley*, 3:46–50; and "Louisiana," *Carlisle Gazette*, December 21, 1791.

27. Barón de Carondelet quoted in Hilton, "Loyalty and Patriotism," in Smith and Hilton, *Nexus of Empire*, 12. Barthelemi Tardiveau to Baron de Carondelet, July 17, 1792, in Kinnaird, *Spain in the Mississippi Valley*, 3:61; Din, "Immigration Policy of Governor," 174; and Gilbert C. Din, "Spain's Immigration Policy in Louisiana and the American Penetration, 1792–1803," *Southwestern Historical Quarterly* 76 (1973): 256 and 267.

28. Baron de Carondelet to Zenon Trudeau, June 8, 1792, in Kinnaird, *Spain in the Mississippi Valley*, 3:51–52.

29. On the Abenaki after 1783, see Colin G. Calloway, *The Western Abenakis of Vermont, 1600–1800: War, Migration, and the Survival of an Indian People* (Norman: University of Oklahoma Press, 1990), 224–37; Fernand Ouellet, *Lower Canada, 1791–1840: Social Change and Nationalism*, trans. Patricia Claxton (Toronto: McClelland and Stewart, 1980), 9–10.

30. Ouellet, *Lower Canada*, 20–22; and Harris, *Reluctant Land*, 232–33.

31. "Instructions to Lord Dorchester as Governor of Lower Canada," in Arthur G. Doughty and Duncan A. McArthur, eds., *Documents Relating to the Constitutional History of Canada, 1791–1818* (Ottawa: C. H. Parmelee, 1914), 21.

32. Harris, *Reluctant Land*, 309; Little, *Loyalties in Conflict*, 5–6; and Rieko Karatani, *Defining British Citizenship: Empire, Commonwealth and Modern Britain* (London: Routledge, 2003), 52 and 60.

33. "Report of the Executive Council Respecting Crown Lands," February 4, 1792, in Doughty and McArthur, *Documents*, 59–60; and "Proclamation" in Doughty and McArthur, *Documents*, 60–61.

34. G. F. McGuigan, "Administration of Land Policy and the Growth of Corporate Economic Organization in Lower Canada, 1791–1809," *Report of the Annual Meeting of the Canadian Historical Association* 42 (1963): 66–67; Harris, *Reluctant Land*, 287; and Ouellet, *Lower Canada*, 37–38.

35. Constitution of Vermont, July 8, 1777, in *Vermont State Papers; Being a Collection of Records and Documents, Connected with the Assumption and Establishment of Government by the People of Vermont: Together with the Journal of the Council of Safety, the First Constitution, the Early Journals of the General Assembly, and the Laws from the Year 1779 to 1786, Inclusive. To Which Are Added the Proceedings of the First and Second Councils of Censors. Compiled and Published by William Slade Jun. Secretary of State* (Middlebury, 1823), 241–55; and Constitution of the State of Vermont, July 9, 1793.

36. *Lower Canada, Declaration of Aliens-H-1154*, Images 41 and 18, Library and Archives Canada; Marcus Lee Hansen, with John Bartlet Brebner, *The Mingling of the Canadian and*

American Peoples (New Haven, CT: Yale University Press, 1940), 1:72; and McGuigan, "Administration of Land Policy," 72.

37. Milnes to Portland, November 1, 1800, in Doughty and McArthur, *Documents*, 254; Gerald F. McGuigan, "Land Policy and Land Disposal under Tenure of Free and Common Socage, Quebec and Lower Canada, 1763–1809" (PhD diss., Laval University, 1962), 120; Hansen, *Mingling of the Canadian*, 72; Ouellet, *Lower Canada*, 37; Little, *Loyalties in Conflict*, 5–6; Harris, *Reluctant Land*, 287; and J. I. Little, "Contested Land: Squatters and Agents in the Eastern Townships of Lower Canada," *Canadian Historical Review* 80 (1999): 381–412.

38. Land Committee Regarding Survey, Brome County Historical Society Fonds, Library and Archives Canada (hereafter BCHS-LAC), Townships Papers, Eastern Townships, A. Minutes and Minute Books, 1792–99.

39. Samuel Willard to Abel Willard, April 15, 1793, and Samuel Willard to Abel Willard, October 6, 1793, in BCHS-LAC, Samuel Willard Papers, 1783–1899, A. Correspondence, 1783–1870; Isaac Weld, *Travels through the States of North America, and the Provinces of Upper and Lower Canada, During the Years 1795, 1796, and 1797* (London, 1800), 1:407–11.

40. Berezly to Samuel Gale, August 9, 1798, in BCHS-LAC, Samuel Gale Papers, 1774–1903, A. Correspondence, 1787–1840.

41. Executive Council Printed Notices, October 20, 1794, in BCHS-LAC, Township Papers, E. Township Papers by Township, Stukely Township, G. Miscellaneous Papers. Library and Archives Canada, Executive Council Office of the Province of Lower Canada (RG 1 L3L): Oath at Missisquoi Bay, 26 April–25 July 1795, Vol. 194, 92515–22; Oath at Missisquoi Bay, 26 July–25 October 1795, Vol. 205, 95964–65; Oath at Missisquoi Bay, 26 April–25 July 1796, Vol. 42, 21507–09; Oath at Missisquoi Bay, 26 July–25 October 1796, Vol. 205, 95967–69; Oath at Missisquoi Bay, 26 October 1796–25 January 1797, Vol. 205, 95966–69.

42. "Canada Lands," *Rutland Herald*, January 4, 1796; Samuel Willard to Sam Dickinson, March 2, 1795, in BCHS-LAC, Samuel Willard Papers, 1783–1899, A. Correspondence, 1783–1870; Simeon Strong Recommendation for Amherst Petitioners, July 7, 1795, in BCHS-LAC, Township Papers, E. Township Papers by Township, Stukely Township, C. Petitions and Petitioners; *Lower Canada, Declaration of Aliens-H-1154*, Images 399 and 413–14, Library and Archives Canada; and *Land Petitions of Lower Canada, 1764–1841* (RG 1 L3L), 50361 and 59666, Library and Archives Canada.

43. Orford Associates, no date in BCHS-LAC, Township Papers by Township, Orford Township, D. Miscellaneous; BCHS-LAC, Township Papers, E. Township Papers by Township, Stukely Township, C. Petitions and Petitioners; Land Committee of the Council-Stukely in BCHS-LAC, Township Papers, E. Township Papers by Township, Stukely Township, A. Minutes; Samuel Willard Petition to Dorchester, July 23, 1795, in BCHS-LAC, Township Papers, E. Township Papers by Township, Stukely Township, C. Petitions and Petitioners.

44. Charles Stewart, *Prominent Features of a Northern Tour* (Charleston, 1822), 12–13; *Le Canadien*, November 28, 1807, quoted in Ouellet, *Lower Canada*, 75–76.

45. Luke Knowlton to Samuel Willard, July 6, 1795, in BCHS-LAC, Samuel Willard Papers, 1783–1899, A. Correspondence, 1783–1870; Calvin Knowlton to Samuel Willard, July 7, 1795, in BCHS-LAC, Samuel Willard Papers, 1783–1899, A. Correspondence, 1783–1870; "Petitions for Grants of Land in Upper Canada. Second Series, 1796–99," with

Introduction and Notes by Brig.-General E. A. Cruikshank, LL.D., F.R.Hist.S., in Ontario Historical Society, *Papers and Records*, vol. 26 (Toronto, 1930): 170 and 272.

46. "Attention!," *Rutland Herald*, June 8, 1795; and Weld, *Travels*, 407–11.

47. Land Committee of the Council-Stukely, in BCHS-LAC, Township Papers, E. Township Papers by Township, Stukely Township, A. Minutes.

48. Land Committee of the Council-Stukely, in BCHS-LAC, Township Papers, E. Township Papers by Township, Stukely Township, A. Minutes.

49. Samuel Willard to Luke Knowlton, August 1, 1797, in BCHS-LAC, Knowlton Family Papers, Luke Knowlton, 1783–1809, A. Correspondence, 1783–1801; and Luke Knowlton to Samuel Willard, December 5, 1797, in BCHS-LAC, Samuel Willard Papers, 1783–1899, A. Correspondence, 1783–1870.

50. Land Committee of the Council-Stukely, in BCHS-LAC, Township Papers, E. Township Papers by Township, Stukely Township, A. Minutes.

Chapter Four

1. 7 Annals of Cong. 354 (1851); Talbot v. Janson, 3 Dall. 133 (1795), 135–36. Histories of expatriation debates in the United States during the 1790s often explain their significance to federalism or the acquisition of citizenship rights. See James Kettner, *The Development of American Citizenship, 1608–1870* (Chapel Hill: The University of North Carolina Press, 1978), 271–81; Rogers M. Smith, *Civic Ideals: Conflicting Visions of Citizenship in US History* (New Haven, CT: Yale University Press, 1997), 155–59; Douglas Bradburn, *The Citizenship Revolution: Politics and the Creation of the American Union* (Charlottesville: University of Virginia Press, 2009), 104–6.

2. Genet's mission is summarized in Stanley Elkins and Eric McKitrick, *The Age of Federalism* (New York: Oxford University Press, 1993), 333–34. See also Harry Ammon, *The Genet Mission* (New York: W. W. Norton, 1973).

3. "Henfield's Case," in Francis Wharton, ed., *State Trials of the United States during the Administrations of Washington and Adams* (Philadelphia, 1849), 52.

4. "Neutrality Proclamation," April 22, 1793, in Christine S. Patrick and John C. Pinheiro, eds., *The Papers of George Washington: Presidential Series* (Charlottesville: University of Virginia Press, 2005), 12:472; and *An Act in Addition to the Act for the Punishment of Certain Crimes against the United States [Neutrality Act, 1794]*, United States Statutes at Large, 3rd Cong., Sess. I., 381–84.

5. Edmond Charles Genet, *United States, 15th January, 1794. Gentlemen of the Senate, and of the House of Representatives. I lay before You, as Being Connected with the Correspondence, Already in Your Possession between the Secretary of State, and the Minister Plenipotentiary of the French Republic, the Copy of a Letter from That Minister, of the 25th of December, 1793; and a Copy of the Proceedings of the Legislature of the State of South-Carolina. Go: Washington* (Philadelphia, 1794), 11; *City Gazette and Daily Advertiser* (Charleston, SC), June 30, 1794; and Alexander Moultrie, *An Appeal to the People, on the Conduct of a Certain Public Body in South Carolina, Respecting Col. Drayton and Col. Moultrie* (Charleston, SC: 1794), 8. For background on the South Carolina events, see Robert J. Alderson Jr., *This Bright Era of Happy Revolutions: French Consul Michel-Ange-Bernard Mangourit and International Republicanism in Charleston, 1792–1794* (Columbia: University of South Carolina Press, 2008), 133–40.

6. *Dunlap's American Daily Advertiser* (Philadelphia), September 4, 1793; and "For the Gazette of the United States," *Gazette of the United States and Daily Evening Advertiser* (Philadelphia), December 30, 1794.

7. Edmund Randolph to George Washington, June 24, 1793, in Christine S. Patrick, ed., *The Papers of George Washington: Presidential Series* (Charlottesville: University of Virginia Press, 2007), 13:140.

8. "Henfield's Case," 49–89; Bradburn, *Citizenship Revolution*, 109–14.

9. "Henfield's Case," 85, 80–82, and 89.

10. "For the Columbian Herald," *Columbian Herald* (Columbia, SC), August 29, 1793; James Monroe to Thomas Jefferson, June 27, 1793, in John Catanzariti, ed., *The Papers of Thomas Jefferson* (Princeton, NJ: Princeton University Press, 1995), 26:384; "A Second Address from Real Republicans in Boston, to Citizen Genet," *Columbian Herald* (Columbia, SC), October 10, 1793; and John Adams to Charles Adams, February 13, 1794, in Margaret Hogan et al., eds., *Adams Family Correspondence* (Cambridge, MA: Harvard University Press, 2011), 10:24.

11. *Talbot*, 135. On Guadeloupe, see Laurent Dubois, *A Colony of Citizens: Revolution and Slave Emancipation in the French Caribbean, 1787–1804* (Chapel Hill: The University of North Carolina Press, 2004).

12. Jansen v. The Vrow Christina Magdalena (USDCSC, 1794), 5. See also Bradburn, *Citizenship Revolution*, 116.

13. *Jansen*, 8, 9, 10–11, and 12.

14. *Talbot*, 150–51.

15. *Talbot*, 136 and 145.

16. *Talbot*, 162 and 163.

17. *Talbot*, 165, 169, and 152.

18. "For the Gazette of the United States," *Gazette of the United States* (Philadelphia, PA), January 18, 1797; and "For the Time Piece," *Time Piece* (New York, NY), January 24, 1798.

19. "Expatriation," *Albany Centinel*, July 21, 1797; "Thomas Paine," *Gazette of the United States* (Philadelphia, PA), February 20, 1797; and "Congress—House of Representatives," *American Minerva* (New York, NY), December 26, 1794.

20. "The Drone–No. XII," *New York Magazine, or Literary Repository*, March 1793; "On Expatriation," *City Gazette and Daily Advertiser* (Charleston, SC), December 3, 1799; and "Expatriation," *Albany Centinel*, July 21, 1797.

21. Charles Pinckney, *Three Letters, Written, and Originally Published, under the Signature of A South Carolina Planter* (Philadelphia, 1799), 28–29; and "NO. 11. Remarks on Judge Ellsworth's Late Judicial Decision, That an American Citizen Cannot Expatriate Himself," *Alexandria Times*, October 29, 1799.

22. *Gazette of the United States* (Philadelphia, PA), December 20, 1799; "Congress—House of Representatives," *American Minerva* (New York, NY), December 26, 1794; and "Expatriation," *Albany Centinel*, July 21, 1797.

23. "Extract," *Gazette of the United States and Daily Evening Advertiser* (Philadelphia, PA), June 12, 1794.

24. *Talbot*, 169 and 154.

25. *A Bill to Prohibit Citizens of the United States from Entering into the Military or Naval Service of Any Foreign Prince or State* (Philadelphia, 1797).

26. 7 Annals of Cong. 349–50 and 354 (1851).

27. 7 Annals of Cong. 354–55 (1851).

28. For the diplomatic history of the Jay Treaty, Samuel Flagg Bemis, *Jay's Treaty: A Study in Commerce and Diplomacy* (New Haven, CT: Yale University Press, 1962); on related political controversies, Todd Estes, *The Jay Treaty Debate, Public Opinion, and the Evolution of Early American Political Culture* (Amherst: University of Massachusetts Press, 2006); on how the treaty related to free trade ideas in the early United States, Paul A. Gilje, *Free Trade and Sailors' Rights in the War of 1812* (Cambridge: Cambridge University Press, 2013), 52–56.

29. Treaty of Amity, Commerce, and Navigation, Between His Britannic Majesty and the United States of America, Conditionally Ratified by the Senate of the United States, at Philadelphia, June 24, 1795. To Which Is Annexed, a Copious Appendix (Philadelphia, 1795), 27–28.

30. United States v. Williams, 29 F. 1330 (U.S.C.C.Ct., 1799), in Francis Wharton, *State Trials of the United States During the Administrations of Washington and Adams* (Philadelphia, 1849), 653–54.

31. On the Jay Treaty's implications for citizenship and state formation, see Lawrence B. A. Hatter, "The Jay Charter: Rethinking the American National State in the West, 1796–1819," *Diplomatic History* 37, no. 4 (2013): 693–726; on economic implications of the Jay Treaty for the Champlain Valley, see H. Nicholas Muller III, "Jay's Treaty: The Transformation of Lake Champlain Commerce," *Vermont History* 80 (2012): 33–56; John C. Ogden, *A Tour Through Upper and Lower Canada* (Litchfield, CT, 1799), Introduction, 36, and 88; and Luke Knowlton to Samuel Willard, July 6, 1795, Brome County Historical Society Fonds, Library and Archives Canada (hereafter BCHS-LAC), Samuel Willard Papers, 1783–1899, A. Correspondence, 1783–1870.

32. Missisquoi Bay Proceedings, November 29, 1797, and January 18, 1798, BCHS-LAC, Township Papers, Eastern Townships, A. Minutes and Minute Books, 1792–1799; Marie-Paule R. LaBrèque, "PENNOYER, JESSE," in *Dictionary of Canadian Biography*, vol. 6, University of Toronto/Université Laval, 2003, www.biographi.ca/en/bio/pennoyer_jesse_6E.html; Marie-Paule R. LaBrèque, "HYATT, GILBERT," in *Dictionary of Canadian Biography*, vol. 6, University of Toronto/Université Laval, 2003, www.biographi.ca/en/bio/hyatt_gilbert_6E.html.

33. Missisquoi Bay Proceedings, January 19, 1798, BCHS-LAC, Township Papers, Eastern Townships, A. Minutes and Minute Books, 1792–99.

34. Letter to Robert Prescott from Jesse Pennoyer, Gilber Hyatt, and Oliver Barker, October 6, 1798, Missisquoi Bay Proceedings, BCHS-LAC, Township Papers, Eastern Townships, A. Minutes and Minute Books, 1792–99; and "Congressional News," *Worcester Intelligencer*, January 13, 1795.

35. Samuel Willard Commissioners Certificate, June 26, 1799, BCHS-LAC, Township Papers, E. Township Papers by Township, Stukely Township, G. Miscellaneous Papers; and Samuel Willard Loyalty Certificate, January 8, 1800, BCHS-LAC, Samuel Willard Papers, 1783–1899, B. Land Papers, 1786–1826.

36. S. Phillips to Samuel Willard, March 25, 1800, BCHS-LAC, Samuel Willard Papers, 1783–1899, A. Correspondence, 1783–1870; Committee Approval of Knowlton Petition, March 22, 1800, BCHS-LAC, Township Papers by Township, Orford Township, A. Minutes; Samuel Phillips to Samuel Willard, November 6, 1800, BCHS-LAC, Samuel Willard Papers, 1783–1899, A. Correspondence, 1783–1870; Orford Township Minutes, 1792–95, BCHS-LAC, Township Papers by Township, Orford Township, A. Minutes; Samuel Gale

to Samuel Willard, June 17, 1799, and Samuel Gale to Samuel Willard, September 27, 1799, BCHS-LAC, Samuel Willard Papers, 1783–1899, A. Correspondence, 1783–1870; Samuel Gale Petition, January 1800, BCHS-LAC, Township Papers, E. Township Papers by Township, Stukely Township, C. Petitions and Petitioners; Samuel Gale to Samuel Willard, February 15, 1800, BCHS-LAC, Samuel Willard Papers, 1783–1899, A. Correspondence, 1783–1870; Samuel Gale Petition to Privy Council, November 28, 1800, BCHS-LAC, Township Papers, E. Township Papers by Township, Stukely Township, C. Petitions and Petitioners.

37. Nathaniel Taylor to Samuel Willard, December 29, 1803, BCHS-LAC, Samuel Willard Papers, 1783–1899, A. Correspondence, 1783–1870; Henry Ruiter to Samuel Willard, November 1, 1807, BCHS-LAC, Samuel Willard Papers, 1783–1899, A. Correspondence, 1783–1870; Jimmy W. Manson, *The Loyal Americans of New England and New York Founders of the Townships of Lower Canada* (Brome County Historical Society, 2001), 32–36.

38. "The Surest Way of Getting Rich," *New Hampshire Sentinel*, June 12, 1802; "The Surest Way of Getting Rich," *Connecticut Courant*, July 12, 1802; and "Lands For Sale, In the Province of Lower Canada," *Green Mountain Patriot*, June 6, 1805.

39. David J. Weber, *The Spanish Frontier in North America* (New Haven, CT: Yale University Press, 1992), 289; and Gilbert C. Din, "Empires Too Far: The Demographic Limitations of Three Imperial Powers in the Eighteenth-Century Mississippi Valley," *Louisiana History* 50 (2009): 288.

40. Manuel Gayoso de Lemos, Proclamation to Natchez Settlers, March 29, 1797; and Baron de Carondelet, Proclamation to Natchez Settlers, May 24, 1797, in Andrew Ellicott, *Journal of Andrew Ellicott* (Philadelphia, 1803), 66–67 and 95.

41. Winston De Ville, ed., *Mississippi Valley Mélange: A Collection of Notes and Documents for the Genealogy and History of the Province of Louisiana and the Territory of Orleans* (Ville Platte, LA, 1995), 1:57–58.

42. On Henry Hunter, see "Report of Americans Arriving at Natchez, April 17, 1792," in Dorothy Williams Potter, ed., *Passports of Southeastern Pioneers, 1770–1823: Indian, Spanish and Other Land Passports for Tennessee, Kentucky, Georgia, Mississippi, Virginia, North and South Carolina* (Baltimore: Gateway Press, Inc., 1982), 37.

43. Ellicott, *Journal*, 44; and Isaac Guion, "Military Journal of Captain Isaac Guion, 1797–1799," Mississippi Department of Archives and History, *Annual Report*, 1907–1908: 82; Jack D. L. Holmes, *Gayoso: The Life of a Spanish Governor in the Mississippi Valley, 1789–1799* (Baton Rouge: Louisiana State University Press, 1965), 199.

44. Ellicott, *Journal*, 69–70.

45. Ellicott, *Journal*, 104–5, 107–8, and 74.

46. Manuel Gayoso de Lemos to Andrew Ellicott, March 31, 1797, and Manuel Gayoso de Lemos to Andrew Ellicott, June 13, 1797, in Ellicott, *Journal*, 70 and 105–6.

47. Ellicott, *Journal*, 114–18.

48. Ellicott, *Journal*, 115.

49. "Lists of Persons Taking the Oaths of Allegiance in the Natchez District, 1798–99," *National Genealogical Society Quarterly* 42 (1954): 108–16.

50. Ellicott, *Journal*, 153–54.

51. The Secretary of State to Governor Sargent, May 10, 1798, in Clarence Edwin Carter, ed., *The Territorial Papers of the United States: The Territory of Mississippi, 1798–1817* (Washington, DC, 1937), 5:32–33.

52. Josef Vidal to Marqués de Casa Calvo, September 27, 1800, in Louis Houck, ed., *The Spanish Regime in Missouri*, 2 vols. (New York: Arno Press, 1971), 2:289–90.

53. Vidal to Casa Calvo, September 27, 1800, in Houck, *Spanish Regime*, 2:289–90.

54. "Memorial to Congress by Citizens of the Territory," November 25, 1803, in Carter, *Territorial Papers*, 5:279; William Lattimore to Thomas Jefferson, March 9, 1807, in Carter, *Territorial Papers*, 5:524–25; and "Petition to the President and Congress by Inhabitants of Washington County," February 7, 1809, in Carter, *Territorial Papers*, 5:693.

55. William Lattimore to Thomas Jefferson, March 9, 1807, in Carter, *Territorial Papers*, 5:524–25.

Chapter Five

1. Jean Francis Dumoulin, *An Essay on Naturalization and Allegiance* (Washington, 1816), Appendix No. 4, xv; and John F. Dumoulin to Thomas Jefferson, May 31, 1816, in James P. McClure and J. Jefferson Looney, eds., *The Papers of Thomas Jefferson, Retirement Series*, vol. 10 (May 1, 1816–January 18, 1817) (Princeton, NJ: Princeton University Press, 2004–15), 101.

2. *Columbian Centinel* (Boston, MA), January 26, 1814. For prominent histories of the War of 1812, see Alan Taylor, *The Civil War of 1812: American Citizens, British Subjects, Irish Rebels, and Indian Allies* (New York: Alfred J. Knopf, 2010); Nicole Eustace, *1812: War and the Passions of Patriotism* (Philadelphia: University of Pennsylvania Press, 2012); J. C. A. Stagg, *The War of 1812: Conflict for a Continent* (Cambridge: Cambridge University Press, 2012); Paul A. Gilje, *Free Trade and Sailors' Rights in the War of 1812* (Cambridge: Cambridge University Press, 2013). This historiography considers the right to expatriation but generally from the perspective of impressment and naturalized citizens of the United States instead of how natural-born citizens expatriating themselves shaped perceptions of the war.

3. St. George Tucker, *Blackstone's Commentaries: With Notes of Reference to the Constitution and Laws of the Federal Government of the United States, and of the Commonwealth of Virginia* (Philadelphia, 1803), Note K: Of the Right of Expatriation, II: 96.

4. Hugh Henry Brackenridge, *Law Miscellanies* (Philadelphia, 1814), 404; and John Pickering, *A Vocabulary, or Collection of Words and Phrases Which Have Been Supposed to Be Peculiar to the United States of America* (Boston, 1816), 200.

5. Prize cases: Murray v. The Charming Betsy, 2 Cranch 64 (U.S., 1804); *The Venus*, 8 Cranch 253 (U.S., 1814); *The Frances*, 8 Cranch 335 (U.S., 1814); U.S. v. Gillies, 25 F. 1321 (U.S.C.C.PA, 1815); *The Mary and Susan*, 1 Wheat. 46 (U.S., 1816). Property inheritance cases: McIlvaine v. Coxe's Lessee, 2 Cranch 280 (U.S., 1805); and Dawson's Lessee v. Godfrey, 4 Cranch 321 (U.S., 1808).

6. *The Venus*, 8 Cranch 253 at 295–96.

7. *Gillies*, 25 F. 1321 at 1322; and *Murray*, 2 Cranch 64 at 120.

8. *Murray*, 2 Cranch 64 at 66–67.

9. *Murray*, 2 Cranch 64 at 71, and 93–94.

10. *Murray*, 2 Cranch 64 at 82–85 and 109–10.

11. *Murray*, 2 Cranch 64 at 68–69.

12. *Murray*, 2 Cranch 64 at 119–21.

13. *McIlvaine*, 2 Cranch 280 at 286–87.

14. *McIlvaine*, 2 Cranch 280 at 323–28.

15. *McIlvaine*, 2 Cranch 280 at 301–3, 320, and 316.

16. *McIlvaine*, 2 Cranch 280 at 306 and 320.

17. Fish v. Stoughton, 2 Johns. Cas. 407, 408 (NY, SC, 1801).

18. Nancy Jackson v. Archibald Jackson, 1. Johns. Cas. 424, 426–28, and 432–33 (NY, SC, 1806).

19. Samuel Shepherd, ed., *The Statutes at Large of Virginia, from October Session 1792, to December Session 1806* (Richmond, 1836), 3:251–53; Murray v. M'Carty, 2 Munford 393, 394–95 (VA, Ct. App., 1811).

20. *Murray*, 2 Munford 393 at 396–400 and 402–6.

21. Ainslie v. Martin, 9 Mass. 454 (MA, S.J.C., 1813).

22. Denver Brunsman, *The Evil Necessity: British Naval Impressment in the Eighteenth-Century Atlantic World* (Charlottesville: University of Virginia Press, 2013), 246–47.

23. *Observations on the Impressment of American Seamen* (Baltimore: Dobbin & Murphy, 1806), 26; *The Rights of a Government to the Services of its Citizens or Subjects, Who Have Emigrated beyond Its Territorial Jurisdiction* (Boston, 1808), 14 and 9; and Charles Jared Ingersoll, *A View of the Rights and Wrongs, Power and Policy, of the United States of America* (Philadelphia, 1808), 64. See also Denver Brunsman, "Subjects vs. Citizens: Impressment and Identity in the Anglo-American Atlantic," *Journal of the Early Republic* 30 (2010): 557–86.

24. On the Monroe-Pinkney Treaty, Stagg, *The War of 1812*, 31–33.

25. "Expatriation and Naturalization," *Essex Register*, December 24, 1807.

26. "The Honest Politician. No. III," *North American and Mercantile Daily Advertiser* (Baltimore, MD), April 15, 1808; "Original Miscellany," *Balance* (Hudson, NY), December 13, 1808; and "No. III," *Salem Gazette*, August 11, 1807.

27. Charles Brockden Brown, *The British Treaty* (Philadelphia, 1807), 74; "Lycurgus," *War or No War? Introduced with a View of the Causes of Our National Decline and Present Embarrassments* (New York, 1807), 58–59.

28. H. N. Muller, "Smuggling into Canada: How the Champlain Valley Defied Jefferson's Embargo," *Vermont History* 38 (1970): 5–6.

29. Thomas Jefferson, the town meeting, and the expatriating pig satire are all quoted in Muller, "Smuggling into Canada," 7, 9, and 8. On smuggling in the region, see Muller, "Smuggling into Canada," 17–18.

30. "From the Country–To the Editor," *Columbian* (New York), December 5, 1811; and "Unexampled Prosperity of Canada," *Connecticut Courant* (Hartford), May 29, 1811.

31. J. I. Little, *Loyalties in Conflict: A Canadian Borderland in War and Rebellion, 1812–1840* (Toronto: University of Toronto Press, 2008), 5–6; Herman Ryland to Samuel Willard, September 24, 1807, Brome County Historical Society Fonds, Library and Archives Canada (hereafter BCHS-LAC), Township Papers, E. Township Papers by Township, Stukely Township, B. Correspondence; Notice to Take Oath, October 28, 1807, BCHS-LAC, Township Papers, E. Township Papers by Township, Stukely Township, G. Miscellaneous Papers; Oath of Allegiance with Signatures, November 6, 1807, BCHS-LAC, Township Papers, E. Township Papers by Township, Stukely Township, G. Miscellaneous Papers; Samuel Willard to Herman Ryland, November 10, 1807, BCHS-LAC, Township Papers, E. Township Papers by Township, Stukely Township, B. Correspondence.

32. *New England Palladium* (Boston), August 21, 1807; "From the Quebeck Gazette," *Republican Watch-Tower* (New York), December 25, 1807; and *Kline's Carlisle Weekly Gazette*, October 30, 1807.

33. "Our Canadian Brethren," *New Jersey Journal*, August 20, 1811; and *Green Mountain Farmer* (Bennington, VT), July 22, 1812.

34. "The Canadas," *Farmer's Repository* (Charlestown, VA), December 20, 1811; and "Respecting the Canadas," *National Intelligencer* (Washington, DC), February 8, 1812.

35. Regulating American Subjects, July 10, 1812, BCHS-LAC, Township Papers, E. Township Papers by Township, Stukely Township, G. Miscellaneous Papers; Samuel Willard to Sir John Johnson, February 8, 1813, BCHS-LAC, Samuel Willard Papers, 1783–1899, A. Correspondence, 1783–1870; Samuel Willard to Herman Ryland, August 15, 1812, BCHS-LAC, Township Papers, E. Township Papers by Township, Stukely Township, B. Correspondence; George Prevost to Samuel Willard, October 9, 1812, BCHS-LAC, Samuel Willard Papers, 1783–1899, A. Correspondence, 1783–1870.

36. Samuel Willard to Sir John Johnson, February 7, 1813, BCHS-LAC, Samuel Willard Papers, 1783–1899, A. Correspondence, 1783–1870; Little, *Loyalties in Conflict*, 9, 20–21, and 36–37.

37. "From The Regulations Established by Sir George Prevost," *Baltimore Patriot*, March 15, 1813.

38. "Our Affairs with Great Britain," *Northern Whig* (Hudson, NY), December 1, 1812; "No. 1–Fools All!," *Poulson's American Daily Advertiser* (Philadelphia, PA), February 5, 1813; and "The Road to Ruin," *Columbian Centinel* (Boston, MA), January 26, 1814.

39. Joshua W. Toomer, *An Oration, Delivered in St. Michaels Church* (Charleston, 1814), 17; and Gouverneur Morris, *An Oration, Delivered July 5th, 1813, before the Washington Benevolent Society, of the City of New-York, in Commemoration of American Independence* (New York, 1813), 19.

40. *Report of the Committee of the House of Representatives of Massachusetts, on the Subject of Impressed Seamen* (Boston, 1813), first page, unnumbered; and "Amherst Resolutions," *Evening Post* (New York, NY), January 24, 1814.

41. *The Charge Delivered to the Grand Jury* (Baltimore, 1813), 7.

42. *Charge Delivered*, 10–11.

43. *The Address of the Grand Jury, to the Court of Oyer and Terminer, for Baltimore County* (Baltimore, 1813), 7, 5, 6, 22, and 18–19. See also William Pechin, *An Address of William Pechin, a Member of the Late Grand Jury, to Luther Martin, ESQ. On the Subject of the Rejoinder, to the Reply of That Body to the Charge, Delivered at the Opening of the Court* (Baltimore, 1813).

44. "A Gentleman of the City of New-York," *An Inquiry into the Natural Rights of Man, as Regards the Exercise of Expatriation, Dedicated to All the Adopted Citizens of the United States* (New York: Pelsue & Gould, 1813), 12 and 5; Alexander B. Johnson to James Madison, August 13, 1813, in Angela Kreider et al., eds., *The Papers of James Madison, Presidential Series*, vol. 6 (February 8–October 24, 1813) (Charlottesville: University of Virginia Press, 1984–), 519.

45. George Hay, *A Treatise on Expatriation* (Washington, DC, 1814), 38, 42, 80, and 30.

46. Hay, *Treatise on Expatriation*, 89–90 and 15.

47. "A Massachusetts Lawyer," *Review of a Treatise on Expatriation* (Boston, 1814), 8 and 29. On Lowell Jr.'s identity as the author of this pamphlet, see William Cushing, *Initials*

and Pseudonyms: A Dictionary of Literary Disguises (New York: Thomas Y. Crowell & Co., 1885), 485–86.

48. "A Massachusetts Lawyer," *Review*, 3–4.

49. 26 Annals of Cong. 1094–95 (1854).

50. 26 Annals of Cong. 1095–97 (1854).

51. 26 Annals of Cong. 1095–97 (1854).

52. Max M. Edling, *A Hercules in the Cradle: War, Money, and the American State, 1783–1867* (Chicago: University of Chicago Press, 2014), 126–27. Loan Bill was H.R. 35 introduced on February 1, 1814.

53. *Speech of the Hon. T. B. Robertson, of Louisiana, on the Loan Bill, in the House of Representatives of the United States, February, 1814* (Washington, DC, 1814), 16–17 and 21.

54. T. H. Palmer, ed., *Historical Register of the United States*, vol. 3 (Philadelphia, 1814), 167, 176–77, and 169–70.

55. Thomas K. Harris, *The Address of Thomas K. Harris, of Tennessee, to His Constituents* (Washington, DC, 1814), 7, 10–11; and William Findley, *The Cause of the Country Truly Stated. Speech of Mr. Findley, (of Pennsylvania) in the Congress of the U. States, the Loan Bill Being under Consideration* (New York, 1814), 9–10.

56. Findley, *Cause of the Country*, 11; and Alexander McLeod, *A Scriptural View of the Character, Causes, and Ends of the Present War*, 2nd ed. (New York, 1815), 165–82.

57. 31 Annals of Cong. 1029–30 (1854); and "A Bill by Which the Right of Citizenship May Be Relinquished," 31 Annals of Cong. 1817 (1854).

58. 31 Annals of Cong. 1059 and 1068 (1854).

59. 31 Annals of Cong. 1082 and 1064 (1854).

60. 31 Annals of Cong. 1044 (1854).

61. *Speech of the Hon. William Gaston of North Carolina, on The Bill to Authorise a Loan of Twenty-Five Millions of Dollars, Delivered in the House of Representatives of the United States, February, 1814* (Washington, DC, 1814), 31. On regional voting patterns, see I-Mien Tsiang, *The Question of Expatriation in America Prior to 1907* (Baltimore: Johns Hopkins Press, 1942), 61.

Chapter Six

1. Asa Brigham to Brothers and Sisters, February 28, 1832, Asa Brigham Papers, 1832–1837, Dolph Briscoe Center for American History, University of Texas at Austin. See also L. W. Kemp, "BRIGHAM, ASA," *Handbook of Texas Online*, www.tshaonline.org/handbook/online/articles/fbr49. Parts of this chapter about Texas were developed and first appeared in Eric R. Schlereth, "Privileges of Locomotion: Expatriation and Politics of Southwestern Border Crossing," *Journal of American History* 100 (2014): 995–1020; and Eric R. Schlereth, "Voluntary Mexicans: Allegiance and the Origins of the Texas Revolution," in Sam W. Haynes and Gerald D. Saxon, eds., *Contested Empire: Rethinking the Texas Revolution* (College Station: Texas A&M University Press, 2015), 11–41.

2. On Mexico's border troubles during the 1820s, see Andrés Reséndez, *Changing National Identities at the Frontier: Texas and New Mexico, 1800–1850* (Cambridge: Cambridge University Press, 2005), 20–21 and 29; Pekka Hämäläinen, *The Comanche Empire* (New Haven, CT: Yale University Press, 2008), 151–56 and 190–201; David J. Weber, *The Mexican Frontier, 1821–1846: The American Southwest Under Mexico* (Albuquerque: University of

New Mexico Press, 1982), 162–66. On the larger history of mobility in the US-Mexico borderlands, see James David Nichols, *The Limits of Liberty: Mobility and the Making of the Eastern U.S.-Mexico Border* (Lincoln: University of Nebraska Press, 2018). Caddo leader quoted in Jack Johnson, ed., *Texas by Terán: The Diary Kept by General Manuel de Mier y Terán on His 1828 Inspection of Texas*, trans. John Wheat (Austin: University of Texas Press, 2000), 80. On Long, see William C. Davis, *Lone Star Rising: The Revolutionary Birth of the Texas Republic* (New York: Free Press, 2004), 45–53; and Ed Bradley, "Fighting for Texas: Filibuster James Long, the Adams-Onís Treaty, and the Monroe Administration," *Southwestern Historical Quarterly* 102 (January 1999): 323–42.

3. On Long's activities and the later history of filibustering, see Robert E. May, *Manifest Destiny's Underworld: Filibustering in Antebellum America* (Chapel Hill: The University of North Carolina Press, 2002), 5–8; "Communication," *Louisiana Advertiser*, May 16, 1820; Josefina Zoraida Vázquez, "The Colonization and Loss of Texas: A Mexican Perspective," in *Myths, Misdeeds, and Misunderstandings: The Roots of Conflict in U.S.-Mexican Relations*, ed. Jaime E. Rodríguez O. and Kathryn Vincent (Wilmington, DE: Rowman & Littlefield, 1997), 50–51; and Weber, *Mexican Frontier*, 177.

4. On economic motivations for migration, see Weber, *Mexican Frontier*, 166; and Gregg Cantrell, *Stephen F. Austin: Empresario of Texas* (New Haven, CT: Yale University Press, 1999), 176–77. For an apt description of Texas migrants as émigrés and for the view that "patriotism was negotiable" for Americans in the trans-Appalachian West, see Andrew R. L. Cayton, "Continental Politics: Liberalism, Nationalism, and the Appeal of Texas in the 1820s," in *Beyond the Founders: New Approaches to the Political History of the Early American Republic*, ed. Jeffrey L. Pasley, Andrew W. Robertson, and David Waldstreicher (Chapel Hill: The University of North Carolina Press, 2004), 303–4 and 308.

5. The relationship between expatriation and colonization in Mexican Texas provides further evidence that "the possibility that Tejanos may have had an agenda separate from, though compatible with, the recently arrived Anglo Americans has been ignored or dismissed," observed by Jesús F. de la Teja, "The Colonization and Independence of Texas: A Tejano Perspective," *Myths, Misdeeds, and Misunderstandings*, 80. On malleable allegiance as a feature of "volitional" citizenship, see James H. Kettner, *The Development of American Citizenship, 1608–1870* (Chapel Hill: The University of North Carolina Press, 1978), 191–92.

6. Benito Jerónimo Feijóo y Montenegro quoted in Tamar Herzog, *Defining Nations: Immigrants and Citizens in Early Modern Spain and Spanish America* (New Haven, CT: Yale University Press, 2003), 74. On Spanish concepts of allegiance, naturalization, and landownership, see David J. Weber, *The Spanish Frontier in North America* (New Haven, CT: Yale University Press, 1992), 280–81; Herzog, *Defining Nations*, 198, 73–75, 118, 202, 198, 163, 145, and 200; and Carolina Castillo Crimm, "Fernando De León: Leadership Lost," in *Tejano Leadership in Mexican and Revolutionary Texas*, ed. Jesús F. de la Teja (College Station: Texas A&M University Press, 2010), 104. The discourse concerning "good" character in Latin American naturalization laws drew from similar assumptions about the nature of membership as did naturalization laws in the United States, beginning with the United States' first federal statute adopted in 1790. For an exploration of the relationship between Hispanic and Anglo-American assumptions regarding loyalty from the perspective of late eighteenth-century Spanish colonial policy, see Sylvia L. Hilton,

"Loyalty and Patriotism on North American Frontiers: Being and Becoming Spanish in the Mississippi Valley, 1776–1803," in *Nexus of Empire: Negotiating Loyalty and Identity in the Revolutionary Borderlands, 1760s–1820s*, ed. Gene Allen Smith and Sylvia L. Hilton (Gainesville: University Press of Florida, 2010), 12, 15, and 26.

7. On the constitution of the Federal Republic of Central America, see Jordana Dym, "Citizen of Which Republic? Foreigners and the Construction of National Citizenship in Central America, 1823–1845," *Americas* 64 (2008): 488; on choice as the basis of membership in the Mexican body politic, see "General Law of Colonization, August 18, 1824," Article 1, and "Law of Colonization of the State of Coahuila and Texas, March 24, 1825," Article 1, in *The Laws of Texas, 1822–1897*, ed. H. P. N. Gammel (20 vols., Austin, 1898), 1:97 and 99; and on good intentions and residence, see "Law of Colonization of the State of Coahuila and Texas, March 24, 1825," Articles 5 and 31, *Laws of Texas*, 1:100 and 103; Weber, *Mexican Frontier*, 20–22; and Vázquez, "Colonization and Loss of Texas," 50–51.

8. James Kent, *Commentaries on American Law* (4 vols., Boston, 1826–30), 1:49; "Gen. Long and the Province of Texas," *Louisiana Advertiser* reprinted in the *Richmond Enquirer*, August 17, 1821; and 31 Annals of Cong. 1044 (1854).

9. Johnson, *Texas by Terán*, 1–3.

10. Johnson, *Texas by Terán*, 99 and 31–32.

11. José María Sánchez, "A Trip to Texas in 1828," trans. Carlos E. Castaneda, *Southwestern Historical Quarterly* 29 (1926): 260 and 271; and Rafael Antonio Manchola quoted in Andrés Tijerina, "Rafael Antonio Manchola: Tejano Soldier, Statesman, Ranchero," in de la Teja, *Tejano Leadership*, 47–48.

12. Johnson, *Texas by Terán*, 97 and 17; and Sánchez, "Trip to Texas," 283.

13. Johnson, *Texas by Terán*, 37.

14. Johnson, *Texas by Terán*, 38–39; and Edith Louise Kelly and Mattie Austin Hatcher, eds., "Tadeo Ortiz de Ayla and the Colonization of Texas, 1822–1833," *Southwestern Historical Quarterly* 32 (1928–29): 158 and 78.

15. Council of State quoted in Vázquez, "Colonization and Loss of Texas," 51; and Kelly and Hatcher, "Tadeo Ortiz de Ayla," 318.

16. Jesús F. de la Teja, "Introduction," in de la Teja, *Tejano Leadership*, 4; Andrés Tijerina, *Tejanos and Texas Under the Mexican Flag, 1821–1836* (College Station: Texas A&M University Press, 1994), 113–15; and de la Teja, "Colonization and Independence of Texas," in de la Teja, *Tejano Leadership*, 84–86.

17. Hämäläinen, *Comanche Empire*, 196; and Reséndez, *Changing National Identities*, 3 and 265.

18. Article 5, "Law of Colonization of the State of Coahuila and Texas, March 24, 1825," *Laws of Texas*, 1:100.

19. Anglo colonists quoted in Samuel Harman Lowrie, *Culture Conflict in Texas, 1821–1835* (New York: AMS Press, 1967), 57. On religion and slavery, the Constituent Congress of Coahuila and Texas "chose to employ language that permitted maximum flexibility in the admission of new colonists," argues de la Teja. "Colonization and Independence of Texas," 87.

20. Eugene C. Barker, *The Life of Stephen F. Austin* (Nashville: Cokesbury Press, 1925), 292; Cantrell, *Stephen F. Austin*, 115–16; Benjamin R. Milam, *A Statement of the Advantages to Be Derived from the Employment of £50,000, upon the Security of Lands in the Mexican Province*

of Texas (London, n.d.), 4; and Lois Garver, "Benjamin Rush Milam," *Southwestern Histori-cal Quarterly* 38 (1934): 109–10; Saucedo quoted in Raúl A. Ramos, "José Antonio Saucedo: At the Nexus of Change," in de la Teja, *Tejano Leadership*, 21.

21. Saucedo quoted in Ramos, "José Antonio Saucedo," in de la Teja, *Tejano Leadership*, 21; Francisco Ruiz quoted in Weber, *Mexican Frontier*, 158; Galveston Bay and Texas Land Company, *Address to the Reader of the Documents Relating to the Galveston Bay and Texas Land Company* (New York, 1831), 3–5 and 32.

22. Robert Owen, "Memorial to the Republic of Mexico," in *Robert Owen's Opening Speech, and His Reply to the Rev. Alex. Campbell, in the Recent Public Discussion in Cincinnati* (Cincinnati, 1829), 178 and 181.

23. Lyman Bostwick to Anthony Dey, November 18, 1834, Box 1, folder 8; and Nelson Briant to the Agents of the Empresarios for Colonizing Texas Residing at the City of New York, February 16, 1835, Box 1, folder 10 in the Anthony Dey Galveston Bay and Texas Land Com-pany Records, Yale Collection of Western Americana, Beinecke Rare Book and Manuscript Library.

24. Gifford White, ed., *Character Documents in the General Land Office of Texas* (Balti-more: Genealogical Publishing Company, 1989), 3.

25. Carolyn Reeves Ericson, ed., *Citizens and Foreigners of the Nacogdoches District, 1809–1836* (Nacogdoches, TX: C.R. Ericson, 1981), 1:47 and 65–66.

26. Petition No. 329, Eli Russel seeking land and colonist status in David G. Burnet's colony, October 16, 1835, in Eleazer Louis Ripley Wheelock Papers, Dolph Briscoe Center for American History, University of Texas at Austin; Milam Letters and Papers, 1827–35, Box 2 R117, in Milam and McKinney Collection, Dolph Briscoe Center for American His-tory, University of Texas at Austin; and Johnson, *Texas by Terán*, 52–53.

27. Milam Letters and Papers, 1827–35; Mary Paxton to Stephen F. Austin, Auburn, Lincoln County, MO, October 3, 1831, in David Gouverneur Burnet Papers, Dolph Briscoe Center for American History, University of Texas at Austin; and Wynn v. Morris, 16 Ark. 414 (1855), 426.

28. Alsberry v. Hawkins, 39 Ky. 177, 9 Dana 177, 33 Am. Dec. 546 (Ct. App. 1839).

29. Moore v. Tisdale, 5 B. Mon. 352 (1845), 354.

30. "Texas," *Washington City Gazette*, reprinted in the *Richmond Enquirer*, October 21, 1825; and Johnson, *Texas by Terán*, 80.

31. Reséndez, *Changing National Identities*, 40–45; and Sam W. Haynes, *Unsettled Land: From Revolution to Republic, The Struggle for Texas* (New York: Basic Books, 2022), 45–58.

32. Richard Ellis et al. to Austin, January 22, 1827, in Eugene C. Barker, ed., "The Austin Papers, Vol. II, Part 2," *Annual Report of the American Historical Association for the Year 1919* (Washington, DC: US Government Printing Office, 1924), 1586–87; and "Resolutions of Loyalty," January 27, 1827, in Barker, "Austin Papers," 1594–95.

33. Austin to Citizens of Victoria, January 1, 1827, in Barker, "Austin Papers," 1558–59.

34. Reséndez, *Changing National Identities*, 146–49.

35. *Proceedings of the General Convention of Delegates Representing the Citizens and Inhabit-ants of Texas* (Brazoria, TX, 1832), 12–16; and John Austin quoted in David B. Edward, *The History of Texas* (Cincinnati, 1836), 184.

36. Reséndez, *Changing National Identities*, 150–58.

37. On centralist notions of allegiance, see Reséndez, *Changing National Identities*, 170.

38. Agustín Viesca quoted in Reséndez, *Changing National Identities*, 158; and "Mina Pronouncement of Loyalty to Mexican Constitution," in Chester Newell, *History of the Revolution in Texas* (New York, 1838), 207.

39. Columbia Citizens to the Citizens of Brazos, July 15, 1835, in John H. Jenkins, ed., *The Papers of the Texas Revolution, 1835–1836* (Austin, TX: Presidial Press, 1973) (hereafter cited as *PTR*), 1:242; Mina Resolutions, July 4, 1835, *PTR*, 1:191–92; Representatives of Brazos, San Felipe to the Commander at Bexar, July 17, 1835, *PTR*, 1:250; and Columbia Meeting, June 28, 1835, *PTR*, 1:169–71. See also Gonzales Meeting, July 7, 1835, *PTR*, 1:214–16; and Columbia Statement to delegates at San Felipe, July 14, 1835, *PTR*, 1:240.

40. Manuel Diez de Bonilla to the Municipality of Gonzales, August 5, 1835, *PTR*, 1:310; Martín Perfecto de Cos to Domingo de Ugartechea, July 7, 1835, *PTR*, 1:214; Cos, Address to the Public in Texas, July 5, 1835, *PTR*, 1:203; Cos to the Political Chief of Brazos, August 1, 1835, *PTR*, 1:297–98; Cos, July 12, 1835, *PTR*, 1:232–33; and Thomas M. Thompson to the Citizens of Anahuac, July 26, 1835, *PTR*, 1:278–79.

41. "Mr. Editor," *Texas Republican*, August 8, 1835.

42. San Jacinto Resolutions, August 8, 1835, *PTR*, 1:318–20; and Stephen F. Austin to Mary Austin Holley, August 21, 1835, *PTR*, 1:359–60. See also Austin to H. Meigs, August 22, 1835, *PTR*, 1:362–63.

43. "Declaration of the People of Texas," November 7, 1835, *PTR*, 2:346–47.

44. "Declaration of the People of Texas," 346–47.

45. Stephen F. Austin to the Provisional Government, December 2, 1835, *PTR*, 3:70–72.

46. James Kerr to the People of Texas, January 4, 1836, *PTR*, 3:415–21.

47. Proclamation of the Federal Volunteer Army of Texas, January 10, 1836, *PTR*, 3:467; Military Affairs Committee Report, December 6, 1835, *PTR*, 3:102–4; and Volunteers to the Convention, February 1836, *PTR*, 4:473–74.

48. San Augustine Address from the Committee of Vigilance and Public Safety, December 22, 1835, *PTR*, 3:287–92; and [William H. Wharton] "Curtius," *Texas: A Brief Account of the Origin, Progress, and Present State of the Colonial Settlement of Texas*, in *PTR*, 9:240–41.

49. San Augustine Address from the Committee of Vigilance and Public Safety, December 22, 1835, *PTR*, 3:287–92; and [Wharton] "Curtius," *Texas*, 239–40.

50. Reséndez, *Changing National Identities*, 165–66; Weber, *Mexican Frontier*, 251–55; and "The Unanimous Declaration of Independence made by the Delegates of the People of Texas," *Laws of Texas*, 1:1063–66.

Chapter Seven

1. "Substance of the Remarks of Mr. Menefee of Kentucky," *Niles' National Register* (Baltimore, MD), January 27, 1838, and "Twenty-Fifth Congress," January 13, 1838.

2. "The Times," *Rhode Island Republican*, January 3, 1838; and "Twenty-Fifth Congress," *Niles' National Register* (Baltimore, MD), January 13, 1838. On the larger contest for control of Texas in the early nineteenth century, see Sam W. Haynes, *Unsettled Land: From Revolution to Republic, The Struggle for Texas* (New York: Basic Books, 2022). An earlier version of the argument in this chapter regarding the Texas Revolution first appeared in Eric R. Schlereth, "Voluntary Mexicans: Allegiance and the Origins of the Texas Revolution," in

Contested Empire: Rethinking the Texas Revolution, ed. Sam W. Haynes and Gerald D. Saxon (College Station: Texas A&M University Press, 2015), 11–41.

3. On the composition of the army of the Texas Revolution, see Paul D. Lack, *The Texas Revolutionary Experience: A Political and Social History, 1835–1836* (College Station: Texas A&M University Press, 1992), 132–33. On Tejano participation, see Raúl A. Ramos, *Beyond the Alamo: Forging Mexican Ethnicity in San Antonio, 1821–1861* (Chapel Hill: The University of North Carolina Press, 2008), 149–53.

4. George C. Childress to Sam Houston, February 13, 1836, in John H. Jenkins, ed., *The Papers of the Texas Revolution, 1835–1836* (Austin, TX: Presidial Press, 1973) (hereafter cited as *PTR*), 4:322. On Childress's background, see Joe E. Ericson, "CHILDRESS, GEORGE CAMPBELL," *Handbook of Texas Online*, www.tshaonline.org/handbook/online/articles/fch28.

5. R.R. Royall to Citizens of the United States of the North, October 26, 1835, *PTR*, 2:224–26.

6. Gregg Cantrell, *Stephen F. Austin: Empresario of Texas* (New Haven, CT: Yale University Press, 1999), 343 and 334.

7. "The Texans," *Farmer's Cabinet* (Amherst, NH), November 13, 1835; "A Citizen of New Orleans," *New York Times* reprinted in *Richmond Enquirer*, November 13, 1835; and "Texas," *Journal of Commerce* (New York, NY) quoted in *New Hampshire Sentinel*, November 6, 1835.

8. For the April 20, 1818, act, see "An Act in Addition to the 'Act for the Punishment of Certain Crimes against the United States,' and to Repeal the Acts therein Mentioned," in Richard Peters, ed., *The Public Statutes at Large of the United States of America* (Boston, 1846), 3:447–50.

9. John Forsyth to Henry Carleton, October 27, 1835, *PTR*, 2:234–35; and Edward D. White to the Public, November 13, 1835, *PTR*, 2:404–5.

10. José María Ortiz Monasterio to John Forsyth, November 19, 1835, *PTR*, 2:468–69.

11. *Daily National Intelligencer*, July 17, 1819, quoted in Ed Bradley, "Fighting for Texas: Filibuster James Long, the Adams-Onís Treaty, and the Monroe Administration," *Southwestern Historical Quarterly* 102 (January 1999): 339; and *The Mexican Side of the Texan Revolution*, 2nd ed., trans. Carlos E. Castañeda (Austin, TX: Graphic Ideas Incorporated, 1970), 55–56.

12. "Texas," *Connecticut Courant*, November 16, 1835; "From Texas," *Farmer's Cabinet* (Amherst, NH), November 20, 1835; and "Texas," *New York Advertiser* quoted in *Farmer's Cabinet* (Amherst, NH), November 6, 1835.

13. H. Meigs to Stephen F. Austin, November 15, 1835, *PTR*, 2:424; Stuart Perry to David G. Burnett, April 16, 1836, *PTR*, 5:490; and George C. Childress to David G. Burnet, April 18, 1836, *PTR*, 5:501.

14. For the district court opinion from the Southern District of New York, see "Important Opinion," *Richmond Enquirer*, November 1835; "Texas," *New Hampshire Sentinel*, November 19, 1835; "Texas in Revolution," *Richmond Enquirer*, October 23, 1835; and *New Orleans Bee* quoted in "Texas," *Richmond Enquirer*, December 19, 1835.

15. New Orleans Meeting, October 13, 1835, *PTR*, 2:116; and Nashville Meeting Address, November 17, 1835, *PTR*, 3:56.

16. "Proceedings of a Meeting of the Citizens of Nashville, Tenn. in Favor of Recognising the Independence of Texas," in *Public Documents Printed by Order of the Senate of the United*

States, First Session of the Twenty-Fourth Congress (Washington, DC, 1836), 6: document 418, page 4.

17. L. R. Kenny to Stephen F. Austin, October 20, 1835, *PTR*, 2:171; and Voluntary Auxiliary Corps enlistees, January 14, 1836, *PTR*, 4:13–14.

18. Sam Houston to Amasa Turner, December 5, 1835, *PTR*, 3:73; Sam Houston to P. S. Wyatt, December 28, 1835, *PTR*, 3:351; and Sam Houston to Isaac W. Burton, December 19, 1835, *PTR*, 3:258.

19. *Constitution of the Republic of Texas*, PTR, 5:113; Asa Brigham to Sister, April 4, 1837, Asa Brigham Papers, 1832–1837, Dolph Briscoe Center for American History, University of Texas at Austin. The changing meaning of voluntary allegiance in the Texas republic provides an additional way to frame the problem of race in the Texas Revolution. Specifically, the widening gap between citizenship as a formal legal identity and patriotism as a cultural expression following independence suggests the role of legal ideas in bringing about racial tensions between Tejanos and Anglos. For two historiographic positions on the problem of race in the Texas Revolution, see Ramos, *Beyond the Alamo*, 155; and James E. Crisp, "Race, Revolution, and the Texas Republic: Toward a Reinterpretation," in *The Texas Military Experience: From the Texas Revolution through World War II*, ed. Joseph G. Dawson III (College Station: Texas A&M University Press, 1995), 38–46.

20. Scholarship on the rebellions in Lower and Upper Canada is vast. My thinking about these events as part of a single rebellion is influenced by Allan Greer, "1837–38: Rebellion Reconsidered," *Canada Historical Review* 76 (1995): 1–18. See also Maxime Dagenais and Julien Mauduit, eds., *Revolutions across Borders: Jacksonian America and the Canadian Rebellion* (Montreal: McGill-Queen's University Press, 2019).

21. "An Address by Marcus Child," *Stanstead Historical Society Journal* 6 (1975): 23; J. I. Little, *Loyalties in Conflict: A Canadian Borderland in War and Rebellion, 1812–1840* (Toronto: University of Toronto Press, 2008), 67–95.

22. Colin Read, *The Rising in Western Upper Canada, 1837–38: The Duncombe Revolt and After* (Toronto: University of Toronto Press, 1982), 20–21 and 178–80.

23. "Alphabetical Arrangement of Districts—Political Stat of Inhabitants," May 1840, in *The Arthur Papers*, vol. 2, ed. Charles R. Sanderson (Toronto: University of Toronto Press, 1957), 141 and 136; R. B. Sullivan to the Lieutenant Governor [Arthur], June 1, 1838, "Mr. Sullivan's Report on the State of the Province 1838," in *The Arthur Papers*, vol. 1, ed. Charles R. Sanderson (Toronto: University of Toronto Press, 1943): 152–53; and Arthur to the Archbishop of Canterbury [William Howley], August 11, 1838, *Arthur Papers* 2:254.

24. Lillian F. Gates, "SUTHERLAND, THOMAS JEFFERSON," in *Dictionary of Canadian Biography*, vol. 8 (University of Toronto/Université Laval, 2003), www.biographi.ca /en/bio/sutherland_thomas_jefferson_8E.html; and Gates, *After the Rebellion: The Later Years of William Lyon Mackenzie* (Toronto: Dundurn Press, 1988), 17 and 20.

25. "Proclamation by William Lyon Mackenzie, Chairman Pro. Tem. of the Provincial Government of the State of Upper Canada," Appendix G in Charles Lindsey, *The Life and Times of Wm. Lyon Mackenzie*, vol. 2 (Toronto, 1862), 363–69.

26. Thomas Jefferson Sutherland, *A Letter to Her Majesty the British Queen, with Letters to Lord Durham, Lord Glenelg, and Sir George Arthur* (Albany, 1841), 164–65; *A Narrative of the Adventures and Sufferings of Captain Daniel D. Heustis and His Companions, In Canada and*

Van Dieman's Land, During a Long Captivity; With Travels in California, and Voyages at Sea (Boston, 1848), 28–29 and 12–14.

27. Edward Alexander Theller, *Canada in 1837–38, Showing, By Historical Facts, the Causes of the Late Attempted Revolution, and of Its Failure; the Present Condition of the People, and Their Future Prospects, Together with the Personal Adventures of the Author, and Others Who Were Connected with the Revolution*, vol. 1 (2 vols., Philadelphia, 1841), 1: 98–99, 208–29, and 110–11.

28. Kenneth R. Stevens, *Border Diplomacy: The* Caroline *and* McLeod *Affairs in Anglo-American-Canadian Relations, 1837–1842* (Tuscaloosa: University of Alabama Press, 1989), 25–26.

29. Oscar A. Kinchen, *The Rise and Fall of the Patriot Hunters* (New York: Bookman Associates, 1956); Edwin C. Guillet, *The Lives and Times of the Patriots* (Toronto: University of Toronto Press, 1968); John Duffy and H. Nicholas Muller, "The Great Wolf Hunt: The Popular Response in Vermont to the *Patriote* Uprising of 1837," *Journal of American Studies* 8 (August 1974): 153–69; Marc L. Harris, "The Meaning of Patriot: The Canadian Rebellion and American Republicanism, 1837–1839," *Michigan Historical Review* 23 (Spring 1997): 33–69; and Andrew Bonthius, "The Patriot War of 1837–1838: Locofocoism with a Gun?" *Labour/Le Travail* 52 (Fall 2003): 9–43.

30. "Canada," *Portsmouth Journal of Literature and Politics*, January 13, 1838; and "Memorial of Citizens of Niagara County, New York, Complaining of Outrages and Murders of American Citizens in Burning the Steamboat Caroline, at Schlosser, in that County, by the British Authorities of Canada, and Asking Redress," February 19, 1838, *American State Papers*, Senate, 25th Congress, 2nd Session, *Military Affairs*, Vol. 7, 972–73 [emphasis in the original].

31. "Mackenzie's Trial: Judge Thompson's Charge," *Niles' National Register* (Baltimore, MD), July 6, 1839; and "The President's Proclamation," *Burlington Free Press* (Vermont), December 14, 1838.

32. February 20, 1838, *Congressional Globe*, 25th Congress, 2nd Session, 144; Charge to Grand Jury—Neutrality Laws, Case No. 18, 265, Circuit Court, D. Ohio, 30 F. Cas. 1018, 1838 U.S. App. LEXIS 304, 2 Mc Lean 1, December, 1838; and "Late From the Frontier," *Newport Mercury*, February 24, 1838.

33. Extract of a Letter, from George Rykert, Esq., M.P.P., to Colonel Jones, A.D.C., St. Catherine's, December 24, 1837, in Great Britain, Parliament, House of Commons, *Irish University Press Series of British Parliamentary Papers: Colonies Canada*, IUP Library of Fundamental Source Books (Shannon: Irish University Press, 1969), 266.

34. Testimony of Thomas Moxey to John Powell, Stamford, Upper Canada, January 9, 1838, in *Irish University Press Canada*, 289; K. Cameron to the Adjutant-General of Militia, Toronto, Chippewa, Upper Canada, December 23, 1837, in *Irish University Press Canada*, 266–67; and F. B. Head to Henry Fox, December 23, 1837, in *Irish University Press Canada*, 264.

35. "Twenty-Fifth Congress," *Niles' National Register* (Baltimore, MD), January 13, 1838. See also Samuel Watson, "United States Army Officers Fight the 'Patriot War': Responses to Fillibustering on the Canadian Border, 1837–1839," *Journal of the Early Republic* 3 (Autumn 1998): 485–519.

36. "By the President of the U. States of America," *Niles' National Register* (Baltimore, MD), January 6, 1838.

37. "Communications," *Burlington Free Press*, August 24, 1838.

38. "Twenty-Fifth Congress," *Niles' National Register* (Baltimore, MD), January 20, 1838.

39. "The Neutrality Bill," *Niles' National Register* (Baltimore, MD), March 24, 1838, and February 24, 1838.

40. Memorial of the Citizens of Erie County [NY], February 12, 1838, HR25A–G6.2; Memorial from Citizens of Tuscarawas County, Ohio, referred on February 4, 1839, and Memorial from Citizens of Franklin County, Vermont, HR25A–G6.6; Petitions and Memorials, 1822–1968; Records of the US House of Representatives, 1789–2015; Petitions and Memorials, Resolutions of State Legislatures, and Related Documents Which Were Referred to the Committee on Foreign Affairs During the 25th Congress, National Archives Building, Washington, DC.

41. Archibald McLean quoted in F. Murray Greenwood, "The Prince Affair: 'Gallant Colonel' or 'The Windsor Butcher'?" in *Canadian State Trials, Volume II: Rebellion and Invasion in the Canadas, 1837–1839*, ed. F. Murray Greenwood and Barry Wright (Toronto: University of Toronto Press, 2002), 170. On the "outlawry doctrine," see Greenwood, "Prince Affair," 164–65. On the "local allegiance" doctrine, see Colin Read, "The Treason Trials of 1838 in Western Upper Canada," *Canadian State Trials*, 111.

42. Greenwood, "Prince Affair," 165–66; John Beverly Robinson quoted in Rainer Baehre, "Trying the Rebels: Emergency Legislation and the Colonial Executive's Overall Legal Strategy in the Upper Canadian Rebellion," *Canadian State Trials*, 45.

43. "Twenty-Fifth Congress," *Niles' National Register* (Baltimore, MD), February 2, 1839; and "The Canada Troubles," *New Hampshire Sentinel*, January 11, 1838.

44. "Twenty-Fifth Congress," *Niles' National Register* (Baltimore, MD), January 13, 1838.

45. "Twenty-Fifth Congress," *Niles' National Register* (Baltimore, MD), January 13, 1838, and "Twenty-Fifth Congress," January 20, 1838; and "Communication," *Burlington Free Press*, January 12, 1838, and "Communication," January 19, 1838.

46. H. S. Fox to Francis Bond Head, March 11, 1838, in Sanderson, *Arthur Papers* 1:60; Fox to Lieutenant-Governor Arthur, January 31, 1839, in Sanderson, *Arthur Papers* 2:31; and Lieutenant-Governor Arthur to Lord Fitzroy Somerset, November 24, 1838, in Sanderson, *Arthur Papers* 2:397–98.

47. *A Narrative of the Adventures and Sufferings of Captain Daniel D. Heustis and His Companions, in Canada and Van Dieman's Land, During a Long Captivity; with Travels in California, and Voyages at Sea*, 12–14 and 55–56; Proceedings of the Convention of the People in Montpelier and Vicinity in relation to Canadian Affairs, the "Neutrality Law" and the burning of the Caroline, February 18, 1839, HR25A–G6.2; Petitions and Memorials, 1822–1968; Records of the US House of Representatives, 1789–2015; Petitions and Memorials, Resolutions of State Legislatures, and Related Documents Which Were Referred to the Committee on Foreign Affairs during the 25th Congress, National Archives Building, Washington, DC; *The Trial of General Th. J. Sutherland, Late of the Patriot Army, Before a Court Martial* (Buffalo, 1838), 72–73; and Caleb Lyon, *Narrative and Recollections of Van Deiman's Land, During a Three Years' Captivity of Stephen S. Wright* (New York, 1844), iv. See also Harris, "Meaning of the Patriot," 55.

48. Theller, *Canada in 1837–38*, 2:315–16.

49. John Prince and Sandwich residents quoted in Greenwood, "Prince Affair," 173–74. On the Morreau case, see Read, "Treason Trials," 109–10 and 112–14.

50. Theller, *Canada in 1837–38*, 1:203–4, 242–44, and 208–9.

51. Theller, *Canada in 1837–38*, 1:206–7.

52. Theller, *Canada in 1837–38*, 2:267–69 and 315–16.

53. Robert Marsh, *Seven Years of My Life, or Narrative of a Patriot Exile* (Buffalo, 1848), 6–7, 13, 31–32, and 20. On the US citizens sent to Van Diemen's Land for their participation in the Canadian Rebellion, see Cassandra Pybus and Hamish Maxwell-Stewart, *American Citizens, British Slaves: Yankee Political Prisoners in an Australian Penal Colony, 1839–1850* (East Lansing: Michigan State University Press, 2002).

54. Robin W. Winks, *The Blacks in Canada, A History* (New Haven, CT: Yale University Press, 1971), 149–52.

Chapter Eight

1. "Speech by Lewis Richardson," March 13, 1846, in John W. Blassingame, ed., *Slave Testimony: Two Centuries of Letters, Speeches, Interviews, and Autobiographies* (Baton Rouge: Louisiana State University Press, 1977), 164–66.

2. Thomas H. Jones to Daniel Foster, May 5, 1851, in Peter C. Ripley, ed., *The Black Abolitionist Papers, Volume 2: Canada, 1830–1865* (Chapel Hill: The University of North Carolina Press, 1986), 133–35.

3. On the efforts of Black Americans to establish and protect their claims to birthright citizenship in the United States, see Martha S. Jones, *Birthright Citizens: A History of Race and Rights in Antebellum America* (Cambridge: Cambridge University Press, 2018).

4. On the Black population of Canada West, see Michael Wayne, "The Black Population of Canada West on the Eve of the American Civil War: A Reassessment Based on the Manuscript Census of 1861," *Histoire Sociale/Social History* 28, no. 5 (1995): 469–70. On the broader history of Black life in the Great Lakes borderlands emphasizing the Detroit River region, see Karolyn Smardz Frost and Veta Smith Tucker, eds., *A Fluid Frontier: Slavery, Resistance, and the Underground Railroad in the Detroit River Borderlands* (Detroit: Wayne State University Press, 2016). On the general history of Black Canadians, see Robin W. Winks, *The Blacks in Canada: A History* (New Haven, CT: Yale University Press, 1971). On the appeal of the British Empire for Black Americans, see Van Gosse, "'As a Nation, the English Are Our Friends': The Emergence of African American Politics in the British Atlantic World, 1772–1861," *American Historical Review* 113 (2008): 1003–28. On Mexico as a destination for enslaved runaways from the United States, see Alice L. Baumgartner, *South to Freedom: Runaway Slaves to Mexico and the Road to Civil War* (New York: Basic Books, 2020). On the limits to Black freedom in Mexico, see Sarah E. Cornell, "Citizens of Nowhere: Fugitive Slaves and Free African Americans in Mexico, 1833–1857," *Journal of American History* 100 (2013): 351–74.

5. Manisha Sinha, *The Slave's Cause: A History of Abolition* (New Haven, CT: Yale University Press, 2016), 131–34, 161–63, and 168–71; Sara Fanning, *Caribbean Crossing: African Americans and the Haitian Emigration Movement* (New York: New York University Press, 2015), 1. On the importance of "international free soil" to abolitionist thought, the choices Black Americans made to leave the United States, and the advent of Black emigration movements within the United States, see Elena K. Abbott, *Beacons of Liberty: International Free Soil and the Fight for Racial Justice in Antebellum America* (Cambridge: Cambridge University Press, 2021).

6. Sinha, *Slave's Cause*, 163–68.

7. On Black opposition to the ACS, see Ousmane K. Power-Greene, *Against Wind and Tide: The African American Struggle against the Colonization Movement* (New York: New York University Press, 2014).

8. "Correspondence of the Colonization Society," *Anti-Slavery Reporter* (New York, NY), July 1833; William Lloyd Garrison, *Thoughts on African Colonization* (Boston, 1832), 15–16; "What Colonization Means," *Anti-Slavery Record* (New York, NY), July 1835.

9. "A Colored Man's Views on Colonization Remarks on Gov. Matteson's Message," *Frederick Douglass' Paper* (Rochester, NY), March 2, 1855.

10. "Convention in Butler County," *Aliened American* (Cleveland, OH), April 9, 1853; and "Resolutions," *National Era* (Washington, DC), May 13, 1852.

11. "Right of Suffrage," *North Star* (Rochester, NY), February 8, 1850, and "Colonization," September 14, 1849.

12. "Colored Emigration to Canada and the West-Indies," *Voice of the Fugitive* (Sandwich, C.W.), November 19, 1851.

13. On curtailing Black suffrage, see Alexander Keyssar, *The Right to Vote: The Contested History of Democracy in America* (New York: Basic Books, 2000), 54–55. On black laws, see Kate Masur, *Until Justice Be Done: America's First Civil Rights Movement, from the Revolution to Reconstruction* (New York: W. W. Norton, 2021), 1–41 and 230–31; and "On the Condition of the Free People of Color in the United States," in William Jay, *Miscellaneous Writings on Slavery* (Boston, 1853), 375.

14. On the declining status of free Black people in southern states before the Civil War, see Ira Berlin, *Slaves Without Masters: The Free Negro in the Antebellum South* (New York: Vintage Books, 1974).

15. Cleland v. Waters, 19 Ga. 35 (1855), 38.

16. "Private Judgment on the Fugitive-Slave Law," *Independent* (New York, NY), February 13, 1851; and "Independent Lectures on Slavery," *Liberator* (Boston, MA), November 30, 1855.

17. Willis v. Jolliffee, 11 Rich.Eq. 447 (1860), 4.

18. Aristide R. Zolberg, *A Nation by Design: Immigration Policy in the Fashioning of America* (Cambridge, MA: Harvard University Press, 2006), 161; and "The Fugitive Slave Law," *National Era* (Washington, DC), June 5, 1851.

19. Cass to Wright, July 8, 1859, *British and Foreign State Papers, 1861–1862* (London, 1862), 52:1332 and 1334; and "That Naturalization Question," *Independent* (New York, NY), July 21, 1859.

20. "That Naturalization Question," *Independent* (New York, NY), July 21, 1859.

21. "Underground–More Arrivals," *Detroit Tribune* reprinted in *Provincial Freeman* (Toronto, C.W.), December 16, 1854.

22. "Canadian Colonization," *Voice of the Fugitive* (Sandwich, C.W.), July 30, 1851.

23. "Petition From American Exiles in Canada," *Voice of the Fugitive* (Sandwich, C.W.), February 26, 1851.

24. On Upper Canada as a Black emigrant destination through the 1840s, see Abbott, *Beacons of Liberty*, 50–99. On the early history of enslaved people in Upper Canada and the United States seeking freedom through border crossing before imperial abolition, see

Gregory Wigmore, "Before the Railroad: From Slavery to Freedom in the Canadian-American Borderland," *Journal of American History* 98 (2011): 437–54.

25. On Black settlement in Nova Scotia, see Harvey Amani Whitfield, *Blacks on the Border: The Black Refugees in British North America, 1815–1860* (Burlington: University of Vermont Press, 2006).

26. John J. Moore to Amor de Cosmos, February 8, 1859, in Ripley, *Black Abolitionist Papers*, 401–5. On the larger history of Black settlement in Victoria, see Winks, *Blacks in Canada*, 272–87.

27. John W. Lewis to Frederick Douglass, March 20, 1855, in Ripley, *Black Abolitionist Papers*, 310–11; Winks, *Blacks in Canada*, 486.

28. "Good Growing out of Evil-Filmorism," *Provincial Freeman* (Toronto, C.W.), October 14, 1854; Wayne, "Black Population of Canada West," 465–85.

29. *Constitution and Bye-Laws of the Anti-Slavery Society of Canada* (Toronto, 1851), 5.

30. "North American Convention," *Voice of the Fugitive* (Sandwich, C.W.), September 24, 1851, and "An Address to the Colored Inhabitants of North America," October 22, 1851.

31. "Fugitive Slaves in Canada West," *Voice of the Fugitive* (Sandwich, C.W.), January 1, 1851. On the lives and activism of Henry and Mary Bibb, see Afua Cooper, "The Voice of the Fugitive: A Transnational Abolitionist Organ," in Frost and Tucker, eds., *A Fluid Frontier*, 135–53.

32. Peter C. Ripley, "Introduction," in Ripley, *Black Abolitionist Papers*, 16; and William Wells Brown, "The Colored People of Canada," in Ripley, *Black Abolitionist Papers*, 480–81.

33. *Minutes and Proceedings of the General Convention, for the Improvement of the Colored Inhabitants of Canada* (Windsor, C.W., 1853), 7–8.

34. *Minutes and Proceedings of the General Convention*, 11–12.

35. Mary Ann Shadd, *A Plea for Emigration; or, Notes of Canada West* (Detroit, 1852), 8 and 36. On Shadd's family background and public life, see Jane Rhodes, *Mary Ann Shadd Cary: The Black Press and Protest in the Nineteenth Century* (Bloomington: Indiana University Press, 1998).

36. Shadd, *Plea for Emigration*, 41.

37. "Emigration," *Provincial Freeman* (Toronto, C.W.), March 17 and "Emigration," April 7, 1855. On the differences of opinion and activism regarding how best to secure Black emigrant life in Canada West that divided Shadd and the Bibbs, see Sinha, *Slave's Cause*, 332–33; and Abbott, *Beacons of Liberty*, 208–9.

38. "For the Provincial Freeman," *Provincial Freeman* (Toronto, C.W.), May 27, 1854, "Brooklyn, NY, April 12th, 1854," May 6, 1854, and "To the Provincial Freeman," July 15, 1854.

39. "Windsor, C. W.," *Provincial Freeman* (Toronto, C.W.), April 22, 1854, and "Rev. C.C. Foote's Begging Operations," September 9, 1854; and Benjamin Drew, *A North-Side View of Slavery* (Boston, 1856), 373.

40. *Proceedings of the National Emigration Convention of Colored People* (Pittsburg, 1854).

41. Martin R. Delany, *The Condition, Elevation, Emigration, and Destiny of the Colored People of the United States* (Philadelphia, 1852), 172, 187–88, and 203.

42. "The Emigration Convention," *Provincial Freeman* (Chatham, C.W.), July 5, 1856; and Delany, "Political Aspect of the Colored People of the United States," in *Martin R. Delany:*

A Documentary Reader, ed. Robert S. Levine (Chapel Hill: The University of North Carolina Press, 2003), 289–90.

43. Samuel Ringgold Ward, "A Recent Tour," March 24, 1853, in Ripley, *Black Abolitionist Papers*, 258, and Ripley's note 25 on 263–64 for details about King Street; William Wells Brown, "The Colored People of Canada," in Ripley, *Black Abolitionist Papers*, 470–75; and Drew, *North-Side View*, 234 and 244–47.

44. On land availability and Indigenous dispossession in Upper Canada and Canada West, see Cole Harris, *The Reluctant Land: Society, Space, and Environment in Canada before Confederation* (Vancouver: UBC Press, 2008), 307–8 and 329. On the Mississauga in particular, see Donald B. Smith, "The Dispossession of the Mississauga Indians: A Missing Chapter in the Early History of Upper Canada," in J. K. Johnson and Bruce G. Wilson, eds., *Historical Essays on Upper Canada: New Perspectives* (Ottawa: Carleton University Press, 1989), 23–51.

45. Drew, *North-Side View*, 14. On the institutions of local government in Upper Canada, see Lyndsay Campbell, "Governance in the Borderlands: Upper Canadian Legal Institutions," in Tony Freyer and Lyndsay Campbell, eds., *Freedom's Conditions in the U.S.-Canadian Borderlands in the Age of Emancipation* (Durham, NC: Carolina Academic Press, 2011), 121–22.

46. Samuel Ringgold Ward, *Autobiography of a Fugitive Negro* (London, 1855), 158; "Introductory," *Provincial Freeman* (Toronto, C.W.), March 24, 1853; and Drew, *North-Side View*, 38.

47. Winks, *Blacks in Canada*, 168–74.

48. "An Act to Repeal a Certain Act therein Mentioned, and to Make Better Provision for the Naturalization of Aliens," November 23, 1849 (12 Vic.—Cap. 197), in Robert A. Harrison, ed., *The New Municipal Manual for Upper Canada* (Toronto, 1859), 387–92.

49. "An Act to Amend the Naturalization Laws of this Province," December 18, 1854 (18 Vic.—Cap. 6), *Statutes of the Province of Canada* (Montreal, 1854), 48; "An Act to Amend the Naturalization Laws of this Province," June 30, 1858 (22 Vic.—Cap. 1), in Harrison, *Municipal Manual Canada*, 663; and Drew, *North-Side View*, 179.

50. Shadd, *Plea for Emigration*, 27–28 and 36; *Minutes and Proceedings of the General Convention, for the Improvement of the Colored Inhabitants of Canada* (Windsor, C.W., 1853), 12 and 8; and "Relations of Canada to American Slavery," *Provincial Freeman* (Toronto, C.W.), March 24, 1853.

51. Drew, *North-Side View*, 39, 179, 49–50, and 177.

52. Drew, *North-Side View*, 29 and 51.

53. Ward, *Autobiography*, 127 and 135; and Mary Jane Robinson to Sarah Ann Harris, March 23, 1854, in Ripley, *Black Abolitionist Papers*, 279–282.

54. "The 1st of August in Toronto," *Provincial Freeman* (Toronto, C.W.), August 5, 1854; J. R. Kerr-Ritchie, *Rites of August First: Emancipation Day in the Black Atlantic World* (Baton Rouge: Louisiana State University Press, 2007), 118–63.

55. "The Duties of Colored Men in Canada," *Provincial Freeman* (Chatham, C.W.), March 28, 1857; and Ward, *Autobiography*, 205.

56. Shadd, *Plea for Emigration*, 8–11; "Yankees in Canada," *Provincial Freeman* (Toronto, C.W.), October 21, 1854, and "To the Editor of the Provincial Freeman," February 7, 1857.

57. For accounts of Black farmers who owned one-hundred-acre farms, see Drew, *North-Side View*, 190, 218, and 307. On average farm size in Canada West, see Harris, *Reluctant Land*, 347. On Abel B. Jones, see Drew, *North-Side View*, 149–52.

58. Lyndsay Campbell, "The Northern Borderlands: Canada West," in Freyer and Campbell, *Freedom's Conditions*, 205–9. For a historiographic assessment of broader questions in the political history of nineteenth-century Canada, see Colin Grittner, "Greater Expectations: Politics, the New Political History, and the Structuring of (Canadian) Society," *Canadian Historical Review* 100 (2019): 602–19.

59. "The Election," *Voice of the Fugitive* (Sandwich, C.W.), January 15, 1851.

60. "The Coming Political Contest," *Provincial Freeman* (Chatham, C.W.), March 29, 1856; Drew, *North-Side View*, 86–87; and Shadd, *Plea for Emigration*, 27.

61. Editorial by William P. Newman in Ripley, *Black Abolitionist Papers*, 322. On Black voters and provincial politics more broadly, including opposition to Larwill, see Winks, *Blacks in Canada*, 212–15.

62. "Something New Under the Sun," *Provincial Freeman* (Toronto, C.W.), October 28, 1854. For discriminatory tax assessments, see Brown, "The Colored People of Canada," in Ripley, *Black Abolitionist Papers*, 478–49; and Campbell, "Northern Borderlands," 206–7.

63. Ward, *Autobiography*, 149–50; Drew, *North-Side View*, 273 and 375; and Campbell, "Northern Borderlands," 209–10.

64. Ward, *Autobiography*, 307; "The Coloured People of Hamilton" to Charles T. Metcalfe, October 15, 1843, in Ripley, *Black Abolitionist Papers*, 97–98; Wayne, "Black Population of Canada West," 472; Kristin McLaren, "'We Had No Desire to Be Set Apart': Forced Segregation of Black Students in Canada West Public Schools and the Myths of British Egalitarianism," *Histoire Sociale/Social History* 37, no. 73 (2004): 27–50.

65. Brown, "Colored People of Canada," 479; and "The Things Most Needed," *Provincial Freeman* (Chatham, C.W.), April 25, 1857.

66. "Colored Men of the States," *Provincial Freeman* (Chatham, C.W.), April 4, 1857, and "For the Provincial Freeman," April 25, 1857.

67. Thomas Smallwood, *A Narrative of Thomas Smallwood* (Toronto, 1851); and "Colored Convention in Iowa," *Provincial Freeman* (Chatham, C.W.), March 21, 1857.

68. For the larger history of enslaved people seeking freedom through mobility during the Civil War but from a view of them as refugees, see Amy Murrell Taylor, *Embattled Freedom: Journeys through the Civil War's Slave Refugee Camps* (Chapel Hill: The University of North Carolina Press, 2018). On the Black Americans transforming the Civil War into a war for abolition, see Sinha, *Slave's Cause*, 543–85.

69. Wayne, "Black Population of Canada West," 471.

Epilogue

1. "Postmaster General Blair and Frederick Douglass," *Douglass' Monthly* (Rochester, NY), October 1862; Kate Masur, "The African American Delegation to Abraham Lincoln: A Reappraisal," *Civil War History* 56 (2010): 117–44.

2. Richard Keith Call, "Letter to John S. Littell" (Philadelphia: C. Sherman & Son, 1861), in Jon L. Wakelyn, ed., *Southern Pamphlets on Secession, November 1860–April 1861* (Chapel Hill: The University of North Carolina Press, 1996), 189–90.

3. On secession as an act of collective expatiation, see James H. Kettner, *The Development of American Citizenship, 1608–1870* (Chapel Hill: The University of North Carolina Press, 1978), 334–35 and 343–44. On secession as a nationalist movement, see Paul Quigley,

Shifting Grounds: Nationalism and the American South, 1848–1865 (Oxford: Oxford University Press, 2012); Texas v. White, 74 U.S. 700 (1869).

4. Crandall v. State of Nevada, 73 U.S. 35 (1867); and 15 Stat. 223 (Expatriation Act of 1868). For the complete history of the origins, adoption, and implications of the Expatriation Act of 1868, see Lucy E. Salyer, *Under the Starry Flag: How a Band of Irish Americans Joined the Fenian Revolt and Sparked a Crisis over Citizenship* (Cambridge, MA: Harvard University Press, 2018).

5. On the naturalization treaties and the interpretation that they marked a turn against individual rights to free movement and expatriation, see Salyer, *Under the Starry Flag*, 189–226.

6. Lucy E. Salyer, *Laws Harsh as Tigers: Chinese Immigrants and the Shaping of Modern Immigration Law* (Chapel Hill: The University of North Carolina Press, 1995); Erika Lee, *At America's Gates: Chinese Immigration during the Exclusion Era, 1882–1943* (Chapel Hill: The University of North Carolina Press, 2003); Mae M. Ngai, *Impossible Subjects: Illegal Aliens and the Making of Modern America* (Princeton, NJ: Princeton University Press, 2004); S. Deborah Kang, *The INS on the Line: Making Immigration Law on the US-Mexico Border, 1917–1954* (Oxford: Oxford University Press, 2017); and John C. Torpey, *The Invention of the Passport: Surveillance, Citizenship and the State*, 2nd ed. (Cambridge: Cambridge University Press, 2018), 2.

7. Article 13, United Nations, *Universal Declaration of Human Rights* (1948); Article 12, United Nations, *International Covenant on Civil and Political Rights* (1966); Aristide R. Zolberg, *A Nation by Design: Immigration Policy in the Fashioning of America* (Cambridge, MA: Harvard University Press, 2008), 454–55; and Charles S. Maier, *Once Within Borders: Territories of Power, Wealth, and Belonging since 1500* (Cambridge, MA: Harvard University Press, 2016), 280.

8. Willem Maas, "Varieties of Multilevel Citizenship," in Willem Maas, ed., *Multilevel Citizenship* (Philadelphia: University of Pennsylvania Press, 2013), 2; Ayelet Shachar, *The Birthright Lottery: Citizenship and Global Inequality* (Cambridge, MA: Harvard University Press, 2009), 16; and Jacqueline Stevens, *States without Nations: Citizenship for Mortals* (New York: Columbia University Press, 2010), 77–78.

9. Institute for Economics and Peace, "Ecological Threat Register 2020: Understanding Ecological Threats, Resilience and Peace" (2020), 1–91; General Assembly Resolution 73/195, Global Compact for Safe, Orderly and Regular Migration, A/RES/73/195 (January 11, 2019), undocs.org/en/A/RES/73/195; and UN High Commissioner for Refugees (UNHCR), *Legal Considerations Regarding Claims for International Protection Made in the Context of the Adverse Effects of Climate Change and Disasters*, October 1, 2020, www.refworld.org/docid/5f75f2734.html.

10. Emigrant rights claims in the context of contemporary needs ultimately helps build a legal and theoretical foundation for citizenship rights distinct from nations and protected by international law. On broader developments in this area, see Peter J. Spiro, "A New International Law of Citizenship," *American Journal of International Law* 105 (2011): 694–746.

11. Abrahm Lustgarten, "How Climate Migration Will Reshape America," *New York Times Magazine*, September 15, 2020; Thomas Jefferson to John F. Dumoulin, May 7, 1816, in *The Papers of Thomas Jefferson, Retirement Series*, vol. 10 (May 1, 1816–January 18, 1817), ed. James P. McClure and J. Jefferson Looney (Princeton, NJ: Princeton University Press, 2004–15): 20; and "Postmaster General Blair and Frederick Douglass," *Douglass' Monthly* (Rochester, NY), October 1862.

Index

Printed in the USA
CPSIA information can be obtained
at www.ICGtesting.com
CBHW021615110424
6759CB00004B/52